Constance Frederica Gordon Cumming

Two happy Years in Ceylon

Vol. 2

Constance Frederica Gordon Cumming

Two happy Years in Ceylon
Vol. 2

ISBN/EAN: 9783337237066

Printed in Europe, USA, Canada, Australia, Japan

Cover: Foto ©Andreas Hilbeck / pixelio.de

More available books at **www.hansebooks.com**

TWO HAPPY YEARS
IN CEYLON

BY

C. F. GORDON CUMMING

AUTHOR OF
'AT HOME IN FIJI,' 'A LADY'S CRUISE IN A FRENCH MAN-OF-WAR,'
'FIRE FOUNTAINS OF THE SANDWICH ISLES,'
'GRANITE CRAGS OF CALIFORNIA,' 'IN THE HIMALAYAS AND ON INDIAN PLAINS,'
'IN THE HEBRIDES,' 'VIA CORNWALL TO EGYPT,'
'WANDERINGS IN CHINA'

ILLUSTRATED BY THE AUTHOR

IN TWO VOLUMES

VOL. II.

NEW YORK
CHARLES SCRIBNER'S SONS
743 & 745 BROADWAY
MDCCCXCII

CONTENTS OF THE SECOND VOLUME.

CHAP.		PAGE
XIV.	RATNAPURA—GEMS,	1
XV.	BADULLA AND HAPUTALE,	23
XVI.	SOME PAGES FROM A BROTHER'S DIARY,	56
XVII.	BATTICALOA,	76
XVIII.	POLLANARUWA,	107
XIX.	TRINCOMALEE—SAAMI ROCK,	140
XX.	TRINCOMALEE TO GALLE,	163
XXI.	SOUTHERN COAST,	192
XXII.	RETURN TO COLOMBO,	227
XXIII.	NATIVE POLICE,	243
XXIV.	IN THE PLANTING DISTRICTS,	272
XXV.	ASCENT OF ADAM'S PEAK,	310
XXVI.	THE TUG OF WAR—THE BATTLE OF DIVERSE CREEDS IN CEYLON,	346
XXVII.	CHRISTIAN WORK IN CEYLON,	389
	INDEX,	431

ILLUSTRATIONS TO THE SECOND VOLUME.

SHRINE ON THE SUMMIT OF ADAM'S PEAK, AND THE SHADOW OF THE PEAK,		*Frontispiece.*
THE GAL-VIHARA, ROCK TEMPLE AT POLLONARUA,	*to face page*	106
THE WATA DÁGÉ OR ROUND TREASURE-HOUSE,	"	116
THE JETAWANARAMA VIHARA AND KIRI DAGOBA,	"	120
THE SAAMI ROCK AT TRINCOMALEE — WORSHIP AT SUNSET,	"	142
THE LILY SHORE NEAR TRINCOMALEE,	"	160
DOUBLE CANOES,	"	196
COFFEE FIELDS ON THE SLOPES OF ALLEGALLA PEAK,	"	276
ADAM'S PEAK, FROM MASKELYA,	"	324

TWO HAPPY YEARS IN CEYLON.

CHAPTER XIV.

RATNAPURA—GEMS.

To Ratnapura—The City of Rubies—Adam's Peak apparently triple—Rest-houses—Full moon festival—Fireflies and glow-worms—Visit to the gem-pits—Red sapphires and blue rubies—Other gems.

THE Bishop most kindly arranged that I should accompany him and his daughter on one of his extensive rounds of visitation, riding and driving circuitously right across Ceylon; the journey from Colombo on the west coast, to Batticaloa on the east of the Isle, to occupy a month; thence travelling inland through the district of Tamankadua to visit the ruins of the ancient city of Pollanarua, and so *via* Trincomalee to Jaffna, in the extreme north of the isle.

We accordingly started from Colombo in the beginning of August, following the course of the beautiful Kelani River right inland, *i.e.*, due east, halting the first night at Hanwella, and the next at Avissawella, all the time rejoicing in lovely river scenery, embowered in most luxuriant and infinitely varied foliage—all manner of palms, feathery bamboos with bright yellow stems, and fine trees, with the richest undergrowth of bananas, ferns, caladium, and innumerable beautiful plants.

One fairy-like detail was the abundance of exquisitely delicate climbing ferns, of several varieties, which in some places literally mat the jungle and veil tall trees with their graceful drapery. One of these is identical with that whose beauty is so fully recognised by the Fijians that they call it the Wa Kalou, "the fern of God," and in heathen days wreathed it around the ridge-pole of their temples.

In Ceylon it is cut wholesale, and laid as a covering over thatch, its long, glossy, black stems, like coarse horse-hair, acting as rain-conductors. Near Avissawella I sketched a very peculiar covered bridge, with wooden pillars supporting a high thatched roof, which was thus protected.

Our route lay thence south-east to Ratnapura, skirting so near the base of Adam's Peak that we obtained a succession of grand views of it towering above white clouds beyond the nearer wooded ranges. As seen from this side, a group of three stately peaks tower so conspicuously above all their blue brethren, that they seem to form one majestic triple mountain, and one of these peaks, known as the Bana Samanala, or "nephew" of the Sacred Mount, appears somewhat higher than the true Sri Pada (the mountain of the Holy Foot).[1] A grand view of this group is obtained from below a wooden bridge at Ratnapura, looking up the Kalu-Ganga or Black River, the whole framed in dark trees, whose stems and boughs are covered with parasitic ferns. Picturesque groups of natives of divers nationality, in bright draperies and with gaily-coloured umbrellas or palm-leaf sunshades, crossing the bridge, add life to the scene. All

See chapter xxv.

around are abrupt rocks, high peaks, and hills clothed with forest. A small fort on a rocky hillock protected the village at its base during the Kandyan wars, and is now a pleasant spot from which to watch a peaceful sunset.

(After leaving Ratnapura, still driving in a south-easterly direction, these three peaks, now more distant, tower to a greater and apparently uniform height, with fewer intervening ranges. For the benefit of future sketchers, I may mention that they are seen to great advantage from the 57¼ mile-post, with a foreground of luxuriant rice-fields surrounded with clumps of bamboo and all manner of palms.)

Here, as in all mountainous countries, one's enjoyment of these glimpses of the upper regions is perhaps intensified by their uncertainty. After watching a glorious sunrise or sunset, when these lofty summits are glorified by the flood of golden light, or one of those clear mornings when every crag and ravine can be plainly discerned, you turn away for a little while, and when you look again, there is nothing whatever to suggest the existence of a mountain —only quiet banks of fleecy clouds. So he who would sketch such scenes must have his materials ever at hand, and take for his motto, "Ready, aye ready."

We found all the rest-houses along this route delightfully situated, and commanding such views that there was comparatively little temptation to leave their cool shade during the hottest hours of the day. As I write, I have before me sketches of the Kalu-Ganga from the rest-house at Ratnapura, of the Kelani-Ganga from Hanwella Fort, and many another suggestion of cloud-reflecting rivers and dreamy shores, where foliage of all loveliest forms blend in visions of delight.

These rest-houses for the accommodation of travellers are kept up all along the principal roads, under the occasional supervision of a committee of the gentlemen in charge of the district roads. They are each in charge of a native, with one or more coolies to assist him. The furnishings consist of table, chairs, crockery, knives, forks, spoons, and very rude bedsteads, every traveller being supposed to carry his own bedding and musquito-nets. Where there is bedding, it is essential to turn over the cushions and anything of the nature of a mattress, as being only too likely to conceal centipedes and scorpions—possibly snakes. The rest-house keeper provides food, but of course in unfrequented districts it is only fair to let him have notice beforehand when guests may be expected. Each detail is charged according to a fixed tariff.

On the principal roads some of these houses are quite luxurious, but in out-of-the-way districts we halted at some which were very much the reverse. Some of the road bungalows yield shelter and nothing more; for instance, that at Aralupitya, on the Batticaloa road, which consisted of two minute rooms of sun-dried mud (whitewashed), one on each side of the open space which acted as dining-room. Happily the projecting thatch, supported on rude wooden posts, afforded some shelter from the blazing sun. Of course such houses are liable to be inhabited by many creatures, more objectionable than even swarms of flies, and their natural spider foes, while the high-pitched thatch is invariably the home of a menagerie of divers reptiles, from graceful little lizards to large and energetic rat-snakes, which are the true rat-catchers of Ceylon. The verandahs of even the best rest-houses are invariably haunted by pariah dogs and carrion crows, all too familiar, and all seeking what they may devour. An *ambulam* is a rude rest-house for native travellers, raised eight or ten feet on a foundation of masonry, so as to be above the miasma which always clings to the ground.

However, I need not have digressed into the matter of rest-houses while speaking of Ratnapura, where we were so speedily carried off to the charming home of a most kind family (Mrs. Atherton). A very pretty Singhalese princess, Kumarahami Eckmalagoda, came with her father, Eckneligoda, to luncheon, and to invite us to their house for the evening festivities, namely, the Perehera, or procession in honour of the August full moon.

These continue every evening for a week. I have already described the festival as observed at Kandy,[1] when the treasures from all the temples are carried to the river, and at an auspicious moment the priests cut the water with golden swords, and rapidly empty and refill their temple water-vessel at the very spot thus struck.

At Ratnapura the ceremony was very weird. First there was a rather pretty dance by a company of women. These were quickly succeeded by a very horrible apparition of men dressed to represent demons and wearing hideous masks suggestive of divers diseases. It is odd to see the conventional expression by which every variety of bodily ailment is depicted—fever by a red face, deafness by a vacant look, lameness or paralysis by twisted faces, idiotcy by distorted features, projecting eyes, and mouth drawn up.

The masquers who thus personated the powers of evil each carried a three-pronged flaming torch, which they brandished while dancing a wild whirling dance, occasionally refreshing the torches by throwing on them a resinous

[1] See chapter x.

gum, which produced a burst of flame and smoke. The whole scene was truly demoniacal.

After the dance we adjourned to the temple, which is a Dewale or Saami house (*i.e.*, a house of Hindoo gods), with a small Buddhist Vihara alongside.

I think that no priest of either religion was present, only temple headmen, of whom our host, Eckneligoda, was chief. First from the Buddhist temple a silver relic-shrine was brought forth with great pomp, carried by the temple headman, before whose footsteps white carpets were spread and sprinkled with white jessamine blossom; above the relic was borne a white canopy and an umbrella.

Then from the temple of Saman Dewiyo, *alias* Rama, a much-venerated gilt bow and three arrows were solemnly brought forth. They are said to have been placed here by Rama himself after he had therewith slain Rawana, the demon king of Lanka, who had carried off the beautiful Sita, wife of Rama. These precious relics were sprinkled with the holy water preserved since the previous year, and placed in the mysterious ark, very much like those used in Arkite ceremonies in the Himalayas. It is really a palanquin with rich hangings, about 4 feet 6 inches by 20 inches, and slung on a central pole. The four bearers who carried it were each robed in white, and had their mouth covered with a strip of white linen. The foremost couple carried a large silver umbrella of honour. A strip of white carpet was also spread for these to walk on.

Each temple possesses one of these sacred arks, which is only used on this festival. We had seen a party of pilgrims start from Colombo some time previously, in order to reach Kataragam, far in the south-east, in time for this feast, and they carried their deo or god in a similar ark.

The precious arrow having been satisfactorily started, the bow was next carried downstairs with equal solemnity, and the mystic wand of the Kapuwas followed. Then the small Juggernath car was dragged out—rather a pretty object, only 12 feet high, with a crimson body on very large gilt wheels, and forming a three-storied square pagoda, each storey having a white roof with bells at the corners.

Amid much blowing of horns and shouting, the procession then formed in the moonlight, elephants bearing headmen who carried large honorific umbrellas above precious objects, devil-dancers with astounding head-masks going before the ark, and men on foot carrying more umbrellas, one of which overshadowed another precious arrow. They made a sun-wise procession round the temple, and then, as it was Saturday night and somewhat late, we had to come away.

The drive home by moonlight, through vegetation of marvellous loveliness, was a dream of beauty, and the breeze was scented with a general perfume of orange blossom, citron, and lime, blossoms of the areka palm, temple flowers, and jessamine, each by turn sending us a breath of delicious fragrance; and the dark foliage overhead and around us was illuminated by the dainty green lanterns of myriads of luminous beetles, flashing to and fro in mazy dance, like glittering sparks, while from many a roadside bank came the far more brilliant, but likewise intermittent, light which tells of the presence of a glow-worm, a fat white grub about two inches in length. As in the case of our own garden centipede, the light is more attractive than the light-bearer.

When captured, the light of the Ceylonese firefly proves to be a very tiny glimmer, but that of the glow-worm is so brilliant as to enable one to read even small print by its light. Scientific men have experimented as to whether this light was extinguished on the death of the creature, and so have killed poor glow-worms, and extracted from the tail a gelatinous fluid so highly phosphorescent that they could read by its light.

I returned on Monday to the Dewali to sketch the car and the ark, and found a great fair going on, at which I invested in sundry oddities.

But previously the great Gem-Notary of Ratnapura (owner of three-fourths of the native town) had sent his carriage in the early morning to convey us to his gem-pits, where white awnings had been erected, carpets spread, and all made ready that we might sit in the utmost comfort to see the whole process of digging and washing the gemmiferous gravel, and its various stages of examination. First the "illan," as it is called, is dug up, and placed in wicker baskets, which are washed in a stream close by to get rid of the clay; then the gravel is washed in long sloping wooden troughs, with divisions, at intervals, of perforated zinc, with holes of various sizes. By these first the largest and then the smaller stones are kept back, so that only the fine gravel passes through the last grating, thence to be transferred to the final trough for critical inspection.

It is a curious sight to see the keen, eager faces of the Moormen (Mahommedans), to whom most of the gem-pits belong, and who sit perched on raised seats overlooking the great troughs wherein a long row of coolies (all but naked) are sifting and washing the gravel, which, perchance, may yield some priceless gem, only to be recognised in its rough exterior by experienced eyes, but which a clever coolie would detect as quickly as his master, so that the latter needs to practise keen vigilance to prevent any attempt at concealment of treasure-trove. Should his attention be distracted for a second, some precious gem may be swallowed, as the only possible means of securing it. So the man on duty sits with hawk-like eyes intently fixed on the trough, and must not even wink till his successor relieves guard. Another walks about keeping a general look-out, just to "mak' sicker."

These Moormen, who are fine, tall, well-built men, dressed in white, with high white calico hats and large sun-umbrellas, look quite the superior race among their squad of workers, with neither clothes nor turbans. They keep the trade of polishing and cutting gems chiefly in their own hands; the commoner stones are intrusted to provincial lapidaries, but all really good gems are forwarded to the masters of the art, most of whom live in Colombo. Unfortunately they adhere with rigid conservatism to their primitive tools and system of cutting, so as to retain the largest possible size and weight at the sacrifice of brilliancy; consequently the size of Ceylon gems is generally greatly reduced, and their value equally enhanced, when they have been re-cut by European lapidaries.

No stone of any value was found on the occasion of our visit, but the Gem-Notary invited us to breakfast at his house, and there exhibited his own priceless collection of sapphires of every size and shade of colour, and also showed us the whole process of cutting and polishing. This great "gemmer" is said to have amassed a fortune of twenty lacks of rupees. He confesses to having cleared 800,000 rupees from one alluvial mine near Ratnapura; and one of his relatives pointed out some huge gneiss rocks from beneath which he had washed out 20,000 rupees' worth of sapphires, the average price in Ceylon of a good sapphire being £6 a carat; but of course a specially fine or large stone commands a purely fancy price, according to what some wealthy purchaser may be willing to pay for it. Ceylon is, *par excellence*, "The Land of the Sapphire," these being so abundant and rubies comparatively rare, therein proving the converse of Burmah, where the ruby is pre-eminent and sapphires comparatively scarce.

Ratnapura, as is implied by its name, "The City of Rubies," is the centre of the district chiefly noted for the abundance and value of the precious stones which have been found in its alluvial deposits, chiefly in the beds of clay or of fine gravel washed down from inaccessible mountain crags—which of course suggests that if these only could be reached, such wealth of gems could be obtained as would outshine all fables of Eastern romance.

Though gem-bearing deposits exist in other provinces, and many precious stones are annually collected from the beds of rivers and from extemporised gem-pits in many parts of the Isle, this province of Sabaragamuwa and some parts of the Morawa Korale have supplied the largest number and the most perfect gems.

I believe that in no other country is there found so great a variety of gems as in Ceylon; in fact, true diamonds, emeralds, and turquoise are said to be the only absentees. Sapphires, rubies, topazes, amethysts, garnet, alexandrite, chalcedony, chrysoberyl, pleonaste, jacinth, carbuncle, diamond-spar, aquamarine, cat's-eyes, moonstones, and tourmalines are abundant, and every now and again some fortunate "gemmer" picks up a treasure worth a fortune. The total absence of diamonds is singular, as the famous Golconda diamond-mines lie so near in Southern India.

But Nature keeps all these treasures enfolded in such ugly crusts that only a practised eye can ever guess which of all the fragments of coarse gravel is in truth the priceless gem. I think that the garnet and its first cousin, the cinnamon-stone, are almost the only exceptions to this jealous concealment. Here and there in the forests of the eastern and southern provinces there lie masses of gneiss which literally gleam in the sunlight by reason of myriads of tiny sparkling garnets embedded in the rock. The cinnamon-stone presents itself in the same unveiled style, certain great rock-masses being so thickly encrusted therewith that gem collectors occasionally carry off large pieces in order to extract the cinnamon-stones at their leisure.

Very beautiful masses of garnets were found while cutting the tunnels on the new line of railway above Haputale, with individual crystals about a quarter of an inch in length, and there too were found lumps of quartz ranging in colour from a rich red to a milky white, and some of a clear blue, said to prove the presence of true cobalt.

If only Mother Earth would yield all her crystals ready polished like the glittering garnet, then Ceylon would really be a fairy Isle of Gems; for not only do her hidden treasures include almost every recognised precious stone save the three I have named, but her list acquires inconceivable variety owing to Nature's freaks in the matter of colouring, whereby she assimilates different stones so closely as to prove hopelessly confusing to the eye of any ordinary mortal.

For instance, when we talk of sapphires, we naturally think of lovely rich blue crystals; and though it is easy to recognise as legitimate members of the family innumerable shades ranging from the deepest invisible blue, too dark to be of any ornamental use, to the palest clear azure, it becomes extremely perplexing to be shown pure white crystals, strangely resembling diamonds, and yellow crystals, exactly like cairngorms or topazes, and to be assured that they are all sapphires. Mr. E. W. Streeter, who is the great authority on these matters, enumerates the colours of Ceylon sapphires as "azure-blue, indigo, dark-red, violet-blue, poppy-red, cochineal, carmine, rose-red to rose-white, milk-white, yellow-white, French-white, lemon-yellow, and green!" I have also seen a clouded sapphire of a greenish opalesque colour, said to be due to water in the stone.

In like manner true rubies are found of every shade of colour. A spinel naturally suggests a lovely rose-coloured gem, but here we may see sparkling bright blue spinels. In point of commercial value the rose-tinted rubies of Ceylon rank lower than the blood-red rubies of Burmah, and I am told that the Singhalese have discovered a method of enriching their colour by wrapping them in shell-lime and exposing them to intense heat. The Ceylonese stone, however, is considered to excel that of Burmah in brilliancy and fire, and very valuable blood-red rubies are sometimes found. One weighing 26 carats, and valued at £5000, was found at Ratnapura in 1889.

There is one variety both of ruby and sapphire which is, I am told, peculiar to Ceylon, namely, the asteria or star-ruby and star-sapphire, both of which, when skilfully cut and polished, reveal a luminous six-rayed star of light on a blue or red ground. It is a very lovely gem.

I do not know whether the starry rays are due to the same cause as the beautiful light in the luminous olive-green cat's-eye; that, I am told, is attributed to the presence of particles of asbestos, a theory which seems confirmed by the successful imitation of this gem which is manufactured from crocidolite, a mineral closely related to asbestos.

On the other hand, the Chinese succeed in so cutting a pearly shell as to produce a very pretty so-called cat's-eye, with a luminous internal ray.

The true cat's-eye is peculiar to Ceylon. Very fine stones are often found at Ratnapura and in Rakwane, though the finest specimens have generally been found in the gem-pits of Morowa Korale district, considerably farther south. This is one of the gems the value of which is specially affected by the caprice of European fashion, according to which its price rises and falls in a manner exasperating to gem speculators. In the Oriental market, however, it holds a steady place, being especially prized by the Malays.

In 1889 a splendid cat's-eye was found in the coffee district of Dikoya, said to be the largest and most valuable yet discovered. It was picked up by a man who was unloading a cart of earth, and at once sold for thirty rupees. The purchaser resold it for 700 rupees, and the next owner secured for it 3000. In its uncut state it weighed 475 carats. When cut, it was reduced to 170 carats, and was purchased for 9000 rupees by a merchant who valued it for the London market at 30,000 rupees. A small piece of the original stone weighing $6\frac{1}{2}$ carats was sold for 600 rupees. (The nominal value of the rupee is 2s., but owing to the depreciation of silver its value when transmitted to England is at present about 1s. 5d.)

Another lovely luminous stone, supposed to have been formerly found in other countries, but now, I believe, only in Ceylon, is the moonstone, which has a soft silvery lustre suggestive of moonlight. It is found in some places so abundantly that the supply exceeds the demand, so it commands a very low price, and exceeding pretty ornaments in really good taste can be bought for a very small sum.

The Morowa Korale has also yielded almost all the fine specimens of a very lovely gem, the alexandrite, so called in honour of the Czar, in whose dominions it was first discovered in the far north. The peculiarity is that by daylight its colour is a rich bronzed green, whereas by gas or candle-light it appears to be of a vivid crimson—a phenomenon attributed to the presence of copper and oxide of lead. Beautiful and interesting as is this stone, I am told that its commercial value is barely one-twentieth that of a ruby of good quality. Sometimes a stone is found, and distinguished as an alexandrite cat's-eye, which by daylight is dark-green, with a cross line of white light. This at night assumes the ruby colour aforesaid.

A very remarkable feature in the beautiful collection of gems exhibited in the Ceylon Court at the Indian and Colonial Exhibition in 1886 was the extraordinary variety of sapphires of various colours, no less than fifty different tints being there exhibited. Beautiful specimens of all the gems of the Isle were gathered together under the watchful care of Mr. Hayward, who, with unwearying courtesy, endeavoured to teach me and many another inquisitive pupil how to recognise familiar stones, all disguised in unwonted colours, as if bent on a masquerade.

Even the topaz, departing from its traditional golden hue, comes out in fancy dress. Not satisfied with assuming every variety of colour, from pale amber to the richest brown, it occasionally indulges in various shades of red or blue, and there have been found harlequin specimens combining blue and yellow in the same crystal! Occasionally the topaz assumes a faint sea-green, so exquisitely delicate that even experts disagree as to whether such a stone is really a precious blue topaz or "only an aquamarine," in which case, by a freak of the gem-market, its value would be greatly deteriorated.

How truly absurd are these fantastic standards of value! I remember one of my sisters taking a number of Welsh topazes to be set by an eminent jeweller, who admired them greatly, and, assuming them to be Oriental, gave her a large estimate of their value. But on her mentioning where she had found them, and expressing regret that she had not collected more, his countenance fell as he exclaimed, "Welsh topazes! Oh, in that case they are worth a mere trifle!"

You can understand that here, where, in addition to the innumerable skilful frauds of the trades in sham gems, Nature herself does so much to puzzle the unwary, the purchase of precious stones is not altogether a wise form of investment for non-professional travellers. In fact, the Moormen take very good care that these shall never even see their really valuable stones, which they keep securely concealed, and like to retain as secure property.

As regards the topaz, not only are its own varieties of colour perplexing, but there are other stones amongst which the untutored eye finds it hard to distinguish. Such is the little-prized cinnamon-stone, a crystal of a rich warm orange-brown tint—a description which also applies to the zircon or jacinth, which, however, ranges in colour from clear gold or delicate pink to fiery sparkling red. The latter are very rare, and consequently highly valued. Some specimens are tinged with olive-green. The zircon is sometimes worn as an amulet to guard its owner from evil spirits and to assure the blessing of sound sleep. Closely akin to it are the red jacinth and the white or grey jargoon, which is commonly known as the Ceylon or Matara diamond.

Then comes the tourmaline, a lovely sparkling gem which, however, not being the fashion, is of small value. It is so like a yellow zircon or a Scotch cairngorm, that I for one despair of ever being able to distinguish one from the other, or indeed from the chrysoberyl, though the latter sometimes assumes an æsthetic sage-green peculiar to itself. These lead on to chrysolites, and to sundry other stones more or less precious.

In some alluvial districts where the promise of gems seems abundant, they are found to have undergone the same process of disintegration as the rock in which they were once embedded, and crumble to atoms at a touch; so that there are streams, such as the Manick-Ganga, or River of Gems, in the south-east of the Isle, the sands of which are literally composed of glittering particles of quartz, mica, rubies, sapphires, and other crystals, which, gleaming in the sunlight beneath the rippling waters, seem like the realisation of some Eastern fable, till closer inspection proves them to be so thoroughly pulverised as to be literally worthless to the gem-seeker, albeit so fascinating to the eye which can recognise beauty apart from intrinsic value. These crystal sands are the trainers of the great gem family, for though not destined to be themselves exalted to high estate, they supply a polishing material of great value in the hands of the gem-cutter.

Such rivers suggest that somewhere near their rock-cradles there must be abundance of such lovely rose-coloured quartz as is occasionally found in large blocks near Ratnapura, as if Nature had wished to carry out her ruby colouring on a wider scale. She certainly must have established her favoured laboratory somewhere among the great hills of Sabaragamua, whose crumbling crags have scattered such precious fragments in every rocky ravine and over all these alluvial plains.

To a race so keenly addicted to gambling as the Singhalese, the possibilities of such glorious prizes as may reward the gem-seeker are irresistible, and so a very large number of the natives adopt this profession, somewhat to the neglect of their fields and gardens. During the dry season between Christmas and Easter, when the streams are well-nigh dried up and their gravelly beds laid bare, hundreds of the poorer classes devote themselves to searching for such crystals as the sweeping torrents of the previous months may have brought from many a remote mountain.

But the wealthier gem-seekers, who can afford preliminary outlay, find it more remunerative to work systematically by sinking pits in the plains at such points as they judge to be hopeful. They dig through layers of recently deposited gravel, soil, and cabook till they reach the "illan" or gemmiferous gravel, which lies from five to twenty feet below the surface. Ratnapura stands in the centre of a great gravel-bed some thirty miles square, and all thus buried; but pits have been sunk in every direction by gemmers, ancient or modern. Of the latter, some are now being sunk to a depth of 80 to 100 feet. The cabook is a hard deposit of plum-pudding stone formed of water-worn pebbles embedded in hard clay. In this are many circular hollows or pockets—natural jewel-cases—washed out by the eddying currents of ancient rivers, and in these many of the finest gems have found a resting-place. The illan is generally found beneath the cabook.

I spoke of "preliminary outlay," but indeed this is not

excessive. The necessary equipment of a gemming party consists of a few mamotees or spades, a few crowbars, a long iron sounding-rod, called "illankoora," for gauging the illan, and a few baskets of split bamboo. When they have dug to a depth of five or six feet, should the sides seem likely to give way, four jungle-posts are inserted, one at each corner, and cross-beams round the sides and centre-beams. As the digging goes on, this frail support is likewise deepened till the gravel is reached, where it is scooped up and washed in the bamboo baskets. As with all other mining, gemming is exceedingly speculative. A pit may prove workable in a few days, or it may involve months of toil, and finally be abandoned as useless. It is said that of every ten pits sunk, only one pays.

In that one, however, there is scarcely a basketful of gravel which does not contain some inferior kind of gem, and these are called "dallam" and sold by the pound, at about nine rupees, after having been minutely searched for any precious stones, which are found in the proportion of one per cent., and of course really valuable ones are very much more rare. However, even the occasional find of a real treasure suffices to keep up the excitement. For instance, about two years ago, quite a poor man tried his luck in a gem-pit, and straightway lighted on a sapphire of such value that a knowing hand at once secured it for £600, and a few days later doubled his money by selling it in Colombo for £1200. It was expected to fetch £3000 in London.

Unfortunately, although some very poor agricultural labourers certainly eke out their scanty living by working in gem-pits, most of the money thus won by gemmers of the poorer class is said to be squandered in gambling and drinking, so that perhaps (though some injustice is apparently involved) it is not altogether to be regretted that recent Government ordinances have imposed a certain check on promiscuous digging.

Under the rule of the Kandyan kings, the right of digging for gems was a royal monopoly, and the inhabitants of certain villages were told off for this purpose. The office was hereditary, as was also that of the headmen who superintended the work. Under British rule this monopoly was dropped, and the gemming industry was thrown open to all men, with the sole restriction that no one might dig on Crown waste lands without a license. Portions of Government land were sold at high prices expressly as gem-lands, and the right of private individuals to seek for gems in any way they pleased on their own land was never questioned.

In 1890, however, when European companies decided to bring European capital to commence systematic mining for gems, a Gem Ordinance was enacted, which is said to be equal to an initial tax of 10 per cent. on problematic gains, and is said to have practically killed the native industry and stopped the work of some 20,000 diggers. It enacts that a license costing five rupees must be obtained for every pit opened, in whatever locality—even in a man's own garden—and a further sum of 75 cents. per head is levied for every person taking part in the work in the next three months. Should the number of persons thus licensed for employment in that pit be exceeded, the whole license may be cancelled, and the extra worker may be fined fifty rupees or suffer six months' imprisonment. One of the chief dangers of mining is that of a sudden influx of water into the pit, necessitating an immediate accession of helping hands; but of course no men would care to risk such penalties in helping their neighbours, and as the formalities to be observed in altering a license generally involve a delay of three or four days, the immediate result of this legislation has been the abandonment of a very large number of pits.

At present, reports concerning systematic work vary considerably, one company being reported to have recovered £1000 worth of gems in a week, while another, which had expended about £5000 on sinking pits, only recovered gems worth about £100, and one gentleman who had sunk £1000 got nothing at all. These not being endowed with the lynx eyes of the Moormen, are naturally suspicious that their gems have been pilfered, and regret that the regulations of the African diamond-fields are not introduced into Ceylon. There, they say, a man is locked up for having in his possession a gem for which he cannot account satisfactorily, while in Ceylon the man who holds a gem can prosecute the man who dares to suggest that it has not been honestly obtained.

Doubtless a solution for all these difficulties will be found in course of time, and there seems every prospect that the gem treasures of Ceylon will from this time be developed on a more scientific system. The great object is to try and discover those mountain geese which lay these precious eggs; in other words, to find the matrix whence the sun and rains and rivers have extracted those specimens from which we gather such suggestions concerning that hidden treasury. It has been proved that in Burmah limestone forms the matrix of the ruby, so the first thing to be done in Ceylon is to examine all the veins of limestone along the course of the Ratnapura River from its source in the heart of the mountains. If once rubies and sapphires can be detected in these, then the work of mining could be begun in real earnest, with good prospects of remunerative results.

Those who are interested in mineralogy find abundant food for study in the very varied minerals thrown out of the gem-pits, including infinitesimal atoms of gold, which, however, is not found in quantities that would pay to work. Mica is found pretty freely, and iron is abundant in certain districts.

But the only mineral of much importance in Ceylon is plumbago, in which there is a very large trade, hitherto almost entirely in the hands of natives, who dig for it in the plains. It is thought probable that the companies who go to the mountains in search of gems will there also find the cradle of the plumbago, which they hope to work by horizontal tunnels at far less expense, and without the danger from water which attends the deep excavations in the low country. In some of these, shafts have been sunk to a depth of upwards of 200 feet, necessitating the free use of pumping machinery. It is estimated that, including carters, packers, and carpenters, who manufacture casks for the export of this mineral, about 24,000 persons are employed in connection with this industry, which is chiefly carried on in the north-western and western provinces, though the southern province likewise yields a fair share. But three-fourths of the whole supply is dug from pits in the Kalutara and Kurunegala districts.

It is often found at Ratnapura and elsewhere in large kidney-shaped masses lying loose in the soil, and also forms so large an ingredient in the gneiss rocks that these seem speckled with bright silver. When this rock decomposes, it resembles yellow brick, and is so soft that, when newly dug out, it can be cut to any shape, but quickly hardens when exposed to the air. It is a valuable material for the manufacture of firebricks, as it resists the greatest heat.

The annual export of pure plumbago from Ceylon (chiefly to the United States and Europe) amounts to about 240,000 cwts., valued at about two and a half million of rupees. Many and varied are its uses, in supplying the lead for our best Cumberland pencils, blacking for our stoves, and an important requisite in polishing steel guns and steel armour for warships; it is also largely used in colouring dark glass in photographic studios, in piano and organ factories, and even in hat factories, where it is used to give a peculiar softness and smoothness to felt hats!

So what with plumbago and gems, the minerals of Ceylon travel over a very wide range of the earth.

23

CHAPTER XV.

BADULLA AND HAPUTALE.

Ratnapura to Batticaloa—Festival cars—Polite priests—Belihul-Oya—
A pink rainbow—Badulla—Haldummulla—Haputale Pass—The
railway—The Happy Valley Mission—The Ella Pass—Badulla—
Ants and ant-eaters—In Madoolseme—Burning the forest—A Roman
Catholic procession—Strange compromises—Forest conservancy—
Chena-farming—Lantana—The Park Country—Rugam tank.

FROM Ratnapura we travelled by easy stages to Haldummulla, halting for the nights at Pelmadulla, Belangoda, and Belihul-Oya, passing through most beautiful scenery and meeting many exiles from the old country, to whom the sight of other white faces was an unmistakable pleasure.

At Pelmadulla we explored the Buddhist Vihara, and noted with interest the prevalence of triple symbolism: saints sitting on clouds, each holding three lotus blossoms; three gods looking down from heaven on a murder scene; three fishes, &c. To this the priests seemed to attach no significance; and yet in their ordination service each question is repeated thrice, which is surely suggestive of some mystic meaning.

I sketched a great gilded festival car, three storeys high, and two very odd great gilded candelabra on wheels, each five storeys high, *i.e.*, with five tiers of crystal lamps on gilded and painted branches. These are wheeled in procession with the great idol car, which is only taken out once a year, at the April–May festival, which is that of the Singhalese New Year.

The priests gathered round to watch the sketch, and my attendants enlarged on the many sacred shrines which I had visited and sketched in many lands. They declared that I had thereby indeed acquired much merit![1] They were guilty of making such very complimentary speeches that I could not resist putting the courtesy of one friendly priest to a cruel test by asking whether he would be very sorry if, in his next transmigration, he should be born a woman; whereupon he craftily answered that *when* that happened, *then* he would be glad, which I thought a very neat answer. But he dared not shake hands with anything so bad in this life!

In all this district the climate is peculiarly favourable to the growth of tropical plants; for while the great rock-ramparts receive and refract the full heat of the sun's burning rays, numerous streams rush down from the mountains, keeping up an abundant supply of moisture. So in this warm damp atmosphere all lovely things of the green world flourish—exquisite tree-ferns and wonderful creepers, which interlace the larger trees in an intricate network. Strange orchids find a niche on many a bough, as do also very brilliant fungi, purple, yellow, or red. One remarkable feature of these jungles is that one never sees a dead tree;

---

[1] Some are more discriminating. I was one day sketching in the temple of Tiendoug, a great Buddhist monastery in China, when a kindly old priest, who had watched my work with great interest, asked quite sadly what was the good, and what merit could there be in my doing all this, if I did not really reverence the Poossas, *i.e.*, the saints and their images? See "Wanderings in China," vol. ii. p. 41.

the white ants dispose of them all, except in the plantation districts, where whole forests have been felled and burned, and the number of charred trees fairly beats even these industrious workers, whose huge nests, or rather castles, form such conspicuous features in the forest.

In swampy places and along the banks of streams hereabouts there grows a peculiar sort of bamboo, very tall and slim, and devoid of all lateral branches. It seems to exist in order to supply ready-made fishing-rods.

The view from the rest-house at Belihul-Oya is especially charming; the house stands on the brink of a clear rocky stream, which rising in the grand Maha-Eliya, *alias* Horton Plains, rushes down a deep-set valley from a grand amphitheatre of intensely blue hills. A little lower it assumes the name of Welawe-ganga, and so traverses the green province of Uva.

Just before sunset the whole scene was transformed. Looking eastward, the sky and hills were all flooded with the loveliest rose-colour, the valley bathed in ethereal lilac, while the whole was spanned by a strangely luminous yellow and pink rainbow, losing itself in a mass of dark trees. I have never seen anything else in the least like that fairy archway.

Brilliant dragonflies—some pure scarlet, others emerald-green—skimmed over the surface of that bright stream, and many splendid butterflies floated joyously in the sunshine. We also saw strange leaf-insects, so like green leaves, that, till they flew away, it was impossible to believe them to be alive; and grasshoppers with red bodies and bright yellow crests hopped about us in most inquisitive style.

On the following day we drove on, always through lovely country and along the base of great hills, whose tumbled fragments lay in huge boulders at the base of precipitous crags, till we came to Haldummulla, 3250 feet above the sea, where we were enfolded in genial kindness, Miss Jermyn and I in one hospitable home, and the Bishop at another. A number of the neighbours had assembled to meet the Bishop and attend the Sunday services, which were held in the courthouse, and bright hearty services they were.

It is a beautiful spot, lying as it does at the foot of a grand mountain range, yet looking down over a vast expanse of cultivated land, chiefly coffee, and a sea of forest through which flow hidden rivers, and far away, seventy miles distant, lies the glittering sea, on which we could sometimes distinguish ships, and before sunrise we could discern the sea both to the east and south. From our next halt, at Haputale, we could distinguish the exact position of far distant Hambantota by the gleaming light on the saltpans.

We women-folk had two days of delightful rest amid these pleasant surroundings, while the Bishop diverged to meet a party of planters and hold service at Lamastotte. This was the first district in which coffee estates struck me as really beautiful, these grand sweeping hillsides, rising far above us on the one side, and on the other sloping down to the low district outstretched before us, all clothed with the glossy verdure of the low bushes, something like small Portugal laurels, and all covered with fragrant blossom, white as newly fallen snow.

At that time King Coffee reigned supreme, and every available foot of land was given up to this one culture, producing in most districts an effect of great monotony. Since then it has passed through very evil days, and in large districts has been wholly supplanted by tea and other products; but it is pleasant to learn that in this district, where it was so pre-eminently luxuriant, a large proportion has recovered, so that coffee once more holds a foremost place in the province of Uva.

We left Haldummulla and all the warm-hearted friends there with much regret, and mounted the steep ascent (all by admirable roads, both as regards engineering and upkeep) till we reached the famous Haputale Pass, 4550 feet above the sea, where a small roadside village offered rest and shelter to weary wayfarers, and a halting-place for the tired bullocks which had dragged up heavily laden waggons.

Never has any place undergone more rapid change than has been wrought here within the last two years. For the long-desired railway, which is to open up the province of Uva and bring it into direct communication with Colombo, is to cross the dividing range at Patipola, which is just above Haputale, at a height of 6223 feet above the sea, thence descending to the south-western plains.

Hitherto the railway terminus has been at Nanuoya, five miles from Nuwara Eliya, and the difficulties of making a railway over the twenty-five miles of mountain and crag which separate Nanuoya from Haputale seemed well-nigh insurmountable. Now, however, all difficulties are being conquered by skilful engineers and the patient toil of an army of five thousand workers, chiefly Tamil coolies, but including many Singhalese and Moormen—all, of course, under European direction. And for all this great body of men daily rice and all other necessaries must be provided, and the once quiet village of Haputale is now a centre of busy life, and also unfortunately of a nest of too tempting arrack, beer, and gin shops, to say nothing of an opium den, all of which are responsible for a grave amount of crime and lawlessness.

The railway work is divided into two sections—one from Nanuoya to Summit, passing below the Elk Plains, and crossing comparatively tame grassy hills and patenas, but involving a rise of about 1000 feet, the other from Haputale to Summit, rising 1673 feet over a rocky chaos of shattered cliffs and ravines. At the actual summit there is a level of about three miles, and at a point not far from there, in the direction of Nanuoya, will be the station for the Horton Plains, the grand sanatorium of the future, which lies only about three miles off the line of railway; so that the weakest women and children will be able without any conscious effort to breakfast at Colombo and sleep on these breezy plains, where already a comfortable rest-house and most lovely garden await their coming.

Little will travellers over the completed line dream what tremendous difficulties have been overcome in preparing the way for their easy journey over a region which can only be described as a chaos of huge crags, break-neck precipices, dangerous and impassable gorges, necessitating a continuous series of heavy cuttings, viaducts, embankments, and long tunnels through solid rock. In the course of a single mile seven tunnels follow in such rapid succession that travellers will be sorely tantalised by too rapid glimpses of the magnificent scenery all around—mountains seamed with rocky ravines, clear sparkling streams glancing among huge boulders or dashing in foaming cataracts over sheer precipices to the cultivated lands far below; tea and coffee estates all sprinkled over with enormous rocks, each as large as a cottage, and then the vast panorama of the sunny lowlands of Uva, its vast expanses of grass-land and rice stretching far, far away to the ocean.

But whatever they see can convey no idea of the toil

and danger faced by those who traced this road and commenced its construction—of their hair-breadth escapes as they crept along rock ledges of crumbling quartz or gneiss, with a wall of mountain above, and a sheer precipice below from 300 to 500 feet in depth, or zigzagged by giddy tracks down the face of crags where goats could scarcely climb for pleasure.

Still less will they realise how pitiless rains disheartened the coolies and soddened the earth, occasioning terrible landslips, in one of which seven poor fellows were buried alive, while another brought down a thousand cubic yards of boulders, earth, and gravel. Awful gales likewise, for days together, have positively endangered the lives of the workers, and proved a powerful argument in favour of adhering to the heavier carriages of a "broad gauge" line, rather than yield to the temptation of constructing a cheaper "narrow gauge" as was urged by some economists, and most vigorously and ceaselessly opposed by the veteran Editor of the 'Ceylon Observer.'

It is said that "a turn begun is half ended," and great was the joy of the isolated planters on this side of the island when the long-desired railway was actually commenced; and energetically has it been pushed on by all concerned.

So my recollection of Haputale as a lonely mountain village will seem as a dream of a remote past to those who now anticipate the time when it will rank as a busy town.

Thence, leaving all beautiful scenery behind us, we drove about a couple of miles down the pass to Bandarawella, which is all grassy, like an average tract of English downs.

In this immediate neighbourhood another amazing transformation has occurred, namely, the formation of the Haputale Happy Valley Mission, where the Rev. Samuel Langdon of the Wesleyan Mission has originated a whole group of excellent institutions, as a beginning of good work in this hitherto most grievously neglected region—neglected because so remote and isolated that till very recently comparatively few Europeans found their way here, and still fewer knew anything of the wretchedly poor and utterly ignorant inhabitants. Even old residents were startled when they realised the existence of an agricultural population of about 180,000 Singhalese, besides many Tamils, inhabiting upwards of 800 villages, which are scattered over the numerous valleys among the grassy foothills and downs which lie between the mountainous Central Province and the ocean, forming part of a region about the size of Wales, which has quite recently been created a distinct province, namely, that of Uva.

In the whole of that vast district there were till within the last year or two only eight schools for boys—not one for girls; and although in some villages there are *pansala*, *i.e.*, Buddhist-temple schools, in most cases the priest in charge can neither read nor write himself; indeed, in some large villages not one man, woman, or child can read.

Could Christian schools now be established in these villages, a very great step would be gained, as otherwise the Government grant will go to aid this wretched *pansala* system of indigenous education, and it will then be far more difficult to secure a footing than in the now vacant field. But except in the town of Badulla and its immediate neighbourhood, very little Christian work was attempted till quite recently, the various missionary bodies being totally unable to find men or money to carry it on.

AN OPEN DOOR. 31

Now small beginnings have been made by a very limited number of Episcopal and Wesleyan missionaries, whose work consists chiefly in walking from village to village, preaching to all who will listen to them, and almost everywhere they are received with kindness, and their message is often heard with apparent interest. Only in some places the people are so sunk in misery and immorality that all their faculties are dormant and amendment seems to themselves impossible. They say, "We must steal and sin if we would live. What you say is good, but it cannot help us, surrounded as we are by poverty and vice and disease." The almost invariable attitude towards religion of any sort is one of total apathy, and even temporal discomfort is accepted as the inevitable result of having failed to obtain merit in a previous stage of existence.

Nowhere have these preachers met with any active opposition, but they find a wide-spread dissatisfaction with Buddhism, and especially with the priests, of whom these people frequently speak in terms of contempt. Though some are nominally Roman Catholic, the majority, while professedly Buddhist, are in truth devil-worshippers, sunk in depths of gloomy superstition, and praying only to malignant spirits in order to avert evil. As regards the beneficent teaching of Buddha, not only the people, but even many of the priests, are so ignorant of its first principles, that any argument founded thereon is utterly wasted; but many listen gladly to preaching which tells of hope both for this life and for the future. So the report of these pioneers is that everywhere they find an open door, and that nothing save lack of men and of means to support them prevent them from carrying the Word of Life to all these 800 villages.

Some years ago the Wesleyans opened a successful school for girls in Badulla, till quite recently the only one in the whole of Uva, which, as I have just observed, is a district about the size of Wales. Here about fifty bright, happy-looking girls are now being well brought up in a good Christian home, where they are taught clean, tidy habits, and are trained to definite work, so as to be able in after years to earn their own living.

Mr. Langdon, however, could not rest satisfied till a definite footing had been obtained in the heart of the most neglected district, and gradually his grand scheme took definite form.

Having obtained from Government a grant of 200 acres of fine valley-patena at this spot, noted for good soil and a perfect climate, with an annual rainfall of 90 inches, and within easy reach of about 9000 of these poor villagers, he has established a home for orphans and destitute children, where all shall receive "such a training as, under God's blessing, shall make them good, honest, and industrious men and women." The children under nine years of age are taught in an elementary school, and older ones in the industrial school.

Here also are a convalescent hospital and a hospital for children, where bright wards gay with coloured prints and the loving care of skilful attendants seem like a foretaste of heaven to the poor little sufferers who are brought here from their miserable homes. But owing to scarcity of funds, only a few wards are as yet furnished, and from the same cause the devoted superintendent and his wife are often compelled to refuse admission to the other departments, in many cases, especially that of sorely tempted half-caste girls, where they know that rejection means perdition.

In his very latest letter, Mr. Langdon tells of his grief at having been compelled to refuse admission to poor little orphan children who were without food or shelter, too young to work, but old in suffering; but he had already received as many as he dared to undertake till funds improve. This is the only home in Ceylon where starving children are received without payment, but it is evident that it stands in great need of further support.

At nine years of age girls are drafted off from the elementary school at Haputale to a girls' home and orphanage in Badulla, which was opened in 1889 to receive orphans and destitute girls; but so excellent is the training there given, that the managers are besieged with requests to receive the daughters of respectable parents as boarders, and it already numbers fifty pupils. The tuition is the same as that given in the Wesleyan Industrial School for girls at Kandy, namely, all that can fit girls for domestic service as nurses and under-ayahs, or for wise housekeeping. They are taught cooking, biscuit-making, dressmaking, sock and stocking knitting, sewing, and mat-weaving.

No caste prejudices of any kind are allowed; the education is religious throughout, without compulsion, no preference whatever being shown to Christian children.

Boys are in like manner transferred when nine years of age to the industrial school, which can receive nearly a hundred, but they remain in the Happy Valley, and in its workshops are duly instructed in various branches of industry, such as carpentry, smith-work, shoemaking, and agriculture, and instead of growing up to be loafers and lying vagabonds, they are taught to earn their own living, and to be truthful and useful, and a comfort to their friends and neighbours.

Boys and girls are also educated according to the requirements of the Public Instruction Code.

Many of the poor little creatures arrive at the Home in a most filthy condition, apparently not having been washed for months, but allowed to run wild in the villages, and even for weeks together in the jungle, with no one to look after them in any way. Such is the raw material from which Mr. Langdon hopes to produce valuable agents for the regeneration of Uva, taking for his motto the verse, "A little child shall lead them."[1]

A very important feature of the Mission is a reformatory home, the first thing of the sort ever commenced in Ceylon. Its dormitories, offices, teaching, and workrooms are all pronounced admirable, as are also the flourishing farm and orchard, which are being worked entirely by lads who, under the former system, would have been serving their apprenticeship in crime in the various prisons of the Isle. The farm is well stocked with cattle, sheep, goats, pigs, and poultry, and it has a small tea and coffee estate, rice-fields, garden, and dairy.

This reformatory, which is capable of accommodating a hundred boys, is about three-quarters of a mile distant from the orphans' home, so there need not be injudicious amalgamation of young criminals with other lads, till the former have started on a new tack, which is rarely long delayed amid such totally new influences. The situation of the Mission is perfect, being a beautiful elevated plateau in a very healthy isolated situation. There is, however, a resident doctor to watch over the health of this rapidly increasing community, and every account of it tells of

---

[1] Story of the Happy Valley Mission. By the Rev. Samuel Langdon. London.

bright, happy young faces, already proving how truly they respond, physically and morally, to the care bestowed on them.

Another good work now commenced for the benefit of various districts of Uva and other hitherto neglected parts of the country has been the establishment by Government of field-hospitals. A group of cottages with mud walls and thatched roofs are erected in some isolated spot. These are the wards, beside which a larger bungalow acts as dispensary and dwelling for the medical officer and dispenser. Of course there is always a little preliminary prejudice against foreign methods of treating the sick, but very soon this is overcome, and the wards are sometimes crowded with poor sufferers, thankful to have the opportunity of obtaining skilled relief.

Leaving Bandarawala, we drove to the head of the Ella Pass, and suddenly found ourselves looking down a magnificent valley formed by a whole series of mountains, some crowned with majestic crags, some still partially clothed in forest, others all terraced with infinite toil for the cultivation of mountain-rice, and all alike vanishing from our view in the deep blue gloom of the ravine far below. I am told that "Ella" means a waterfall or rapid, which in this case must apply to the great Magama River, which rushes down the gorge far out of sight, suggesting during what countless ages the mountain torrent must have toiled and fretted ere it carved for itself this mighty channel.

Beyond these nearer mountains lay outspread the beautiful Park Country, stretching right away to Batticaloa and the sea. The district is well named, for in truth it is one broad expanse of fine open park of good pasture-land and sweet short grass, well watered by several large rivers and numerous clear streams, and interspersed with clumps of fine old trees. Near the base of the great central mountains are ranges of low rocky ridges, partly clothed with tall lemon-grass, much higher than a man, sometimes growing to a height of twelve feet. It is terribly punishing to those who have to force a way through it. In some places it is dense and tangled, in others it grows in tall tufts from the rock crevices. Some of the plains are so covered with lemon-grass that, as the wind sweeps over it, it is like an undulating sea of waving corn.

Right away from the mountains the Park itself is studded with detached masses of granitic gneiss, like fortresses of giants, but beautified by trees of large growth, which have contrived to find root in the crevices.

There being no rest-house at this place, quite an ideal temporary bungalow had been prepared for the Bishop—a framework of bamboos and strong posts filled in and thatched with stout aloe leaves and jaggary and talipot palm leaves, all the inside being draped with calico, and decorated with the graceful blossoms of the cocoa and areca palms (like bunches of splendid wheat). This large bungalow was divided into central dining-room, with side bedrooms and dressing-rooms all complete. A very handsome pandal (arch of welcome) was erected in front of the house, and a comfortable stable and house for the servants at the back. This really was luxurious camping in the wilds!

Hearing of a small rock-temple in the Ella Pass, I started in search of it. It proved rather a long expedition, ending in a scramble across paddy-fields and along a hillside. It proved to be a very small temple amid most picturesque surroundings, huge rock-boulders, fine old Bo-trees, temple-trees loaded with fragrant blossom, and tall palms. Within the temple are sundry odd paintings and images of coloured clay; amongst others, one of a large cobra coiled up, with its head forming the canopy above a small image of Buddha sitting cross-legged upon the coils.

In looking over my sketches, I see that under a crag at the head of the pass I have written Sri Pada Keta, which suggests its possession of a holy footprint, probably a modern imitation of that on Adam's Peak.

Descending the pass by a steep zigzag road, and following the course of a river fringed with luxuriant clumps of bamboo, we came to Oodawere, a pretty and hospitable home, further embellished by a number of "potato-trees," which, as I have already mentioned, are really gorgeous trees, robed in purple and gold,—that is to say, they are loaded with blossoms like our brightest potato-flowers, only three times as big. (This was in the month of August.)

Thence we drove on to Badulla, the capital of Uva, a very pretty little town in the midst of a grassy and well-wooded and well-watered plain, about 2200 feet above the sea-level, and surrounded on every side by fine hills of very varied form. There is a considerable amount of rice culture round the town, which seems like an island crested with cocoa-palms rising from a sea of velvety green. It was here that the Buddhist people erected a neat Christian church to the memory of Major Rogers, in token of their appreciation of his wise and impartial rule in this district.[1]

That church, which has now been considerably enlarged and beautified, was charmingly decorated in honour of the Bishop's arrival, and an exceedingly graceful pandal was erected at the entrance to the churchyard, the road for a considerable distance being bordered with fringes of torn

[1] See chapter viii.

yellow banana leaves, the effect of which, in connection with the pandal, is very light and characteristic.

A number of Europeans had assembled to meet the Bishop, so there were full congregations and pleasant social gatherings. Several Kandyan chiefs appeared in their gorgeous full dress, with the large-sleeved brocade jackets, "peg-top" shaped swathing of fine muslin, and wonderful jewelled hats.

I sketched the whole scene from the old fort, which is now used as a courthouse, where many very varied groups of Moormen and Malays, Tamils, Singhalese, and Burghers came and went the livelong day. Fine hills, rich foliage, tall cocoa and areca palms, and cosy-looking red-tiled buildings combined to make up a very attractive scene, blue and white convolvulus matting the nearer shrubs, and the balmy air fragrant with the scent of rosy oleanders.

I am told that among many recent improvements have been the formation of a small lake, always a pleasant feature in a landscape, and also of a park and racecourse. An excellent new feature is a botanic and experimental garden for the acclimatising of all possible novelties in the way of desirable fruit-trees and vegetables. Already the apples and pears of Badulla are making their mark, and potatoes weighing upwards of a pound each are a delightful reminder of Britain, dearer to her exiled sons than the most ambrosial tropical fruits.

I found another sketching ground at the Kataragam Devale, an old Hindoo temple to Skanda, the god of war, which attracted our unwilling attention by the deafening noise of its "services" daily at 5 A.M. and all the evening—truly a very odious neighbour. The Buddhist Vihara was happily less noisy. It and a dagoba of considerable size date from about A.D. 200, so they are distinguished by some of the calm of old age; otherwise Buddhist temples are wont to rival those of the Hindoo gods in the terrific noise produced by the roar of shell-trumpets, the beating of drums, and the shriek of shrill brass pipes.

I was told of a curious carved stone at another temple, on which is sculptured a short two-headed snake, a sight of which was "good for broken bones;" so of course we set out in search of this interesting object, but failed to find the temple.

But there are stones of more pathetic interest in the old cemetery, some of which date as far back as the "rebellion" of 1817–18, a time when the lives of British officers and their wives in these remote forts must have been sorely beset with anxieties. One crumbling stone marks the grave of a young bride only sixteen years of age. Another marks that of Mrs. Wilson, who came here from her home at Stratford-on-Avon, and died in 1817, aged twenty-four. She was the wife of the Government Agent, who shortly afterwards was shot by an arrow, and whose head was cut off and exposed on a tall pole. Her grave is protected by the roots of a fine old Bo-tree, which have enfolded it, thus marking it as sacred in the eyes of the natives, to whom otherwise a neglected cemetery is simply a valuable quarry whence to abstract ready-hewn flat stones just suitable for grinding curry-stuffs upon! Of course this sacrilege is punished when detected, but its perpetration is easy and the temptation ever-recurring, so that many and many an old gravestone has vanished in all parts of the Isle.

In all this district we heard grievous complaints of the ravages wrought by white ants, and of the ceaseless vigilance necessary to guard against their advances. In native houses an extra plaster of cow-dung is applied to the floors and walls, and is considered efficacious; but somehow superfastidious Europeans do not appreciate this remedy sufficiently to introduce it into their homes! But certainly the white ants do muster strong, their great earth castles, five or six feet in height, and six or eight in circumference at the base, being common roadside objects. Near some of the tanks the ground is strewn with little green hillocks about three feet in height; these also are ant-hills overgrown with grass.

The ants, of all sizes and colours, have two singular and very different foes. One is the strange little ant-lion, which is the hideous larva of an insect like a small dragonfly. It is an oblong hairy creature, only about half an inch long, with a very large stomach and a very small head. It has two large arms and six legs, with which it contrives to move backward, but so slowly that it could never capture a dinner without stratagem. So it makes a small funnel-shaped pit in the sand, and buries itself at the bottom with only its eyes and arms visible. There it lies in wait for any rash ant which ventures too near the edge; as soon as one does and begins to slip down-hill, the ant-lion throws sand at it and so helps it down, when he sucks its life-juices and then jerks out the corpse.

The other foe is on a much larger scale, and is known as the great-scaled ant-eater [1]—a very different creature, however, from the ugly hairy ant-eater [2] of South America, although, like it, it has no vestige of teeth, only a long glutinous tongue with which to lick up the ants. The Ceylonese and Indian ant-eater is clothed in a coat of mail, being covered with hard plates of clear horn, and when frightened it hides its head between its legs and curls its tail beneath

---

[1] *Manis pentadactyla.*   [2] *Myrmecophaga.*

it and right over its head, which it covers completely, presenting the appearance of an armour-plated ball. The strength of several men combined could not uncoil that little creature against its will. Hence its common name, "pengolin," which is derived from a Malay word meaning "to roll up."

It breaks into the ants' citadels with its sharp powerful claws, and licks out the garrison with its long slender tongue. It is a pretty creature, and grows to about three or four feet in length. Being easily tamed and very gentle, it makes rather a nice pet, though its habit of burrowing seven or eight feet into the ground makes it somewhat troublesome, its claws being so powerful that it can dig through anything. It climbs trees as nimbly as a cat, but is never seen by day. It wanders about during the night, but steals back to its hole at dawn.

The Bishop's next work lay in the district of Madoolseme. The first stage was right up-hill to Passara, where there was a school to be examined; then on to Yapane, above which rises a hill naturally fortified by most singular ridges of gneiss. Then "upward, still upward," till we reached Mahadova, where the owner of many nice dogs gave us cordial welcome and most luxurious quarters.

Here we witnessed one of the most characteristic sights of Ceylon, and one which remains stamped on my memory as one of the most awesomely grand scenes it is possible to conceive. A tract of 160 acres of dense forest, clothing both sides of a deep mountain gorge, had been felled, and had lain for some weeks drying in the sun.

I may mention that the method of felling is ingenious as a means of economising labour. Beginning at the lowest level, all the trees are half cut through on the upper side;

gradually the regiment of woodcutters ascend, till at last they reach the summit, when the topmost trees are entirely cut, and fall with a crash, carrying with them those below, which in their turn fall on the next, and so on, like a row of ninepins crashing all down the hillside, till the last ranks have fallen, and the glory of the beautiful forest is a memory of the past, only a few trees here and there remaining standing for a little longer.

When the timber is fairly dry, then the planter waits for a day when the wind is moderate and in the right direction to blow the flames away from his plantations or reserved forest, and then the blaze begins.

On the present occasion we were posted well to windward, and then fire was applied simultaneously in many places, and spread with amazing velocity, till all the fires joined in one wild raging sheet of flame in the depths of the valley, whence fiery tongues shot heavenward mingled with dense volumes of smoke of every conceivable colour, white, blue, yellow, orange, and red, changing every moment and covering the whole heaven with a hot lurid glow, while the thundering crash of falling timber and roar of the mad flames were deafening.

We ran rather a narrow risk of contributing some particles of charcoal to the coffee, having taken up a commanding position, so as to look right down the gorge, in a corner of reserved forest, beneath the cool green shade of a group of beautiful tree-ferns and beside a clear streamlet, in which it was refreshing to bathe our scorched faces. Happily we obeyed a shout from more experienced friends, who bade us come down quickly, which we most unwillingly did, and only just in time; for hardly had we done so, when the flames swept upward in resistless fury like corkscrews,

CLEARING THE FOREST.

twining upward and onward. We rushed away half-suffocated, and soon the whole patch of reserved forest was one sea of fire, which even extended its ravages to some neighbouring coffee. Next morning we had occasion to ride along a narrow path overlooking the scene, and only a veil of blue smoke curling from among the blackened ruins of the forest told of the mad conflagration of the previous day.

There is great luck in the matter of burns. Sometimes the fires die out too soon, and the timber is insufficiently burnt. Sometimes they rage too furiously, and the soil is scorched to such a depth as to be grievously injured. No sooner is the land cooled than an army of coolies overspread it, and cut square holes in every possible corner, no matter how rocky the soil (indeed, the rockier the better), or how dizzy the precipitous height; wherever a crevice can be found, there a precious little bush must be inserted, and after a while, as its roots expand, a small artificial terrace must probably be built, to afford them space and prevent the rains from washing all the earth from their roots. Nothing can be more hideous than the country at this stage.

After a while, however, matters improve, and by the time the coffee shrubs attain their proper size, the whole country becomes densely clothed with glossy green, and though the black stumps and great charred trunks remain standing for many a year, they do gradually decay, or else become so bleached by the sun that the coffee-fields resemble a gigantic cemetery, with headstones utterly without number.

Twice a year the whole country appears for a few days as if covered with a light shower of snow, each bush being veiled with wreaths composed of tufts of fragrant white blossom. These in due time give place to bunches of green berries, which eventually become scarlet cherries, very tempting to the eye, but insipid to the taste. Within these lie two precious coffee-beans; the red pulp is removed by machinery, and is useless, except as manure for the bushes—a sort of cannibalism is it not? The beans are then dried in the sun, and the skin or "parchment" with which each is coated must be removed, after which they are ready for roasting.

When the coffee is dry, it is tied up in sacks of a given weight (each so heavy that few Englishmen would care to carry it half a mile), and these are carried by the coolies on their heads for many a weary mile over hill and dale to the nearest cart-road.

The dress of the coolies is remarkable. Some indeed have little clothing save an old grain sack covering the head and shoulders, and affording a miserable shelter from the pitiless rain; but the majority are provided with an old regimental coat, scarlet, blue, or green, no matter what colour. So this is the final destination of our military old clothes! I think their original wearers would scarcely recognise their trig apparel when thus seen in combination with a turbaned head and lean black legs swathed in dirty linen.

You cannot think what a new sensation in coffee it is to go and rest in one of the great coffee stores, where the clean, dry beans are piled up in huge heaps, like grain in a granary at home. The stores come in useful for everything. All manner of public meetings, from church services to balls, are held in them, and coffee-bags are the most orthodox seat; rather hard, however; for comfort, commend me to the good honest coffee heap, on which many a tired planter has slept without a sigh for spring mattresses.

On that same day (August 30), at Mahadova, we chanced

to witness another strangly characteristic scene, namely, what the Tamil coolies themselves described as a Catholic Saami (*i.e.*, idol) festival. This was a Roman Catholic procession, in which, however, I believe all the coolies, of whatever creed, took part. We heard their shouts in the far distance, and presently they came in sight, winding down a steep path through the coffee, or rather winding up hill and down dale, in order to visit all the Saami houses (*i.e.*, idol shrines) in the neighbourhood, carrying with them four almost life-sized images, in very tall, open shrines, which were simply canopies on poles, painted crimson and yellow. Much the largest of these, shaped like a gigantic crown, contained an image of the Blessed Virgin; two of the others contained St. Sebastian, and a fourth St. Anthony. All were borne on platforms on men's shoulders.

With the exception of the cross on the top of each shrine, and of innumerable gaudy banners, there was nothing whatever to indicate that this was not a Hindoo festival, accompanied by all the usual adjuncts—the firing of guns, the beating of tomtoms, and wild dancing of half-naked brown men with white turbans, dancing all the way, precisely as at the festivals in honour of their gods, and led by the temple-dancers.

When they had visited all the idol shrines, and danced a while at each, they were to halt beside a stream, where all would bathe, preparatory to a great feast of curry and rice, after which dancing was to be resumed by torchlight.

Often when I hear thoughtless persons, who certainly cannot have looked below the surface, compare the results of Protestant and Roman Catholic missions in heathen lands, greatly to the credit of the latter, I wish they could have a few opportunities of really observing the radical change required in the converts of the former as compared with the mere change of denomination which is accepted by the latter in every country where I have seen the working of both missions. No wonder that their converts are numerically large.

In Ceylon we were told of one Roman Catholic chapel in which, during the temporary absence of the priest, the congregation had introduced three images of Buddha and several others; and we ourselves saw a small Roman Catholic chapel with the image of Buddha on one side and that of the Blessed Virgin on the other, apparently receiving equal homage. I fancy, however, that that also must have been without the leave of the priest.

The curious policy of seeking to beguile heathen nations into accepting a spurious so-called Christianity by the closest possible assimilation to their national pagan rites has unfortunately been very widely sanctioned by the Church of Rome in all ages, but nowhere has it been carried to such excess as in Southern India, whence these Tamil coolies have immigrated.

In A.D. 1606, with the full sanction of the Provincial of the Jesuits, and of the Archbishop of Goa, a Jesuit priest, Robert de Nobili, established himself at Madura, where he asserted that he was a Brahman of the West, directly descended from Brahma, and of the highest possible caste.

He forged a sacred Veda purporting to be of high antiquity, in which some Christian doctrines were cunningly blended with much Hindoo imagery. In presence of a large assembly of Brahmans he swore to having received this Esur Veda from Brahma himself.

This Brahman of Rome assumed the yellow robe of the venerated Saniassees, and daily marked on his forehead the circular spot of powdered sandal-wood which denotes caste.

His small crucifix, hidden in his waist-cloth, was suspended from a twisted thread very similar to that worn by Brahmans. He carefully performed all ceremonial ablutions, and certainly shrank from no self-denial in working out his strange compromise, for he abjured all animal food—meat, fish, and even eggs, confining himself to the vegetables, milk, and clarified butter which is the fare of true Brahmans.

Moreover, the better to assert his superior position, and assuredly forgetting the teaching of his Master, he associated only with Brahmans, feigning the utmost contempt for all pariahs and other low-caste people.

He soon obtained credit for great wisdom and sanctity, and gained so many adherents that he is said to have baptized 100,000 persons, largely drawn from the higher castes—converts who naturally were not to be distinguished from their heathen brethren in aught but name.

On the authority of his forged Veda, he prohibited the worship of the Hindoo idols, but freely incorporated all the processions most dear to the people. Amongst others he adopted all the tumultuous ceremonies of the Juggernath night-festival, when huge gaily-decorated idol cars were borrowed from the Tamil temples. So-called Christian images having been temporarily substituted for those of the idols, and loaded with offerings of flowers, the ponderous cars were dragged in procession by excited crowds, amid the blaze of rockets and fireworks, the din of tomtoms, drums, and trumpets, and the acclamations and shouts of the people. Half-naked dancers streaked with vermilion and sandal-wood powder danced wildly before the cars, and all the crowd wore on their foreheads the marks symbolic of idol-worship. Yet these, with the exception of the dancers and musicians, who were hired from the nearest heathen temple, were the so-called Christians of Madura, and the images borne on the cars were supposed to represent the Saviour, the Blessed Virgin, and the Apostles.

Franciscans, Dominicans, and other religious orders having complained of his methods of carrying out mission-work, the matter was referred to Rome, but after an inquiry which lasted thirteen years, the Pope pronounced a decision which practically left things as they were, even approving the wearing of the Brahminical thread by converts, provided it was sprinkled with holy water, and that the converts were invested with it by a Romish priest. They might also continue to mark their foreheads with ashes of sandal-wood, provided they abstained from using ashes of cow-dung.

Thus sanctioned, this sham Christianity flourished, till after forty-two years of vain toil, de Nobili retired, sick at heart, and his followers for the most part returned to their primitive Hindooism.

But till the expulsion of the Jesuits from India in 1759, there was no limit to the compromises by which they sought to gain nominal converts.

Not content with attracting the heathen to their churches by elaborate mystery-plays and theatrical representations of the great events in the life of our Lord, these very adaptive teachers endeavoured to appeal to popular prejudice by blending with their own religious ceremonials all the most striking pageants of Hindooism, and, notwithstanding all the edicts of Pope Gregory and his successors, these were retained until, in 1704, Pope Benedict XIV. issued a most rigorous Bull commanding their suppression.

The Jesuits frankly confessed that obedience to the Papal decree would result in the loss of most of their adherents, and so it proved. Multitudes to whom the adoption of Christianity had been solely a change of name resumed that of "Hindoo," and ere long the stringent regulation was relaxed and the pitiful compromise resumed.

From Mahadova we rode to various other estates, sometimes through lovely bits of ferny jungle, sometimes across great tracts of burnt forest, with their wreaths of blue smoke still curling upwards from the blackened waste which had taken the place of all the fair vegetation, the growth of centuries.

To all lovers of beautiful nature it must be sad to think of the hundreds of square miles of primeval forest which have thus been totally destroyed in clearing ground for the growth of coffee, cinchona, and tea, in all the mountain districts, the greater part of the belt of the Isle between the altitudes of 3000 to 5000 feet being now totally denuded.

But looking down from high mountains on the great plains seaward, we still overlook vast expanses of forests—in fact, about three-fourths of the eastern lowlands are said to be still forest or scrubby jungle, from which the fine timber has all been cleared for commercial purposes. Till quite recently there was no fully organised Forest Department to regulate the ravages of the woodcutters, and certainly no sentimental pity or reverence led these to spare either the monarchs of the forest or the trees of tender years; consequently many of those most valued for the beauty of their timber have now become exceedingly rare.

The necessity for such supervision was recognised so far back as 1858, when Sir Henry Ward appointed my brother to act as timber and chena inspector. But in those days travel was exceedingly difficult, and no man could really attempt to do more than make himself acquainted with the forests of his own province, which in my brother's case meant the neighbourhood of Batticaloa. Moreover, as his sole assistants were two Government peons, it was evident that, keenly interested as he was in this work, he could not do very much.

It was not till 1873 that Sir William Gregory laid the foundation of a more systematic conservancy of forests by the appointment of four foresters for the four northern provinces, and assistants for other districts, whose duties include not merely checking improvident destruction of existing timber, but also establishing in the neighbourhood of the great tanks, nurseries for valuable forest trees.

My brother's appointment as chena inspector refers to the singular method of cultivation known as " chena-farming," which is a system of nomadic farming involving perpetual locomotion, inasmuch as, owing to the poverty of the soil, the same ground is never occupied for more than two years at a time, and is then left to itself for fifteen years! This strange custom has been adhered to for upwards of two thousand years, so it follows that "primeval forests" had been cleared off the plains long before European planters felled those on the mountains. The extent of ground which has been subject to this treatment is enormous.

The process of chena-farming is that the inhabitants of a district proceed to fell and burn a tract of two or three hundred acres of forest. This space is then fenced and apportioned to the number of families concerned, each of whom erects a temporary hut. In these they live in a cheery sort of gipsy fashion, some making and baking earthenware vessels, and others spinning thread or rearing poultry, while waiting for the growth of the crops they have sown.

In a few months the newly reclaimed land is rich with

cotton plants, sugar-cane, Indian-corn, pumpkins, sweet potatoes, millet, yams, melons, and other vegetables. Some of these are ready for the market within four months; so they are gathered, and fresh seed is sown for a second crop, which is ready four months later, the cultivators all the while keeping sentinels posted in little huts, ceaselessly watching day and night to ward off incursions from thievish beasts and birds.

In the second year the company divides, some remaining to guard and gather the cotton, which does not come to maturity for two years, the others proceeding to clear new ground by felling and burning more forest. When the cotton crop is gathered, then the last farm is abandoned, and luxuriant natural growths rapidly spring up.

A good deal of chena is devoted to the growth of plantains, which are very fine the first year, but deteriorate so much in the second year, that by the third they are generally abandoned.

A marked characteristic of all land which has been thus suffered to relapse is the density of the thorny jungle, with few, if any, large trees, but a thick matting of rope-like creepers, many of which, and of the bushes, are armed with wicked hooked thorns of every variety, making the scrub impassable to any creature but an elephant.

Masses of prickly cactus grow luxuriantly on such clearings, as does also the much-reviled lantana, which was introduced only about sixty years ago, solely as an ornamental shrub. It is uncertain whether it was brought from Brazil by Sir Hudson Lowe or from the West Indies by Lady Horton. Its original home is the Cape of Good Hope, where, however, it is by no means so rampant as in these lands of its adoption. It is a pretty plant, covered with little bunches of orange and rose-coloured flowers or small dark berries; the latter find great favour with birds, who carry the seed in every direction, and it has acclimatised to such good purpose, that now it springs up unbidden on every morsel of neglected land, so that from the sea-level up to a height of 3000 feet, thousands of acres are covered with impenetrable thickets of this too luxuriant colonist. Naturally all cultivators consider it an intolerable nuisance, and rue the day of its introduction to Ceylon; but nevertheless the lantana has its own useful mission to perform, in securing for the land both shade and moisture, while by the ceaseless decay of its rich foliage it gives new life to the worn-out soil, preparing it afresh for the service of ungrateful humanity.

Since Government has awakened to the necessity of guarding the remaining forests, this chena-cultivation is under control of surveyors, and the sanction of the Government Agent is required before a new tract can be thus treated; so the villagers are gradually learning to grow their vegetables on more economic principles.

Leaving the mountainous region, we travelled north-east across that known as the Park Country, on which we had looked down from the high grounds—a great tract partly of forest, partly of open grass country and of swampy ricelands, but all intersected by very picturesque hill ranges.

Until very recently, all this district abounded with game of all sorts, which, however, has been so ruthlessly slaughtered, that it is now said to be, practically speaking, exterminated. There are still large herds of spotted deer and a good many of the Sambur deer—here called elk—but very few compared with even ten years ago. A close season has been appointed for the preservation of all manner of deer and other useful and beautiful animals, but this ordinance is apparently respected only by Europeans, and not invariably by them. As to the natives, they harry the poor wild tribes day and night, in season and out of season, large parties with guns, dogs, and nets lying in wait at the waterholes and tanks where they must come to drink, so that the poor beasts have no chance.

A Ceylon paper for July 1891 quotes advertisements showing that "27,453 Ceylon elk hides" had been offered for sale in London since January, and, while discrediting the figures, comments on the ruthless wholesale slaughter which is undoubtedly carried on all the year round. It seems probable that here, as in the United States, the wild creatures are destined to be exterminated, and eventually replaced by more prosaic herds of domesticated animals— cattle, sheep, and horses—who would doubtless thrive in this grassy and well-timbered region, all of which is apparently admirably adapted for pastoral purposes.

A minor drawback to these grassy plains in dry weather are the innumerable "ticks," which swarm in some places. These scarcely visible black atoms get on to one's clothes, and continue their travels till they succeed in burying their heads in one's skin, the sensation of the victim being that of being pricked with a red-hot needle. Any attempt to pluck them out only produces irritation, so it is best to leave these unwelcome guests in peace till you can touch them with a drop of oil, when they relax their hold. (The natives always have cocoa-nut oil at hand to anoint their hair, and oh! the aroma thereof.) There is a larger variety of this pest called the buffalo, but its bite is not nearly so painful as that of its minute cousin. One comfort of rainy weather is that these creatures then disappear.

One very annoying family are the innumerable minute "eye-flies," which take pleasure in dancing as close as possible to one's eyes, as if they really found pleasure in beholding themselves mirrored therein.

It must be confessed that after a while the daily routine of marching is apt to become somewhat tedious, almost every morning having to be up soon after 5 A.M. packing, swallowing a hurried breakfast, and then starting on a march which rarely exceeds twelve or fourteen miles, but which is necessarily so slow that it is probably past ten before you reach your destination, by which time the sun is pouring down in scorching heat, and you are thankful indeed for the shadow of the palm-leaf hut, or any other rough and ready rest-house.

Half the coolies always march at night, starting as soon as you have dined, and the cook and table-servant can get the cooking pots and dishes packed; so that you find your real breakfast ready on arriving, and right welcome it is. By the time you have fed and washed, you are so tired that you generally are thankful for an hour's sleep, that you may be fresh for the afternoon's work or ramble, as the case may be.

Day by day, riding or driving, we moved from point to point. One pretty drive lay through most charming jungle, literally swarming with butterflies. We had to cross the Maha-Oya just at its junction with the Dambera-Oya. A fine wide river-bed overshadowed by large trees suggested what this stream must be when swollen by heavy rains in the mountains, but now all was drought, and there was not even a trickle of water. We walked across the sandy channel, while the horses dragged the empty carriage, and a well-trained elephant, who was assisting in building a bridge for the use of future travellers, lent his great strength to shove the baggage-carts while the patient bullocks pulled them across.

I was struck here, as in many another district in the hot plains, with two peculiar characteristics of several of the principal trees. One is the thinness of their bark, as though Mother Nature knew they would only require summer coats; the other is the extraordinary size and height of their massive roots, which are thrown out on every side like buttresses, evidently to enable the tree to resist the rushing of floods. These buttresses are so high that full-grown men could stand in one compartment unseen by their neighbours in the next division.

We had slept the two previous nights in miserable rest-houses, so it was delightful to find this night's quarters at Pulawella in a clean new house, cosily placed in a patch of quiet jungle with peaceful meadows on either side.

On the following day we found equally pleasant quarters at Rugam, near the Rugam tank, to which we were escorted by a fine old village headman, who remembered my brother vividly, as did also all the villagers, by whom, said the old chief, he was immensely loved. They said he often came here at night for sport in the days when the long-neglected lake lay undisturbed in the silent forest and game of all sorts abounded.

At the time of our visit the tank was being restored, so we saw no large animals, only a goodly family of crocodiles, and many radiant birds—oriole, barbet, kingfisher, &c. The officer in charge of the works was rejoiced to see white faces, the first he had seen for two months. He bade a fisher cast his net in the now clear waters, and each cast enclosed a multitude of fishes, which we carried back for the use of the whole party.

CHAPTER XVI.

SOME PAGES FROM A BROTHER'S DIARY.

DURING his eighteen years' residence in Ceylon, until his death, October 6, 1865, John Randolph Gordon Cumming kept regular diaries full of most interesting notes on natural history and sport, as were also his numerous letters to the old home. By some lamentable accident, the whole of these have been lost or destroyed, with the exception of a few pages of an early journal and half-a-dozen letters—by no means the most interesting, being chiefly on business. Nevertheless, as no word from his pen has ever been published, I here quote a few passages from these, to show how worthily he filled his place as one of the race of Nimrods—the brothers who were all born sportsmen.

"*July 6th*, 1818.—*Batticaloa.*—On the 4th inst. I slept at Terricoil, where there is a large temple. On the following morning I met five Moormen, one of whom told me that a leopard had entered their village the night before, and had so alarmed his bullocks, which were confined in a kraal close to his house, that they broke loose and ran away in all directions. Next morning he found one of the finest killed and partly devoured in the centre of a large plain across which I would have to pass. I rode on, and found his words verified. On examining the ground, I saw that there had evidently been a desperate struggle, the chetah[1] having twice thrown the bullock ere he killed him.

"My first consideration was how best to conceal myself for a shot at the spoiler, in case he should return to feast on his prey. This was no easy matter, on account of the nature of the ground. Fortunately there was one small bush within thirty yards of the spot; this I enlarged with the help of some fresh branches from the neighbouring jungle, forming a very natural-looking crescent, which would effectually conceal several men when once fairly settled down in it.

"I then sent for some villagers to drag the bullock within range of my ambuscade. The moon being in her first quarter and very hazy, I was obliged to take a very near shot, and, to the horror of the Moormen, made them place it within nine yards of the bush, exactly between me and the nearest point of the jungle.

"A few minutes before sunset I took my seat, in company with three other men who were anxious to see the sport. We expected that, according to custom, the chetah would make his appearance immediately after dark, and we were not disappointed. Half-an-hour after we were fairly settled, the sudden retreat of a number of wild hogs and jackals warned us of his approach, and a few minutes after I could just discern him through the darkness, crawling up stealthily with his belly to the earth, like an enormous cat.

"The light was so bad that I did not dare to fire. After

[1] Leopards in Ceylon are habitually miscalled "chetah." See vol. i. p. 237.

licking the flesh two or three times, he retreated out of sight in the darkness; presently he returned, but unfortunately got the wind of us, and after growling most savagely for ten minutes, vanished for the night—so at least I was told by one of the men, an old hand, who added that if he did return, he would examine our hiding-place carefully. So there was nothing for it but to depart in disgust. Returning to the spot the following morning, I found that the chetah had returned, and polished off the best part of the carcase, not, however, before making a careful survey of the bush, as the tracks proved.

"As there was still a chance of his coming back the following night, I determined to take it and fire on him at any risk, whether the light were good or bad. I had, however, a long day before me, and spent it examining different holes and dens of bears and chetahs in the forest, without success, although several of them bore marks of very recent visits from both parties. Came on a small herd of elephants, and shot two, right and left.

"At sunset I again retreated to my hiding-place in company with my former attendants, my hunter and two Moormen. On our arrival at the ground, we found it already occupied by upwards of thirty pariah or village dogs, and as they set us completely at defiance, we allowed them to feast at their leisure. They went on very quietly for some time, till a herd of wild hog, including three large boars, came forward, determined to dispute the field with them. A most exciting scene followed, the dogs ranged on one side of the carcase and the pigs on the other, neither party daring to put a nose on the meat. Every now and then a boar made a rush forward, only to be driven back in double-quick time by the dogs.

"Suddenly the scene changed; the dogs beating a hasty retreat and the pigs moving off to a respectful distance, again warned me of the approach of my game. A few minutes afterwards I discovered him crawling up in the darkness. The moon was cloudy, but I had determined to fire upon him at any risk; so the moment his nose touched the carcase, I did so. The report was followed by most fearful roars and growling, but the smoke coming back in my face prevented me from seeing the actual result. On turning round to spring out of the bush to take a second shot, I found that my attendants had fled, taking with them my spare gun and pistol!

"The smoke having dispersed, I saw that the chetah was gone, but my followers coming up a few minutes afterwards, consoled me by telling me that he was mortally wounded, otherwise he would have sprung forwards, and that we would find him the following morning within a short distance of the place. This proved to be the case. Returning at dawn, we found him stiff and cold within two hundred yards of the spot. He turned out to be a full-grown male; the ball, entering the neck a little behind the ear, had passed through the whole length of the body.

"Returning home, I found that a bullock had been killed by two chetahs the night before. I tracked and shot one of them, a fine male."

"*October* 10*th*, 1848.—Crossed the lake to Nathany. Proceeded to Narvalgennie, and went out bear-shooting with hunting-buffaloes. Shot one bear mortally, but did not bag him owing to the darkness. I found him sitting at the side of a small tank in the middle of an old chena farm; we immediately tacked up towards him with the buffaloes, but owing to the nature of the ground we could not get within thirty yards, so at that distance we lay down to watch his actions.

"The bear, apparently wondering what we were about, approached to within twenty yards of us, and then sat down. The buffaloes began to snort and toss up their heads. I took a hasty shot at his head and missed, the light being bad. As he continued to advance sideways, I fired my second barrel, aiming behind his shoulder. The ball told well, as he rolled heels over head, roaring and groaning. (Poor brute!)

"Before a second gun could be put into my hands, he had disappeared in the darkness, and I saw him no more. On the bear's giving vent to his feelings, the men lost all restraint over the buffaloes; they tore up to the spot, apparently bent upon annihilating the unfortunate brute, and were as much disgusted at his escape as I was myself."

"*October* 14*th*, 1848.—*Charrelacaddi, near Batticaloa.*— Two nights ago, just before sunset, a leopard knocked over a buffalo beside the jungle, in an old chena close to the village above named. The herd, on hearing the noise made by their unfortunate companion, dashed up to the spot in a body, doubtless hoping to polish off the cat by goring him with their horns. He, finding himself hard pressed, first sprang up into a tree, but as the buffaloes continued to butt it and plough up the ground around it, he made a bound over their heads and dashed into the jungle.

"The chetah had broken the neck of the buffalo, but apparently had not tasted blood, for he did not return that night to his feast. Next evening, however, passing that way on his rounds, he carried the carcase into the thick jungle and devoured about one-half. I lay in wait for him next day, but he did not return. The meat was evidently too gamey for his taste, as, instead of eating it limb by limb, according to custom, he had only selected the daintiest bits. This, I find, is a sure sign that a leopard will not return to his quarry."

"*November* 29*th*, 1848.—A farmer in this neighbourhood sent a herd of goats to feed on a small peninsula. A chetah getting wind of them, swam over from the mainland, and laid himself up for the day in a small patch of jungle. The herdsman having discovered him, reported the matter to his master, who immediately collected a party with guns and spears in order to dislodge the enemy. They hastened to the spot, taking the herdsman as their guide.

"The poor fellow, being more bold than prudent, went up to the chetah's place of ambush, and while he was in the act of pointing out the direction of its head, the brute sprang upon his shoulder, sending him heels over head into the shallow water. The man regained his legs, and staggered forward a few paces, the chetah still holding on, and then both rolled over into the deep water.

"The cat not relishing the cold bath, let go his hold and bolted back into the jungle. The other men, on going up to their companion, found his back much cut and torn, and in their anxiety to convey him home and have his wounds dressed, they forgot all about the leopard, who took advantage of their absence to leave the peninsula.

"That same evening a chetah having killed a bullock at Kalarr, two men tied a seat in a tree and lay in wait to shoot him. On the enemy making his appearance a little after nightfall, they fired at him, whereupon he bolted into the jungle. The following morning, on examining the place, they found drops of blood, and followed up the trail, which led them into the middle of a thick rattan jungle. While they were busily engaged in examining the ground, the chetah sprang upon one man, and with one stroke of his paw knocked out his left eye, at the same time taking off one half of his nose. He then disappeared.

"This morning the coolies killed a rock-snake fifteen feet long. His body was all scarred by the protrusion of the horns and bones of different animals which the reptile had swallowed in the course of his lifetime. These snakes are rarely seen by day, but come out at night in search of prey, and seize any animal they can, even a deer. Coiling round him, they crush him, lick him into a shape convenient for swallowing whole, and eventually disgorge his bones.

"*December* 10*th*.—Rather a curious thing happened the other day. A leopard struck down a young buffalo,[1] and while dragging it off to thick jungle was attacked by the mother. The poor beast, in her zeal to defend her calf, missed the cat and stuck her horns several times through her own calf, the leopard meanwhile disappearing into the jungle, doubtless with the intention of returning to feast at leisure after dark.

"Another chetah having struck down a buffalo, the herd, hearing the noise, dashed up to the spot. The cat finding

[1] The Ceylon buffalo is a large, clumsily-built, very strong animal, with black, shining, leathery skin, and scarcely any hair. It carries its head horizontally, nose forward, so that its large, ribbed, heavy horns bend backwards, resting on the shoulders, and it makes good use of them both for defence and to attack man or beast, so it is by no means an enemy to be despised by man or leopard.

himself hard pressed, bolted up a tree. Some labourers who were at work in a neighbouring paddy-field saw the commotion among the cattle and ran to the spot. As soon as the chetah found their eyes fixed upon him, he bounded over their heads and bolted into the thicket.

"*December 15th*, 1848.—I went last week to Karativoe, and the headman of Pantroup, a neighbouring village, sent me word that a chetah had killed a buffalo there the previous night. I ordered my horse and rode off post-haste, but did not reach the spot till an hour before sunset. I found the carcase, which was that of an old bull, half-way between the village and the sea.

"The soil being light and sandy, and rain having fallen on the previous night, I had a famous opportunity of observing the manner in which the leopard had waylaid and secured his prey. So distinct indeed were the tracks, that I could almost fancy I saw the monster taking the spring. They had met on a jungle path; the buffalo, of course unconscious of danger, had approached at a steady pace, stopping occasionally to crop the herbage. The chetah, on the other hand, having winded his game from a distance, had crawled along, *ventre-à-terre*, trying the stunted bushes on either side of the path, till at length he got himself comfortably lodged in the middle of a low thick bush commanding an angle of the path.

"Thence he had sprung, and I could actually see the marks of his tail lashing the sand preparatory to so doing. The buffalo on receiving the shock had staggered forward a few paces and then fallen heavily to the ground. He was unable to regain his feet, and the struggle had evidently been a desperate one, the ground being literally ploughed up and branches of a large size broken.

"The chetah having only sucked the blood of his victim. I knew from former experience that he would return early in the night to make a meal, and as the day was so far advanced, I had little time to form plans or take precautions in self-defence, and the jungle was so low that I could only fire at him from the ground. Hastily shaping out a seat in the middle of a bush within twelve yards of the carcase, I made a screen all round with live branches, which would effectually conceal me and at the same time look quite natural to the eye. I then loaded my guns, and ensconced myself with my attendant in the bush.

"Just as the sun was setting, we heard a distant snorting like that of a horse, only rougher. The sound approached nearer and nearer, and a minute afterwards the head and shoulders of the magnificent brute appeared through an opening in the jungle, within thirty yards of us. Although I had judged from his track and the strength of the buffalo he had laid low that he was one of unusual size, I was quite unprepared for such a grand sight; in truth, he reminded me of a diminutive prize-ox at a cattle-show— such a breadth of chest and shoulder.

"I took aim several times, but judging from the immense size of his limbs and muscles how little effect a ball could have unless it struck a vital part, I reserved my fire for a more convenient season. He continued sitting in sight, snorting for more than five minutes, and then turned round, and with a growl disappeared in the jungle.

"The sun had by this time gone down, and we lay for fully two hours without either hearing or seeing anything of the enemy. We watched the rise of the lovely full moon and the proceedings of a pack of jackals which had been prowling about when we first came to the ground. These became emboldened by the long absence of the chetah, and began to approach the carcase, keeping a good look-out, however, in the direction from which they expected he would come. Every now and then one of them would summon up pluck to give a tug at the buffalo, letting go his hold again as quickly as if it were hot iron, and then running off to a distance, would sit down nervously.

"At length we heard distant growling, which, of course, put us on the alert. As for the jackals, they disappeared in a twinkling. The growling grew louder and louder, till at length the very air seemed to shake, and presently the head and shoulders reappeared at the same place as before. Then the beautiful beast sat in silence for more than half an hour in all the dignity of leisure, as if wishing to make sure that the coast was clear. Then, apparently suspecting danger, though he could not possibly have winded us, he rose and recommenced growling as if in defiance. After standing thus for several minutes, he turned round and disappeared.

"We listened to his growling till at length the sound was fairly lost in the distance. The mosquitos had feasted upon me so long and earnestly that I had grown callous to their attentions, and I was so weary that I was just dropping off to sleep, when my attendant silently touched my shoulder. Listening intently, I again heard the sweet melody, although at a great distance and in an opposite direction from that in which we had last heard it.

"This time he appeared to have made up his mind, as immediately on arriving at the opening he walked up to within a few paces of the carcase and sat down. All on a sudden it apparently occurred to him that it would be as well to reconnoitre the neighbourhood once more before commencing supper, for he rose and walked forward a few paces in the direction of our hiding-place.

"I saw that there was no time to be lost, so, quickly screwing up my nerves for a steady shot, I allowed him to advance within nine yards or so. As good luck would have it, he swerved a little to the right, thus affording me the opportunity of giving him a very favourite ball. I fired. With one terrific roar he bounded into the jungle to the right of us.

"His voice had such an effect on my attendant that he made a desperate attempt to bolt past me out of the bush. I, however, seized him by the wrist and held him fast, apparently much to his horror and disgust. I find that remaining quiet at such a moment is of the utmost importance, as in the event of the cat discovering his enemy, he will spring upon him to a certainty.

"After remaining quiet for ten minutes listening, so as to be sure that he was either dead or had crawled away into the jungle, we got out and walked home. At daybreak we returned in company with a numerous retinue, and were at no loss to find the trail, as, independent of the tracks upon the light soil, blood-stains were not wanting. These continued for about thirty yards and then ceased. That was easily accounted for, as he had then evidently sat down and licked his wounds.

"After following the trail a little further, we lost it in thick jungle. There the natives drew back, and no offer could tempt them to proceed. I made a long and vain search single-handed, but was obliged to give it up for the moment as a bad job. Feeling certain, however, from various circumstances, that he could not have crawled far, I offered a reward of two rupees to any one who would bring me his head. This step had the desired effect, as, on the third morning after, a man came to my bungalow and demanded payment, as he had found the cat.

"I rode off with him to the spot, being anxious to see the noble brute, and also how the ball had taken effect. To my surprise, he had hardly gone 250 yards from the scene of action, and was lying in an old chena by the side of a dense jungle. The poor animal had evidently survived the shot some time, as he lay in a crouching attitude, as if preparatory to making a spring. He was a full-grown male, and measured upwards of eight feet seven inches from nose to tail. The ball had entered the left shoulder and passed out below the ribs on the left side.

"The headman of the village told me that £200 would not cover the damage this leopard had done by the slaughter of cattle in that and the neighbouring villages."

Here ends the only fragment I possess of my brother's diary.

From a small packet of letters I give the following extracts:—

"*July* 27*th*, 1852.—*Kandy*.—I came up to the Kandyan country ten days ago upon business. It is a great relief to have one's nerves braced up after the fearful heat of the low country. I have had a few days' elk-hunting with a friend, and enjoyed myself very much. It is one of the noblest and at the same time the hardest sport I know. We run down the deer with fox-hounds, which gives us a run on foot of eight or ten miles over mountains and rocks, through rugged glens and along precipices. Deer-stalking in Scotland is comparatively tame work."

"1857.—*Batticaloa.*—Christmas alone in the backwoods is not a cheerful season, so I was glad to seek a little excitement in the jungle. Had I chosen to stick to elephants, I could easily have made a large bag (of their tails), but I prefer variety, and to get that, one has to go to work quietly. As it was, I killed four elephants, eight buffaloes, two elk, six leopards, and a considerable number of deer and pigs; of these I only kill what I require for feeding my men.

"While out, two of my friends from Kandy joined me. They stuck to elephants, and killed four, one of which was a small tusker. Shipton nearly came to grief; he was knocked over by an elephant, which afterwards walked over his body, but got confused, and fortunately left him. Two months ago, a native, under almost similar circumstances, was taken up by the elephant in his trunk, and deliberately pounded to death between the brute's knees.

"I was very sorry to hear of poor Bill being hugged by a bear and getting his wrist chawed up;[1] but it is well it was not worse, as these horrid creatures invariably try to get at your face. In my night excursions, generally in the early morning, when they are on the prowl in search of prey, I have had some extraordinary escapes, especially on one occasion, when, just as the brute flew at me open-mouthed, I sent a ball down its throat. The Ceylon bears are enormously strong and very savage, often attacking men without provocation. Sometimes they drop on natives from trees and lacerate them frightfully.

"They are omnivorous, eating fruit, roots, and honey,

---

[1] See "Wild Men and Wild Beasts." By Colonel William Gordon Cumming. Published by David Douglas, Edinburgh.

supplemented by ants, which give a formic acid relish, but they are always ready for raw meat if they can get it.

"They are very jealous of human poachers on their preserves of wild honey, and often attack natives while honey-hunting in the forests.

"Several accidents happened while I was out last. One poor fellow, whom I saw on my way out, was killed before my return by a bear, which literally tore him to pieces, and yet the poor wretch lived for ten days afterwards. He was in a fearful condition: his right eye was gouged out, and the side-bone of the face torn away—features could scarcely be distinguished; his arms and legs were also frightfully mangled.

"Another man had his stomach torn out by a buffalo, and died immediately. Another was killed by a crocodile, which caught him while fishing in a tank. He was rescued, but died in the course of the night. During the same time I heard of four deaths from snake-bite. So, you see, a sportsman in this country has to keep a good look-out; but I find endless delight in watching beasts, birds, reptiles, and nature in general.

"It was the season for birds' nests, and my men feasted freely on the eggs of pea-fowl and many sorts of water-fowl. I myself robbed a lot of pelicans' nests, just for the fun of the thing, but the eggs were rather strong for my taste. It is so absurd of these large birds to build their nests in trees, and their nests are small in proportion to the size of the bird.

"While passing through a low, swampy jungle I came on a crocodile's mound, and the proprietrix, a very large one, was lying quietly on guard. I gave her an elephant ball, which blew her brains away, and she never moved a muscle. With a good deal of trouble, we dug out the eggs from the centre of the mound, and then smashed them. There were fifty-eight in all. A crocodile lays from fifty to a hundred eggs, very much resembling those of a common goose. Fancy all these horrors coming to years of discretion!

"Another day I passed two very fine specimens of rock-snake, from fifteen to eighteen feet long. I could easily have secured them, but left them undisturbed.

"I kill a considerable number of crocodiles by the aid of a hook baited with raw meat and attached to a strong rope made of a great number of small cords so loosely twisted as to get between the teeth of the brute, who is thus unable to bite them. A wooden float attached to the line indicates the whereabouts of the too-confiding crocodile who has swallowed the bait. I draw the float gently ashore, and with it the head of the poor reptile, when a well-directed shot aimed at the back of the neck breaks the spine and secures an easy victim."

"*January* 1863.—*Batticaloa*.—This is our monsoon or wet season. Fancy that for nineteen days we have had no *tappal*—that is, post—from Colombo on account of the low country being flooded, and at the same time our port is closed, so we are effectually cut off from communication with the world. Speaking of post, delightful as it is to receive letters from home, you really must all remember to have your letters weighed, as I have sometimes had to pay as much as six shillings for a single letter, and that's no joke in these hard times."

"*April* 1863.—The last two months have been, as usual,

most oppressive, owing to the reflection of the sun and drying up of the waters after the monsoon. However, vegetation is at its fullest, and all nature rejoices. Birds of all sorts are busy building and rearing their young. It is commonly said that tropical songsters are inferior to those of Europe. I find, on the contrary, that some of the birds here are the most powerful and melodious I have ever heard. But as regards human beings, the only time when a white man can have any enjoyment of life, is the first hour of the morning and the last at night, the glare and heat of the intervening hours being insufferable."

"*July* 1863.—I often wonder how you would relish a week of such weather as we have at present. During May, June, and July our hot winds prevail, the blasts of which are just such as you might imagine coming from the lower regions. At this moment it is blowing in full force, apparently, as one would think, carrying desolation and destruction along with it. I can tell you that a man leading an almost solitary life in such a sultry and exhausting climate has to ' make an effort ' to keep body and soul together. I occasionally go out shooting, but it is more for the sake of exercise and excitement than real pleasure, such is the effect of an unnatural temperature upon the constitution.

"I went out about a fortnight ago and killed various troublesome beasts, amongst others five very large elephants, all with single shots. I also bagged a very large crocodile with baited hook and line.

Some people seem to imagine that the life of a cocoa-nut planter must be a very easy one. That certainly is not the case if you happen to be settled in a part of the country where wild animals abound, and where, for want of sufficient timber to make fences, you are obliged to be constantly on the alert to protect your property.

"I generally rise at 4.30 A.M. and take a saunter in the jungle, watching the habits of any animals or birds I may see. Returning to coffee, I start my men at 6 A.M. to their various duties. Meanwhile a watcher has gone all round the estates, and reports any damage done by buffaloes, wild-hog, or porcupines. When he has anything to report I go to inspect, and if buffaloes have broken in we summon a village headman, who values the damage done and fines the owners accordingly. Sometimes these buffaloes are savage and knock the men down right and left. When the same animals return too often we shoot them.

"Wild-hog are the worst enemies we have to contend with. Those which enter the estates are generally the large single boars, and as they are ferocious to a degree, especially when surrounded, we run considerable risk in effecting their destruction. You can fancy what their strength must be when one rip is sufficient to cut open a horse or a bullock.

"I have had so many dogs cut to pieces that I have given up keeping them, and in general I now shoot as many boars as I can. Some, however, are such cunning old hands that they only come on dark nights, and go away again before morning. For these we prepare pitfalls filled with sharp stakes. This causes a very horrible death.

"A curious thing happened lately. A large boar had been giving much trouble. Two pitfalls were prepared at low parts of the fence where he was in the habit of jumping over. A porcupine fell into one and got staked, but he slipped in so quietly as not to disarrange the branches and grass placed over the top. In the course of the night the boar fell into the other trap, and although badly staked he managed to get out; but while seeking for a hole in the fence by which to get out he fell into the other pit on to the porcupine, and must have attacked it furiously, for his mouth and nose were all transfixed with quills. After all, he managed to get out of the pit, and in the morning we found him at some distance lying in a bush, too weak to charge. The poor creature's tongue and throat were literally riddled with quills.

"It was very horrible, and I much prefer shooting them when it is possible. I lately shot five large ones in one morning. The natives are always glad to get pig's flesh, though Europeans generally object to it, as the wild pigs are filthy feeders, and feast on putrid carrion quite as readily as on young cocoa-palms (so that their trespassing on the latter is inexcusable). They even gobble up the enormous earth-worms, which are as large as small snakes.

"As a matter of sport, pig-hunting in this island is a very different thing from Indian pig-sticking, which is all done on horseback by men carrying spears. Here the sportsmen follow on foot, and the only weapon in use is a long, sharp hunting-knife. Young boars and sows go about in large herds of perhaps a couple of hundred, but the old patriarchs prefer wandering about independently.

"Porcupines also do serious damage on a cocoa-palm plantation, as they have a special weakness for the heart of young palms; and there is no keeping them out, as they gnaw their way through fences or burrow under walls in the most determined manner. They can be tamed, but are troublesome and mischievous pets.

"At 11 A.M. I return to breakfast, and the men do likewise, resuming work at 1. If possible I remain indoors till 3 P.M., when I go out again till sunset at about 6.30.

"Then, unless there is any night shooting to be done, I am glad to get to bed early, and so take refuge inside the nets to escape the mosquitos and other playful insects. At the present moment I can hardly see my paper for eye-flies."

I think there are few sportsmen who will not share my regret that these meagre notes are all that remain to record the experience and observation of one who landed in the Isle while it was still a true paradise for sportsmen—when the multitude of wild animals was as described by Sir James Emerson Tennant—when there were no game-laws, no need of licences, only a grateful people, not, like the villagers of to-day, provided with rifles, powder, and shot, but ready to bless the white man, who freed them from the incursions of dangerous foes and provided them with abundant food, in the form of wild pigs and sundry kinds of deer. For his own camp fare there was a most appetising variety of birds, jungle and pea fowl, red-legged partridges, plover, and pigeons, quails, parroquets, fine fat wild-ducks, snipe, cranes—in short, ample materials for savoury stews and roasts; and of these also we occasionally received amusing notices, as, for instance, when one day he had shot a lovely rose-tinted marabout stork that he might send me its feathers, and its body had furnished an excellent stew. After dinner his servant remarked that fish must surely be very scarce this season. On his asking "Why?" the reply came, "Because in cleaning that bird for master's dinner I found a large rat inside of it!" Now, even in the jungle, that was not a very pleasant suggestion!

Besides all the animals that can be classed as game, that quiet observer of nature found a never-failing delight in studying the habits of all manner of creatures which a mere hunter would pass unnoticed, or probably destroy as vermin. My brother's delight lay in taming many such, and his rough-and-ready bungalow was not only adorned with all manner of trophies of the chase, but also was the home of a most singular variety of pets of all sorts—his companions in many a lonely hour.

CHAPTER XVII.

BATTICALOA.

Musical shell-fish—Shooting fish by torchlight—Baptism of villagers at Navatknda—Tamil caste persecution—Honorific umbrellas—Life on a cocoa-palm estate—Visit to the Veddahs—Dread of the evil eye—Singhalese castes—Dhobies prepare huts for travellers—Bad water causes divers diseases—Pollanarua.

FROM Rugam we drove to Batticaloa; part of the distance was to have been accomplished in a borrowed carriage, but as the horse totally refused to move, and finally lay down in the middle of the road, we had to wait several hours under the palm-trees till another could be procured. These little difficulties are of such frequent recurrence whenever it is necessary to hire horses, and the many unpleasant methods to which the horse-keepers resort to persuade obstinate, or perhaps half-starved, animals to proceed have been so often described, that it is needless to refer to them, and, personally, my own experience was generally confined to the well-cared-for and well-trained horses of friends.

The country towards Batticaloa is a dead-level plain, which (thanks to the restoration of the tanks, and of the ancient system of irrigation) has been transformed from an unhealthy marsh, overgrown with low jungle, to a vast expanse of luxuriant rice.

Sir Henry Ward (who first suggested the necessity of a forest protection) was also the first to attempt any restoration of the old irrigation works in the Eastern and Southern Provinces. In the Batticaloa district the repair of the great tanks at Irakkamam and Amparai restored prosperity to all the country round, converting a district where malarious swamps alternated with arid wastes into a smiling expanse of fertile land. Now the eye may rest on a plain of about 20,000 acres of lovely green rice, in addition to all other varieties of cultivation, and a well-fed, prosperous, healthy population replaces the half-starved and diseased villagers of fifty years ago.

Parallel with the coast for about thirty miles lies one of those strange fresh-water lagoons or "gobbs" similar to those on which we sailed up the western shores of Ceylon,[1] formed by the confluence of some of the many rivers, which, meandering through this vast verdant plain, 200 miles in length by about twenty in width, have changed their course in many a flood, and yet continue to supply their former channels, thus forming a natural network of navigable canals—quiet waterways fringed with dense thickets of evergreen mangroves whose curiously arched and wide-spreading roots grow right into the water, the home of innumerable crabs and shell-fish, and also swarming with crocodiles. Lovely blue kingfishers and snowy or rose-coloured cranes, pelicans, and other aquatic birds here find quiet covert whence they can fish unmolested.

The united waters are prevented from entering the sea (except when in flood) by a harbour-bar of their own creating, which effectually forbids the entrance of any vessel—a grave inconvenience to those whose business is

---

[1] See chapter iv. A glance at the map will well repay the trouble.

occasionally interrupted by the raging breakers on the bar, but a feature which secures a beautifully calm lake, in which all the ranges of blue distant hills and wooded headlands lie faultlessly mirrored.

The name of Batticaloa is said to be derived from the Tamil words *Matta Kalappa*, meaning "Mud-Lake," and the little isle on which the Portuguese built their town and fort is called Puliyantivu, or "The Isle of the Tamarind-trees." This they did in 1627 without permission of the King of Kandy, who thereupon invoked the aid of the Dutch. These in 1638 arrived in force from Java with six ships-of-war, captured and destroyed the fort, and then proceeded to build one for themselves, which remains to this day, with the invariable uncompromisingly plain chapel within its precincts.

Likewise within the fort, and scattered round three sides of a grassy common, are white houses all roofed with red tiles, each bungalow standing in its own pleasant garden. The peaceful cemetery occupies a prominent position on this green common, one side of which is washed by the lake, whose farther shores are densely clothed with cocoa-palms.

One of those red-tiled houses and one little corner in that still God's acre possess a very special interest in our family history, as the scenes of the close of this first chapter in the life of one very dear to us.[1]

After watching a gorgeous sunset from the ramparts of the old Dutch fort, when earth and lake and sky seemed transformed to glowing gold and the rosy oleanders shone red as rubies, we rowed in the quiet moonlight to listen to the faint notes of the far-famed "musical shell-fish," which are only to be heard in the dry season, so we were

[1] See page 169.

fortunate in the time of our visit. When the lake is swollen by the rains the depth of water deadens the faint submarine chorus.

That night there was not a breath of wind nor the least ripple to disturb the dead calm, and we distinctly heard the tiny voices, each apparently producing a succession of notes, as if you gently tapped a tumbler with a steel knitting-pin, the combination of these producing faint rippling thrills, just like the vibration when you rub the rim of a finger-glass with a moist finger.

We rowed very gently, halting at different points where alone the sounds were audible, whence we inferred that the musicians live in colonies. The Tamil fishermen attribute the notes to the inmate of a small pointed shell which they call *ooria coolooroa cradoe*, "the crying-shell;"[1] but this shell is found in other lagoons where it shows no talent for singing, and, in truth, no one seems able to identify this little minstrel of the Batticaloa lake.

Less pleasant inhabitants of the lake are the crocodiles, which are large and numerous, ranging from six inches to twenty feet in length. The former, of course, are the newly hatched babies.

We were much interested in watching the fishers shooting fish by firelight, which they did with almost unerring aim. They go out at sunset, and having kindled a bright fire in a brazier in the centre of their boat, they stand at the prow with a large bow and arrow—the latter attached to a long string, whereby they draw in the silvery fish which, moth-like, have been attracted to their doom by the glare on the dark waters. The strangely shaped boats and dark figures, and the reflections of these moving fires, with

[1] *Cerithium Palustre.*

the bright moonlight just silvering the tall dark palms, presented a succession of very striking scenes.

A few days later we were privileged to witness a scene of far more enduring interest. On Sunday the Bishop held service in English for the general community of Britons and Burghers, and afterwards in Tamil for the converts of that race, assisted by their own native clergyman.

The latter had the happiness of telling him of the remarkable (and in Ceylon quite unique) conversion of all the inhabitants of a neighbouring village—that is to say, that all had resolved *en masse* to give up the worship of the Tamil (Hindoo) gods, and to become the faithful servants of the One True God. They had already given substantial proof of being thoroughly in earnest, for although very poor people—only despised toddy-drawers—of the Nallavar caste, they had quite of their own accord subscribed so liberally that they had raised sufficient money to buy a piece of land as the site for their village church, and had already built a temporary house in which to meet for service.

These earnest converts now craved Christian baptism, and the native clergyman requested the Bishop to go to their village and admit thirty men to that holy Sacrament. About 130 women and children were kept back for fuller instruction.

On a lovely afternoon[1] we proceeded by boat to the village of Navatkuda (*i.e.*, the Bay of the Jambu-tree or Rose-apple,[2] a waxy pink fruit with a flavour like the perfume of rose-leaves), which lies on the shores of the lake, about two miles from Batticaloa.

[1] September 10th, 1873.
[2] "The Malay Apple" (*Eugenia Malaccensis*).

There, on the grassy palm-fringed shore of the clear blue lake, we found the 160 men, women, and children who had resolved on this great step, assembled to receive the servant of their newly-found MASTER. Brown men with large turbans and waist-cloths of bright-coloured calico, and brown women and children with glossy black hair and brilliant drapery, and of course (however poor) adorned with some sort of metal bracelets and anklets, always ornamental. They were a very nice-looking lot, and all reverently escorted the Bishop to their little temporary chapel, which was hung with white calico ("the honours of the white cloth"), and prettily decorated with palm leaves in the native style.

Nothing could have been more impressive than the baptismal service which followed, and all listened with the deepest and most earnest attention to the Bishop's address, charging one and all to stand steadfast unto the end, in the face of whatever difficulties might await them. Then, as the sun set, we bade them farewell, and rowed back to Batticaloa in the stillness of rapidly-deepening twilight, watching the gleaming reflections of many boat-fires as the fishers started for their evening sport.

Very shortly after this the Bishop's health became so seriously affected that he was compelled to resign his charge in Ceylon and return to Britain; and though the remembrance of the scene on the shores of the lake has often come back to me, it is only quite recently that I have obtained details of the grievous and pitiless persecution which (albeit under protection of the Union Jack) these our fellow-subjects and fellow-Christians have endured during all these long years, for no other reason than that, being of very low caste

—toddy-drawers [1]—they had presumed to support a resident schoolmaster, and they and their children had obtained a little rudimentary education. For religious teaching they were dependent on the visits of a catechist, and occasionally of a Tamil clergyman, the Rev. A. Vethacan.

From the time of their conversion they declined to carry wood to the idol temples, and they abstain from Sunday-work, except the necessary collection of the sap in the early morning. But worst of all, it is averred that some of these low-caste people have actually ventured to carry umbrellas to shelter them from the blazing sun! These are the sole offences of which they have been guilty, and for which they have repeatedly been cruelly beaten and insulted by unneighbourly neighbours of the Fisher caste, who (taking advantage of their sometimes prolonged absence at different cocoa-nut plantations, where they have been employed in the dangerous work of toddy-drawing) have again and again maliciously destroyed their poor palm-leaf and mud huts, so that on their return they have found their houses all wrecked.

The persecution can scarcely be ascribed to envy of any advantages conferred on these poor Christians by their profession of faith, for they do not seem to have received any sympathy or support from the large Christian community in Batticaloa, and they have never yet been able to improve on their original rude school-chapel, though years ago they collected a great heap of bricks, hoping soon to be able to build a simple church.

To this effort they were encouraged by the present Bishop,[2] who visited them in 1889, and being deeply touched

---

[1] The work of collecting the sap of the palm-blossoms is described in page 158.

[2] The Right Rev. R. S. Copleston, D.D.

by manifest proofs of their genuine Christianity, earnestly commended their work to the sympathy of the Church in Batticaloa. But beyond the collection of a small sum of money by the Bishop himself, nothing seems to have been done, and probably the very fact of the Bishop's visit stirred up the jealousy of the Fishers, who perhaps were also influenced by the somewhat general revival of caste distinctions, owing to their unfortunate recent formal recognition by the British Government. Anyhow, on January 6, 1890, they commenced a most unprovoked series of attacks on the poor Christians, two of whom were so seriously wounded that they had to be carried to the hospital at Batticaloa, their assailants proceeding to burn the school-chapel with its benches and simple furnishings, and totally destroy the village.

Nevertheless, on the following Sunday the catechist assembled his congregation as usual, and held service beneath the shadow of the trees beside the calm lake.

Of course, as in duty bound, the Rev. A. Vethacan reported the disgraceful business to the Magistrate and Government Agent, and the ringleaders having been secured, several were deservedly sentenced to long terms of imprisonment. None of the Christians were found to be at all in fault, having acted solely in self-defence.

As they did not dare to return to rebuild their village on the former site, the Government Agent determined at first to provide for them a new settlement on Government land in another part of the district; but believing that after the leader of the aggressions had been committed to prison all would be peaceful, he resolved to erect new huts on the old site, and having done so, invited the Christians to return. This they were afraid to do, and the headman, whose duty it was to bring them back, asked Mr. Vethacan to come over and persuade them to do so.

Bound on this peaceful errand to his sorely-tried flock, the good old clergyman started, as he had so often done, to cross the calm lake to Navatkuda, and at 7.30 A.M.[1] he landed on the grassy shore, expecting to find the headman waiting for him. That official was late, but Mr. Vethacan perceived a man coming towards him armed with a gun and brandishing a sword, and recognised one of the most bitter aggressors, and one, moreover, who had been hurt by one of the Christians in self-defence (as had been proved in the court).

On seeing this truculent-looking person approach, Mr. Vethacan returned to his boat and shoved off from the land, whereupon the assailant began pelting him with stones, and threatening to fire if the boatman did not at once return, which the cowardly fellow, being in mortal terror, did. The miscreant then fell on Mr. Vethacan with his sword, wounding him very severely, and then went off, leaving him on the ground half dead.

There he lay in the blazing sun for about two hours before any one came to his assistance, his boatman having gone off to Batticaloa to inform the Government Agent of the assault. The latter started at once, but met another boat in which the victim was being brought to the hospital, his clothes all saturated with blood. He was found to have received several severe wounds on the arms, the first finger of the left hand had been cut off, and several others were severely injured, and he had lost so much blood and received so grave a shock that at first it was feared his life was in danger.

[1] On the 1st December 1890.

Happily, however, all went on well, and with good care and nursing he has made a good recovery, and after five months was able to resume his duties. Ten months elapsed ere the case was tried, when it is satisfactory to learn that the cowardly assailant was then sentenced to ten months' imprisonment. It is equally satisfactory to learn that this long delay was due to the fact that there was no spring assize either at Trincomalee or Batticaloa, owing to the general absence of crime in the Eastern Province, and the fact that there was no other case for trial. In order to teach the people to keep the peace, a police force has been quartered in the village, for which they will have to pay about 1600 rupees a year—a salutary lesson.

The Christians very naturally refuse to return to their old quarters, so it has been decided to remove them to the other side of Batticaloa. Their chief regret is that they will thus be removed from the neighbourhood of a large Mahommedan village, where they have hitherto got work from employers who happily ignore caste questions.

Surely it would be well that some proof of sympathy was extended to these long-suffering Christians, and the Bishop earnestly hopes that funds may be placed at his disposal to enable him to build their church, though not on the site which they secured so many years ago, and also to secure the salary of a catechist who may endeavour to turn the hearts of the persecutors, and win them also to the knowledge and love of the MASTER, Whose love recognises no distinction of caste.[1]

For the whole difficulty has really arisen from these wretched petty caste privileges, and the determination of

---

[1] Any donations for this object will be gladly received by Mrs. Coplestone, 16 Denmark Place, Brighton.

the fishers that no lower caste should rise in the social scale or presume to encroach on their prerogatives. Of these, none is so jealously guarded as that of carrying an umbrella in scorching sun or pitiless rain!

A few years ago some men of the Barber caste presumed thus to offend on the grand occasion of a wedding. The fishers took umbrage, smashed the umbrellas, and a mêlée ensued in which several of the " higher caste " were stabbed. This led to a riot in which sundry houses were burnt, and all barbers punished for becoming proud. Natives in good position declared it "served them right." A number of fishers were sent to prison, but to this day the barbers dare not carry umbrellas. It is alleged that the Nallavars of Navatkuda had been guilty of this offence, and that consequently the fishers resolved to give them a lesson.[1]

As an example of how low caste acts as a social disability even in the professional world, I may instance the case of a man whose father, although a toddy-drawer by birth, has made money in plumbago, and educated his son as a proctor. His Tamil brethren of the law, however, would not allow him to sit at the table with them in his native town, and he has been compelled to seek practice elsewhere.

Such a detail in an English court of law sounds strange in Britain, where we are so effectually learning that "money maketh man," and where

> "Gold hath the sway
> We all obey."

Imagine the son of a rich ironmaster being professionally scouted on account of his father being a self-made man!

Leaving Batticaloa at sunrise in a wretched palanquin, one execrable horse dragged us four miles along the lake,

[1] See chapter xxii., Subdivisions of Fisher Caste.

and then was replaced by one rather worse, till we came to a deep sand track, impassable for wheels. There the Bishop's horses met us, and we rode to the shores of the Moondim Aar lake or river, where a boat was waiting to take us to Chandivelle, a large cocoa-palm plantation belonging to one of my brother's old friends.

A hospitable welcome awaited us in a real rough-and-ready bungalow beneath the palms, a smaller separate one being assigned to Miss Jermyn and myself, which formed our comfortable headquarters for several days. It was my first experience of living on a cocoa plantation, and was quite "a new sensation" in nuts! Every morning the great elephant-cart went round the estate, collecting such cocoa-nuts as had fallen during the night, and by midday a huge pile had accumulated. These nuts being fully ripe, were then broken up wholesale with hatchets by a band of almost nude coolies, and very hard work they had, the outer husk being so thick. Then another lot scoop out the kernel, either to be dried in the sun as *copra* for curry-stuff, or sent off to the oil-mill. On every side picturesque brown Tamil men in big turbans, women in bright draperies with ear-rings and nose-rings, bangles and anklets of silver or base metal, and children with silver charms but little drapery, gave life and colour and interest to the scene; and I for one was never weary of watching these ever-varying groups in their daily avocations, especially when they gathered round the primitive well to fill their great red earthenware chatties or brass lotas, cooling themselves by emptying these over their heads.

A baby elephant wandered about as a playful pet, and one day a snake-charmer brought a whole family of deadly cobras to dance before the verandah, whereon lay the ugly heads of several gigantic crocodiles with large white teeth, and other hunting trophies. These and many other characteristic details, such as prickly aloes and tall cotton-trees, were our surroundings, all bathed in the mellow sunlight streaming through the golden and brown lower leaves of the tall palms, which being right above us, revealed all their wealth of nuts and blossom.

Then at night the stars and the clear moonlight were so perfect that we could scarcely go indoors. Specially attractive were the great bonfires (made of palm leaves and the outer husks of the nuts), round which about a hundred of the estate black cattle were picketed as a protection against leopards. It would be difficult to imagine a more striking scene for an artist's brush than these groups of dark animals beneath the palms, which glowed so red in the firelight, while a silver shimmer of moonlight played on ever-waving fronds.

One night we approached that living picture too quickly, and the cattle mistook the strange white women for leopards, and some in their terror broke loose and stampeded.

I should perhaps mention, as a practical though unromantic detail, that these large herds of estate cattle are kept on various plantations solely for the sake of manure. I visited one estate where 180 head were kept at a cost of about £500 per annum, their sole other duty being to supply milk and butter for one couple, though doubtless the coolies profited by the surplus. They are also allowed a limited supply of cow-dung for coating the floors and the inner walls of their houses, this being an effectual preventive of vermin; it is far too precious to be used as fuel, as in India. When coffee began to be sickly, this manure fell into disfavour, as being productive of obnoxious white grubs, and many estates sold their herds. Now, however, it is proved that as a fertiliser for tea it is of inestimable value.

I regret to learn that the grievous murrain which in 1890 decimated so many herds has not spared this district, which reports a decrease of 14,000 buffaloes and 6200 black cattle. In the district round Pollanarua and Minery 5581 buffaloes and 5223 black cattle died, and many thousands more perished in the villages round Haputale and throughout Uva. The mortality has been unnecessarily great owing to the superstitious belief of the people that the murrain is the work of demons, who would be incensed by direct interference with their doings by any attempt to minister to sick beasts or observe rational precautions, so that all efforts of the afflicted cattle-owners are limited to making propitiatory offerings to the "ill, vile, evil devils."[1]

Our meat supply consisted largely of the flesh of wild pig, which we did not consider equal to good English pork, so we were very glad when the entertainment was varied by snipe, which are abundant in the wet rice districts and all marshy places in the Eastern Province, sometimes rising in flights of a dozen. I recently saw a letter from this very estate in which the writer describes a sudden arrival of unexpected guests, for whom, naturally, he had no provisions. He, however, went off trustingly to his favourite preserve, and in half an hour returned, having bagged 17½ brace, which enabled him to feast his friends on roast snipe, stewed snipe, grilled snipe, and snipe curry!

[1] For the benefit of any Southron who may not recognise the quotation, I may explain that it refers to a Scotch minister's exposition of the character of Satan, and how appropriately he was named. "For, my brethren, if you take one letter from his name, you find *evil*—he is the father of evil; and if you take away a second, you find *vile;* and take yet another, and there remains *ill;* so that he is just an *ill, vile, evil devil.*"

When Colonel Meaden was stationed at Trincomalee in 1872, within easy reach of the brackish lake Tamblegam, he went out snipe-shooting on seventeen days between January and April, and bagged 482½ couple, the highest record being fifty-two couple one day, the lowest being two couple.

And in occasional days in March, April, and May 1891, our kinsman, Hector Macneal, of the Gordon Highlanders (grandson of "The Old Forest Ranger"), bagged 375 couple in the low country round Bentotta, in the south-west of the isle.

The bungalow stands close to a broad reach of the river, where in the early morning and in the delicious cool of the evening I practised rowing, under the able tuition of my host, and very soon had an opportunity of turning my powers to good account on the occasion of our visit to the Veddahs.

The Park Country through which we had travelled on our way to Batticaloa lies on the southern verge of the region haunted (I can scarcely say inhabited) by that strangely primitive race, supposed to be descendants of the aborigines, who, upwards of two thousand years ago, retreated to these wilds when the Singhalese conquerors arrived here from Bengal, and have ever since maintained their isolation from all contact with civilisation, only desiring to be left unmolested in their own deep solitudes. At least this is still the attitude of the pure-blooded Rock Veddahs, who conceal themselves in the caves and forests among the foot-hills at the base of the great mountain centre—a region known as "Bintenne," which describes broken country at the base of the highlands, answering to "The Terrai" at the base of the Himalayas. It used to be so pestilential that even camping there generally resulted in jungle-fever, but now its character in that respect has greatly improved, owing to considerable clearings of forest.

This remote secluded region was, till very recently, untrodden save by these wild shy tribes, themselves shunning the human presence, and waging a noiseless warfare with wild beasts, silently stalking till within ten paces of their quarry, then shooting with noiseless bow and arrow—no disturbing firearms—and rarely letting a wounded animal escape to be a living warning to his fellows.

They live in caves or in temporary grass huts (not in trees, as has been sometimes stated), but they rove to and fro, following the migration of game, which travels from one district to another in search of water-pools. When the water on the low ground is all dried up, and the streams and pools are transformed to beds of dry sand, the game betakes itself to the moist mountain pastures, and the Veddahs follow, some of them owning small dogs to help them in the chase.

They have long bows and arrows for big game, and very small ones for birds. As regards the former, the bows, which are of very flexible wood, are over six feet in length; taller than the ugly little archers, who are often under five feet in height. The bowstring is of twisted bark fibre greased, and the arrow (which is a light shaft two and a half feet in length, and winged with feathers from the peacock's wing) carries a broad flat arrow-head fully six inches in length, and sometimes twelve or even fifteen inches long. These iron arrow-heads used to be the only manufactures of the civilised world which they at all appreciated, and certainly in the hands of keen marksmen they can do great execution.

The archer holds his bow in the right hand and pulls the string with the left hand.

Even the giant elephant does not escape, for the hunter glides stealthily close up to him, and aiming at the heart, does his business more swiftly than many a keen rifle-shot, who vainly seeks the little brain in that thick skull.

Sometimes these archers fall in with elephants when they had expected only small game, and when their quiver is stored only with little short-headed arrows. Then they wait till the giant slowly lifts his great foot, when, swift as thought, the winged shaft pierces his sole. An angry stamp only drives the barb farther home, and the hunter, well satisfied with his work, is content to wait, knowing that very quickly the wound will fester, and that the poor brute, no longer able to support his own ponderous weight, must lie down, an easy victim to his foes.

Strange to say, this nice clean vegetarian, whose flesh is so greatly appreciated in Africa, is despised by all races in Ceylon; even the Veddahs never eat elephant, buffalo, or bear, though squirrels, mongooses, and tortoises, kites and crows, owls, rats, and bats are highly esteemed, while a roast monkey or a huge hideous iguana-lizard is an ideal dainty.

They also catch fish in the rivers and neglected tanks, but their chief store is deer's flesh cut in long strips and dried on a scaffolding of sticks over a fire. It is then securely packed in bark and stowed away in hollow trees, with a top-dressing of wild honey to exclude the air. Then the hole is filled up with clay—a safe repository till the next time their wanderings lead them to the same district.

When the chase fails to supply them with meat, they seek wild berries and roots, and failing these, they allay the pangs of hunger by chewing bark, which also supplies their clothing. After being soaked and beaten till it becomes pliable, it is stitched together with fibres of the jungle-vines, which hang so ready for use in all the forests. But even this simple raiment was formerly considered *de luxe*, for when my brother used, in his solitary forest wanderings, unexpectedly to come on Rock Veddahs, men and women alike were quite naked and truly hideous; their mass of long, shaggy black hair, and the men's long, uncombed beards, all filthy and matted, making their head seem too large in proportion to their ill-shaped limbs. All are insignificant in stature, and their wide nostrils, large jaws, and projecting mouths and teeth, are certainly not according to *our* idea of beauty!

Now, however, they so far condescend to contact with civilisation that they are willing to accept a certain amount of calico and earthenware chatties, as well as the much-prized iron arrow-heads, hatchets, and salt, supplied by Moormen, as the Mahommedan traders are called, and in exchange for which they place beeswax, elk's horns, deer's flesh, and occasionally an elephant's tusk in some conspicuous place.

Lucifer-matches, however, have not yet superseded the ancient way of obtaining fire by rapidly twirling a long pointed stick in a hole made in a piece of dry old wood, held by the feet. Atoms of dry wood are thrown in as tinder, and after a few minutes of hard work a spark appears and fire is kindled.

The language of this strange race consists chiefly of a very limited range of guttural sounds, quite incomprehensible to the Singhalese; and as regards religion, they have literally none, having no knowledge of any God, nor any instinct of worship beyond offering propitiatory sacrifices to certain spirits of earth and water, as their forefathers, the Yakkas, did in bygone ages, to avert thunder and lightning; and they also perform some devil-dances on behalf of sick persons.

These really wild Rock Veddahs are now few in number, and are very rarely seen. Hideous and filthy as they are, the Singhalese, with their intense reverence for high position and ancient blood, acknowledge these gentlest of savages as of very high caste, ranking next to the Vellales, or cultivators, who rank highest of all.

The Village Veddahs, with whom we had several interviews, are a stronger, more manly-looking race, but are not of pure blood, having frequently intermarried with Kandyans and Singhalese, whose language (in a very corrupt form) they have adopted. The Coast Veddahs, who work to a certain extent with the Tamil fishers, speak a Tamil *patois*. These support themselves by fishing and by weaving mats and baskets.

The total number of Veddahs is now estimated at about two thousand, but I need scarcely say that Rock Veddahs do not furnish census statistics! Even the Village Veddahs have a gipsy-like love of migration, and think little of moving, their frail homes being simply constructed of mud, reeds, and palm leaves. Efforts have, however, been made to induce them to settle by allotments of land for cultivation. Wells were dug for them, cocoa-palms and bread-fruit trees planted, as were also fields of Indian-corn, kurukkan, rice, and other grain, manioc and cassava roots, plantains, gourds, and sundry vegetables : seed and agricultural implements were provided for them—in short, everything done in the endeavour to tame them, with the result that a considerable number of them are becoming reconciled to a stationary life, with some simple comforts around them.

In 1838 the Wesleyan missionaries at Batticaloa began to try teaching them, and have continued the effort ever since, with moderate success, a few having embraced Christianity.

Many of those who were formerly scattered along the sea-coast were persuaded to congregate in villages prepared for them in forest clearings near the shores of beautiful Vendeloos Bay, to the north of Batticaloa. At one of these villages the Bishop had, in the previous year, opened a school for the bright, intelligent Veddah children, and to inspect this was one of the objects of the present journey.

So we started from Chandivelle at early dawn one lovely morning and rowed about nine miles down the Nattoor River to Vallachena, two miles from Vendeloos Bay, where the river enters the sea. (The river is quite salt even at Chandivelle.) The shores and many little isles are clothed with mangrove, acacia, and other trees, and the scenery is pleasant.

Many Veddahs had assembled to welcome the Bishop on his return, and presently some women arrived and very shyly came forward to see their white sisters (probably the first who had visited them).

First the Bishop examined the school-children, and some of the most advanced wrote sentences for us in Tamil on the "ola" or strips of prepared palmyra leaf, which form the substitute for paper not only for copybooks, but for precious manuscripts, though the talipot-palm is preferred for the most valuable books.

Then we all squatted on the dry grass beneath a white awning which was suspended from the trees, and the native clergyman read service in Tamil, selecting Genesis i. and St. Mark i. as the Lessons. Then the Bishop spoke on these, Mr. Samonader interpreting.

After service we begged for an illustration of the farfamed skill of the Veddahs as archers in the use of their little bows, which they had brought with them. This, however, proved a lamentable failure, which we charitably attributed to the awe of our presence, but which seems to be generally the case in presence of Europeans, their success in bringing down game being rather due to their extreme caution in creeping close to their quarry ere hazarding an arrow.

In the afternoon, the Bishop, being ill and very tired, was obliged to rest, so the native clergyman offered to row Miss Jermyn and me some distance up the river in a small boat to a Veddah village of palm-leaf and mud huts, overshadowed by tall palm and other trees. Some of the men's huts were like those erected in the fields for the sentinels watching the crops, namely, two platforms, one above the other, raised on a scaffolding of rough-hewn poles, the upper platform shaded by a light thatch. The regular dwelling-houses are very low, only about eight feet high, and almost all consisting of palm-leaf thatch, the upright side walls being so very low. The people were quite friendly, but very shy.

When we had gone round one village (and of course sketched a little), we rowed on a little farther to another, and saw the people making mats, grinding grain, &c. (korrakan, the small grain on which the poorer villagers chiefly subsist; it is made into hard uninviting cakes, occasionally compounded with a good deal of dirt).

We thought to win a mother's heart by admiring her

baby, but found we had done quite the wrong thing, as admiration is supposed to imply covetousness and involves great danger of the "evil eye,"—a baneful influence which is as sorely dreaded in Ceylon as in Italy, or indeed in most other countries, including even Scotland.[1]

In almost all Eastern countries some device is resorted to to draw aside this malign influence; children are loaded with jewels, or they are purposely left with dirty faces; the trappings of camels and horses are adorned with cowrie shells; Mahommedans suspend ostrich eggs from the ceilings of their rooms, and here in Ceylon earthenware jars daubed with white paint are conspicuously stuck on the roof to attract the eye which might cast the dreaded glamour on the house.

As evening drew on, we started on our homeward row down the river, the native clergyman, as before, taking the oars, till, as we passed a village, the headman came out and remonstrated on his doing so, he being a high-caste man. The argument was evidently effective, for the worthy man appeared quite perplexed, evidently fearing to lose influence with his flock. So to solve the difficulty (though I fear, perhaps, establishing a bad precedent), I took the oars myself and rowed home—an easy task, being downstream.

Though "caste" distinctions are by no means so obtrusive in Ceylon as on the mainland of India, they are, nevertheless (as I have already proved), sufficiently marked to be the occasion of many difficulties, especially in the formation of missionary schools, where almost naked little brown brats

---

[1] As I noted when "In the Hebrides," p. 261. Certainly, judging from such verses as Mark vii. 22 and Proverbs xxviii. 22, the "evil eye" must also have suggested some very definite ill to the Jewish mind.

of high caste sometimes begin by displaying the most amazing spirit of contempt and persecution towards those of lower caste.

The Singhalese (as worshippers of Buddha, who entirely condemned caste distinctions) ought to be free from these distinctions, but practically they make as much of them as any Hindoo, which is perhaps not to be wondered at, seeing that they are descended from the Brahminical conquerors who, under the leadership of Wijayo, came from Bengal about the year 543 B.C., and overran Ceylon.

Then it was that the aborigines fled for refuge to the forests and caves of the interior, and to the outlying isles of the north. The former (who are supposed to be the ancestors of the Veddahs, were thenceforward known as Yakkas, or demons, because their sole religion consisted in propitiating the powers of evil. To the Yakkas (whether demons or aborigines) is ascribed everything of unknown origin, whether ruins of constructions which are deemed too great to have been created by unaided human power, or too rude to be the handiwork of any existing race, such as certain huge dams, rock-fortresses, &c.

Those who fled to the extreme north rendered special worship to the cobra, and were accordingly named the Nagas, or cobras, and the northern part of the isle was called Nagadipo, "The Isle of Serpents." (As I have previously mentioned, on one at least of the small isles near Jaffna there is still a temple where live cobras are reverently tended by priests and priestesses, and receive devout worship.)

To this day, as we have seen, the Singhalese recognise the hideous and filthy Veddahs to be worthy of all honour, as being of very high caste; so much so, that it would be no disgrace for a woman of good social position to marry one of them, should her strange taste incline her to do so. But on the other hand, the most cruel and indelible disgrace that could possibly be inflicted on a high-caste woman was to give her to an outcast Rodiya (or Rodilla), a singularly beautiful race (at least both men and women are so in youth), who nevertheless have ever been regarded as the lowest scum, their name even being derived from *rodda*, " filth."

Under the Kandyan kings every phase of ignominy that could be devised was heaped on these poor people, who are said to have been degraded for ever and ever because one of their ancestors having, on one occasion, about two thousand years ago, failed in procuring venison for the king's table, substituted the flesh of a nice fat baby, of which his Majesty partook with much relish. But the crime was discovered, and the whole clan of the miscreant shared in his disgrace, and thenceforward all their posterity were ceaselessly persecuted and oppressed till English rule freed them.

They were forbidden to enter a Buddhist temple or any village; they might not till the soil, or draw water from a well, or even cross a ferry; even the stream on which their shadow fell was defiled for a while; they must get off the path to avoid the possibility of any one brushing against them, and so being polluted; they were compelled to salute *every one* by raising their joined hands above their head and then making lowly obeisance; men and women alike were forbidden to wear any clothing below the knee or above the waist; and they might not even build a decent cottage with a wall on each side, but only hovels constructed of palm-leaf hurdles leaning against a back-wall of mud. A curious detail of petty but very real persecution was the prohibition to divide their burden into two bundles, hanging from each end of the " pingo " or shoulder-yoke, as is done by all other natives, in Ceylon as in China; the Rodiyas might only carry one bundle, and so lost all balance.

They were only allowed to earn their bread by guarding the crops from the ravages of wild beasts, or by the polluting work of burying the carcases of dead cattle, of whose raw hides they manufactured strong ropes for binding elephants. Once these were made, any caste might handle them freely. They were compelled to furnish all Government leather-work, also they might kill monkeys and prepare their skins for covering native drums. For a member of another caste to touch a Rodiya was accounted such pollution, that when in the early days of British domination it was necessary to arrest some of them on a charge of murder, the native police refused to lay hands on them, but offered to shoot them down from a distance. This was strictly correct from a native point of view, any man being at liberty to shoot a Rodiya as freely as though he were a noxious animal.

Any Government orders or other communications to be made to Rodiyas were generally sent by charcoal-burners, as being the lowest of all recognised castes, and the messenger, if possible, delivered it across a flowing stream, to save his own respectability. Yet, as they were deemed to be fortune-tellers and dealers in witchcraft, doubtless many consulted them on the sly.

Whatever may have been the true origin of these beautiful outcasts, it is certain that their ranks have been recruited in later ages by whole families of the highest castes, who have been degraded to the rank of Rodiyas as a punishment for treason, sacrilege, or other grievous crimes.

As they were forbidden to till the soil, it was enacted that in time of harvest each cultivator should bestow on them a small gift of rice, and very small it sometimes was.

On one occasion, however, a stingy man was paid-out for having given a Rodiya an exceptionally small dole. The angry man walked up to the threshold floor and scattered it broadcast over the grain which was there heaped up, thereby polluting the whole. Happily British rule was firmly established, so the infuriated farmer dared not shoot the outcast, as he wished to do. He was recommended to sue him before a law-court, but this he deemed quite too derogatory to his own dignity, so the Rodiya escaped.

Of course, under British rule caste distinctions are nominally ignored, so the Rodiyas now have better houses and some home comforts; some even own small farms and a few head of cattle, but the old influence asserts itself, and their proud Kandyan neighbours make them mark their cattle by hanging round their necks a cocoa-nut-shell fastened with a strip of leather, and in many petty ways contrive to remind them of their inferiority.

(When Ernst Haeckel, the naturalist, was living in the rest-house at Belligama, pursuing the study of marine zoology, his devoted assistant was a beautiful Rodiya lad, to whose unfailing zeal and dexterity in everything he bears the highest testimony. The amazement of the villagers was unbounded when this despised outcast was promoted to such honour as that of being the right-hand of the man of wondrous scientific knowledge, and the grief of the poor lad when his employer departed may well be imagined.)

Strange to say, low in the social scale as these poor people rank, two castes rank so much lower that the Rodiyas refuse to have anything to say to them. These are the Hanomoreyos of Uva (manufacturers of betel-boxes) and the Ambetteyos or barbers. What they can have done worse than inveigling a king to eat human flesh no one can imagine. Just fancy entrusting your face and head to be shaved by a man whose very touch at other times would be pollution! The village dhobies or washermen, here as in India, are another example of how the highest castes depend on the low castes for their cleansing and beautifying. Strange to say, all castes, even the lowest, employ the dhobie, and would consider it quite wrong to do their own washing!

One singular duty of the chief dhobie in each district is that of preparing temporary bungalows for the reception of such officials as are entitled thereto in out-of-the-way places where rest-houses are not available, and we were now entering on a series of marches right into the interior of the isle, where we were entirely dependent on these for our night quarters. While travelling with the Governor, I had seen "mushroom villages" of such forest bungalows provided for all the suite, albeit to be occupied for one night only.

Of course, the preparations for the Bishop and his party were on a much smaller scale, though answering their purpose equally well. These huts are lightly constructed of bamboos, reeds, and plaited palm leaves or "cadjans" on a framework of wood, and the interior is all hung with white calico. This is called "the honour of the white cloth," which is accorded to all persons to whom special honour is due. At first I marvelled how so much white calico could be obtained in the heart of the forest, but we soon discovered that each strip was the spare garment of some villager. The village washerman knows exactly who is possessed of such extra property, and he goes round borrowing, and so the temporary guest-house looks delightfully cool and clean to welcome the tired travellers.

Within an hour of their departure the huts are demolished; perhaps the woodwork and palm-leaf cadjans, and certainly all the white cloths, are restored to their proper owners, probably with an infinitesimal share of the vale bestowed on the dhobie.

Sometimes, however, mischievous monkeys begin the work of demolition without waiting for the departure of the travellers. I specially remember one day when we returned to our grass-thatched home on the embankment of the great tanks at Pollanarua, where we halted for some days, and found a whole troop of monkeys on the roof in wildest glee, tearing up all the thatch!

Of course, in such a hut the floor is simply dry earth (or in some cases very wet earth), but for such an expedition a traveller's luggage must include a roll of taliput palm-leaf mats, in addition to a coolie-load of simple bedding, pillow, mosquito-net, &c.

Of course, travelling on these unbeaten tracks, where roads are still unknown, was specially interesting; day by day we rode by jungle-paths, perhaps following the slow footsteps of some dignified headman who was proud to act as the Bishop's guide. Sometimes we followed the course of fine rivers overshadowed by magnificent trees, but in the month of September the streams were well-nigh dry, and we were able to ford them without difficulty. The one exception was when we came to the broad, beautiful Mahavelli-Ganga, the largest river in Ceylon, to which I had already done homage where it flows round the mountain capital of Kandy.

We halted for a delicious rest beneath one of the great trees overhanging the wide glassy stream, while the horses waded and swam across. Then we followed by boat, and again halted on the farther shore in a green glade where the cool moist grass had attracted a swarm of gorgeous butterflies, which floated on their fairy-like wings as though holding a festive assembly. One family of these lovely fairies has large velvety black wings spotted with vivid crimson; another, which measures six inches across the wings, has upper-wings of black velvet, but under-wings of glossy yellow satin.

All insects were not equally attractive. We found minute eye-flies and mosquitos especially irritating, nowhere more so than at the huts where we had spent the previous night, close to two ancient tanks, one quite and the other partially dried up. These huts were literally swarming with long-legged spiders, thousands of them clustered together, like bunches of black hair. Those were not pleasant quarters, but the natives were very kind, and brought most welcome gifts of milk, which, however, we felt sorry to be obliged to accept, as of course the drought affected even their supply of drinking-water, which is at all times a difficulty, and at many places where we halted it was so foul that it had to be boiled and filtered twice over ere we dared to use it. But under any circumstances we were strictly forbidden ever to drink a drop of water which had not been both boiled and filtered once. Where it was obviously impure, obedience was comparatively easy; but where it looked clear and sparkling, and we were parched with thirst, we were sometimes sorely tempted, though well aware of the necessity of strict obedience, bad water being the prolific cause of divers diseases, such as fever and dysentery, in the mere traveller, but too often, in the case of poor villagers compelled to use it habitually, it is in a great measure responsible for the far more terrible diseases known as Beri-beri and " parangi," resembling leprosy. Perhaps the most blessed result of the recent restoration of so many of the great tanks is that, with the abundant supply of good water, and consequently of wholesome grain, this awful malady has almost disappeared from the districts thus favoured.

The natives purify drinking-water for their own use by rubbing the inside of the earthen water-vessel with certain seeds which have the virtue of attracting to themselves all noxious properties, and in five minutes all impurities sink to the bottom, leaving the water clear. One of the seeds is a small nut called Ambu-prasa-dana, the other is the fruit of a large forest tree, the Ingenni-gedia. It is a gelatinous berry in a woody outer case.

A good many years ago an admirable village filter was invented by G. W. R. Campbell,[1] consisting simply of three large wicker baskets, each one foot smaller than the last, the space between the two outermost being tightly packed (below and on every side) with clean sand; the space between the next two being similarly packed with charcoal. This was sunk in a foul village tank, leaving the surface above water, and in a little while the innermost basket filled with pure clear water, whence all comers might draw. Simple as is this contrivance, the natives, however, generally prefer their own ways, and the use of the purifying seeds which Nature provides all ready for them.

I am told that in preparing such a filter, vegetable charcoal, freshly burned and powdered, suffices (with sand and gravel) to remove vegetable matter, but that only charcoal of animal substance can remove animal impurity. Whether this is true, however, I cannot say.

I may mention, as a hint for thirsty travellers, the advan-

[1] For many years Inspector-General of Police in Ceylon.

tage of carrying bottles of cold tea for use on the march, each bottle being wrapped in a wet towel, the evaporation from which in the burning sun secures most welcome coolness.

Having crossed the "Great Sandy River," a short beautiful ride brought us to our bourne, namely, the ruins of the ancient city of Pollanarua, where we found that a group of most delightful huts had been erected for us beneath the cool shade of large trees growing actually on the embankment of Topa-Wewa, the great artificial lake, on whose still waters floated the loveliest waterlilies, and across which we looked away to the lovely blue ranges of the far-distant Matale hills, rising above the wide expanse of dark forest which encompasses the lake on every side.

107

CHAPTER XVIII.

POLLANARUA.

King Prakrama Bahu—Small-pox—Rain charms—Devil-bird—Legend—Inscription on the stone book—Temple of the Tooth—Divers temples, relic-shrines, baths — Porcupine trap — Rock-temple— Gigantic images—Intercourse with China—Minery Lake—Oath-stone—Temple of the tank gods—Circles of pottery—Crocodiles— Kantalay tank—Tamblegam oysters.

ALTHOUGH Pollanarua (or Toparé, as the modern village is now commonly called by the islanders, from Topa-Wewa, the artificial lake on which it stands) is less interesting to the antiquarian than Anuradhapura, from the fact that its glory as a city only commenced when that of the latter had waned, to less critical eyes it is equally amazing, as being a mighty city now literally buried beneath many feet of soil, and all covered with green turf and jungle ; the busy streets and their inhabitants have alike disappeared beneath the sod, and the whole is, as it were, one vast cemetery for houses and men.

Only here and there stately ruins remain to tell of the vanished glories ; and though these are on the whole less impressive than those of Anuradhapura, in that the imperishable stone sculptures have in many cases been replaced by brickwork and very fine stucco, the general effect of the place is more attractive; there are more picturesque "bits" to tempt an artist's brush, owing perhaps to its utter desolation, and to the fact that it has as yet scarcely been touched by the marks of restoration and excavation.

The beautiful lake Topa-Wewa, which was originally fifteen miles in circumference, was formed by King Upatissa II., who reigned A.D. 368; but not till A.D. 650 do we hear of a royal palace having been built here by King Sri Sangabo II. Both these were monarchs of the Sula-Wansae or "Lesser Dynasty," so called in Singhalese records in uncomplimentary contrast to the grand monarchs of the Surya-Wansae or Solar Dynasty (also called the Maha-Wansae or Powerful race), which had so long reigned at Anuradhapura.

That ancient capital was not forsaken in favour of Pollanarua till about A.D. 769, when, weary of battling with continual invasions of the Malabars, the Singhalese monarchs moved south-eastward to this more inaccessible district, and created a new city, more beautiful than that which they had abandoned, with temples and palaces which awakened the wonder of all comers, while the abundant water-supply was secured by the formation of enormous tanks, one of which, the great artificial Lake Minery, is twenty-two miles in circumference. Even now, in its neglected and ruinous condition, that is its size in wet seasons, although in years of great drought it now evaporates to a lakelet barely four miles in circumference.

Of course the Malabar invaders soon made their way to the new city, and the same weary struggle continued for many generations.

This mediæval capital attained its climax of wealth and power in the period between A.D. 1153 and 1240, during the reigns of the mighty King Prakrama Bahu and of his successor, Kirti Nissanga. The former ranks above all others in the love and reverence of the Singhalese, as having been pre-eminent in chivalry, in piety, in wisdom, and in power. He had mastered the various sciences and accomplishments of the age, including medicine, logic, poetry, and music, and the training of the elephant and of the horse.

His reign, which continued for thirty-three years, began amid civil war, from which his energy and popularity brought him forth "sole king of Lanka,"[1] and secured such peace in his own dominions as enabled him to accomplish an incredible amount of work, while at the same time his warlike nature found means to wage successful war against the kings of Cambodia, Pandya, and Chola (the two latter in Southern India). Each of these had given him cause of offence, for which each was forced to make ample reparation, and all three became tributary to Lanka.

Whatever this large-minded king undertook was carried out on a scale so magnificent as to be only rendered possible by the employment of the unpaid labour of the people. I have already referred to those stupendous irrigation works, including 1470 tanks, including lakes so great as to be commonly called "the seas of Prakrama." Besides these, he restored about as many more which had fallen into disrepair during the prolonged wars, and made or repaired upwards of 4000 canals and watercourses.

While thus furnishing his people with an abundant water-supply and securing the means of raising plentiful crops, he built or restored innumerable temples, relic-shrines, and houses for Buddhist priests in every part of the Isle, which was the more remarkable considering the difficulties of communication in those days.

[1] The ancient name of Ceylon.

Amongst other meritorious works enumerated in the national chronicles were the erection of 101 dagobas, 476 images of Buddha, and the building of 300 rooms for the reception of images, besides repairing 6100 such rooms. Besides all the temples which he built, he made 31 rock-temples, with tanks, baths, and gardens for the priests, while for the accommodation of travelling priests he built 230 lodgings, with 50 halls for preaching, and 192 rooms in which to offer flowers. He also built 230 halls for the use of strangers.

At Pollanarua itself everything was done that could enhance the beauty of the city, and very lovely it must have been, rising from the brink of the great lake, which reflected its stately palaces, temples, and dagobas, coated with the cream-coloured cement so like polished marble, and all the gilded spires and cupolas and golden umbrellas. And to right and left of the city lay outstretched a broad expanse of richly cultivated land and verdant pasturage, with groves of flowering trees and palms and clumps of tamarinds, casting the coolest of all shade.

Prakrama encompassed the city with a strong wall, enclosing an area about thirty miles long by twelve in width, and at the four great gates he erected alms-houses for the poor and hospitals for the sick, whom he visited in person, giving them the benefit of his own medical skill.

Within the city were noble streets, with halls for music and dancing, schools and libraries, public baths and pleasant gardens. Prakrama's own palace was seven storeys high, and, according to the chronicles, contained four thousand rooms, supported by hundreds of stone columns, besides outer halls and staircases.

Strange indeed it seems to think of so fair a city, after

reigning as capital of the Isle for five hundred years, being in its turn abandoned to utter desolation. The only probable solution of the mystery is, that in the course of the incessant wars which ravaged the Isle in the centuries succeeding that of the great king, enemies must have devised means for cutting off the water-supplies by diverting the feeding rivers, and so the whole irrigation system would be destroyed, and the millions whose very existence depended on the rice-crops would thus be suddenly reduced to starvation, and either died of famine or were compelled to abandon a district which could no longer yield them food.

Once the inhabitants were gone, the downfall of the city would be swift. Legions of white ants would quickly reduce the woodwork to powder, insidious parasitic plants would take root in many a crevice, and rapidly developing into great trees, would rend the walls, and herds of wild elephants would do their part in hastening the downfall of tottering buildings; then would follow the amazingly rapid growth of thorny jungle, which even in two or three years so effectually overruns all abandoned land, and here the elephants and too luxuriant vegetation have reigned undisturbed for upwards of six centuries.

Even the sparse population which remained, contriving to subsist in dependence on the precarious rainfall, were well-nigh swept away by a terrible visitation of small-pox in the first year of the present century. This infliction being deemed the special amusement of one of the goddesses, it is supposed that any attempt to stay its progress would be specially displeasing to her; so no precautions whatever are taken (or rather would not be, were they not made compulsory), and in that year its ravages were such that the great district of Tamankaduwa, of which Pollanarua is the capital, was literally depopulated, and now only averages five inhabitants to the square mile—5000 to 1000 square miles; and in all that vast desolate district of 640,000 acres, only about 2800 acres are now under cultivation! The people subsist by hunting and chena-farming; the former rapidly leading to the extinction of game, and the latter cruelly destructive of timber.

Happily for land and people, the days of tank restoration are at hand, and the same good work which has brought new life to Anuradhapura and the great district of Nuwarakalawiya, is about to be wrought in this hungry and thirsty region around Toparé, not merely in restoring the eight ancient lakes, sixty of the smaller tanks, several hundred village tanks, and the general system of irrigation canals, but in the still more necessary formation of head-works to regulate the overflow from the rivers in times of flood.

For it is by these ungoverned outpourings from the great rivers, Mahavelli-Ganga and Amban-Ganga, even more than by the lack of a regular water-supply, that the rice-lands are rendered desolate, and it will tax the skill of the ablest engineers to avert these oft-recurring dangers.

At the time of our visit to Pollanarua, the land was suffering from a prolonged drought, the tanks being dryer than they had been for thirty years; fields and jungle were alike parched and burnt up, even the hardy shrubs all scorched and shrivelled by the fierce sun, and all the tender green of ferns and mosses had utterly vanished, except in favoured patches within reach of some leak in a tank, or near the river-banks. For days and days together we scarcely saw a blossom, save the scentless scarlet ixora, whose very loveliness at last became hateful, for it made us hot to look at it, especially as we well knew what colonies of vicious red ants made their home among its blossoms.

In these seasons of sore drought the people of this district have recourse to sundry charms to obtain rain, one of which is that they clear the jungle from a ridge whereon stands a dagoba, to which they then repair and pour out offerings of milk, which they say invariably produce the desired boon. Apparently they deem it unwise to try this remedy too often!

We had suffered considerably in the last few days from the great heat, but all was forgotten now in the delight of finding ourselves in such cool and pleasant quarters, actually on the embankment of the lake, and thus sufficiently raised to command a perfect view, and also to catch every breath of air that rustled through the foliage. It was a joy even to be at rest under the cool shade of wide-spreading trees, looking down on beds of rosy lotus-blossoms, and on humbler blue and white lilies, which floated on the blue waters.

Though disturbed by the preparations for our coming, many aquatic birds soon returned to their homes in the waving reeds and tall flowering water-grasses, and sometimes a flock of long-legged white cranes or of rosy flamingoes, or even a familiar grey heron, would alight and stalk solemnly along the shallows.

When the sun began to lower we went off to explore the wonders of the silent city, returning to our quarters beside the lake in time to watch the glories of sunset colouring and of the gorgeous afterglow, till it faded away in the darkness.

What a standing mystery it is! What can there be about

the horizon to act the part of so wondrous a prism, that, for a few short moments at the outgoing of morning and evening, earth, lake, and sky should thus be bathed in rainbow colours?

How beautiful those nights were, with the brilliancy of glittering starlight and the various voices of the forest, which now and again broke the utter stillness—the whirring of night-moths, the rustling of grasses, the chirping of grasshoppers, the croaking of frogs, the querulous yapping of jackals, the hooting of owls, of which there are several varieties, from the beautifully-marked brown wood-owl, and the rich orange-buff screech-owl, which cries like an infant wailing in distress, to a delightful little creature peculiar to Ceylon (*Scops minutus*), which is only six inches long, and has a little feeble cry. It is brown and grey, and has yellow eyes and a horny feather-crest; it feeds on bats and tiny birds. But the one voice which I did wish to hear was silent, namely, that of the far-famed devil-bird, or Guamala, as the natives call it, whose excruciating cry has been so often described, but whose identity has ever been under dispute. Even Sir Samuel Baker, who says he heard it continually, never succeeded in catching sight of the bird. That cry is sometimes like the shout of a man in distress—a shriek of torture, followed by a gurgling sound as if a victim were being strangled; then follow piercing screams and convulsive cries agonising to hear, so suggestive are they of murder; then follows a silence as of death, perhaps broken once more by dismal wails and pitiful cries.

It is a voice so very eerie that it is said no one can hear it without a shudder, and all natives hold it in superstitious horror, believing it to be a warning of death; and doubtless this awe has been intensified by the mystery as to what creature utters these horrid sounds. At last, however, Mr. Stephens of Gampola has succeeded in shooting a bird in the very act of emitting these unearthly yells, and the victim proved to be the forest eagle-owl (*Bubo Nepalensis*), which is known to the Singhalese as *Loku Bakamuna*, and to the Tamils as *Peria Anda*. It is a large strong bird of beautiful plumage—another proof that fine feathers do not secure melodious voices!

The Singhalese account for a bird being endowed with so agonising a cry by a legend of how a wicked man, being angry with his wife and child, took the child to a wood and murdered it. Then taking some of its flesh, he returned home, and sending his wife out on an errand, he popped the flesh into a curry which she was preparing. Unheeding the child's absence, the woman presently ate of the curry, when the inhuman father told her what he had done. Crazed with horror, the unhappy mother fled to the jungle and there destroyed herself. In her next transmigration her soul passed into a "devil-bird," which thenceforward has made night hideous with its cries of anguish.

If night in the forest is beautiful, how entrancing is the delicious freshness of the tropical dawn, when the stars pale in the clear vault of heaven! Then the hills stand in sombre purple against a primrose-coloured sky, and suddenly the darkness is replaced by a flood of pure dazzling light; all living things in the forest awaken, and a thousand varying notes blend in one harmonious chorus. It is so odd to hear the deep bass supplied by a booming note not to be distinguished from that of the great monkey, but which is really produced by a most gentle dove.

How ethereal were the lovely violet hues of the distant

mountains in that early dawn, changing so rapidly from purple to pink, and then the mellow glow of the risen sun casting clear dark shadows where a moment before all was even-toned, and bringing out the rich greens of the great trees and of the rank succulent herbage all round the muddy shores of the lake, the "moist and reedy grass" fringing the still waters, which form quiet little bays and inlets separated by wooded peninsulas!

Our little regiment of coolies, composed of Moors, Hindoos, Buddhists, and Veddahs, were camped on the brink of the lake beneath the cool shade of overhanging trees, and the blue smoke of their camp-fires added a picturesque touch to the scene.

The embankment on which our huts were built, and which is the dam to which the lake owes its existence, is about sixty feet wide on the summit, and about two miles in length. The whole was faced with hewn stone, but the roots of large trees have dislodged the great blocks, and overthrown this massive masonry.

We were close to the ruins of Prakrama's audience-hall, and lion-throne, marked by a number of dwarf stone pillars and by a solitary finely sculptured lion with curly mane and twisted claws and tail. He is about 7 feet long by 6 feet 6 inches high. We were fortunate in seeing him in the right place, as he was shortly afterwards removed to Colombo, there to grace the museum. His date, in common with that of most of the ruins, must be about A.D. 1153.

On the farther end of the embankment stands a cyclopean statue of King Prakrama, sculptured in full relief from a mass of dark rock. He is represented reading an "ola," i.e., a long scroll, and the sculptor has not given him a pleasant expression. The height of the statue is 11 feet 6 inches.

By some accident the upper half of his head was broken and has been replaced rather on one side. The Government Agent (Sir F. Dickson), who was with us, bade his men climb on to the shoulders of the statue and put it straight. With undisguised horror they refused to stand on the shoulders of a king, but they climbed up the rock behind him, and with great difficulty contrived to reach it and do what was needed.

I found a very attractive spot for a comprehensive sketch at the Wata Dágé or round treasure-house, a circular building of red brick on a raised and terraced mound. It is surrounded by a low wall of huge stone slabs, all covered with a sort of diaper pattern of four-leafed flowers, which is quite unique in my experience of Oriental sculpture. Between each slab stands a tall monolithic column with finely sculptured capital. The terrace wall round the mound is all very richly sculptured with rows of grotesque fat men, lions, and lotus blossoms all round it. It is approached by four very handsome stairways, all most elaborately carved, and with very perfect guardian figures, with the usual headdress or canopy of seven-headed serpents. The moonstones at the base of these steps are also in most perfect preservation, with semicircles of geese, elephants, and horses round a central lotus flower. These stones are 7 feet 8 inches in diameter.

Within the circular building there remain only the mutilated fragments of a sitting image of Buddha, whose head lies on the grass, with stony face upturned to the sky, alike heedless of the gay butterflies that hover around, and of the white woman from a far-away isle who dares to invade his sanctuary.

Beside the broken statue lies an oblong stone marked

with diamond-shaped holes. A similar stone lies in the outer quadrangle of the "Temple of the Tooth." They were probably yoga stones, on which devotees might gaze fixedly to intensify their meditations.[1]

The circular brick wall is only about twenty feet in height, but on its summit a noble banyan has established itself, and throws out such a network of great white roots, reaching to the base of the mound, that its roots are in truth as conspicuous as the wide-reaching arms, which were the chosen playground of a large troop of frolicsome monkeys of all ages and sizes, jumping, swinging, chattering, scolding, grimacing, as if they were trying to show off their accomplishments to the strange invader of their sanctuary. Several had the neatest little babies, which cuddled in the maternal arm, rode on her back, or held on by her long tail, as the case might be.

The clear blue of the sky forming a background to the warm rich reds of the brickwork, the white banyan stems and stonework, and the greens of foliage and grass, made a pleasant scene, and presently a solitary priest ascended the steps, and his brown skin and saffron drapery and palm-leaf fan added just the needful touch of yellow light. To the right of the picture rises the Sat-mahal-prasada, or "Palace of Seven Storeys." It is a small building in very perfect preservation, but it is only 28 feet 6 inches square at the base, and there is nothing to indicate what it was used for; possibly a cell for some fanciful priest.

Between it and the Wata Dâgé lies a very remarkable huge block of stone known as the "Galpota" or stone book. It measures 28 feet in length by 5 in width, and averages 2 feet 6 inches in depth; but only the top and the

---

[1] See chapter xiii.

four sides are hewn so as to represent a gigantic book. For some reason unknown, King Kirti Nissanga caused his "strong men" to carry this enormous stone all the way from the sacred mountain of Mihintale, a distance of upwards of eighty miles. This is recorded on the stone itself, which is entirely covered with writing, except that the inscription is encircled with a procession of sacred geese, and at either end a neat little image of Buddha sits cross-legged between two tall elephants, which uplift their trunks and so form a canopy for his protection.

The inscriptions, which date from about A.D. 1187, are chiefly Oriental adulation of King Kirti Nissanga by his prime minister. After enumerating proofs of his miraculous powers and wisdom, the inscription tells how he re-constructed the embankments of great lakes and watercourses, thus restoring prosperity to the people; how he got rid of robbers by giving them whatever riches they desired (!); how he expelled evil-doers from the monasteries, and provided the priests with food, raiment, lodging, and physic.

Very curious are the details of some of his almsgiving, and also of his care for the prosperity of his own race. We are told how, considering that the continuance of religion and of the sciences depended on the royal dynasty, the king sent to the country of Kaalinga (i.e, Orissa in India), whence he himself had come, and caused many princesses of the Soma Surya Wansae (i.e., the Luni-Solar race) to be brought to his court, and he married these royal virgins to his son, and so increased the royal family.

Then with regard to alms, every year his Majesty, wearing the crown and all royal ornaments, caused himself, his two chief queens, and his son and daughter, to be weighed in a balance, and he bestowed five times their united weight of goods on the Buddhist and Brahmin priests, the blind, the lame, the deformed, and other destitute and friendless people. "He quenched the fire of poverty with showers of riches, gold coin, copper, bell-metal, gold, silver, pearls, precious stones, vestments, and jewels." "Thus he made the poor happy, and caused a constant supply of rain." The last allusion to the favour of the gods is one which would eminently appeal to this rice-growing community in a district so subject to drought.

On the same huge tablet another inscription tells of the numerous temples and relic-shrines which he either built or repaired, of the enormous sums he expended in regilding the seventy-two images of Buddha placed by his predecessor in the rock-temples at Dambulla, and restoring the shrines at Anuradhapura, in building alms-houses, which he furnished with vessels of gold and silver, and where the poor were provided with abundance of victuals, and how he dedicated his son and daughter to the Sacred Tooth, and subsequently redeemed them by offering in their stead a dagoba of solid gold and other precious objects.

This very literal reading of a man being worth his weight in gold seems to have commended itself to the Singhalese sovereigns. The same inscription on the rock at Dambulla which records how the great King Prakrama Bahu made and gilded the aforesaid seventy-two statues of Buddha, also tells of his annual donation of five times his own weight in gold and jewels for the relief of the poor. And here at Pollanarua another rock-tablet tells of another king of the Kaalinga dynasty, who, like his predecessor, Kirti Nissanga, annually distributed five times his own weight of gold, precious stones, jewels, and rich vestments for the good of the needy; and, moreover, for five years

relinquished all his royal revenues in order to relieve the people from the distress occasioned by the exactions of former kings.

Very special interest attaches to the Delada Maligawa, a temple built for the reception of Buddha's famous tooth. It is thought that the Wata Dágé was built for it when it was first brought here from Anuradhapura, for the Mahawanso records how the great Prakrama, arrayed in royal apparel and mounted on an elephant, with a golden umbrella over his head, came with much military pomp to return thanks for his victories at the shrine of the holy tooth. This second temple seems to have been erected in its honour a few years later by King Kirti Nissanga. After the lapse of seven centuries it remains in wonderful preservation, the sculptures on the walls and the very remarkable pillars round the inner shrine being almost perfect.

I found another very pictorial subject in the ruins of the great Jetawanarama Temple, with a foreground of exceedingly ornamental pillars and admirably sculptured stones overgrown with tangled creepers, while beyond these in the near distance stands the Kiri or Milk-white Dagoba, so called from the beautifully smooth white chunam with which the whole huge building was once coated. And very well it must have looked when crowned with its gilded *tee* or symbolic umbrella. The chunam and the gilding have disappeared, otherwise it is almost perfect, though large trees have contrived to root themselves in many a fissure, and veil the now naked brick, or rather tile-work (for the building material here is all tiles), with delicate foliage and a network of roots and branches.

The great Jetawanarama Vihara is likewise almost shorn of its coating of once dazzling chunam, but the rich warm colours of its crumbling brickwork, standing in strong light and dark shade against a blue sky, and all softened by the cool greens of many a tree and creeping plant, are certainly more attractive to an artist than the temple could have been in the days of its glory. A stairway of the usual type, but of which each stone is twenty feet in length and very finely sculptured, leads up to the eastern entrance between two polygonal turrets, which, like the rest of the walls, are about eighty feet in height.

Against the western wall, facing the rising sun, stands a huge and now hideous image of Buddha about sixty feet in height, which when coated with chunam must have resembled polished marble, but is now only broken brickwork. From the fact that some very low windows seem to have been the only means of lighting this shrine, Sir James Tennent infers that the roof was perhaps constructed on the same principle as that of a pagoda on the Irawaddi River known as the "Cave of Ananda," in which a similar statue of Buddha is mysteriously illuminated by means of an opening in the roof, unseen by the worshippers, but so contrived as to throw a full ray of light only on the head and shoulders of the image, thus forming a very effective halo, in striking contrast with the gloom of the temple.

I spoke of the Kiri Dagoba as "huge." It is really about 100 feet high, with a diameter of about 70 feet, which is pretty well for a mass of solid brickwork, but it is effectually dwarfed by the Rankot or Golden-spire Dagoba (which is also called Ruan-welle-saye, "the place of golden dust"). This gigantic pile is 200 feet high, and about 186 feet in diameter. It is surrounded by eight small shrines with conical roofs.

There are several other dagobas of the same type, and

innumerable sculptured pillars, which alone remain to suggest vanished glories, for the buildings which they supported have wholly disappeared. Near the so-called fort were the royal baths. In the centre of the "kumara pokuna," the king's own bathing pond—a stone-lined tank—there is a circular stone on which the king sat and submitted to the delicate attentions of bathers; for one of the penalties of monarchy was that he had not even the privilege of washing himself. Three stone lions which lie close by are supposed to have supported this "bath-chair."

But it is useless to attempt to describe the numerous ruins which lie so thickly scattered all through the jungle, which now overspreads the whole of what was once so great a city—mounds of brickwork, broken columns, an inexhaustible supply of sculptured stones, geese, elephants, lions, horses, lotus-blossoms, and grotesque figures, with here and there fallen images lying prostrate on the earth.

Now temples and palaces are utterly deserted save by the beasts of the forest, which find in these silent sanctuaries the stillness they love, a secure retreat, and deep cool shade where they can make their dens and rear their young undisturbed. Bears, leopards, and porcupines share the inner shrines with owls and flocks of evil-smelling bats. Radiant peacocks and emerald-green parroquets, orioles, barbets, and many other birds of gay plumage, flash athwart the sunlight from the shelter of dark foliage, and herds of wild deer couch fearlessly beside the broken idols with the calm passionless faces which so little heed their own downfall.

In one ruined shrine I collected a handful of porcupine quills as a memento of the spot. These creatures conceal themselves so effectually in the daytime, that even in the districts where they abound many people have never seen one. They are often captured at night by the simple stratagem of digging a deep ditch with perpendicular sides, and narrowing gradually towards one end. The porcupine enters the ditch in search of food, and walks on till he sticks fast, and can by no possibility turn round, as his quills stick in the mud; then the poor " fretful porcupine " fall an easy victim. His flesh, which resembles that of a nice young pig, is prized as a great delicacy.

To me the shrine of greatest interest was the Gal Vihara, which lies to the north of the city, a quite unique rock-temple, hollowed in a mass of dark-brown gneiss rock; from the colour of which the temple is also called Kulagalla, " the black rock." From this rock three gigantic figures have been sculptured in almost full relief. One represents Buddha sitting in contemplation in the usual attitude, arms and legs alike folded in complete repose. This image is 15 feet high, and sits on a pedestal 5 feet deep by 18 wide. The background is almost elaborately sculptured, and all as sharp and clean-cut as though it were the work of yesterday—not a trace of weathering after the lapse of seven centuries.

Then comes the rock-hewn temple, which is built up in front and adorned with columns, but within it is an altar on which is another sedent image of Buddha, all hewn from the rock. It is only about half the size of the image outside, but the whole interior of the shrine is elaborately decorated. Unfortunately, modern piety has renovated ancient art with grievously crude colours.

The temple is approached by rock-hewn steps, and on either side the rock has been smoothed so as to form two inclined planes, one of which, 18 feet high by 13 feet 9 inches in width, is covered with a long inscription in the ancient Pali character, which, however, is not specially interesting.

Next to this, standing at the head of a huge recumbent image of Buddha, is an upright statue, 23 feet high, representing Ananda, Buddha's favourite disciple, with his arms crossed on his breast. He stands on a circular pedestal, edged with the conventional lotus-leaf, which generally marks the throne of Buddha; hence this image has generally been mistaken for Buddha himself, but wise authorities have decided otherwise, chiefly because the Mahawanso records the formation of this rock-temple by King Prakrama, and describes only two images of Gautama, one sitting, the other reclining. All three wear the robe so as to leave the right arm and shoulder bare.

The recumbent statue is forty-six feet in length, and represents Buddha as in the dreamless sleep of Nirvana, his head resting on the right hand, on the palm of which is engraved a lotus-blossom, and the hand resting on a bolster. The attitude is that of perfect repose. The difference of stature between Buddha in contemplation and Buddha in his last rest is very striking. Eastern symbolism always seems to suppose corporeal growth in the holy dead, hence the necessity for graves of preternatural length, as in the case of that of Eve at Jeddah, which measures at least sixty feet.[1]

[1] This great image is, however, a mere pigmy as compared with some in other Buddhist countries, notably at Bamian in Afghanistan, where, on the road between Cabul and Balkh, the early Buddhists excavated monasteries and rock-cells literally by the thousand in the high cliffs of conglomerate, some of which have been fashioned into the likeness of gigantic images of Buddha. One of these, which was measured with the theodolite by the Hon. M. G. Talbot, R.E., was found to be 173 feet in height. Another,

I fear that the mere description of all this may not sound very impressive, but it certainly is so in reality, and so I felt it to be while myself sitting on another great mass of dark chocolate-coloured rock, separated from the temple by a belt of grass and shrubs, and looking above and beyond it to a background of silent solemn forest. One or two brethren of the yellow robe hovered about the door of the inner temple, but the throng of worshippers who in bygone ages bowed before these gigantic idols has passed away; yet there these remain, heedless as ever of the coming and going of men, and of all their joys and sorrows.

To this great capital came embassies from distant lands, even from China, chiefly to do homage to the various objects of Buddhist worship. There is, however, evidence of very early commercial intercourse with China, chiefly gathered from Chinese books of extracts from ancient records now lost, showing how Chinese fleets came to Galle to trade. Swords and musical instruments were among the things imported to Ceylon, and in later days, A.D. 1266, Chinese soldiers served in the army of Prakrama III.

But in 1405 King Wijaya-Bahu VI., who seems to have adopted the Hindoo faith, tyrannised over the Buddhists and maltreated strangers, plundering their ships. Among those thus treated, a Chinese embassy bringing gifts to the shrine of Buddha were treacherously waylaid, and escaped with difficulty. Nevertheless, when, in 1407, the Emperor

also a standing figure, was proved to be 120 feet high. A sitting figure is 90 feet, and of two others now in ruins, one must have been about 60 feet high. All these statues were originally either gilt or covered with metal. Burmah also glories in great images of Buddha, one near Moulmain being fully 120 feet long. It is built of brick, and represents Buddha in Nirvana. In China and Japan also he is represented on a colossal scale.

of China sent his great general, Ching-Ho, with sixty-two junks and a strong military force, on an embassy to Sumatra, Java, Cambodia, Siam, and other places, Ceylon was included, the embassy arriving there in 1408.

Wijaya-Bahu, however, endeavoured treacherously to capture his visitors and to plunder and burn their ships. The tables were turned, and he and his queen, his children, his officers of state, and the Tooth were carried back to China, where the Tooth was long kept in a monastery at Nankin.

The Emperor of China, having compassion on his prisoners, desired the officers of state to elect "the wisest of the family" as their king. This honour was conferred on Pula-ko-ma Bazac Lacha, which is evidently Chinese for Prakrama Bahu Rajah. All the prisoners were sent home, and a Chinese envoy was sent to invest him with regal power as a vassal of China, and thenceforth annual tribute was paid till A.D. 1459, when it suddenly ceased.

Now the intercourse between the nations seems to be limited to the visits of traders, who explore certain caves on the coast in search of the glutinous nests used in the manufacture of soup, and who trade in the sea-slugs or *béche-de-mer* which are turned to similar account. The former, however, form a very small item. From a recent table of exports from Ceylon to China, I see the total value of edible birds' nests for the year was only forty rupees, that of *béche-de-mer* was 27,300 rupees. Sharks' fins were valued at 13,667 rupees. Fish, dried and salted, and fish fins and bones, were 18,327 rupees, and birds' feathers amounted to 1240 rupees.

We made the very most of several long days at Pollanarua, and then abandoned our peaceful, pleasant camp, with much regret. A lovely morning ride of about nine miles brought us to beautiful Lako Minery, halting on our way at Giritale, a charming little lake, with massive stone embankment and some sculptured stones. It has the usual surroundings of fine trees, and view of near wooded hills and blue distant ranges. We had previously visited Sevamputti, another of these minor tanks, beyond which lies Gunner's Quoin, one of the principal hills in the neighbourhood. There the scene had a touch of human interest from the lonely watch-huts on the brink of the swampy ground, mere rudely-thatched platforms of boughs raised on high poles, wherein some lonely watcher kept ceaseless guard to scare marauding animals from the crops. By day he shouts and pulls long lines of clacking rattles, and by night he kindles fires for the same purpose.

The great lake at Minery was made about A.D. 275, and owes its existence to King Maha Sen, who, as we learnt at Anuradhapura, atoned for his early apostasy from Buddhism by most energetic construction of temples and of tanks for the irrigation of temple-lands. It is said that Minery was designed to irrigate twenty thousand fields, belonging to the Jetawanarama Vihara at Pollanarua. In order to form it, he diverted the waters of the Kara-Ganga (now called Amban-Ganga) near Matale, which is distant about forty miles, and formed a great canal by which to convey them to Minery. Besides this, he constructed sixteen other tanks, including that of Gantalawe (now called Kanthalay) near Trincomalee.

So great and numerous were his works, that the people deemed him godlike, and believed that he received supernatural aid; yet strange to say, though all his works were beneficent, yet when, after his death, a pestilence swept the land, they commenced to worship him as an incarnation of the Indian war-god Kataragama—an angry deity to be propitiated, chiefly with a view to the healing of malignantly inflicted bodily suffering (see page 223).

In the very picturesque village of Minery a humble mud-hut is the temple of the deified king, whose iron sword, with a square hilt, peculiarly decorated with small brass chains, is treasured as a precious relic. In presence of his image there is a holy stone, about two feet square, let into a large one for greater security. To this temple persons accused of any crime, or having any cause of dispute with their neighbours, repair, and having kept solemn vigil for a night in an open shed near the temple, deposit on the stone a fanam, which is a very small coin, equal to the sixteenth part of a rupee, and swear their most solemn oaths,[1] with the firm conviction that perjury would involve death within six months. In the village we also saw a curious circular thatched building all closed up, in which, we were told, various sacred relics were stored, including an arrow once used by King Maha Sen.

We had heard a rumour of the existence of a place of exceeding sanctity, known as the Grove of the Tank Gods, and were exceedingly anxious to see it, but the people were unwilling to lead us to it. The headman declared he could not take us, as it would require three months of purification ere he dared approach the spot with necessary offerings! However, having gone off by myself in the evening for a long walk, with only a villager for my guide, I discovered this holy of holies, to his great disgust and my own unbounded satisfaction.

[1] As our ancestors did on the Oath-stone of Iona. See "In the Hebrides," page 70.

And such a poor, contemptible little place as it is! simply a small space cleared in the dense vegetation on the embankment of the lake, and round this are ranged broken fragments of images and a variety of sculptured stones, the body of a headless lion, an odd hunchback figure *minus* legs, a broken image with a seven-headed snake-canopy a rather graceful female figure, and a good many others, all broken, and propped up with heaps of fragments. Two only, namely, the hunchback and the lady, are unusual, and are supposed to represent Maha Sen and his wife. Is it not strange to think that the descendants of the race who constructed these grand tanks and built these splendid cities and temples can rise to no loftier conception than collecting broken fragments of images in some shady corner, which is thenceforth invested with sanctity and mystery, and only approached in trembling dread?

In the same walk I came on several queer little holy places in the forest—mere circles of small stones, within which were deposited a multitude of offerings of rude red pottery, very varied in shape, some being simply water-jars, but the majority resembling the *tee* on the summit of a relic-shrine. I never saw anything of this sort anywhere else; but a few days later, near the tank at Kanthalay, we came on a sandy circle beneath great trees, where red earthenware votive-lamps stood ready for lighting at night. Some of these were such neat little curios that I felt sorely tempted to appropriate one, but, happily, refrained from such sacrilegious theft. It is certainly remarkable that the very monkeys respect those unprotected accumulations of crockery. A sudden impulse on the part of one of the numerous troops would make short work of the whole.

One of these circles was guarded by a familiar spirit in

the form of a splendid lizard, about eighteen inches long, a chameleon, I suppose, as he rapidly changed colour with indignation at my intrusion. To begin with, he was bright green with a crimson head; then he turned brown and yellow, and afterwards appeared of a rich olive colour. After a while he turned black, to frighten me, I suppose, as he stood puffing like a little demon and raising his dorsal spines. When he saw I was not bent on mischief, he once more assumed his green robe and ruby cap, and seemed satisfied. Another of these harmless lizards has a red-and-orange pouch under his chin, and small horns which give him a most demoniacal appearance. They love to lie basking in the noonday sun.

A family of screaming, flying foxes returning to roost in the trees overhead were well in keeping with the scene, and as evening drew on, the large green frogs in the lake commenced their night concert of croaking.

The quaintness of the aforesaid circles was greatly enhanced by their surroundings of huge vines—climbing plants of various sorts—originally mere twisted tendrils, which have swung from branch to branch, thence hanging in huge festoons, till the whole forest is thus linked together by this intricate living cordage. Sometimes the beautiful treacherous creepers crush to death the trees and boughs around which they have twined, and the stem decays and crumbles away, leaving the great coils, now grown into hard wood, old and self-supporting, twisting spirally in every direction, like legions of writhing snakes, and forming a very distinctive feature in the undergrowth. One of these creepers[1] bears a gigantic bean, always suggestive

---

[1] The *Entada pursætha*, called by the Singhalese the Maha-pus-wuel or great hollow climber.

of Jack-in-the-beanstalk. Its pods, which are from four to six feet in length, and about four inches wide, are divided into sections, each containing a handsome chocolate-coloured bean, which, when hollowed out, makes a neat match-box.

Another of these climbing plants, which mounts to the top of high trees, bears large clusters of yellow flowers, which are succeeded by prickly pods containing pretty, smooth grey seeds, so round that they might almost be used as marbles.

The temporary bungalows prepared for us at Minery were less fascinating in point of situation than our last camp, being farther from the lake and much nearer the village. They were, however, near a very picturesque stream, in which groups of natives bathed with infinite enjoyment beneath the shade of pleasant trees all matted with large-leaved creepers, forming ideal "greenrooms." Graceful tree-ferns grew beneath the tall palms and overhung the stream, and the luxuriant elephant creeper, with its large heart-shaped leaves and lilac blossoms, formed the loveliest screen, mingling with the beautiful Granadilla, starred with passion-flowers and with the large green fruits which, with sugar and milk, are very pleasant food. Handsome basket-ferns had niched themselves on the boughs of many trees, from which also hung divers orchids.

I have already mentioned that even now in a rainy season Lake Minery fills so as to have a circumference of fully twenty miles. At the time of our visit the waters had contracted to about a third of that size, so not only was the hewn stone-work of the great embankment all uncovered, but promontories and islets, which then rise charmingly from the waters, were all high and dry. The said embankment is about a mile and a half in length, about two hundred feet wide at the base, and about sixty feet high. The view thence, looking to the mountain ranges of Matala and Kandy, greatly resembles that of the Cuchullin Hills in Skye as seen from Ross-shire, though the latter could not show such a foreground of fine timber.

We had been told that what should really be the bed of the lake was bordered with firm, springy turf on which horses can canter safely, but our experience was of a soft, muddy shore, very bad riding-ground, and in places all undermined and thrown up into soft hillocks, as if an army of moles had been at work: this was due to the boring of huge earth-worms.

But this rich, juicy grass forms delightful pasture, and the swampy ground about this lake used to be one of my brother's favourite hunting-grounds. Then herds of elephants and ungainly, often savage, buffaloes (the latter perhaps numbering a hundred or more) would come to enjoy the delight of wallowing in the thick, soft mud and long grass. But since cheap guns and gunpowder have placed weapons of destruction in the hands of natives as well as foreigners, the harassed, over-hunted survivors have disappeared to forests yet more remote, and now the extensive pasture-grounds here and at Pollanarua, and around all the great tanks, are frequented by very large herds of domestic buffaloes and black cattle brought over from the mainland *viâ* Manaar.

In some places the swampy shores of the lake are edged with cable-rattans, which one would naturally suppose to be bamboos, but which are really members of the palm family —Calamus—long slim canes which grow to a length of a hundred feet or more,[1] climbing to the tops of the highest trees, and all armed with hooked thorns and interwoven so as to form an impenetrable mass. This grows to the very brink, where rank grass borders an expanse of soft dark mud, forming a treacherous crust on which the unwary treads, and sinks through into deep slime and decaying vegetable matter, a mud-bath delightful to the wild elephants, who love to smear their whole bodies with it, and so are protected against mosquitoes.

The apparent extent of the lake is much diminished by the luxuriant growth of the lotus, with its tall, artistically untidy leaves and great rosy blossoms; but here and there lies a reach of very still water, a calm mirror reflecting the pure blue of heaven, and on which float the creamy cups of white lilies—an image of peace, marred, however, by ugly suggestions of scaly monsters swimming languidly to and fro among the lovely lilies.

These horrid crocodiles (the largest of lizards, and oh, how unlike their dainty little cousins!) lie basking on the dry mud, looking so like boughs of fallen trees that it is quite startling to see them glide into the water as one draws near—indeed I often felt rather nervous as I made my way on foot through the low brush and tall grasses which fringe these lagoons, lest I might inadvertently stumble over one and awaken him from his noonday sleep. One snap from

[1] Tennant mentions having seen a specimen 250 feet long and an inch in diameter without a single irregularity, and no appearance of foliage other than the bunch of feathery leaves at the extremity. In the southern forests, where it grows most luxuriantly, these slender canes are used by the natives in the construction of light suspension foot-bridges, consisting of a frail woven platform, with a rattan hand-rail, swaying in such a manner as sorely tries the nerve of any European who finds himself obliged to cross a stream on so frail a roadway (the stream perhaps roaring in a ravine a hundred feet below).

those enormous jaws would be a remembrance not quickly forgotten, even supposing one got away. I had a recollection of hearing of one, measuring $17\frac{1}{2}$ feet in length, which swallowed a native whole, barring his head and one hand which it had previously bitten off. It was killed on the following day, and the remains of the man's body were found inside of it.

These brutes seize their prey and drag it under water to drown it, and then eat it when hungry. But they are not at all particular as to what meat they devour, and being cannibals, are always ready to feast on the carcase of their nearest relation who has been shot and left on the shore. They vary in size from new-born babies just hatched by sun-heat from the sixty to eighty eggs which the mother buried in the sand, to full-grown reptiles, perhaps eighteen feet in length. Strange to say, those which inhabit tanks liable to dry up in summer have the power of hibernating, and bury themselves in the mud, which dries over them, and there they lie torpid till the next rainy season reawakens them. These never grow larger than about eight feet. With regard to longevity, in the case of one recently captured, scientists decided, from certain developments of horny growth, that it must be fully three hundred years old.

One peculiarity of these very unpleasant creatures is, that in the course of their long lives they renew their sixty-eight long sharp teeth several times, so that even in extreme old age those appallingly strong jaws are always well furnished for offensive warfare. When they have something to eat afloat, you see only their noses and foreheads above water, but as soon as they see that they are observed down they drop to the bottom.

Often they lie embedded in mud among tall reeds and

water-grasses, and often only the quivering of these betrays their presence. On land they waddle slowly, but once they take to the water they prove swift swimmers.

To do them justice, they are most diligent scavengers, rejoicing in every sort of decayed animal matter, whether fish, flesh, or fowl. Nevertheless, their numbers are in excess of even this need; and since it is so very desirable to find an incentive for thinning the ranks of these terribly prolific and dangerous monsters (which in the northern lakes, near Mullaitivu, literally swarm), it is satisfactory to know that, although no use has as yet been discovered for their horrid-looking scaly backs, the belly skin has a high commercial value, being the finest, strongest, softest, and most durable of all leathers, and is greatly prized for the manufacture of travelling-bags, portmanteaux, boots and shoes, pocket-books, &c.

The skin must be removed in as large and clean a piece as possible, without any tear or cut; then it must be steeped in strong brine, and afterwards well rubbed with salt and alum, and then forwarded to England in a secure packing-case. The tanning is done in London. The value of a skin is chiefly determined by its width. Sportsmen who have sent consignments to London say that they have received 18s., 20s., and 26s. apiece for them, so that crocodile-hunting is now practically useful in more ways than the mere destruction of dangerous animals.

More agreeable denizens of the waters are sundry kinds of fish, which are good and abundant. The natives catch them with nets and in trap-baskets of bamboo wickerwork rather like lobster-pots, much wider at the base than at the top. The fisherman dexterously drops one of these over a fish as it lies in a muddy shallow, and then inserting a hand through a hole at the top, captures the fish and drops him into a creel slung by his side. The best of these is the "lola," which is rather like a very large ungainly trout, but is considered excellent.

Once more we took the road, or rather what the fine old village chief who led the way on foot was pleased to call the path, sometimes along the dry bed of rocky streams, passing as best the horses could under or over fallen trees, then through parched jungle, all burnt up with the drought, except the scarlet ixora; even the great tree cactii and bare knotted ropes of giant lianas looking more weird than ever without their accustomed veiling of delicate foliage.

At last, after four hours of this slow, hot march, we suddenly emerged on the high-road, with telegraph posts and all other proofs of a return to civilised life, and found ourselves at the village of Gal-Oya, where a most wretched mud-hut was signified with the name of a Government rest-house. There we spent a broiling day, and repeated the programme on the following day in the rest-house at Alutoya. The third day brought us to the margin of the great ancient tank of Kanthalay, which is apparently about as large as Minery, but with a more deeply indented shore-line. I had to explore alone, my companions being too thoroughly exhausted by the great heat.

This also is a very pretty scene—a great ruined embankment of huge cut stones all overgrown with fine old trees; an enormous pile of hewn blocks marking the site of the ruined sluice, masses of dark chocolate-coloured rock, dreamy ranges of far distant hills, and the calm lake reflecting all the beauties of earth and sky. Not a sound to break the stillness save the occasional shrill cry of passing wild-duck or other water-fowl. Now and again a flash of lovely colour as a dainty kingfisher or some other fairy of the bird-world flashed by. Shortly after that date, however, this tank was effectually restored, and though the people were very slow in profiting by the boon, it is now a centre of extensive cultivation and of a flourishing population.

The lake, as I have mentioned, was originally formed by King Maha Sen about A.D. 275, but it, and the great feeding canal connecting it with Minery, were practically remade by Prakrama Bahu about 1153, forming part of that vast series of navigable waters known as the Seas of Prakrama. (I think I have mentioned that he is said to have constructed 1407 tanks, and to have repaired 1395.) Prakrama's great canal is believed to have carried its water-supply twenty-four miles farther, to irrigate the once fertile plains of Tamblegam, close to Trincomalee. But, in some time of overwhelming flood, these plains were transformed to a great lake, whose waters forced a passage to the sea, and then, in turn, received the tribute of the great ocean in an influx of salt water.

Once admitted, it has never again been possible to exclude the sea, so that Tamblegam is now a large, brackish lake swarming with fish, but chiefly notable for its immense beds of small semi-transparent oysters, about six inches in diameter, and very flat. They are largely used in China as a substitute for glass in ornamental windows, so many are exported thither, and many more are burnt as yielding peculiarly fine lime for betel-chewers. So wonderfully are creatures adapted for their varying conditions of existence, that these oysters flourish only in brackish water, and serious mortality results when either fresh or salt water predominates, as happens in season of flood or drought.

We passed this wide, glassy lake on the following day,

on our way from Kanthalay to Trincomalee (a distance of twenty-six miles), the latter a very beautiful spot, which was destined to prove the farthest point of this expedition, and where our stay was considerably prolonged owing to the Bishop's very serious illness.

CHAPTER XIX.

TRINCOMALEE——SAAMI ROCK.

Trincomalee Harbour—Fort Austenberg—Fort Frederick—The Saami Rock—Birds—Hot springs—Palmyra-palms—The Lily shore.

I SUPPOSE that, with the exception of Rio in Brazil and Sydney in Australia, few of the world's harbours excel Trincomalee in beauty and security.

So perfectly is it landlocked that, as we stood on the high ramparts of Fort Austenberg, looking down on the inner harbour, on whose clear, green waters floated several British men-of-war, it was scarcely possible to believe that this was indeed an arm of that sea which lay wrapped in purple gloom beyond a wide expanse of dark palmyra-palms.

One of the officers had kindly provided for me a shelter from sun and rain by spreading a thick matting of palm leaves over one of the embrasures, and as I sat there hour after hour sketching that beautiful panorama, I saw nothing of the passage by which these vessels had entered this calm haven from the great outer ocean, and which is protected by a reef stretching far out to sea, forming a perfect breakwater. My attention was called to the fact that, so deep are these placid waters, large vessels can lie so close inshore as to discharge their cargo without the use of boats, their yard-arms actually projecting over the wharf. I was told (but whether true or not I cannot say) that the depth is really so great that it has never been fathomed, which gives rise to a theory that this harbour is the crater of a submerged volcano.

More tempting swimming-baths could scarcely be imagined than some of the sheltered inlets of this deep, calm sea-lake; but, alas! even here danger sometimes lurks in the form of venturesome ground-sharks, and there is a sad tradition of how once, when a party of soldiers were bathing below the fort, their comrades on shore perceived the dim form of a large shark rising in pursuit of a lad who had just taken a header into the depths. All unconscious of danger, he rose cheerily to the surface, but a moment later a cry of agony rent the air as the lad disappeared, and the waters were reddened with his life-blood. Quick as thought a soldier dived at the very spot, and quickly reappeared, bringing the poor young fellow's head and shoulders— the body having been bitten in two by the shark, who escaped safely with the lower half, and was never seen again, though many days were devoted to the attempt to capture him.

Right below me lay the Dockyard, the Naval Stores Depôt, and the Admiralty. Not the shipping only, but also charmingly wooded isles lay mirrored in that quiet inland lake; while beyond the white sands of the farther shore, red-tiled houses, embowered in pleasant gardens, indicated the direction of a town with some eleven thousand inhabitants, stretching round a horse-shoe-shaped bay, the entrance to which is guarded by two rocky headlands, on the nearest of which, overshadowed by grand old trees, stands the Government Agent's house[1] (a spot endeared to us all by the recol-

[1] The seat of the Government Agency was shortly afterwards removed to Batticaloa.

lection of the sympathetic and considerate hospitality which there enfolded us in a time of grave anxiety.[1]

The farther point of the horse-shoe is a bold peninsula rising from the ocean in a sheer precipice about four hundred feet in height, and thence sloping gently towards the shore, with which it is connected by a long flat neck of grassy sand. Fort Frederick, by which name this fortified crag is known to Europeans, guards the outer harbour, and is the military headquarters. To the natives, however, this bold headland is still, as it has been from time immemorial, the Saami (or, as it would be pronounced in India, Swami) Rock, or ROCK OF GOD, sacred to the worship of EISWARAMA, THE ALMIGHTY GOD.

(It is said the original name of this place was Tirukko-natha-malai, *i.e.*, " the Mountain of Holy Konathar," whoever he may have been.)

Nothing has struck me more forcibly in the course of my travels than the fact of how often the people living in a place take no interest whatever, and probably ignore the existence, of some local custom or legend which to the traveller is the point of chief interest in the district.

This I found to be emphatically the case at Trincomalee. Many years ago I had been told by Mr. Forbes Leslie that he had here witnessed a strikingly picturesque form of aboriginal worship, so one of my first inquiries on arriving in the district was whether the ancient worship on the rock was still carried on. I was assured on all hands that it was entirely given up.

However, on the very evening of our arrival at Fort Frederick, a natural instinct led me past the old Dutch burial-ground, with its moss-grown graves overshadowed by

[1] Owing to the Bishop's serious illness.

flowering surya-trees, to the brink of the highest precipice, which in itself is so very grand that I determined to lose no time in securing a picture of it.

So thither I wended my way at daybreak on Monday, September 29th,[1] returning in the afternoon to colour my morning's pencil sketch. Just as I was finishing my work, or rather was compelled to halt for the evening in order to watch the marvellous loveliness of the sunset lights and colours which flooded the wide sea and rocks with opal tints of dreamy beauty, through which one by one the stars began to glimmer, I observed that first one, then another and another native, both men and women, were taking up positions on the crag, each carrying either a bunch of fruit or a chatty of milk or water.

Ere long about forty had assembled, including one who acted the part of priest. He was clothed with scanty saffron-coloured cloth, and had a string of large black beads round his head. He stood on the utmost verge of the crag, and the worshippers, having laid at his feet their offerings of cocoa-nuts, lovely cocoa-palm blossoms, betel leaves, bunches of plantains, flowers, coins, small baskets of grain, or whatever else they had to give, clustered around wherever they could find a footing on the rock or the slippery grass while the priest performed his ceremonial ablutions for purification in water poured from a brass lota.

As the sunset glories faded and the stars shone out more brilliantly the priest intoned a litany, to which all devoutly responded; then one by one he took the chatties of good milk or water, and poured them out on the rock as a

[1] Sir James Emerson Tennant mentions this worship as occurring once a year, on the 23rd January.

libation.[1] After this, while still chanting the litany, he took each gift, and from his giddy height cast it into the fathomless ocean, far, far below, a true offering to the Almighty Giver.

Then kindling a fire on the rock pinnacle, he thrice raised a blazing brand on high, and all the people threw their arms heavenward. Afterwards he lighted a brazen censer and swung it high above his head, till the still evening air was all perfumed by the fragrant incense. Finally, descending from his post of danger and honour, he took ashes from the sacred fire and therewith marked each worshipper on the forehead, after which they silently dispersed, and in the quiet starlight wended their way back to lower earth.

A more strikingly impressive scene I have never witnessed, and I need scarcely say that to me it proved so irresistibly attractive that again and again I found my way at sunset to the same spot, whence I commanded so perfect a view of the Saami Rock. I found that the worshippers assembled there every Monday and Friday evening, and one night I had the good fortune to witness this ceremony just at the moment when the great full moon was rising from the waters, and nothing more solemn could be conceived. There was the mellow light of the moon flooding the calm sea, and the red firelight glowing on the dark crag and on the brown skin and white turbans and drapery of the wor-

[1] Precisely as was done by our own ancestors—a custom kept up in many a corner of Great Britain long after Christianity was the only recognised religion in the land. For instances of such libations being offered even in the last century in our northern isles and Highlands see "In the Hebrides," pp. 71 and 192 to 194. By C. F. Gordon-Cumming. Published by Chatto & Windus.

shippers, while from across the harbour flashed one vivid terrestrial star from the lighthouse on Foul Point.

It seems that at the time when the Tamil conquerors crossed from the coast of Malabar and invaded Ceylon, they resolved to appropriate a spot so venerated by the aborigines; so having (so they said) proved from their sacred Puranas that Trincomalee was a fragment of the holy Mount Meru, which had been hurled from heaven in a celestial turmoil, they thereon built a stately shrine dedicated to Siva, and which is still remembered as the shrine of a Thousand Columns.

In the year A.D. 1622, however, the Dutch deeming it necessary to erect forts at various important points in order to secure themselves against the Portuguese, took possession of Trincomalee, and ruthlessly appropriated the great temple as the quarry to supply building material for their fortifications. Consequently sculptured and carved stones are still to be discerned here and there in the walls of Fort Frederick (a name said to have been bestowed in honour of Frederick William, Elector of Brandenburg).

One solitary pillar on the highest point of the crag commemorates the suicide in A.D. 1687 of Francina Van Reede, a Dutch maiden of good family, whose betrothed had forsaken her, and had embarked for Europe with his regiment. Ere the vessel could clear the coast, she had to tack, and again ran close inshore beneath this precipice, and at that moment the girl sprang from the dizzy summit, and, in presence of her faithless lover, fell a mangled corpse on the dark rocks which jut through the surging surf far below.

Although the aforesaid pillar bears a Dutch inscription recording this sad event, it is so precisely like some of the most prominent pillars in the ruined wave-washed temple at Dondra Head (the southernmost point of the Isle)—pillars with the identical alternate sections, square and octagonal—that I have little doubt that this was one of the " Thousand Columns " of Siva's shrine.

I ascertained that the officiating priest of the rock, though not a true Brahman, was one of the spurious low-caste Brahmans so common in Southern India,[1] who habitually minister at the blood-stained altars of Siva, with whom Eiswarama has been so artfully identified; indeed, I learnt that the Saami Rock is often described as Kon-Eiswara-Parvatia, thus also honouring Siva's wife, the goddess Parvati.

There is, however, no doubt that the worship of Eiswara is by far the most ancient faith of the island, and there is every reason to believe that this striking ceremonial has continued unchanged from remote ages. Whole dynasties have arisen and become extinct—conquering races from India, Portugal, Holland, and Britain have successively held sway in the fair Isle, and the one thing which has continued the same from generation to generation has been this evening sacrifice.

> " Not 'neath the domes where crumbling arch and column
> Attest the feebleness of mortal hand,
> But in that fane, most catholic and solemn,
> Which God hath planned.
> In that cathedral, boundless as our wonder,
> Whose quenchless lamps the Sun and Moon supply,
> Its choir the winds and waves, its organ, thunder,
> Its dome the sky."

To me it seemed a very impressive and simple act of worship, singularly free from idolatry, and in very marked

---

[1] " In the Himalayas and on Indian Plains," pp. 578–580. Published by Chatto & Windus. For a curious example of a very venerated and most foul Hindoo shrine being enclosed within the great Mahommedan —now British—fort at Allahabad, see p. 75 of the above.

contrast with the many painful forms of devil-worship which met us at every turn in the beautiful Isle of Palms.

I confess to a feeling of real regret when I learnt how, in September 1889, this solemn natural shrine had become the scene of contention between the priests of rival sects, a Pandaram priest appealing against a Brahman for declaring that he alone was entitled to officiate as priest at the Saami Rock, and there to perform Sivite religious ceremonies. The dispute ended in a civil trial before the District Judge, each party being defended by native counsel, and the case was given in favour of the Pandaram priest, to whom were awarded damages to the value of 120 rupees.

Moreover, in consequence of the increased military precautions at Trincomalee, it has been decided that henceforth worshippers will only be allowed access to the Saami Rock on the first and last Fridays of each month, no one being now admitted to Fort Frederick without a pass from the Commandant.

In truth, not for the sake of Ceylon only, but for the protection of the world's mercantile marine, there was much need to strengthen the somewhat antiquated military defences of this magnificent harbour; and as regards Fort Frederick, isolated as it is from the mainland by the low grassy neck of the peninsula, one cannot but fear that, in case of a siege, the beleaguered garrison would find themselves in as difficult a position as were the Dutch when in August 1795, they were here besieged by a British force, consisting of the 71st, 72nd, 73rd, and 77th regiments together with artillery, and two battalions of Sepoys, under command of General Stewart. As they entered the harbour one frigate struck on a sunken rock and was lost. At the end of three weeks the garrison was forced to capitulate since which time the Union Jack has here floated in undisturbed possession.

Previous to that date this beautiful bay had witnessed many a struggle between the covetous European Powers, who each craved a monopoly of Singhalese commerce. First of all, in 1612, the King of Kandy, who hoped by the aid of the Dutch to get rid of the Portuguese, permitted the former to erect a fort at Cottiar, on the southern side of the Bay of Trincomalee. This, however, was no sooner done than it was captured and destroyed by a Portuguese force, which had rapidly marched across the Isle from Colombo or Negombo.

In 1622 the Dutch seized and garrisoned Trincomalee itself, but finding that holding forts on the east coast of the Isle was of no avail in securing the cinnamon trade of the western provinces, they shortly after abandoned both Trincomalee and Batticaloa.

Thus it was that when, in 1657, the *Ann* frigate of London, a trading vessel commanded by Captain Robert Knox for "the Honourable the East India Company," was driven to anchor in Cottiar Bay for necessary repairs, they found there no Europeans, but what seemed at first a very kind welcome from the natives. The story of the treacherous seizure of the captain, his son, and the greater part of the crew, and the graphic account of the then quite unknown interior of the island, and the customs of the king and people of Kandy, which was published by Robert Knox, junior (when, after twenty years of captivity, he at length contrived to escape, and after infinite difficulties reached the Dutch fort of Arrepa, near Manaar, on the north-east coast), is one of the most remarkable and interesting volumes of pioneer travel. The modern Cottiar is a populous village of industrious Tamils.

The Dutch subsequently reoccupied the forts of Cottiar and Batticaloa, both of which, strange to say, they abandoned without a blow in 1672 in their panic at the sudden arrival of the French squadron under Admiral De la Haye. The French at once took possession of Trincomalee, but being unable to maintain a firm hold in the island, they disappeared as unexpectedly as they had arrived. At that time the Dutch had about a hundred ships constantly trading between Cottiar and Coromandel, whence they brought clothes and other wares to exchange for timber, areca-nuts, palmyra-sugar, and rice.

In 1782 Great Britain first appeared on the scene. War having been declared against Holland, a British force, commanded by Sir Hector Munro, took possession of Trincomalee, which, however, was so inadequately garrisoned that it was almost immediately afterwards surprised by the French fleet commanded by Admiral Suffrein, by whom the British force was removed to Madras, and in the following year Trincomalee was restored to the Dutch.

But the time had now come for British rule in Ceylon, and in 1795 Lord Hobart, Governor of Madras, fitted out the expedition commanded by General Stewart, which landed at Trincomalee, and, as I have already stated, captured the fort after a three weeks' siege. Then, in rapid succession, Jaffna, Calpentyn, Negombo, Colombo, Caltura, Point de Galle, Matura, and all other strongholds of the Dutch, were ceded to the English, who thus became the undisputed rulers of the maritime provinces, and no clamour of war has since then disturbed the peace of this fair harbour.

In 1801, however, no less than five thousand British troops assembled here under command of Colonel Arthur Wellesley (the great Duke of Wellington), with the intention of proceeding hence to Java; but this force was ordered to Egypt under Sir David Baird, and Colonel Wellesley returned to India.

Latterly the garrison has numbered about 400 men of the Engineers, Highlanders, Artillery, and Pioneer force, besides those employed at the Naval Depot. Now, however, prudence requires the adoption of necessary precautions, therefore modern science is being brought to bear in all directions; and what with the enlarging and strengthening of the old forts, and building of a new one, and of extensive barracks for a greatly increased military force, while the restoration of the great tank at Kanthalay is bestowing new life on all the agricultural population of the district, Trincomalee is fast becoming a place of very much greater importance than it was at the time of our visit; but whether it will not thereby lose much of its charm is another question.

It is not often that I am attracted by the picturesqueness of Dutch buildings, but within Fort Frederick, beneath the cool shade of large dark trees, there is a most fascinating old well. Two heavy pillars coated with cream-coloured chunam, once polished like marble, but now partially stained with orange-coloured lichen, support a heavy overhanging roof of rounded red tiles, which are the playground of many squirrels. To a stout rafter is attached a pulley over which passes a long rope; to this is attached the bucket wherewith brown men (clothed only in a white waist-cloth and scarlet turban) fill their great red water-pots for domestic use. It is all very pleasant to the artistic sense, though I suppose we must admit that for practical purposes unromantic leaden pipes have their advantages!

But for a never-failing supply of sketchable scenes, one has only to turn to the nearest temple, whether Tamil or

Buddhist, and here at a small Hindoo temple I found a most primitive Juggernath car, adorned with gaudy mythological pictures and thatched with dry palmyra leaves of a pale straw colour. It was drawn on a rude wooden platform supported by four heavy unwieldy wheels, each constructed of three solid wooden planks, fastened together by crosspieces of roughly-shaped wood. A very brown old Tamil priest, with scanty yellow drapery, stood beside the rickety old car, shading himself with part of a dry taliput palm-leaf—a fine study in colour. In the background stood the domed temple with red pillars and red wall, surrounded by cocoa and palmyra palms, each laden with golden nuts.

Close by, a statuesque brown water-carrier was drawing his supplies from a rude well by means of a red jar slung on a bamboo, which creaked ceaselessly as it rose and fell, emulating the harsh cries of sundry birds and insects.

One very attractive small bird which walks tamely about the gardens at Trincomalee has a purple head and breast and sienna back. It roosts in the palms, and we were often startled by its resounding sonorous call—a single note, "Hoop! hoop!"—so deep and far-carrying that on a still evening it is heard very far off. I was told that this was a jungle-crow, but as this name was also applied to a larger bird, somewhat suggestive of a magpie, except that instead of being black and white its colouring is brown and black and its eyes red, I cannot venture to say which bird is entitled to the name.

Still more fascinating are the dainty little sunbirds, which with long brush-like tongue capture insects, and also feed on nectar of flowers. Some have maroon bands on the breast, others primrose-colour; they love the fragrant pink oleander and scarlet hybiscus with glossy dark-green foliage.

The Singhalese call these dainty creatures "Flower-honey birds." One of very brilliant plumage is distinguished as the tiny sunbird, being only three and a half inches long. It is, however, very rare.

Happily the lovely little purple sunbird is more common. Its head and throat are of a bright metallic green, shading into the glossy purple of back and tail, while beneath each wing is a tuft of gold, displayed when the dainty chirping creature is fluttering over flowers to extract their honey. Not that it confines itself to nectar only, for it thoroughly enjoys good substantial spiders. It builds a most artistic pear-shaped nest of grass, interwoven with hair and spider's-web, and lined with feathers and tufts of silky cotton. This is deftly slung from the bough of some shrub, and herein in the month of April it lays two or three greenish eggs with brown specks. Of course in autumn we saw only empty nests.

Then there are the wren-babblers and scimitar-babbler (the latter so called because of its long curved yellow beak), neat little brown birds, common in the low-country jungle, which run up and down trees, hopping and jerking like woodpeckers, hunting for insects. They utter a loud melodious call, with very varied notes, and are cheery companions when one is sitting quietly sketching. There are also exquisite little flower-peckers, peculiar to Ceylon; some very gaily coloured, with dark-blue back, yellow breast, and white throat; others all olive-green except the stomach, which is grey.

Speaking of birds, a kind of swallow was pointed out to me, which is also said to be peculiar to Ceylon, and which not only builds on houses, just as our own do, but also in marshy places and near rice-fields. Its throat and breast are brown, but its back and wings are black, and its general appearance sufficiently suggestive of our own familiar friends to be very pleasant in a far country.

I found so much attractive sketching-ground in the immediate neighbourhood of Trincomalee that I did not care to go very far afield. But one lovely morning we drove at dawn to the Periyakulam, one of the ancient tanks, which is now, like so many others, simply a pretty lake covered with waterlilies. On the embankment stands a gigantic upright boulder, known as the Nine-Pin Rock, which looks as if it must topple over with the first strong gale. It would be curious to know for how many centuries it has held its ground.

One of our pleasantest early morning rides was to visit a group of seven hot springs on a wooded hill-range about eight miles from Trincomalee. Ceylon is so free from any trace of recent volcanic agency that a very special interest attaches to these.[1] The place is called Kannya, some say in " memory of " seven celestial virgins;[2] others say in honour of Kannya, the mother of the arch-demon Ravana, and that she is here worshipped by the Tamils, who come to observe certain rites on the thirtieth day after the death of their kinsfolk. A ruined temple, sacred to Ganesa, the elephant-headed god of wisdom, proves that he received at least a share of homage.

Some distance to the north, at Mannakandal, in the Wanni, there are sundry Buddhist ruins in the heart of the jungle; amongst others, those of seven temples within one enclosure. These are called Kannya-kovil, and are said to

[1] There are also hot springs at Badulla, Patipal Aar, near Batticaloa, Kitool, and Medawewa, near Bintenne, and at Yavi Ooto, in the Veddah country. In all the water is so pure as to be good for cooking purposes.

[2] *Kannee*, " a virgin."

have been erected by, or else dedicated to, seven virgin princesses of the Wanni district.

The seven springs were taken in hand by the Dutch as being healing waters, and were confined within seven tanks of carefully regulated degrees of heat. All are now in ruins, but the springs are found to vary in temperature at different seasons from 85° to 122° Fahr. Marvellous to relate, even when the thermometer has indicated the latter degree of heat, live fish of several species—carp, roach, and others—have been taken from these springs, and in the streamlet which flows from them.

We were not so fortunate as to see any of these eccentric fishes, so contented ourselves with watching the play of some harmless snakes while we sat under the beautiful kitool, areca, and cocoa palms which overshadowed the dilapidated tanks, enjoying our breakfast and tea made with clear pure water from one of the boiling springs.

These families of the great clan Palm are comparatively rare in the neighbourhood of Trincomalee, where the vast cocoa-groves of the southern provinces are replaced by an incalculable multitude of palmyra-palms,[1] which form a belt of dark-green all along the coast, flourishing even on the brink of the salt coral-sand, where at high tide the blue waters bathe the roots of their sturdy black stems, which stand like regiments of well-drilled soldiers, faultlessly upright and unbendingly stiff.

In every respect they present a curious contrast to the graceful cocoa-palm, whose white stems bend in every variety of symmetrical curve, while their long slender fronds (each composed of a multitude of sharp glittering sword-shaped leaves) are rarely for one moment at rest, but gleam

[1] *Borassus flabelliformis.*

in the sunlight while ceaselessly turning and trembling with every breath of air.

The palmyra-palm, on the contrary, rises straight to a height of sixty or seventy feet, and bears a thick crown of stiff fan-shaped leaves, deeply indented. Beneath them hang clusters of beautifully glossy golden-brown nuts, each about half the size of a cocoa-nut, but quite circular, and a full-grown tree bears perhaps eight or ten bunches of these, with a dozen or more in each cluster. Seen half in sunlight and half shadowed by the dark crown of foliage against a vividly blue sky, these brown and yellow nuts are beautiful, but as a fruit they have none of the charm of the cocoa-nut, although they form the staple food of the population on the north-east coast.

The glossy outer skin is so hard that only an expert hand can tear it open. Within it, and mixed with fibre, is a farinaceous pulp, at once oily and gelatinous, which even the natives rarely eat raw, but when roasted or dried in the sun and then smoked, it is largely used in making curries and cakes. It is said to be excellent when half ripe, but is then very liable to produce dysentery. Embedded within this pulp, each nut contains three very hard kernels or seeds, and of the myriads of these which are annually sowed, only a very small proportion are destined to become trees. The main crop is dug up in infancy, when the root resembles a waxy parsnip, and is either eaten as a vegetable, or dried and made into flour something like tapioca. This root is known in the bazaars as *kelingu*, and the dried fruit is *punatu*.

A cruelly wasteful delicacy is obtained from this, as from several other palms, by sacrificing a well-grown young tree for the sake of its tender leading shoot, which much resembles a gigantic stalk of very white celery, with a pleasant nutty flavour.

The palmyra-palm does not begin bearing fruit till it is upwards of ten years of age, and a comparatively small number of the trees are allowed to develop their crop of beautiful nuts, the majority being tortured into yielding only the luscious sap, which when allowed to ferment becomes slightly intoxicating and is known as toddy (doubtless so named by some early Scotch planter, in remembrance of the whisky-toddy of the North!). By exposure to the sun the toddy becomes vinegar, or, if sugar is required, a little lime is mixed with the sap, which is then boiled down to a thick syrup, and poured into baskets made from the palmyra leaf, and allowed to harden. In this state it is sold as *jaggery* sugar, of which a very large amount is used in the island.

In order to obtain this sap, the toddy-drawers, who are marvellously expert climbers, ascend to the crown of leaves, beneath which, each cradled in a long solid sheath or spathe, are the bunches of ivory-like blossom bearing the embryo nuts. Each spathe having been tightly bound to prevent its expansion, is ruthlessly beaten every morning with a heavy wooden mallet, till the immature flower within, instead of developing into a thing of loveliness, is reduced to pulp, but without injuring its outer cover.

After about a week of this maltreatment, the sap begins to flow, much to the satisfaction of swarms of insects, who assemble to feast thereon, and in their turn attract flocks of crows and various insectivorous birds. These again afford many a dainty meal to the palm-cat and sundry other foes, who climb the palms in pursuit of the birds.

Meanwhile, the toddy-drawer having cut off the tip of the spathe to allow the sap to drip, hangs a small clay chattie or a gourd beneath each bleeding blossom, and thenceforth for about five months he ascends day by day at early dawn to collect the sap, emptying each little chattie into one suspended from his waist, and when that is full he lowers it by a cord to an assistant below, who empties it into a larger one. Every day he cuts a thin slice off the poor bruised flower to make it bleed afresh, and each flower continues to yield sap for about a month.

Each tree yields on an average about three quarts a day (the produce of the female tree is, however, considerably more than double that of the male tree).

Only once in three years are these tortured trees allowed to ripen their fruit, in order to save their lives, as otherwise they would die under this unnatural treatment. The sweet juice from about nine hundred trees being collected from the earthen chatties, is poured into a copper still, and distilled three times over to obtain the strong and highly intoxicating spirit called arrack, most of which, however, is obtained from the cocoa-palm, which contains less sugar. Palmyra-toddy is considered by connoisseurs to be too luscious.

The work of the toddy-drawer is no sinecure, for although by the aid of a loop of flexible vine passed round his ankles, so as to enable him to grasp the trunk of the tree with his singularly prehensile feet, he contrives to climb with monkey-like agility, one man can scarcely manage to ascend more than twenty trees every morning. So, in order to lessen the toil of climbing, and enable each man to work a hundred trees daily, half-a-dozen palm-tops are connected by ropes, along which the drawer passes from tree to tree. Sometimes a second set of ropes, some feet higher, are added for security, but even with these it is a work of danger, and many horrible accidents result from this practice, besides the fatalities recorded.

In the annual report of deaths from accident, a considerable number are shown to be caused by falling from trees. I have this list for 1879, 1883, 1887, and 1890, and I see the deaths under this head are respectively 255, 250, 326, and 369, and the majority of victims were toddy-drawers, who in some cases lose their hold of the slender coir rope while collecting the sap, but more often perish from its breaking as they pass from one high tree-top to another. Sometimes the ropes are rotten, sometimes they are injured by rats, and in some cases there has been reason to suspect an enemy of half-cutting the rope.

The men engaged in this work are of very low caste, and in too many cases their hardly-earned wages return to the toddy-merchant. There are, however, some brilliant exceptions, such as that village of stanch Christians whom we visited near Batticaloa.

As a matter of course, the dress of these athletes is reduced to a minimum, but in ascending the palmyra-palm they find it necessary to wear a breastplate of stout leather as a protection against the very rough stems. In ascending the smooth cocoa-palm this is not requisite.

That a tree so precious as the palmyra-palm should ever be sacrificed for timber seems unnatural, but so valuable is its hard black wood in house-building, that an immense trade is done therein, especially for the supply of rafters, as it is found that even white ants scarcely care to attack it. But as its value as timber increases with its age (no tree being worth felling which has not attained at least a hundred years), each tree has done a life-work of good service to man ere it commences a second century of usefulness as an almost imperishable timber. It has, however, one peculiarity, in that it causes nails to rust rapidly.

It is somewhat singular that not only is the female palm so much more generous than the male in her yield of sap, but also her timber fetches a very much higher price, as being denser, harder, and darker in colour. It is said that in order to increase these three qualities in the male palm, the natives immerse the newly-felled timber in the sea, and there leave it to season. Unlike the ebony tree, which conceals its precious heart of black wood within an outer casing of white wood, the palmyra carries its hard black wood externally, enfolding a heart of soft white wood—a pretty subject for a tree-parable.

Great as is the demand for this timber, due care is, of course, taken to keep up the supply of a tree so precious that the Tamils recognise it as the Kalpa or "Tree of Life," sacred to Ganesa, the god of wisdom; and whereas the Singhalese talk of the hundred and fifty good uses to which the cocoa-palm lends itself, a Hindoo poet sings of the eight hundred and one manners in which the palmyra benefits mankind!

It is estimated that there are on the Isle about twelve million palms of this species, and as to the innumerable ways in which they are turned to account (besides those to which I have already alluded), I can only advise you to use your imagination, for you will find it difficult to think of any necessary of life which native ingenuity will not contrive to extract from this priceless tree—anything from a walking-stick or a thatching-needle, to a bedstead, a ladder, a plough, or a water-spout!

As its stem yields timber for house-building, the leaves supply the best possible thatch, and material for weaving mats both for ceiling and for floor; baskets of all sorts, including some which can be used as buckets for drawing water; fans, umbrellas, coolies' hats, ropes, fly-whisks, torches. Strips of these leaves, steeped either in boiling water or in milk to render them pliable, and then smoothed on a heavy wooden roller, form the equivalent of paper and parchment—*olas*—only inferior to those obtained from the huge leaf of the taliput-palm.

As the fruit, root, and sap of the tree supply food, palm-wine, sugar, and oil for the use of man, the young leaves serve as fodder for his cattle, and the hard spathe, wherein the blossom lay cradled, has often been used to good purpose as a baby's bath.

The general effect of a great expanse of palmyras is certainly dull and monotonous, but when seen near, nothing can be more picturesque than a group of these, especially when, as is so frequently the case, overgrown by some parasitic tree. During its prolonged youth, the palmyra retains its great fan-shaped leaves, set spirally round the stem like a huge corkscrew. When, with advancing years, these die off, the solid leaf-stalk and coarse net-like fibre remain, giving the black trunk a rugged, untidy appearance, but also affording support to a great variety of delicate climbing plants, and offering a cradle wherein many seeds lodge and germinate, especially those of the banyan, which take root so effectually that ere long the parent stem is completely enfolded, often strangled, by the too close embraces of the long white arms and roots which twine around it in every direction.

Such marriages of the sacred banyan and palm-tree, though by no means uncommon, are regarded by the natives, whether Tamil or Singhalese, with extreme rever-

ence, and great was the interest evinced by some who found me sketching a very remarkable grove on the shore about a couple of miles from Trincomalee, where scores of black palmyras were each thus enfolded by white banyans twisting around them like contorted snakes. Sooner or later the ungrateful parasite strangles the protector of its infancy, and is left standing alone, twisted into every conceivable fantastic form.

In this particular instance the scene was absolutely fairy-like by reason of the exquisite undergrowth of tall white lilies, like our lovely virgin lily, but streaked with most delicate pink—truly a vision of delight. These were growing luxuriantly all along the shore, which, moreover, was richly carpeted by the goat's-foot, Ipomea, a large lilac convolvulus, whose glossy green foliage, with profusion of delicate blossoms, mats the sands to the very brink of the sea, affording shelter to thousands of tiny crabs. This pretty plant flourishes on the seaboard in all parts of the Isle, and constitutes one of the many charms of the beach.

As to the crabs, they were a constant source of amusement, especially one odd little creature with one claw longer than all the rest of its tiny body. It sidles along at a great pace, holding up this great claw as if to attract attention; hence it is generally known as the calling crab. (I saw myriads of these crabs in Fiji, but far more brilliantly coloured.)[1]

I only wish it were possible for words to convey any impression of the fascination of such a shore as that of the calm bay on which we looked down from the Government Agent's house—clear glittering waters rippling on sands strewn with pearly Venus-ear and many another shell;

[1] "At Home in Fiji," vol. i. p. 257, and vol. ii. p. 2.

brown children paddling tiny canoes made of rudely hollowed logs; a lilac-and-green carpet of the marine convolvulus losing itself beneath the shadow of a grove of tall, graceful cocoa-palms bending in every direction; and then the rocky headlands, so inviting for a scramble, with their broken crags, rock pinnacles, and at least one great natural archway offering cool shade beneath which to rest while revelling in the loveliness of all around.

Just above it stands the pleasant home, with its red-tiled roofs and pillared verandah, overshadowed by beautiful trees and surrounded by aloes and flowery shrubs. Add to all this the vivid light and colour of sea and sky, and surely you can realise something of the charm of many a home on this sweet Isle.

CHAPTER XX.

TRINCOMALEE TO GALLE.

Trincomalee—A Tamil play—A luminous sea—Batticaloa—Flying-fish—Galle—Buona Vista—A kabragoya—Green corals—Uses of the cocoa-palm.

I HAVE seen some curious specimens of plays and theatres in many lands, but none more singular than an evening open-air performance at Trincomalee by a company of Tamil actors. The ground formed a grassy amphitheatre gently sloping down to the centre, where a large circular stage was erected, and protected from possible rain by a canopy of matting. The spectators were closely seated in circles all around, those at the back being sufficiently raised to command an excellent view of the stage, which was divided into six imaginary sections, the players actually performing each short scene six times over, facing each section of the audience by turns. Wearisome as such a performance would prove if seen too often, it was certainly interesting for once, and the native spectators were evidently delighted, and waited with exemplary patience while each scene went the round of the other five sides.

A few of the actors were very handsomely dressed, to represent ancient Tamil kings and queens, and loaded with gorgeous jewellery of real old patterns. Some wore large richly jewelled animals placed on each shoulder or on the head, the front of the stage being dimly lighted by rude lamps fed with cocoa-nut oil, and stuck on plantain stems about five feet high. These details would have been invisible had not each of the principal actors been escorted by a coolie in the ordinary undress, whose duty it was to carry a small earthenware lamp fastened to the end of a stick, and this he thrust right in the face of his master that all might be able to see him and his finery.

A number of other coolies in the lightest of raiment stood about on the stage to help in various ways, and as the orchestra (which consisted of a chorus of discordant voices and musicians beating tomtoms and other drums, blowing shells and shrill pipes) was also on the stage, and all moved round together, the effect was most confusing, and the richly dressed actors were almost hidden by the scantily draped subordinates.

It is difficult to realise that it is not so very long since our own drama was even more primitive than this, and yet our kings and their courtiers could sit out a "morality" or a "mystery" continuing for nine or ten hours.[1]

Happily for the success of this open-air entertainment, the weather proved perfect, which was more than we could count upon, for (it was now the end of September) heavy

[1] On such occasions the stage was a rush-strewn scaffolding, with a light cloth canopy, and that scenic effects were not costly may be inferred from such entries in the accounts of the play-giving guilds as the following :—" Paid for mending of Hell, 2d. For keeping fire at ditto, 4d. For setting the world on fire, 5d. To Crowe for making three worlds, 3s." The chief actors received 3s. 4d. each, but the *prima donna* only 2s.

It is curious to learn that, as in China at the present day, so in Britain prior to A.D. 1661, no women might appear on the stage, so that for at least half-a-century all Shakspeare's daintiest dames were impersonated by youths !

tropical thunderstorms were pretty frequent, and were certainly no joke. Sometimes they came on very suddenly. Dark clouds gathered with surprising rapidity, and then the blinding glare of vivid lightning and the crashing thunder-peals were succeeded by such a pitiless deluge as defied the stoutest waterproofs. Such storms, however, passed away as quickly as they arose, and seemed only to add fresh charm to the fragrant stillness of the night, illuminated by a thousand points of glittering pale-green light, as the light-giving beetles which we call fire-flies flashed to and fro, and the whole air was perfumed with the fragrance of orange, lime, and shaddock blossoms.

But the chance of such soakings and the amount of "roughing" which is inevitable in jungle travel form a grave risk for any one not endowed with very robust health, and even before we reached Trincomalee it was evident that the Bishop would be compelled to abandon his northward journey to Jaffna, in the extreme north of the Isle. When, therefore, at the end of an anxious month of severe illness, the kindest and most careful of doctors (Dr. Goodwin) was able to sanction his leaving Trincomalee, it was clear that he must return to Colombo by the easiest route, namely, by the Government steamship *Serendib*,[1] which had only to call at Batticaloa and Galle. So, after a regretful parting with many friends whose kindness at such a time can never be forgotten, we embarked one evening at sunset, and some hours later sailed out of the beautiful harbour in the clear starlight.

The sea there is intensely phosphorescent, and it seemed that night as though the sea-gods were holding high revel,

[1] One of the many names by which Ceylon was known to the ancients and to the writers of "The Arabian Nights."

and we poor mortals strained our eyes in the effort to peer down through the waves, which were all aglow with marine fireworks and illuminations. I never saw anything more lovely. The sky was very dark, with stormy clouds scudding before a pretty stiff breeze, but the sea was all full of dancing, glittering, points of pale white fire, with here and there large dazzling stars, which gleamed suddenly, then faded away into darkness, like the intermittent flash from some beacon-light. Wave beyond wave, right away to the horizon, was plainly defined in pallid light, here and there crested with brighter fire, where the breeze had caught the curving billow and tossed it back in glittering spray.

As we looked down through the waters and watched the myriad points of light rushing upwards, some one suggested a comparison to champagne or some such effervescing drink alive with air-bubbles. But these luminous globules frequently start on independent careers, and dash to right or left, according to some impulse of their own devising.

Often as I have watched the phosphoric wonders of our dark Northern seas (when, sailing through a shoal of herring, each separate fish has seemed a thing of living light), I had never seen the light so widespread as here. It seemed as if the sea-gods had issued large supplies of phosphorus for the occasion, for creatures which on other nights are quite invisible to-night shone, probably with borrowed lustre. Large families of flying-fish darted from the water as we passed, suggesting flights of luminous birds, and here and there a school of great, heavy porpoises rushed by, leaving a trail of living fire; and thousands of delicate little jelly-fish floated peacefully along, like inverted cups fringed with fire—most lovely, fairy-like creatures.

On a night like this I always, if possible, take up a position either at the bow or stern of the ship. From the former you look sheer down, as from the edge of a precipice, and watch the dividing of the waters as the vessel cuts her way through the waves, and the startled creatures of all sorts awaken, but in their hurried flight they quickly light their lamps, and the white spray that is thrown off from the bows, in a ceaseless fountain, glitters like a shower of radiant stars. It always reminds me of the Ancient Mariner's lonely watch, when from his eerie ship

"The elfish light fell off in hoary flakes!"

Coleridge must assuredly have watched on such nights as these.

Then, if you make a pilgrimage to the stern, and can endure to stand just above the throbbing, thumping screw, you see the most wonderful sight of all. For the great propeller literally churns the waters far, far below the surface; and each stroke produces a body of clear green and blue light, which rolls upwards in a soft brilliancy quite indescribable—like dissolved opals. As each successive globe of this fairy-like green fire rises to the surface, it breaks in bubbling, hissing spray, and spreads itself over the surface, leaving a pathway of fire, which remains visible for a long time after the vessel has passed, fading away in the distance, like a reflection of the Milky Way, that spans the dark sky above it.

Some of my far-travelled companions, who had sailed in many seas, were talking one evening of the various forms in which this beautiful phenomenon appears. One of the officers had the good luck to see what is known as "white water" as he crossed the Arabian Sea. It was a dark moonless night in summer, only the stars were reflected on the calm waters, when suddenly a soft, silvery light overspread the ocean—a tremulous, shimmering light; the waters lay smooth as a mirror. He drew up a bucketful of this gleaming water, and found it was clouded, as if tinged with milk, and luminous with phosphorus. When he emptied the bucket it continued to glow for some time.

Another officer said he too had seen a milk-like sea, in about the same part of the ocean, but when some of the men on board drew up water for examination it was perfectly clear, and they concluded that the curious appearance of the sea was due to the fact that they were passing through a soft hazy mist, and though the night was so dark that they were scarcely conscious of its influence, they supposed that it in some way refracted the starlight on to the surface of the waters, and to this they attributed the quivering of the pallid light—tremulous as a mirage.[1]

If this was really the cause of the light, it must have been due to some very strange condition of the atmosphere, as even in the tropics such a phenomenon is very rarely seen, and we cannot say as much for mists!

I am told that a similar appearance has occasionally been observed in the North Sea, and even on the Northumbrian coast; and the fishers have noted that its presence indicated a very poor herring season, and that the temperature of the sea was unusually high during its duration. It proved to be a very tangible form of whiteness, for when

---

[1] I have myself witnessed just such an effect of dazzling light, illuminating the whole surface of the water, during two midnight storms in New Zealand. *Vide* "At Home in Fiji," vol. ii. p 169.

they drew up their nets they found them coated with a substance resembling lime.[1]

We reached Batticaloa about noon on the following day, and were once more cordially welcomed to the same pleasant quarters which had been assigned to us on our previous visit.

On the following morning, Captain Varian having most kindly undertaken to show me some of my brother's cocoa-nut estates, we started before dawn in one of the *Serendib* boats, towed by the steam-launch a long way ahead of us —a delightful mode of travel, securing perfectly smooth, gliding motion. The morning was exquisite, and all the ranges of blue, distant hills and wooded headlands were faultlessly mirrored in the calm sea-lake.

About eighteen miles from Batticaloa we landed at the first estate, then proceeded to another, and ploughed our way through an apparently interminable grove of cocoa-palms all planted in straight lines, at regular intervals, in deep, hot sand —endless rows of tall palms, all of much the same height, extending for miles and miles as far as the eye could see, and much farther, all growing out of the arid sand—very different from lovely half-wild groves where trees of all ages grow at their own will from a cool, deep carpet of the greenest guinea-grass by the brink of some cool lake; the young ones like huge clumps of great ferns growing cup-wise, others in every stage of growth, the middle-aged ones strongly resembling tree-ferns with fronds fully twenty feet in length. It would be difficult to imagine richer vege-

[1] The fisher-folk of Shields and Tynemouth, and the villages immediately to the north, noticed this peculiar condition of the water in the summer of 1878, which proved an exceptionally bad year for the herring-fishers.

tation than that, but these orderly plantations are quite another thing.

It was very fatiguing even to walk once along that sand-track, and I realised as I had never done before what must have been the sinking loneliness of the brave young heart, exiled from one of the cheeriest and most beautiful homes in Scotland, to settle quite alone on these desolate sand-banks, and commence the toil of planting them with the nuts about which so little was then known that speedy remuneration was expected, whereas the experience of the next fifteen years was one of continual outlay, ceaseless watchfulness to defend the young plantations from the ravages of most mischievous boring beetles,[1] rats, white ants, herds of wild hogs, porcupines, troops of elephants, and other foes, and no remuneration whatever.

Then, when the day of his emancipation came, the estates passed to other hands, and strangers now reap the abundant fruits of his long years of weary toil.

Planters of the present day, profiting by the experience of their predecessors, find that by a liberal application of oil-cake, ashes, sea-weed, salt mud, and various other manures they can induce young palms to commence flowering about the seventh year (some which have been fed as carefully and liberally as prize oxen have actually flowered in the fourth year), and, moreover, that the trees thus nourished will bear at least twice as many nuts, but the work at the time to which I refer was in a great measure experimental.

Even now cocoa-nut planting is a very uncertain venture, for not only do many estates wait twenty years ere yielding a full return (though probably about half the trees commence bearing in the fourteenth year), but the crop is also

[1] *Oryctes rhinoceros.*

very variable, some estates yielding only one candy of copra to the acre, while others yield three.

The fact is, that there are in Ceylon a vast number of nameless varieties of cocoa-palms, and unless almost impossible care is observed in the selection of nuts for planting, the crops will always be variable. An experienced planter says: "One tree begins to flower in its fifth year on four feet of stem; its nearest neighbour, equally vigorous, runs up to fifteen or even twenty feet, and only begins to flower in the tenth year. One will have fertile germs on its first flower, and its neighbour will only produce barren flowers for twelve months. One will, within a year of opening its first flower, fall into a regular yield of a hundred nuts per annum of medium size, while another close by carries from thirty to forty very large ones, and the next in the same line carries above two hundred very small ones."

Besides these differences in the nuts themselves, varieties of soil are responsible for many disappointments, some planters having wasted much energy on swampy or clayey soils, only to find that after ten or twelve years the palms gave no promise of fruit, while sandy soil, moist but not too wet, is the most favourable.

In Ceylon the cocoa-nuts are gathered six times a year, and when liberally manured and carefully tended should continue in bearing for upwards of a century.

We trudged through deep sand till we reached the small bungalow of the present owner, who gave us refreshing cocoa-nuts to drink, and lent us the cart, drawn by an elephant, which daily collects the fallen nuts; but I cannot say we found it pleasant, as the elephant had a faculty for bolting first on one side, then on the other, against the palms, thereby keeping us constantly on the jerk; so we very shortly agreed that even the fatigue of walking was preferable, and accordingly descended from our uncomfortable quarters, and trudged through the hot sand till we reached the site of my brother's original house, now marked only by the fruit-trees which he planted round it.

We returned to Batticaloa at sunset, and in the peaceful moonlight I stood by the grassy grave in the little "God's acre," with an intensified sympathy for many of "our boys" leaving the happy home-nest to carve their fortunes in distant lands.

Amongst minor details in a day of so great interest, I may mention the multitude of fresh-water snail-shells which we found on the banks of a small tank, and also the pleasure of finding a number of turtle's eggs, each containing a perfect miniature turtle quite ready to be hatched—the neatest tiny creatures.

On the following evening we took leave of our many kind friends, and returned on board the *Serendib*, which was lying outside the harbour-bar, and fully did we realise the sudden change from the dead calm of the sea-lake thus guarded to the tossing ocean beyond.

This bar is often the occasion of very grave inconvenience to the inhabitants of Batticaloa, for when a strong sea-breeze is blowing the waves dash upon it so tumultuously that no boat dare face those raging breakers. In this comparatively tideless sea, high or low tide afford very slight variation in the depth of water on the bar, which in the spring months is sometimes barely three and a half feet. Moreover, owing to the usual deposit of silt, the mouth of the river is growing daily narrower, notwithstanding the strong current which sweeps the shore.

Happily, the singular regularity in the variation of the direction of the wind affords some security, as the boatmen well know that the sea-breeze will attain its height shortly before noon, when the bar will probably be impassable. But at night the land-breeze sets in and quiets the tumult, so that by morning there is comparative calm, and from dawn till about 9 A.M. the bar can generally be crossed in safety. But, of course, it is not always that a steamer can lie in the open roadstead to await these possibilities, and so it occasionally happens that passengers and cargo cannot get on board, while other passengers and goods cannot be put ashore. At other times the transit is effected at the cost of an hour's hard rowing and a general soaking.

Happily for us, at the end of October, we had no such unpleasant experience, wind and waves combining to speed us on our way.

All the next day was taken up in beating about in search of a reported rock, which we failed to find; but to a sketcher "all is fish that comes to the net," and I was thus enabled to secure sundry reminiscences of the coast as seen from the sea or the inland mountain ranges.

Speaking of fish, I never remember seeing so many flying-fish as on that voyage. They rose from the waves, at our approach, like flashes of silvery spray, and flew perhaps two hundred yards, just skimming the surface of the water—then again, just touching the wave to moisten their transparent wings. They looked so like flights of darting birds that I can well understand the ancients describing them as "sea-swallows."

It seems barbarous to think of these graceful little creatures from a gastronomic point of view, but certainly they are the very daintiest fish-morsels that ever rejoiced an epicure. (In the West Indies they are so highly prized that a special method of capturing them has been devised. The fishers go out at nights in their canoes, carrying blazing torches, to allure these inquisitive "sea-moths," who come flying to the light, and are captured in small nets fastened on to poles, like our landing-nets).

I saved some of their wings (I suppose I ought correctly to say "pectoral fins"), which are formed of a tissue of curious gauze-like membrane, stretched on a folding framework, and must, I think, have inspired Chinamen and other early sailors with the original design for folding sails of matting on movable bamboos.

We reached Galle on the following afternoon, and found it beautiful as ever, but the masts of yet one more newly sunken steamer rose from the waters of its lovely, treacherous harbour, wherein so many fine ships have met their doom.

Archdeacon Schrader "the Good" came to welcome the Bishop, and to fetch us all to his hospitable roof, and to service at the beautiful church, All Saints', which owes its existence to his energy. It is by far the finest in the island, and one whose constant and hearty services have come as a breath of home to many a wanderer from far-distant lands, pausing here on his voyage.

On the following day the Archdeacon drove us to see the large Orphanage at Buona Vista, which crowns the summit of the steep headland which forms the southern arm of the harbour, and commands a lovely view of Galle. We were most kindly received by Mr. and Mrs. Marks,[1] who showed us their troop of very nice-looking boys and girls. This is a mission-station of the S.P.G. Society,

[1] The Orphanage is now under the care of Miss Callender.

and supplies Christian teachers, both male and female, for the surrounding village schools. We were told that, of the children who attend these village schools, about one-sixth are Christians, and it is found that, even among those who at the time appear quite uninfluenced by Christian teaching, a considerable number receive impressions, which, at a later period, develop into active principles.

Strange to say, the heathen parents, though perfectly aware of the heart's desire of the teachers, make no objection whatever to their children being carefully instructed in all Christian knowledge until the day comes when the young student, being fully of age to make his own decision, desires to be baptized. Then every possible means is adopted to counteract his newly awakened faith. Buddhist priests are called in to reason with him; expulsion from home and disinheritance are all threatened, but rarely overcome the resolution once formed, and eventually the relations, finding they cannot shake the faith of the young convert, abstain from active persecution.

On another hill, bearing the very British name of Richmond, and also commanding a lovely view, stands the Wesleyan Mission and its schools. It is in connection with a large chapel in the town, at which services are alternately held in English, Portuguese, and Singhalese.

Greater interest in point of antiquity attaches to the fine old cruciform Dutch church, which is paved with tombstones of bygone generations, whose monuments also crowd the walls. Here services according to the form of the Presbyterian Church of Holland are held in English, recalling the autocratic manner in which the Dutch conquerors strove to "convert" the islanders by the aid of interpreters, utterly refusing themselves to learn their language.

About ten miles inland from Galle lies Baddegama, a lovely spot on the Gindura river, where, in 1818, the Church Missionary Society commenced England's first effort on behalf of her newly annexed colony. A very satisfactory feature of this station is the boarding-school for Singhalese girls, which has provided many well-taught Christian wives for the young men trained in Christian colleges. Some years ago the fine old church tower was struck by lightning, as was also the verandah of the mission-house, and the missionary in charge, Mr. Balding, narrowly escaped being killed, an incident of which he and his parishioners are perpetually reminded by the sound of a cracked bell, said to have previously been well toned.

Another point of interest near Baddegama is the oldest sugar-cane estate in the Isle, a cultivation which has not been largely taken up in Ceylon.

On our homeward way, as we drove through a cool shady glade, the horses started as a gigantic lizard, or rather iguana, of a greenish-grey colour, with yellow stripes and spots, called by the natives kabragoya,[1] awoke from its midday sleep, and slowly, with the greatest deliberation, walked right across the road just in front of us. It is a notoriously slothful reptile, and on this occasion fully sustained its reputation, for it did not hurry itself in the smallest degree; so we had to wait its time, and had full leisure to observe the lazy movements of this strange creature, which was fully seven feet in length, with a general resemblance to a crocodile.

Like that very unattractive monster, the kabragoya is amphibious, and when in danger tries to make for the water. It is quite harmless, however, except in the matter

[1] *Hydro saurus salvator.*

of eating fowls, and is eminently peaceful in its disposition, unless roused at close quarters, when, in self-defence, it can turn on a foe and administer a tremendous blow with its armour-plated tail, which, being provided with a sharp crest, can inflict a very serious wound on the lightly draped natives. Occasionally a rash aggressor receives a broken arm or leg, as a warning against molesting harmless fellow-creatures; consequently the Singhalese treat these huge lizards with considerable respect. The all-destroying foreigner occasionally shoots one, and notes its strange tenacity of life, the head being apparently the only vulnerable, or at any rate the only vital, spot. I believe, however, that the Veddahs are the only people who have sufficient strength of mind to eat the ugly monster.

I had not been in Galle since the memorable occasion when I first landed there on my way to India, and received my never-to-be-forgotten very first impressions of palm-trees and the tropics—first impressions of perfect novelty and fairy-like enchantment—so of course I longed to return to Wakwalla, to which we accordingly drove in the evening. But, alas! as with all else in this world, familiarity does wear off the keen sense of delight even in palm-trees, and exquisite as such a drive through mazes of tropical foliage must ever be, I felt on this second visit to Wakwalla that my own appreciation of its loveliness was somewhat dulled by the many visions of tropical beauty on which my eyes had feasted since I had first beheld it.

Nevertheless, it was with great pleasure that I accepted invitations from several kind friends in Galle and its neighbourhood, with the prospect of returning to Colombo by the lovely road along the sea-coast—a drive of seventy miles all shadowed by the graceful palms which droop right over the sea.

So the *Serendib* sailed *minus* one passenger, and I made my way to the farthest point of the ramparts to watch her safe out of the ill-fated harbour with her precious freight of truest friends. Afterwards I ascended the lighthouse, and thence looked down on the coral-reefs clearly visible through the shallow, lustrous, emerald-green water-reefs which come too near the surface for the safety of the harbour, as many a good ship has proved to her cost.[1]

But beautiful as is such a bird's-eye-view of the reef (which, when lighted by the rays of the noonday. sun, gleams like a lost rainbow, held captive by water-sprites) its treasures of delight are only to be fully appreciated by floating over it at low tide, in a boat drawing only a few inches of water, and regardless of paint (for the sharp cutting points of the coral are fatal to a trig ornamental boat). Only thus is it possible to realise the loveliness of these submarine gardens, where coral-trees, coral-shrubs, and coral-flowers of every hue, violet and rose, red and brown, gold and lemon colour, are the homes and play-grounds of all manner of strange, beautiful fishes, crabs, sea-snakes, star-fish, sea-urchins, and innumerable other creatures, of every conceivable shape and size and colour.

Naturalists, however, note with interest the remarkable predominance of green in the colouring of many of these creatures, as though by assimilation to the prevailing verdure of the Isle. They find green water-snakes and green fishes, crustacea and star-fish, sea-anemones and

---

[1] I am told that no less than twelve steamers have been wrecked in Galle Harbour, *i.e.*, more than one-third of the total number of thirty-four which have been lost on the shores of Ceylon.

sea-urchins, sea-slugs and several shells of various shades of olive or emerald greens, while a considerable number of corals are verdant as the plants they so closely resemble.[1]

All too fleetly the pleasant days slipped by with drives and boating expeditions to many a lovely scene, and temptations for an artist on every hand. After one long morning in search of the best point for a panoramic sketch of Galle, I came to the conclusion that the very finest view of the town and harbour was that from the verandah of Closenberg, a delightful bungalow, where we landed at some risk, as the surf was running high and dashing in cataracts of spray against the black rocks. However, skilful steering ran our boat in safety between the biggest breakers, and I was soon most cosily ensconced for my day's work.

Looking along the lovely palm-fringed shore, I could not but think that if man does "mark the earth with ruin" in some places, as in the central districts of this Isle, and wherever primeval forests are cleared by planters beginning work, we often forget how deeply we are indebted to those of past generations for much of what we accept as natural beauty. As in New Zealand, Taheiti, and other isles, where imported vegetation is even more luxuriant than that which was indigenous, so here the improving hand of the foreigner has not been confined to acclimatising the beautiful flowering shrubs which adorn the gardens, but even the multiplication of the palms, which now seem so natural a feature of Ceylon, was really greatly due to the commercial instincts of the Dutch, who, finding that about nine-tenths of the west coast, from Galle right up to

[1] Such are the Montipora, Madrepora, Millepora, Macandrina, Astræa, Alcyonia, Anthophylla, Heteropora.

Calpentyn (the whole of which is now one succession of luxuriant cocoa-groves), was then waste uncultivated land, offered Government grants thereof to all persons who would undertake to plant cocoa-palms, and thereon pay a certain tax.

It would appear that strong pressure must have been brought to bear to awaken the easy-going natives to the necessity of carrying out this extensive scheme of cultivation of a crop which brings such slow returns (ten years to wait at the very least). However, the plantations were made, and the waste lands transformed to their present beauty. But even now the apathy of the villagers is such that, although the shore may be strewn with masses of seaweed, which, if collected and dug into the earth round the roots of the palms, would materially increase the crops, they will scarcely ever exert themselves to utilise the manure thus laid ready to their hand.

At Jaffna and Batticaloa, where the cocoa-palms are now ubiquitous, and might well be supposed to be indigenous, European planters only commenced work in 1841, and, as I have already shown, many of the early plantations ruined their first owners.

It is certainly remarkable how rarely the cocoa-palm is mentioned in old Ceylonese history; it is never alluded to as food, whereas the palmyra and taliput palms are frequently referred to. Not till the twelfth century is it named as a tree worthy of cultivation. At all events its merits are fully recognised in this nineteenth century!

At Galle the heavy rainfall, attracted by the neighbouring hill ranges (and which is three inches in the year in excess of that at Colombo, the respective measurements being ninety and eighty-seven inches), must always have favoured the luxuriant vegetation, and no tree is more gratefully responsive for an abundant supply of rain than is the cocoa-palm, of which it has been calculated that those bearing fruit in this district alone exceed 5,300,000. The total number of fruit-bearing palms on the shores of Ceylon is estimated at 50,000,000, besides 200,000,000 which are either unproductive or are forced to yield their life-blood in the form of toddy, chiefly for the manufacture of arrack. But it is estimated that, even at the low average of twenty-four nuts to a tree (and very many bear from sixty to eighty), one thousand millions of nuts are annually allowed to ripen for the good of man. Unlike the date, the cocoa-palm bears male and female flowers on the same tree—in fact, on the same cluster. The number of actually barren or male palms in Ceylon is singularly small, being said not to exceed one in three or four thousand.

I speak of this palm as belonging to the shore, for it is emphatically a coast tree, flourishing in a belt about fifteen miles in width. The places where it has been successfully planted inland are so few as to be quite exceptional. Such are Mihintale, the sacred hill near Anuradhapura, where groups of graceful palms wave around the great dagobas which crown the summit. I also saw large flourishing plantations in good bearing at Matele, which is about a hundred miles inland and about 1274 feet above the sea-level; they also bear well at Kandy, Gampola, Kurunegalla, and Badulla, all of which are far inland, and the latter 2241 feet above the sea. A few scattered cocoa-palms have been grown as high as 3500 feet, but these bear no fruit.

The Singhalese have a saying that this friendly palm cannot live far from the sea, or from the sound of the human voice, and in proof thereof point out that wherever you see a cluster of these tall crowns you are sure to find a human house not far off. And what can be more natural, seeing that each tree is somebody's private and very valuable property,[1] the precious provider of "golden eggs" in the form of material for all things needful to existence?

The half-ripe fruits (in their hard outer cover, green or golden as the case may be) supply food of the consistency of jelly, and cool refreshing drink in a natural cup. The older brown nuts (as we know them in Britain) give the hard white kernel which is scraped as a flavouring for curry, or mixed with sugar (obtained from the sap) to make cakes, or else scraped and squeezed through a cloth to obtain delicious cream which is excellent in tea when cow's milk is not to be obtained. I believe that the Singhalese anoint their glossy black hair with a fine oil obtained by boiling this cream, but the regular oil of commerce is extracted from the kernel after it has been left to dry in the sun, when it is known as copperah.

The small native oil-mills, or "chekku," as they are called, are of the rudest construction, and turned by bullocks. Being entirely made of wood, they creak in the most ear-splitting fashion, but they do their work so efficiently and so cheaply that, happily for all who appreciate primitive Oriental scenes, they hold their ground against the costly steam oil-mills, steam crushers, and hydraulic presses set up near Colombo by foreigners, so that about nine hundred

[1] Here is a case in point:—
"MURDER ARISING OUT OF A CLAIM FOR A COCO-NUT TREE.—On the 11th September 1890 Josappu, a tavern-keeper of Payyagala, was severely assaulted by his cousin Bachappu and two others. The injured man was removed to the Kalutara Hospital, where he died the following day. It would seem that Josappu claimed a share of the profits of a coco-nut tree which Bachappu was exclusively enjoying. The latter could not or would not see the validity of his cousin's claim. A quarrel ensued, with the result aforesaid."

of these quaint mills are still creaking and grinding in the southern and western provinces. (In 1876 it was stated that there were in the whole Isle 1930 chekkus worked by bullocks, besides about a dozen steam mills with hydraulic machinery.)

Many of these chekkus are quite small, and worked by man-power, and very picturesque they are, with a miniature thatch of palm-leaves over the small vat containing the copperah, and perhaps two or three brown children perched on the long handle by which their father turns the vat, and so crushes out the oil. The clothing of such groups is reduced to a minimum, that of the children often consisting only of some charm against the evil eye or to protect them from devils. The refuse left after extraction of the oil is called poonac, and is either used as food for cattle and poultry or for manuring the soil.

No refining process is required beyond a week's exposure to the sun, by which time all impurities will have sunk to the bottom, and the oil can at once be drawn off into casks. It is largely exported, to be used in the manufacture of soaps and lubricants, also in the preparation of stearine candles, and for these purposes is in increasing demand. In Ceylon it is much used as a liniment wherewith to rub the body in cases of rheumatism and other ailments, and the Tamils, not the Singhalese, habitually oil their bodies after bathing; but as regards light, the simple lamp formed of a cocoa-nut shell, and fed with cocoa-nut oil, is now very generally replaced, even in native huts, by a kerosine lamp, as the imported mineral oil, even after all its long journey from America, is cheaper than the native product.

It is not only in rheumatism that cocoa-nut oil is esteemed as a remedy; it is also applied to counteract insect stings, and when mixed with the juice of the leaves is used in cases of ophthalmia. Another sort of oil, extracted from the bark, is applied in skin diseases, and even the root yields a medicine for the fever-stricken. An astringent lotion, bitter as alum, is obtained from the flower, which also (when bruised in the manner I described when speaking of the palmyra-palm) yields toddy, vinegar, sugar, and, when distilled, the intoxicating spirit called arrack.

Toddy, which when first drawn in the early morning forms rather a pleasant drink, commences fermentation before noon, and is highly efficacious as a leaven for bread. After standing a few hours it becomes highly intoxicating, and is frequently made more so by adulteration with nux-vomica, seeds of Indian hemp, datura, and other poisons. A fine of fifty rupees is, however, incurred by any person detected in thus drugging either toddy or arrack.

But the simple mixing of toddy and arrack (*i.e.*, the unfermented with the distilled juice of the beautiful cocoa-flower) produces a very "heady" drink, on which a man can get exceedingly drunk for a very small sum; and sad to say, here as in Lower Bengal, where Buddhism and Christianity have successively done so much to break down the restraints of caste, that gain is in a measure neutralised by the fact that the sobriety once characteristic of the people is rapidly disappearing, and intemperance is grievously on the increase.

It is a sore subject that, whereas Hindoo, Mahommedan, and Buddhist conquerors have ever abstained from deriving any revenue from the intoxicating spirits which are forbidden by each of these religions, a Christian Government should so ruthlessly place temptation at every corner both in Ceylon and in India, where, as has been publicly stated by an Archdeacon of Bombay, the British Government has created a hundred drunkards for each convert won by Christian missionaries.

The toddy is converted into arrack in small local distilleries with copper stills capable of containing from 150 to 200 gallons, which is about the daily produce from a thousand trees, to which a small quantity of sugar and about one-third of rice is generally added. When distilled, a liquor is produced which is called polwakara. A second distillation produces talwakara, a spirit about twenty degrees below proof. When the process has been repeated a third time, arrack of the desired strength is obtained, at first very crude in flavour, but after having been stored in wood for several years it mellows, and even finds favour with Europeans. It is exported from Ceylon to Madras and served to the native troops as a daily ration.

The arrack trade is entirely under control of the Ceylon Government, which derives a considerable revenue from the sale of licenses to distillers (each of whom pays a yearly fee of one hundred rupees), and from the annual sale by auction of the right to farm arrack taverns in all parts of the Isle, a privilege which, being annually sold to the highest bidder, of course makes it to his interest to push the odious trade and establish fresh centres of temptation wherever he can possibly do so. Never was the old proverb that *l'occasion fait le larron*[1] better exemplified, and many a planter has good cause to complain of the temptation thus brought to the very door of his coolies, who now too often barter the very food provided for them, in order to obtain fiery liquor.[2]

[1] Opportunity makes the thief.
[2] I see that, at the auction of arrack rents for 1890, the successful bidder for

Nor is this true only of the intoxicants natural to the country. Government holds a monopoly of the whole liquor traffic of the Isle, and has therefore a direct interest in pushing the sale of drink. Hence railway refreshment-cars and refreshment-rooms at railway stations are exempt from paying license, and the stations themselves (which are Government property) are placarded with advertisements of the whisky which, as has been so truly said, has dug more British graves in Ceylon than malaria, sunstroke, and cholera put together, and there is no doubt that these widely scattered "suggestions" are largely responsible for the practice of dram-drinking, which is said to be so much on the increase.

As regards the natives, who are always so largely influenced by any indication of the will of the ruling power, the mere fact that drinking-places are sanctioned by Government gives them a measure of respectability altogether contrary to unbiassed native opinion.

the privilege of farming Kandy paid 43,000 rupees; Nuwara Eliya fetched 70,000; while the whole of the Central Province was knocked down for 380,000 rupees. All the provinces of the Isle collectively realised 1,803,625, being an increase of 242,171 rupees since 1838.

But "the appetite doth grow with that it feeds upon," and when the rents for the Central Province were put up for sale by auction from July 1891 to June 1892, with the strong recommendation of the Government Agent to the renters to put in good bids, and not trouble Government to call for higher tenders, his advice was so well received that 470,000 rupees were offered for the lot, being 90,000 rupees in excess of the previous year.

In further proof of the steady increase of this baneful traffic, I may also quote the sales of arrack rents for the North-Western Province in April 1891. At Kurunegala there was a large gathering of renters from all parts of the island, the Government Agent presiding. There was brisk bidding, with an exciting finish. The result was 112,200 rupees for the district of Seven Korales (*i.e.*, 14,700 more than last year); Yagampattu and Chilaw districts, 102,000 rupees (*i.e.*, 21,800 rupees more than last year); and Puttalam rents were purchased for 35,900 rupees, being an advance of 4000 on last year.

For plain speaking on so grave a subject, I may refer to the official report on the Negombo district for 1890, in which Mr. Lushington, Assistant Government Agent for the Western Province, expresses his deliberate conviction that by scattering arrack taverns broadcast over the land, Government is itself encouraging the real source of crime, namely, the habits of drunkenness which lead to gambling, cockfighting, divers forms of theft, cattle-stealing, quarrels, and murders.

He finds that men who would not go a mile to procure intoxicants yield readily to the temptation when brought to their very doors, and while pointing out that more than half of the total revenue of the Western Province (apart from customs and railway receipts) is made up of licenses chiefly for the sale of intoxicants and such narcotics as bhang and opium, he proves that an increase in such revenue means simply a corresponding increase in demoralisation and every form of crime, and increased expenditure on its repression by police and legal machinery. " Rather than give up a few thousand rupees of revenue, we encourage the people to sink deeper and deeper in crime by increasing their facilities for drinking."

Mr. Lushington believes that nine-tenths of the serious crimes of the Isle are committed within a mile of a tavern, and that quite one-half arise from the desperation caused by losses at gambling. He says that in the maritime districts every village has its cockpit, every group of villages its gambling den, and near to each is either a tavern or a place for the illicit sale of arrack.

And here comes in another grave difficulty, for in this strange Isle the very men who have purchased a monopoly for the sale of intoxicants are frequently in league with the smugglers and unlicensed arrack-sellers, actually sharing in their profits. Vigilant and conscientious indeed must be the police who could cope with such a state of things.

To return to the more legitimate uses of the good cocoa-palm. Another form in which the nut is used as food (a form, however, more appreciated in the South Seas than in Ceylon) is when, in the early stage of germination, the kernel is transformed into a puffy ball, quite filling up the shell.

The said shell furnishes the household drinking-cups, spoons, lamps, and musical instruments, if I may so describe the clattering castanets. The outermost husk serves as household scrubbing-brushes and fuel, while the thick fibre in which the nut is so securely embedded is the coir used for making ropes, cables, mattresses, nets, brushes, and matting. This is prepared by soaking the husks for a considerable time, if possible, in tanks or pits on the margin of the sea, as salt or brackish water improves the fibre, whereas steeping it in fresh water deteriorates it and creates an obnoxious smell. When thoroughly steeped, the husks are beaten with heavy wooden mallets and then dried in the sun. The ropes are all made by hand-machinery, chiefly in the neighbourhood of Galle and Colombo, and are used for shipping, housebuilding, lashing bridges, tethering cattle, &c.

So securely is the nut embedded in this outer packing-case, that a hungry man, not provided with a hatchet and uninitiated in the method of extracting it, might very well be sorely tantalised in the midst of plenty. In fact, it requires considerable strength as well as some skill to tear off the hard covering.

For this purpose near every cocoa-grove strong wooden stakes are driven into the ground, leaving two or three feet above ground. Each stake is cut to a sharp point, and the man who has to skin a cocoa-nut takes it in both hands and violently dashes it on to the stake so as to impale it. Then wrenching it from side to side, he succeeds in tearing off the husk, and obtains the hard nut inside with the three eyes familiar to every British boy. On a large estate this forms a serious item of labour. It is said that the coir is less brittle and of a better quality if the nuts are plucked before they are fully ripe, and these also yield a larger proportion of oil.

Such are the principal uses of only the flower and fruit of this generous tree. When we come to reckon the very varied purposes to which every separate portion of the leaves, trunk, and root are applied, we find that the Singhalese enumeration of the hundred uses of their beloved palm is no figure of speech, but a practical fact.

As further varieties of food, the young buds, when boiled, are eaten as a vegetable something like cabbage, and when a tree is blown down or stricken with lightning, a sort of sago is obtained from the pith at the upper end of the trunk. Such windfalls are only too common, but deliberately to fell a fruit-bearing tree would seem too foolish, seeing that from the time a palm commences bearing, at about ten years of age, it yields its full crop annually for about eighty years.

In this region of terrific thunderstorms the value of these tall palms as lightning-conductors is inestimable, and many a home has been saved by their superior attraction.

The Singhalese say that you can build a house and furnish it, or build a ship and freight it, solely from the products of this palm. It would puzzle a European to build a seaworthy vessel without a single nail, but here square-rigged vessels, called dhonies, and large canoes, which resist the heaviest surf, are stitched together with coir yarn, which in salt water is almost imperishable. Small canoes are made from a single trunk hollowed out, and balanced by a smaller stem floating alongside; the cordage, mat-sail, and fishing-net are made of coir; the torch or chule which lights our night-march through the forest, or which the fisherman burns to attract fish, is made of dried palm leaves.

As to the house, the palm trunk supplies all its woodwork, while its thatch is supplied by the leaves plaited so as to form a sort of long narrow mat called cadjan. Garden fences and even small huts are made entirely of these cadjans. From the leaf-stalk is formed the pingo or yoke which a man balances on his shoulder with his fish or vegetables hanging from either end, or else it can be used as the handle for a cocoa-nut fibre broom. Its thick end answers as the paddle of a canoe, or if soaked like coir it furnishes a strong black fibre-like horse-hair from which ropes and fishing lines are manufactured. I must not forget to mention that cocoa-nut water mixed with lime produces a strong cement.

In short, as good George Herbert long ago pithily put it—

". . . The Indian nut alone
Is clothing, meat, and trencher, drink and can,
Boat, cable, sail, mast, needle, all in one."

Well may this grateful Isle adopt the cocoa-palm as the emblem on her coinage!

A very elegant use of the young leaves is in the decoration of pandals and churches, one tall leaf on each side of a window forming a very effective decoration. Of course, a cocoa-nut blossom is always an exquisite object, but besides the cruel wastefulness of sacrificing a whole cluster of embryo nuts, there is the disadvantage that to the native mind it suggests a charm against evil spirits, for which purpose it is placed over the cradle of the new-born babe, and over the grave of the newly buried.

CHAPTER XXI.

SOUTHERN COAST.

Mātara—The leper king—Leper Hospital—Dondra Head—Tangalle—Mulgirigalla—Hambantota—Salt lakes—Magama—Happy hunting-grounds—Kataragama.

BEFORE turning northward to Colombo I wished to see something of the southern coast of the Isle, and gladly accepted an invitation from the same kind friends who had made our stay in Negombo so pleasant, to visit them in a new home at Mātara, a most lovely place at the mouth of the Nilwalla Ganga (*i.e.*, the river of blue sand), and only four miles from Dondra Head, which is the southernmost point of the island.[1]

Leaving Galle before daybreak by the royal-mail coach,

[1] During my two years in the Isle this family was subjected to all the trouble and expense of moving three times, that is to say, of selling off their furniture (of course at considerable loss), renting and furnishing a new home, and finding new servants.

This system of continually, and on the shortest notice, moving Civil servants from one corner of the Isle to another, either as a "permanent" appointment or as *locum tenens* for some one temporarily transferred to other work, is a very grave drawback. No sooner has a man begun to understand his duties in one district, and to know something of the people around him, than he is liable to be uprooted and ordered off to take up an entirely different line of work, perhaps among people of another race and language.

I had an exquisite drive of about twenty-five miles, all close by the sea, with its magnificent green waves booming as they broke in dazzling surf on the white sands, only hidden now and again by the wealth of luxuriant vegetation, the whole glorified by the golden light and purple clouds and shadows of early morning, soon replaced by clear sunlight and the vivid blue of sea and sky.

Certainly one great charm of the tropical habit of always being out before sunrise and again at sunset is that we do profit by all Nature's gorgeous but too fleeting displays of colour, which so many people in Britain never see except in winter, simply because they are asleep in the mornings, or tied and bound by the evening solemnities of dinner. Happily the latter offers no hindrance in Ceylon, where the sun sets all the year round at six o'clock.

Much as is written of tropical sunrises, I have seen just as many in Britain, the gorgeousness of which has been quite indescribable. This very morning, in September, looking due east from my window in Scotland at 4.30 A.M., I looked out on a horizon of intense orange verging into sea-green, while the whole upper sky was covered with the loveliest rose-coloured clouds on a pearly-grey ground, and against all this the trees and wooded hills stood out almost black. But when the sun rose at 5 A.M., though the sky was lovely, it was not at all exciting, and by the time the household awoke, all was quite dull and commonplace. So that of these ever-new glories, as of many other things, I can only say people do not see them because they do not look for them.

Sixteen miles from Galle the coach halted at the pretty village of Belligama, now called Welligama, i.e., the Sand Village, at the head of a beautiful bay, wherein lay a crowd of picturesque fishing-boats. There too lies an island known as Crow Island, on account of the multitude of crows[1] which come every night to roost in the tall cocoa-palms, returning to the mainland at early dawn to forage for themselves wherever human homes suggest a prospect of obtaining food by fair means or foul.

The small red-tiled, white-pillared rest-house is pleasantly situated so as to command a good view of the sea, and stands in a shady garden, where large bread-fruit and other trees are matted with graceful climbing plants, hanging in festoons from the boughs. Unfortunately, there are, it is said, rather a numerous supply of black scorpions to be found about the place; but then in Ceylon one has always to keep instinctive watch against noxious creatures of various sorts, with the result that one very rarely comes in contact with any.

The chief interest of the place centres in a statue about twelve feet in height, sculptured in a niche cut into a huge rock-boulder, and shaded by kitool and cocoa palms and flowering shrubs. The statue is that of the Kushta Rajah or Leper King, supposed from his dress to have been a Singhalese king of the twelfth century—some say 589. Tradition is somewhat uncertain concerning his merits, for according to one version, it was he who first imported the cocoa-palm to Ceylon, and here planted a large tract of the coast; whereas another legend tells how it was revealed to the afflicted king, that if he visited the coast of Ceylon and worshipped the relic in the Buddhist shrine at Belligama, and further ate of the fruit of a tree then unknown to him, which proved to be the cocoa-palm, he would be healed of his sore disease. And he was healed, and

[1] *Corvus splendens.*

as his thank-offering he richly endowed the temple at Welligama.

Sad to say, the "tree of blessing" has lost its magic power, and the poor lepers of Ceylon are deemed as incurable as those of other lands. Happily they are not very numerous, only about 1800 in a population of 3,000,000, but it is sad to learn that their number is steadily increasing.

In Ceylon there is no law of compulsory segregation, though all sufferers are encouraged to seek an asylum in the leper hospital at Hendala, about four miles from Colombo, where 208 are well cared for, and are fed and clothed at the expense of the colony. Within the last few years two small chapels have been erected for their benefit, one for the Roman Catholic patients, the other (the gift of Mrs. Copleston, wife of the present Bishop of Colombo) for the use of all Christians, of whatever denomination, whose pastors may be willing to hold services in that sad asylum. About 200 more are at large in Colombo.

In this rock-hewn statue the attitude of the hands is peculiar. Both are uplifted from the elbow; but whereas the left hand is closed, the right is open except that the first finger meets the thumb, as if his Majesty were about to indulge in a pinch of snuff. This is noteworthy, because in Buddhist statues the first and second fingers alone are generally upraised, in the conventional attitude of benediction.

On my return journey, driving leisurely, I was able to secure a picture of the Leper King, and also to note (for the thousandth time) the efficacy of one simple palm leaf, which you must remember is about fourteen feet in length, knotted round the stem of the parent tree for the protection of the tempting clusters of cocoa-nuts, which, but for that leaf would surely prove irresistible to thirsty wayfarers. But the tree so marked is placed under special protection of some guardian spirit, and superstition prevails where honesty might fail, as it is firmly believed that any one eating of the fruit would suffer severely. Sometimes the knotted leaf denotes that the tree is dedicated to some shrine, Roman Catholic, Buddhist, or Hindoo, in which case a selection of the finest nuts is sent as an offering, or sometimes oil is made from the nuts to burn before the altar.

Cordial was the welcome that awaited me in a delightfully situated two-storied bungalow on the very brink of the beautiful Nilwalla River. From its cool upper verandah, where we daily met for very early breakfast, we looked down on a wilderness of glossy large-leafed plants to the reaches of the river, all embowered in grassy groves of most luxuriant palms of all ages, leaning far over the water, with here and there beds of flowering reeds and tall water-grasses and shrubs.

I found most fascinating sketching-ground at every turn, both far and near, and only wish it were in the power of words to convey any idea of those charming scenes, in all their lovely changes of colours, at the "outgoing of morning and evening," and also in the calm beauty of full moonlight. I think the most attractive of all was the meeting of the "broad, and deep, and still" waters of the river with those of the heaving ocean, the faithful palms enfolding the stream to the very last, as if loath to let it glide away. Doubtless such rivers as these carry many a floating nut far out to sea, perhaps to be washed ashore and take root on some distant isle.

So great was the charm of quietly boating in such surroundings, that it needed some effort to turn elsewhere,

although we found beauty on every side. At Mātara, as indeed in all the chief towns or villages along this coast, the hand of the Dutch is still visible in houses and fortifications, and the ramparts of a small fort built of coral-rock were a pleasant point from which to watch the breaking waves bathing the roots of the cocoa-palms overhanging one of the many lovely bays which form so attractive a feature of these shores.[1]

Within the fort is the old Dutch church, originally built for the garrison, but now used by civilians of different denominations, Presbyterian and Episcopal, at different hours.

A very romantic tradition attaches to Mātara respecting a certain King Kutara Daas, who, thirteen hundred years ago, delighted in composing verses. This royal poet having written a very graceful couplet, added beneath his lines a promise of great reward to whoever should complete the stanza. The poet Kalidas saw the couplet, and added another, which he committed to the care of a lady of evil reputation, who resolved to secure the reward for herself, and so she murdered the poet and vowed that the lines were her own.

The king, however, recognised the master-hand, and having detected the murder and discovered the body of the poet, he had it unearthed and gave him a noble funeral pyre. When it was ablaze, he himself rushed into the flames, that he might thus be re-united to his friend. Thereupon his five queens likewise immolated themselves, and thus followed their lord. This happened in the year

[1] On 29th May 1891, a very singular phenomenon occurred at Mātara, namely, *a shower of red rain* which fell on the town, extending over a radius of about two miles. Some of this strange rain-water was preserved by the wondering natives.

A.D. 522, when seven sacred Bo-trees were planted over their seven tombs, which continued to be held in honour till 1783, when a ruthless Dutchman cut these venerable trees and used the tombs as building material! But though now only a plantation of cocoa-palms, the place still retains its old name of Hat-bodin, "the seven Bo-trees."

One of our most interesting expeditions was an early morning drive to Dondra Head, by a coast-road all of the same character, along a shore of wave-kissed palms. Two thousand years ago this southernmost point of the Isle was a place of exceeding sanctity, known as Devi-nuwara, "the city of the gods," also called Tanaveram. A magnificent temple to Vishnu, as incarnate in Rama Chandra, is known to have existed here in the seventh century—a temple so vast that passing ships mistook it for a city. The great central pagoda and towers were roofed with plates of gilded copper, and the temple, wherein were stone and bronze images of a thousand idols, was surrounded by cloisters and colonnades and terraced gardens, where flowering shrubs were cultivated to supply fragrant blossoms for the daily offerings.

Ibn Batuta, a celebrated Moorish traveller, who, starting from Tangiers in 1344, devoted twenty-eight years to travel, came to Dondra and saw this wonderful building. As a good Mahommedan, he could not himself enter an idolatrous temple, but was told that one of the idols, the size of a man, was made of pure gold, and had for eyes two rubies so large and so lustrous that at night they shone like lanterns. There were then a thousand Brahmans attached to the temple, and five hundred dancing and singing girls. The town, which he calls Dinewar, was then a large place inhabited by merchants, and was all temple property.

Pilgrims crowded to worship at a shrine second in renown only to that of the holy footprint on Adam's Peak, and the consequent wealth of the temple in gold and gems, ivory and sandalwood, was such as to awaken the covetousness of the Portuguese, who in 1587, under De Souza d'Arronches, devastated this coast, committing indescribable cruelties. Having plundered all treasures, destroyed the idols, and burnt their gorgeous cars, and whatever else could be so consumed, the soldiers proceeded to demolish the temple and level with the ground its arches, gates, and towers; finally, as a crowning indignity, they slaughtered cows in the sacred courts, thereby defiling the very ground for ever, and thus the famous temple was reduced to a shapeless mass of ruins.

There still remain about 200 granite columns which formed part of the colonnades, and also a finely-sculptured gateway, the lintel of which, when struck, gives a ringing sound like a bell. Other stone carvings lie scattered about over a considerable space, but, sad to say, regardless of all antiquarian interest, these ruins have been regarded as a convenient quarry, and while some sculptured pillars have been carried off to act as milestones, others have been taken by the native fishermen to construct a pier.

Of course the Brahmans were not allowed to monopolise a place so holy, consequently the Buddhists here erected one of their earliest dagobas, the renovation of which by successive sovereigns was recorded in historic annals. Now this ancient relic-shrine is likewise a ruin, and the modern worshippers of Buddha, Vishnu, and Siva make common cause, the shrines of the Hindoo deities flanking those of Buddha and his disciples in the Buddhist temple.

Once a year, at the time of the midsummer full moon,

this quiet village is the scene of a great religious festival and fair, combined attractions which draw thousands of pilgrims and other folk to Dondra Head for a week's holiday; and very picturesque these crowds must be, all in their gayest attire, camped beneath the palms and along the shore.

Rows of temporary sheds are erected and rapidly transformed into hundreds of small shops for the sale of all manner of food, fruit, cakes, curry-stuffs, confectionery, native books, Tangalla brass-ware, tortoise-shell combs, tobacco-leaves, betel-leaves and areca-nuts, cloth, cheap jewellery, and toys.

The religious ceremony is a Perahera, when the shrine containing some precious relic is carried round the village in solemn procession, followed by lay and ecclesiastical officials in their Kandyan state dress, and escorted by a troop of trumpeters, shell-blowers, and tomtom-beaters, making their usual deafening noise.

In 1889 the Queen's birthday was celebrated by a very different event, namely, laying the last stone to complete the finest lighthouse on the coast, one of a series extending from Colombo right round the southern coast of Ceylon as far as the "Great" and "Little Basses," within such moderate distances of one another as to afford all possible security in navigation. The foundations of this latest addition to the lights of Ceylon were hewn in the solid rock at the close of 1887, the Jubilee year, and when this finishing touch was given, the summit of the tower stood 176 feet above the sea-level—a lonely beacon-star for the guiding and warning of many a vessel in years to come.

On the day of our visit, however, all was very quiet. We invested in some curious very coarse red pottery, peculiar to this place, some specimens representing hideous animals. Having inspected the fort built by the Dutch when they had succeeded in driving out the Portuguese, we next strolled to the shore, a succession of lovely bays clothed to the water's edge with luxuriant palms and strange screw-pines. I selected as my sketching-ground a very striking pile of shapeless ruins, literally rising from the waves. They are apparently those of a smaller temple, but now are merely a heap of tumbled stones and pillars sculptured in alternate square and octagonal sections.

The scene gained additional interest from the fact that this headland is the southernmost land of which we know anything—not even a little coral islet is known to lie between this and the South Pole.

Presently my companions summoned me to breakfast in a cosy bungalow which had been decorated in our honour with palm-leaves and cocoa-nuts. We were glad to rest in its cool shade till the noonday heat was over, and then returned to the lonely ruins on the shore, where we lingered till they and the feathery palms alike showed "dark against day's golden death," when we started on our beautiful homeward drive in the mellow moonlight.

Those now wave-washed ruins of the ancient temple are suggestive of the ceaseless battles between land and water, in which Ocean has won so many victories.

There seems little doubt that in early days this beautiful island was of far larger extent than it now is, and that by a series of encroachments of the sea it has been gradually reduced. Native traditions tell how it was originally 5120 miles in circumference, and how, by a terrible judgment of Heaven, it was reduced to less than 3000. According to the legendary records of the Ramayana, this calamity occurred soon after the death of Ravana, B.C. 2387, a date which curiously approximates to that generally received as the year of the Deluge. It is also singular that this measurement should so nearly coincide with that recorded by Pliny as having been taken B.C. 200. The sea, however, not content with having swallowing up half the island, still crept onward, and the native annals tell how, year by year, fresh lands were submerged, till there remained only the comparatively small extent we now see, measuring about 800 miles in circumference.

A multitude of lesser islands are also said to have disappeared. Probably they lay between Ceylon and the Maldive and Lakadive islands, and, forming one great kingdom, may have given to Ceylon the name, by which it was anciently known, of Lanka or Laka-diva, "the ten thousand islands." Certain it is that, at the longitude assigned by old records to the great city of Sri-Lanka-poora, the capital of the island, there is now only a wide expanse of blue waters.

It was in this city that Ravana, the mighty king of the isle, was besieged by Rama, a warrior prince of Oude, whose beautiful wife, Sita, had been carried off by Ravana, in revenge for insults offered to his sister. This city of palaces had seven fortified walls, and many towers with battlements of brass. Moreover, it was surrounded by a great ditch, wherein flowed the salt waters of the ocean. Hence we may infer that the sea had not much ado to encroach on so confiding a city. The native legends both of Ceylon and India tell how, "'twixt the gloamin' and the mirk," the glittering light from these brazen battlements still gleams from the ocean depths, and being reflected on the dark sky overhead, causes the afterglow.

The Brahmans declare that this terrible overflow of the mighty waters was sent to punish the impious Ravana, who had dared to fight against Rama, the peerless king and warrior.

Further calamities befell the Isle about the year B.C. 306, when much of the west coast was submerged. This was in the reign of King Devenipiatissa, who held his court at Kelany, a town which stood seven leagues inland from the point where the River Kelany then entered the sea. According to tradition, King Tissa had good cause to suspect his beautiful queen of an intrigue with his own brother,[1] who accordingly fled to Gampola, whence he endeavoured to send a message to the queen written on a neatly rolled-up palm leaf.

This was conveyed by a messenger disguised as a priest, who was to gain access to the palace on a day when a multitude of priests were to receive the royal alms. Having attracted the queen's notice, the messenger dropped the

[1] In view of the custom of polyandry, formerly prevalent throughout the Isle, Tissa's jealousy was unjustifiable, as every woman was entitled to half-a-dozen husbands, who, as a matter of preference, ought all to be of the same family—brothers if possible. King Wijayo Bahu VII., who was the reigning monarch at Cotta, near the Kelany River, at the time when the Portuguese built their first fort at Colombo, had a wife in common with his brother.

Polyandry and the murder of superfluous female infants were the recognised means of checking the increase of population among a race too indolent to cultivate more land than was necessary for their own support. Thanks to Portuguese and Dutch influence, these obnoxious customs were soon abandoned in the maritime provinces, but in the mountainous Central Province the ancient Kandyan custom prevailed till quite recently, when British marriage-laws were framed with a view to bringing it into discredit.

On the similar custom of certain mountain tribes in Hindostan, see "In the Himalayas," p. 406, published by Chatto & Windus.

letter, but ere she could raise it the king seized and read it. In his fury he declared that the intrigue thus proven was sanctioned by the high-priest himself, who accordingly was seized and thrown into a cauldron of boiling oil, while the queen was pinioned and thrown into the river.

Ere long the innocence of the priest was established, but it was too late to avert the wrath of the gods, who caused the sea to encroach on the west coast of the Isle so rapidly, that the unhappy king strove to avert the terrible punishment from his people by the sacrifice of his own beautiful virgin daughter, Sudhá-Déwi, whom he secured in a covered canoe overlaid with pure gold, and having inscribed this ark with the title "A Royal Maiden," he launched it on the raging waters.

The spirits of air and water protected the maiden thus committed to their care, and landed her safely on a distant shore at Totalu Ferry, where the ark was found by some fishermen. The prince of the land, Ka-wan-tissa Rajah, was so fascinated by the beauty of the damsel, that he married her, and changed her name to Wihari-Dewi. It was her son, Dootoogaimoonoo, who afterwards expelled the Malabars and restored the supremacy of the Singhalese.

But King Tissa's sacrifice proved of no avail, for the encroaching waters never stayed their advance till they had swallowed up 640 flourishing villages and permanently submerged a strip of country extending twenty miles inland, and including some of the richest arable land. According to the Rajavali, no less than 100,000 large towns and 1370 fishers' villages were then destroyed.

That this calamity was due to volcanic agency seems evident, for the tradition further records, that when the king himself went on his elephant to watch the progress of the raging waters, the earth opened and vomited flames which swallowed him up, and he was no more seen.

Of the encroachments of the sea on the coast of Coromandel and other parts of Southern India, we have visible proof in the fact of its having stayed half-way in act of washing away at least one old city which now lies half beneath the waves.[1] These have encroached to the very doors of the great temples, but sculptures and pillars still jutting up from the waters suggest how much of the old city has been altogether submerged. Some of the aged natives of the last generation remembered how in their youth, while sailing far out at sea, they could distinguish the forms of temples and other buildings lying deep beneath the waves. Some of these had cupolas of copper-gilt, which glittered in the early sunlight, but had gradually ceased to do so, and now the fishes vainly peer into those clear depths—the city is no longer visible. They suppose that the copper has corroded or that the foundations have given way.

To return to our peaceful modern life at Mātara on the brink of the broad beautiful river. In such surroundings, rendered yet more attractive by the kindness of many friends, a fortnight slipped quickly by, when we started in force, a whole family party, great and small, to visit a hospitable Scotsman, the District Judge at Tangalle, a pretty little seaside town about twenty miles farther east. Once more we followed the "palm o'er-shadowed way" along the shore, and facing the sun as it rose in glory from the clear calm ocean, which shone like a dazzling mirror, so that we were glad to rest our eyes by gazing into the shady groves to catch pretty glimpses of home-life in the native huts.

We met many native vehicles, always driven by pictur-

[1] Maha-bali-poor or Mavalipuram.

esque people, and drawn by handsome oxen, white or brown, drawing their heavy loads simply by the pressure of the yoke on their much-enduring hump.

Presently (happily when we were near a rest-house) the tyre came off one of our wheels, so we had to halt some hours for necessary repairs, and amused ourselves by watching the fishermen drawing their large seine-nets, several canoes uniting their forces to draw one net on shore. They work all through the burning midday hours to an accompaniment of melancholy song, sometimes indeed pathetic, at others wild, but never very musical. As we rested beneath the cool shade of a great banyan-tree, kind natives brought us a gift of ripe plantains and a great bowl of delicious creamy buffalo-milk, a dainty generally shunned by Europeans, on the ground that buffaloes are not strict vegetarians.

When the glare and heat drove us to seek shelter in the rest-house, we consoled ourselves by watching the antics of many small squirrels who scampered fearlessly about the verandah—pretty little creatures, dark-grey, with three white stripes down the back.

Indoors, the spiders and darling little lizards, "Geckoes,"[1] reigned unmolested—the former splendid specimens of a large dark-coloured hairy spider, with ten thick hairy legs. To the unaccustomed eye they are hideous and alarming, but they really are very useful, as they wage war on cockroaches and such-like unwelcome intruders. They have the oddest way of periodically shedding their whole skin. As the creature grows, its skin fails to expand, so it splits down the back, and then the spider shakes off this outgrown overcoat and steps out in all the glory of a new skin, leaving

[1] *Platydactylus.*

the old one perfect (but for the one long split), and for the moment the spider and the empty case look like twins.

One enormous spider, the *Mygale fasciata*, sometimes miscalled a tarantula, is not content with such small game as cockroaches, but occasionally devotes its energies to ensnaring lizards. It has even been accused of capturing tiny birds, but this charge is not proven. It is a very unpleasant-looking creature, its body and legs being covered with long dark-brown hair, and it is so large that when its legs are extended a full-grown specimen will cover a circle of about eight inches in diameter.

Instead of weaving a web after the manner of spiders in general, this curious creature builds for itself a sort of tubular nest, generally in the crevice of some old wall or gravelly bank, and for this it spins a waterproof lining of the very finest silk, and furthermore constructs a most ingenious door, which opens and shuts on hinges, and which it can close from within and successfully exclude unwelcome intruders.[1]

But of all the spiders (and they are very numerous and varied), none struck me as more curious than a family with tiny bodies and ridiculously long black legs, so slender as literally to resemble coarse hairs. I have seen these in some very neglected rest-houses, and sometimes on gravelly banks in the hills, in such multitudes that the wall or bank seemed to quiver with the tremulous movement of these little bunches of black hair. One long-legged house-spider always reminded me of the old woman who lived in a shoe, because of its innumerable family of the tiniest perfect little spiders, which it carries about with it in a cocoon supported

[1] See nest of the Californian tarantula, in "Granite Crags of California," p. 320, by C. F. Gordon Cumming.

under its legs. When frightened, it drops this little silky cradle, and out scamper a regiment of most active little creatures. I used always to wonder whether the family was ever reassembled, especially as destructive human beings so often with one rough touch rend the dainty nest woven with such skill.

The lizards, of which there are several varieties, green, grey, or chocolate-coloured, spotted or streaked, and ranging from four to seven inches in length, are very abundant on the sea-coast, and every house has its own colony of these pretty little harmless creatures, which suddenly peep out from some unexpected corner, chirping their little note like "Cheeka! cheeka!" On their feet are small suckers, which enable them to walk inverted like flies as they scamper about on the canvas ceilings in pursuit of insects. Occasionally they get on to a loose rag of canvas or a flake of whitewash, and fall violently to the ground or on to the table, and, like Bo-Peep's sheep, leave their tails behind them, wriggling independently, while the proprietor takes himself off as fast as he can.

In the crevices of the walls they lay fascinating little white eggs like sugar-plums, and from these, when hatched by the sun, come forth most minute perfect lizards, who at once scamper off in search of food.

Some of these seaside places are occasionally haunted by musk-rats (*alias* shrews), which utter shrill little cries while diligently hunting for insects, especially for crickets, which are their special weakness; but they are an intolerable nuisance, as they taint everything they touch.

By the time a blacksmith had been found and our repairs complete, a furious rain-storm had set in, which never abated all the afternoon; so there was nothing for it but to face it; but right glad we were when we reached our journey's end, and were hospitably received and dried. Then followed a wild wet night, and the rickety venetians rattled and shook with every gust of rushing wind; but loud above all minor voices of the storm resounded the roar of the mighty waves as they thundered on the shore; for at Tangalle, unlike most of the harbours of Ceylon, there is no bar to check their landward rush.

As if to atone for this night of passion, the days that followed were each enchanting. I awoke to find myself in a comfortable old bungalow, with wide-pillared verandah and red-tiled roof, delightfully situated beneath the cool shade of large trees on the very brink of the sea, from which the glorious sun was just rising

"In one unclouded blaze of living light."

The charms of that shore, with the quaintly-built canoes, with great outriggers and nets hung up to dry, and the picturesque groups of brown figures (fisher-folk, and women carrying red water-jars on their heads and children astride on one hip), to say nothing of the always irresistible attraction of shell-strewn sands, held me captive for some days. There was such a sense of peace in finding a cosy resting-place at the foot of some dark tree, whose great boughs extended right over the sands, and almost dipped into the now gently rippling wavelets.

About fifteen miles inland from Tangalle lies the celebrated old Buddhist monastery and rock-temple of Mulgirigalla, where, to my great delight, I found that our kind host had made all arrangements for our reception. A beautiful drive brought us to the Goagalla or Iguana Rock, whence we obtained a splendid view of the sacred crag, a huge square red rock, towering to a height of 350 feet from the brink of a dark-blue lakelet, which gleamed like a sapphire in its setting of luxuriant tropical foliage. The flat summit is crowned by a great white dagoba of the usual dome-shape, containing a precious relic of some early Buddhist saint or hero. Somewhat lower, conspicuously placed on the face of the crag, are the red-tiled monastic buildings, nestling among fragrant flowering shrubs.

The mighty crag is perpendicular on three sides, but on the fourth the ascent is easy, flights of steps being hewn at the steepest parts. Where the carriage-drive ended we found chairs with bearers waiting to carry us up to the monastery, where we were most courteously received by the high-priest and sundry monks, who escorted us to the famous temples. These are simply a series of overhanging rock-ledges, partially built up so as to form artificial caves, decorated in colour in the same style as those at Dambulla, but on a much smaller scale. Within these are colossal images of Buddha, one of which, a huge recumbent figure, resting beneath the shadow of the dark maroon-coloured rock, and shaded by the light foliage of a sacred peepul-tree, formed a very impressive foreground to a blue distance of endless forests extending to the far-away ocean.

Mulgirigalla has been held in veneration from the earliest ages of Buddhism. In Singhalese chronicles of B.C. 137 it was referred to as being already a very sacred shrine, and throughout the twenty centuries that have glided away since then, with all their manifold changes, the praises of Buddha have been ceaselessly sung by the yellow-robed brethren of this rock-monastery.

Comfortable quarters having been assigned to us for the

night, we were able to wander about at leisure, enjoying each picturesque combination of dark rocks, red-tiled buildings, brown priests robed in yellow, and wonderfully varied foliage, all in vivid light and shadow. One quiet corner especially attracted me, where, among the great rock-boulders and overshadowed by fragrant temple-trees, daturas, plantains, kitool, areca, and other palms, are the fine old tombs containing the ashes of cremated high-priests who have lived and died in this peaceful spot—

> "The world forgetting,
> By the world forgot."

Overhead a troop of merry monkeys were at play in a dark jak-tree, laden with enormous fruit hanging from the branches and trunk. In short, there was much to tempt the pencil at every turn. The view from the summit is magnificent, either looking southward over the Hambantota district to the blue ocean, or inland to the mountain ranges of Kataragama and Uva, while in the far distance beyond the high table-land of the Horton Plains towers Adam's Peak, the holy of holies. We rejoiced in all this beauty as seen in the changing lights of sunset, followed by the quiet starlight, and then again in the stillness of the dawn, and realised how calmly life might glide on in such an eyrie. Nevertheless certain broken palm-trees snapped in two suggested how fiercely the winds must often rave around this lofty crag.

Following the seaboard eastward from Tangalla to Hambantota, a distance of about twenty-five miles, the whole character of the scenery changes. Luxuriant vegetation is replaced by a mere sprinkling of parched scrub and scanty grass on a dead flat expanse of white sand, which seems to dance in the quivering mirage produced by the intense heat of the glaring sun.

Here and there, on rocky islands or on the shore, a few isolated palms seem as if they had been banished from the company of their fellows, to dwell among thorny wild date-palms, fantastic screw-pines, with their strange stilt-like roots, their forked cylindrical trunks, and quaint whorls of drooping spiral leaves, for ever rustling and swaying with every breath of air, and grotesque euphorbias like gigantic candelabra, the ghostliest of all plants when seen in the moonlight, or dark against a red sunset sky.

The most characteristic feature of the district is the chain of shallow lagoons, which furnish about one-fifth of the salt supply of the island. There are about half-a-dozen of these lakes, separated from the sea by a high sandbank clothed with thorny impenetrable jungle. Some are several miles in circumference. Their waters are a solution of the saltest brine, which precipitates and crystallises at the bottom and round the edges, so that when seen from any height, these blue lakes seem to be edged with dazzling white surf.

Beneath the blazing summer sun evaporation is so rapid that the lakes partially dry up, leaving a beach of the purest white salt six or eight inches in depth, the bed of the lake being equally coated. Salt being (as I mentioned when describing the artificial saltpans at Puttalam) a Government monopoly and a considerable source of revenue, the lakes are guarded by watchers, so that no man may help himself to this necessary of life.

So for the greater part of the year these shallow lagoons are utterly undisturbed, and afford sanctuary to innumerable birds and other shy creatures. Great mobs of snowy pelicans and groups of delicately rosy flamingoes stand reflected in the still waters, the latter changing to crimson as they rise and display their brilliant under-wings. Many crocodiles bask on the shores. These are of a peculiarly harmless kind, and, strange to say, they are never known to have attacked any of the salt-collectors who so audaciously invade their quiet retreat.

Whether the stagnation of life in such still waters has a soothing effect on their inhabitants, I cannot say, but it is a well-authenticated fact that the crocodiles which live in the lakes and tanks of Ceylon are by no means so dangerous as those which haunt the rivers, the latter being a source of constant dread to the natives, as are also the sharks, which occasionally venture some way up the broad mouth of the rivers in pursuit of fish, and render bathing exceedingly dangerous. The Singhalese, however, assert that sharks only attack human beings at certain times, so that when man is not in season they bathe with confidence. When possible, however, they hire a charmer to recite incantations, which are supposed to render the brutes harmless; such services are specially sought by the divers, whose work leads them right into Shark-land.

The salt harvest is generally gathered in the month of August, but the exact time depends on the weather, for it is a precarious crop; and whereas in a very dry season the amount collected and safely stored may be very large, unseasonable rains may melt it all away and leave a very poor return—in some cases even none. Thus in the North Province, in 1876, the salt harvest yielded 151,718 cwts. In the following year there was absolutely none, and in the year after, only 11,772 cwts. So in this Southern Province, in 1878, the salt crop proved a total failure, whereas two years later, 136,757 cwts. were safely gathered.

The method of collecting is first to gather the deposit on the shore, and then, by wading into the lakes, collect that which has formed under water—a method grievous to those employed, as, after a few days' work, the intense salt of the water excoriates the feet and legs, causing severe pain. Much of this work is done by the convicts from the Hambantota jail. The salt thus obtained is brought ashore in baskets, and built up into great piles, which are protected from rain by a thick thatch of cocoa-palm leaves till the salt can be carted away to the Government storehouses, whence, after the lapse of three or four months, it is sold to merchants, who supply the retail dealers, the Government profit on the transaction being about 900 per cent. on the outlay.

So rigidly has the price of salt been maintained, that for such purposes as manuring the land, preserving hides, and fish-curing it was for long altogether prohibitive, and it is only quite recently that fish-curing grounds have been established at Hambantota, where, under strict Government supervision, salt is supplied at a nominal price to encourage a native trade in dried salted fish, which hitherto has been imported from the Maldive Islands or the coast of India to an annual value of about 900,000 rupees.

The scenery around Hambantota, though not without interest, is certainly not attractive. The Government Agent's house and court stand on a hot bare hill, looking on the one hand to a long ridge of red drifting sandhills and scrubby jungle, on the other to the heavy breakers thundering on the white beach. On a rocky promontory stands a fortified tower, which overlooks the anchorage where lie the small vessels which come to ship the salt from the salt-water lakes. From this tower you can overlook the sandy world around, in strong contrast with the vivid blues of sea, sky, distant mountains, and salt lakes, the latter edged with a glittering crust of white, and all set in a dark framework of sombre jungle. But except in the early morning, or late afternoon, the heat is grilling.

About fifteen miles farther along the sea-coast is the site of the ancient city of Mahagam, or, as it is now called, Magama, at the mouth of a river of the same name. Twenty-two centuries ago it was a flourishing and important centre of busy life, of which all trace has disappeared, and the ruins which alone remain to mark its vanished glory are in the same style as those of Anuradhapura and Pollanarua, namely, cyclopean dagobas, masses of fallen and crumbling brickwork, lines of erect monoliths, once the supports of temple and palaces, sculptured pillars, blocks of granite, and great flights of steps, once the thronged approach to stately portals, now all overgrown with prickly cactus and thorny jungle.

For the great tanks (or rather artificial lakes) constructed by the builders of Magama for the irrigation of the land have for centuries been left to go to ruin, the whole district, once so densely peopled and so carefully cultivated, has long lain desolate, and the arid jungle, extending from the sea to the foot of the Madulsima and Haputale ranges, is the sportsman's and naturalist's happiest hunting-ground—a vast unbroken forest some sixty miles in width, where the wild creatures, scared from their former haunts by the advance of ever-encroaching planters, still find a comparatively undisturbed sanctuary.

This is especially true of elephants, against whom the necessary war was for many years waged so vigorously, both by European sportsmen and by Moormen, that at length there seemed a danger of their extermination. But though bad masters, they are far too good as servants to be given over to destruction. A close season was therefore instituted, and it was declared illegal to shoot an elephant without a Government license, costing ten rupees for each animal slain—a proviso which has proved sorely trying to sportsmen who have had exceptional luck in falling in unexpectedly with elephants, and whose license perhaps allowed them to shoot one only.

Thus protected, these giants of the forest soon increased, and are now said to be as numerous as ever, though they have retired to the most unfrequented regions, seeking concealment in the dense and frequently malarious jungles which clothe the eastern side of the Isle. They now abound in the South-Eastern Province from Hanbantota as far eastward as the Kombookgam River (now called Kumukkan Aru), and range inland to the forests at the base of the Uva hills near Badulla, whence they wander at will over all the low country extending to Batticaloa.

The largest elephants, however, are said to haunt the forests of Tamankaduwa around Lake Minery and the ruins of Pollanarua, and also those to the north of Trincomalee. Great herds also find covert in the desolate region to the north of Manaar, in the extreme north of the Isle, and in the vast fever-haunted jungles of the Wannie—a term which describes an area of about 14,000 square miles.

The Southern Province is, however, the most popular with sportsmen, and the country about the Nipple Hills to the north of Tissamaharama and between the Kumukkan Aru and the Kataragama-Ganga is now considered to be the finest district in Ceylon for sport, so numerous are all manner of large game, including buffalo, which, like the elephant, are now protected, and may not be shot without a license.

In many districts, however, they have been so decimated by disease as to be now comparatively scarce. The wild buffalo of Ceylon has small horns as compared with that of India, but he is a very dangerous and resolute antagonist. Even the domestic buffalo of the Isle is generally vicious; very different from the meek animal which in China is generally ridden by the smallest child.

Deer of various sorts are here abundant—red deer, axis or spotted deer, and sambur (commonly miscalled elk), hog-deer, barking-deer, and the pretty little mouse-deer, which sometimes starts from the grass almost under one's feet. Chetahs and leopards, porcupines, wild pigs, monkeys, and sloths find their paradise in that region, where jungle, open plains, and lagoons supply all their need. Bears also are numerous in the rocky jungle and in the dense forest, wherever white ants, wild honey, or fruits are to be found, and very dangerous antagonists they often prove, especially from their horrid habit of trying to tear the face of their assailant.

Here, too, birds of radiant plumage still abound; large flocks of gorgeous pea-fowl, jungle-fowl, and many varieties of pigeons, yellow-headed hoopoes, crimson-breasted barbet, and many another shy creature here dwell in peace, while cormorants, spoonbills, ibises, herons, and toucans congregate around the lonely forest tanks, their wild cries alone breaking the utter stillness.

Soon after my return to Britain, I received from Mr. G. W. R. Campbell, Inspector-General of Police, a description of a night journey across this district, which gives some idea of the risks which may be incurred by lonely travellers, and made me realise that there may be cases when it is a matter of congratulation that so few Ceylon elephants own tusks. He says:—

"After inspecting the jail, I left Hambantota for Koslanda, in Haputale. I was to travel the first twenty-eight miles during the night in a bullock-cart, and next morning drive my own horses to the foot of the mountains. The road lay almost all the way through dense forest scrub infested with elephants and other wild animals. I was informed that the elephants, not content with pulling up the milestones, sometimes attacked carts, so I deemed it prudent to desire that an armed constable should escort my cart, which was a high heavy covered spring-cart on two wheels. It was about 7 feet 3 inches in length, and when my cushions were laid along it, made a fair bed. It was drawn by a pair of bullocks, and three other pairs were stationed along the road in advance.

"About midnight I fell asleep, and being thoroughly tired, I was quite unconscious when we halted to change the bullocks and escort.

"Between two and three in the morning the cart was running merrily along the white road in the bright moonlight, the constable following, when a large elephant rushed out from the jungle to the right, and with his trunk struck the cart a heavy blow on the top, trumpeting furiously.

"On his approach the terrified constable took to his heels and fled back along the road by which we had come, but the driver, uttering loud cries, partly of fear and partly in the hope of driving the beast off, ran by the pole urging his bullocks to their best speed, the elephant following.

"Just then I awoke, and for a moment imagined that the darkness and the screaming and swaying of the cart were caused by the bullocks having gone off the road and down some embankment into the jungle, but in another moment I saw that the darkness was caused by the head of an elephant blocking up the back of the cart, and that he was bumping the hood upwards with his forehead.

"Fearing that the whole thing would go over, or that he would seize me, I instantly twisted myself round, and got out beside the driver, intending to run as he was doing by the side of the pole; but I missed my footing, and came to the ground so awkwardly that the cart, which was going very fast, knocked me down, and the off-wheel immediately passed over me.

"Instantly, fearing lest the elephant should also pass over and crush me, I scrambled into the grass, though with difficulty, owing to pain in my legs. The cart had disappeared, and there, about fifteen paces off, facing me, stood the elephant in the moonlight, in the middle of the white road, with a halo of dust round him.

"I stood quite still in the shade of the tall thorny scrub, which formed a high and almost impenetrable wall on either side of the road. I do not know whether he saw me or not, but in less than half a minute he turned, and standing across the road, put up his trunk as high as he could and repeated the horrible screaming which is called trumpeting. Then turning round quickly, he marched back along the road by which we had come.

"I at once went off at a run in the other direction, feeling very stiff and sore, and about 200 yards farther on overtook the cart, which the driver, rather bravely, I think, had managed to pull up within that distance. He hurried me into the cart, and we pushed along as quickly as we could, he shouting every half minute at the top of his voice to scare other wild animals.

"Soon afterwards we came upon a herd of seven or eight huge wild buffaloes, which would scarcely let us pass, and about a mile farther passed another herd, which absolutely blocked the road. I tried to frighten them by lighting matches and throwing them at them; one lighted match actually fell on a buffalo's back.

"About the twenty-second mile-post we found our next bullocks, and two men with guns, who told us they had been visited by a bear while waiting for us.

"When, just at daybreak, we reached my carriage, my knees were so bruised and swollen that I could not walk, nor even stand for a moment without great pain. Nevertheless I had to drive myself twenty-three miles farther to Wellawaya before I could rest. Arrived there, a touch of jungle-fever came on, so that night's sleep was not much better than the previous one; but at daybreak I started to drive myself the remaining twenty-six miles to Haldummulla, halting for some hours at Koslanda for an inspection, though in such pain that I was unable to stand for more than a few seconds at a time."[1]

No wonder that the tappal-runners, the rural postmen of the isle, dread these lonely forest roads, their sole protection being a bunch of small bells at the end of a long stick, which they jingle as they go. A flaming torch is generally effectual in scaring elephants, but in the North-Eastern Provinces, in the days of palanquin-travelling, the bearers

[1] The Inspector-General of Police and of all the Prisons in Ceylon had little time to let grass grow under his feet. I remember Mr. Campbell's driving one morning, quite as a matter of course, from Colombo to Negombo, thence starting on an extensive round of inspection, returning the same evening, having driven upwards of seventy-five miles, besides all his official work at each station. And next morning, long before dawn, he was at work in his office, ready as usual for another long round. Few men in Britain would even attempt to undertake such work as here falls on a few willing shoulders; yet any breakdown in health is invariably attributed, not to overwork, but to the climate!

used to insist on being escorted by a professional elephant-charmer, who, whenever they approached a herd, warned them off by the mystic sentence, "*Om am ari nari saring-ham saravaye*," at the sound of which the boldest elephants turned tail and fled!

This South-Eastern Maritime Province, though only separated from the western coast by a mountain range not 5000 feet in height, is in every respect strangely different; for whereas from April till July the west coast has a heavy rainfall, this too sheltered region can only hope for rain in November and December; so instead of rich luxuriant groves and large timber, the prevailing feature is dry thorny scrub, with here and there tracts of thirsty sand, only partially clothed with stunted grass and huge cactus-like euphorbias, with their odd four-sided stems and fleshy branches, growing to a height of over thirty feet.

These scorched plains are subject to excessive drought, when rivers are reduced to meagre streams meandering through an expanse of burning sand, and their tributaries wholly disappear, leaving only dry watercourses, tantalising to thirsty men and beasts. Then, when the rains do set in, they are apt to fall in such good earnest that the country is flooded, and when half dry, form deep unhealthy marshes, sending up a steaming miasma productive of fever, dysentery, the scourge of the country, and parangi, that dreadful and loathsome complaint said to be peculiar to Ceylon, and greatly due to lack of good food and good water.

An immediate improvement in the condition of the district was looked for when, in 1876, the restoration of the great tank Tissamaharama, six or eight miles to the north of Magama, was completed; but from various causes, chiefly from the scantiness of the population, who were to profit by its water-supply, it for a while proved so unremunerative (in return for the enormous outlay on its restoration) as to have been deemed well-nigh a failure. That, however, is an impression which is fading away before the steadily increasing area of well-watered cultivated land which is now yielding abundant food in the districts where famine so long reigned.

By the beginning of 1890 no less than 1500 acres were yielding two rice crops yearly in return for the precious water supplied by Lake Tissa, and now Moormen as well as Singhalese are coming from other districts to compete for these well-irrigated lands, and it is found necessary to provide fresh storage for the ever-increasing demand for water. In short, there seems reason to believe that in process of time the whole country between Tissa and the sea will become one vast cultivated expanse.

The tank, which is about six miles in circumference, and covers an area of about 3000 acres, was made by King Devenipiatissa, B.C. 307. It lies on a slightly raised tableland 73 feet above the sea-level, where once stood a great city, of which there remain only ruins all overgrown by dense forest. Now its rock-temples and ruined palaces afford shelter only to wild beasts except at midsummer, when the pilgrims halt here on their way to Kataragama to worship at these ruined shrines, and for a few days Tissa is once again thronged, perhaps by thousands, intent on trade or devotion, as the case may be.

A detail of some geological interest is that in the neighbourhood both of Tissa and of Hambantota there are beds of great extent, and many feet in thickness, composed entirely of shells. These are dug out and used instead of gravel in repairing roads. In view of all the traditions of the encroachments of the ocean, we can scarcely suppose the sea to have receded from this particular coast, so the theory of upheaval seems the more probable.

This theory is confirmed by the fact that at Miripenna, just south of Galle, large blocks of coral rock are excavated from the soil fully a quarter of a mile inland; also in the extreme north of the isle, the Jaffna peninsula is found to rest entirely on a foundation of coral, which is supposed to have been upheaved in geologically recent times.

Fain would I have extended my travels twenty miles inland to those blue hill-ranges around the famous shrine of Kataragama (*alias* Maha Sen), one of the demons worshipped by the aborigines, afterwards identified with a mighty Singhalese king, and finally adopted by the Brahmans, who identify him with Siva. Contrary, however, to the custom of the Sivites, this temple contains no image, only a mysterious curtain, before which kneel crowds of pilgrims from every part of India, sometimes even high-caste Brahmans from remote Hurdwar (the holy city near the source of the Ganges, distant well-nigh 2000 miles), who visit this shrine seeking cures for divers diseases, and who present silver models of their various limbs as votive offerings to Maha Sen.[1]

[1] It is curious to observe how widespread is this custom of hanging up models of the limb restored or for which healing is craved. In the long-isolated temples of Japan I have seen thousands of such models. We know that they were offered in ancient Greece, for the British Museum possesses two votive hands made of bronze. They were also common in Egypt, generally entwined with figures of serpents, emblematic of recovered health. Hands, arms, ears, eyes, and other members, modelled in terra-cotta or carved in ivory, have been found at Thebes and elsewhere, with a thanksgiving dedication to whichever deity received credit for the cure effected.

Most remarkable of all is the fact that in many of these heathen

The great annual festival occurs at the hottest season of the year, between June and August, its precise date being regulated by some combination of the full moon with other details. So vast are the crowds which sometimes flock to this shrine, and so great the consequent risk of outbreaks of cholera, that in 1874 it was found necessary to enact a law that in seasons when sickness is prevalent only 400 pilgrims in all were to be permitted to attend, *i.e.*, 100 each from the Western, Central, Eastern, or Southern Provinces, each person being provided with a ticket signed by the Government Agent of the Province, and being further bound to travel by specified routes, and to conform strictly to police regulations, arranging their journey so as not to arrive at Kataragama earlier than the 3rd August or to remain there for more than two clear days, to include the period of the full moon. Any infringement of these rules renders the offender liable to a year's imprisonment or to a fine not exceeding 1000 rupees.

Stringent as are these regulations, it has sometimes been found necessary to render them still more so. Thus in June 1883 upwards of 10,000 pilgrims assembled at Kataragama,

offerings the hand is modelled with the third and fourth fingers closed, while the first and second (the fingers of benediction, as a Ritualist would call them) are upraised in the orthodox attitude of ecclesiastical benediction. Hence we may infer that not only the presentation of such *ex votos* at Roman Catholic shrines, but also this peculiar priestly attitude, are directly borrowed from Paganism, probably introduced into the Alexandrian Church by some Egyptian convert. Those who have travelled in Roman Catholic countries can scarcely fail to recall various churches (such as those of San Publio in Malta or of Notre Dame de la Garde at Marseilles, where votive offerings of every sort, but chiefly of miniature arms, legs, eyes, and ears, modelled in wax or silver, as the case may be, are hung up round the altars of divers saints, as thank-offerings for cures attributed to their intercessions.

but in the following year, when there was fear of cholera, the number was officially restricted to a total of 150 persons, namely, thirty to represent Colombo, thirty for Kandy, and as many for Galle, Kurunegalla, and Batticaloa.

Before this regulation of the pilgrimages commenced they were simply seed-beds for the fostering and spread of disease. Thus in the cholera outbreak in 1858, no less than seventy-six dead bodies were counted on the highroad between Hambantota and Tangalla, and it is certain that very many more must have perished in the jungle-paths and roadside villages.

The following table, though not up to date, shows how the number of pilgrims varies from year to year:—

1872	1873	1874	1875	1876	1877	1878	1883
4000	7000	1200	60	107	44	15	10,000

For a lover of the picturesque this pilgrimage is specially attractive, the favourite camping-ground being the dry bed of the broad Kataragama River, which in the summer-time is totally dried up, but is overshadowed by magnificent forest trees. In Oriental lands such a scene, with all the groups of very varied nationality clustering round their camp-fires, is always full of incident and colour.

That river is more commonly known as the Manick-Ganga or "River of Gems," from the fact that its sandy bed is composed of glittering atoms of quartz and mica, mingled with infinitesimal fragments of rubies, sapphires, garnets, and jacinth. As the sunlight plays on the clear shallow water flowing over this radiant bed of sparkling gems, it seems like the enchanted river of some fairy tale, but so tiny are the precious morsels that it is exceedingly rare to find one worth keeping. The people use this sand to facilitate the labour of sawing through elephants' teeth. Near Hambantota there are tracts of sand which literally are composed of ruby dust.

Certainly it is strange that a gem-loving people should for so many centuries have recognised that these precious fragments were washed down from some of the higher rocks, and yet should never have attempted any systematic search for these hid treasures. Doubtless now that gem-mining is being taken up in good earnest, those hitherto inaccessible crags will be made to yield many a priceless jewel.

CHAPTER XXII.

RETURN TO COLOMBO.

Bentota—Lilies—Mangroves—Kalutara—Fisher castes—Ordeal by
boiling oil—Colombo.

ON my return journey from Mātara to Colombo I proved how comfortable it can be to travel "in charge of the police;" always provided such charge be that of a great Inspector-General who takes special pride not only in every detail of his official work, but also in the excellence of the grey horses which await him at every halting-place.

Not that we had to hurry over the beautiful drive. Happily for my sketching mania, there was so much police inspection to be done on the way, that we were detained a whole day at Galle and another at Bentota, a very pretty fishing-village, with a really luxurious rest-house charmingly situated beneath the cool shade of feathery tamarind-trees and cocoa-palms, on a little rocky headland washed by the waves, and at the mouth of the Alutgama River.

Thence, looking along the shore, there is a fine view of Cape Barberyn, which is the westernmost point of Ceylon. Grand waves breaking round rocky palm-covered islands, glimpses of calm fresh-water pools and green turf, coast villages, and many fishing-boats, successive headlands all clothed with cocoa-palms, pandanus, and other tropical vegetation, and yellow sands carpeted with marine convolvulus, make up as pleasant a picture as can be desired.

Equally fascinating is the view from the bridge looking up the beautiful river flowing so calmly between continuous walls of lovely foliage, to where, beyond many ranges of palm and forest in varied tints of green and blue, rises the clear delicate range of far-away blue mountains, of which the crowning peak is the ever-attractive "Sri Pada" (the Holy Footprint).

Most beautiful of all was a row up the silent river in the clear moonlight, doubly attractive after the great heat of the day. Yet even that heat was tempered by a delicious sea-breeze and an invigorating scent of iodine, and the too dazzling light on sea and sky served to intensify enjoyment of the blessed shade.

Truly exquisite and delightful to eyes wearied with the sun's glare is the endless variety of cool refreshing greens which surround them on every side in this verdant paradise; large golden-green silky leaves, which seem to have embodied the sunlight that plays on their upper surface; sombre dark-green foliage, so thick and heavy as effectually to bar all light, casting a cool deep shadow on the grassy carpet below. There are olive-greens and emerald-greens, indigo and chrome, every tint that can be produced by blending every known yellow with every known blue. Loveliest of all, perhaps, is the exquisitely fresh green of the rice-fields, brighter even than our own wheat-fields in early spring.

As if to harmonise with these all-pervading hues, a large proportion of living creatures—the fairies of the forest—are clad in green, the better to escape the notice of their foes.

Brilliant green birds, butterflies, and dragonflies flit from tree to tree, tasting each honeyed blossom, while green lizards and green beetles find secure homes in crevices of the mossy stems, and green whipsnakes too often glide about among the boughs, perhaps in pursuit of the pretty little green tree-frogs, which try to hide themselves beneath the green leaves.

As to the small green parroquets (which are the only Singhalese representatives of the parrot family), their name is legion, and they are as gregarious as our own rooks, vast flocks assembling towards evening in such trees as they fancy, uttering shrill screams, chattering and fluttering, while apparently fighting for the best places, and dispersing again in the early morning amid a babel of the same ear-splitting screams.

Though all these parroquets are practically green, several varieties have distinguishing marks; thus one peculiar to the mountains in the Central Province has a purple head; another, which is also peculiar to Ceylon, has a deep red plume on the crown of the head; a third has a grey head, and a fourth has a rose-coloured ring round the neck. Occasionally, but very rarely, a pure yellow parroquet is hatched, and is valued on the same principle as the many-headed palm, on account of its rarity.

Attractive to the eye as are these pretty birds, their unmusical voices make them anything but desirable neighbours, whereas some of the pigeons, whose plumage, though less brilliant, is quite as lovely, have most soothing melodious notes. Such is the Kurulu-goya, whose euphonious Singhalese name well expresses its note. These birds fly in flocks, and their colouring is most delicate green flushed with rose-colour. A small pretty pigeon with dark-green metallic plumage is the Batta-goya, while the Mahavilla-goya is also a small green dove. The Kobaiya is a small grey turtle-dove, and the Baila-goya is a grey bird very like our own wood-pigeon.

A very common green and brown bird is the barbet, of which there are at least three varieties in Ceylon, one of which, with red head and green back, goes by the name of "the coppersmith," its strange metallic note being unpleasantly suggestive of hammering metal—a sound which, blending with the incessant creaking, sawing, and buzzing noises produced by various insects, to say nothing of the creaking of wooden cart-wheels and the working of the garden-well, sometimes become almost unendurably irritating.

Among the delicacies provided for us by a most attentive rest-house keeper were some of the oysters for which Bentota is famous, but they are poor little mis-shapen things, somewhat bitter in flavour, as well they may be, from a hereditary intuition of how successive generations of white men persist in tearing them from their homes, and yet never accord them one word of praise; for you never hear a Singhalese oyster named except in disparaging comparison with those of Europe or America. They are, however, allowed to be good when roasted on the shore, in the manner so familiar at Australian seaside picnics.

Alas! how poor words are to convey clear impressions of lovely scenes, with the countless characteristic details to which they owe so much of their charm! As I turn the pages of many sketch-books and portfolios, and feel how vividly the slightest jottings recall places, and all their attractive Oriental inhabitants and interesting customs, I feel how impossible it is to make mere words convey any true idea of what is so fascinating to the eye.

To take one of the most insignificant examples, the ping-tallie or ping-chattie, *i.e.*, "meritorious water-jar," placed at intervals along the roadside by some one anxious to acquire merit by keeping up a constant supply of cold water for thirsty wayfarers. Here is one sketched at Bentota on the brink of the sea. A large red chattie of porous earthenware on a stand to raise it some feet from the ground, and with a miniature roof of red tiles, the whole overshadowed by golden-green banana leaves; a little child carrying a large green leaf as a sunshade stands beside its mother while she refills the great jar, across which lies the wooden scoop with which each traveller takes out water and pours it into his hand, drinking thence, or else pouring it into his mouth from some height, so that men of all castes may drink without defilement.

Here is a very primitive ping-chattie poised on a tripod formed by three sticks, the upper end of which supports a thatch of palm leaves. This is in a cocoa-palm tope, and a thirsty brown man with long silky black hair carries in his arms a kid, whose mother follows close, as does also a little child guiltless of any raiment.

Here is one equally primitive, sketched in a village near Kandy, where the red jar rests in the fork of a small dead tree, across the broken branches of which is poised the yellow fan-shaped leaf of a talipat-palm, to protect the water from the sun. Beside it grows a large aloe, and a datura literally white with large and very fragrant trumpet-shaped blossoms. Just beyond, overshadowed by a great "lettuce-tree," its beautiful lemon-yellow foliage gleaming in contrast with a bright blue sky, is an ambulam or rest-house for Tamil coolies, its solid white pillars supporting a red-tiled roof, on the summit of which is a curious red earthenware ornament, representing three times three cobras arranged in a pinnacle. Well for the merry squirrels who play hide-and-seek among the broken tiles that these are only images of the cobra, and not the genuine article! A troop of monkeys are also careering over the roofs and in the trees, while groups of turbaned men are cooking at small fires in the open air.

This rest-house is at the entrance of a village; all the roofs are red-tiled, and all are shaded either by large-leaved plantains, fragrant white daturas, potato-trees with lovely purple blossoms, or palm-trees loaded with nuts in all stages. On either side of the road flows a narrow stream, across which a separate arched bridge, with steps, leads to each house. In the open shops hang huge clusters of ripe bananas, and piles of huge jak fruit to be used in curries, fragrant pine-apples, bright green ripe oranges, and other fruit to tempt wayfarers, also large cages full of poultry. Among the innumerable, ever-changing groups which make up the kaleidoscope of colour, all in vivid light and shadow, comes a cart drawn by white bullocks, with the usual high-arched cover of dried palm-leaves, which throws such rich dark shadow on the figures crouching within. This one is literally covered, inside and out, with red earthenware jars of all sizes, hung on with cords.

I turn a page and find another village, which, described in words, would seem only a repetition of the last. But in this case the "meritorious water-chattie" stands on a neat white pedestal, built upon one of the little bridges aforesaid, and it is protected by a large native umbrella supported by two sticks.

Just one more page! Here is a ping-tallie sketched at

Dickwella. It is a most elaborately sculptured stone font, which (but that it represents grim heraldic lions) might take a place in any church. It certainly is out of keeping with the broken steps leading up to the rude well from which it is being filled by a bronze lad, clothed chiefly in his own long black hair, and who, by the help of a long rope, draws up his red jar from the deep cool waters far below. A Singhalese woman, barefooted of course, and showing a good deal of brown waist between her white jacket and orange-coloured comboy, is giving her brown little ones a drink from the wooden scoop, and oh! what pretty creatures are some of these, with their large lustrous black eyes. Similarly attractive scenes meet one at every turn, and give human interest to scenes of ever-changing loveliness.

The whole drive from Galle to Colombo, a distance of about seventy miles, is one long dream of beauty. The excellent carriage-road runs so close to the shore that we are constantly catching sight and sound of the vividly blue sea and grand surf, sometimes dashing on headlands of dark rock, sometimes breaking more gently on the yellow sands of peaceful bays, and revealing endless glimpses of fishing life—brown boats with ruddy sails, brown men, chiefly clothed in a yellow palm-leaf hat, drawing brown nets. The whole way is overshadowed by luxuriant vegetation in such varied combinations that the eye can never weary of such a succession of beauty.

Of course the tall slender palms, with their sunlit crowns, are the predominating feature, towering above all to a height of ninety to a hundred feet, bending in every direction, and often overgrown by graceful creepers, which hang in festoons and garlands. The most remarkable of these is the

Gloriosa superba, there called "Neyangalla," a very peculiar climbing lily of a gorgeous scarlet and orange.

Sad to say, on the many thousand palms which clothe the shore from Bentota to Kalutara there is scarcely a nut to be seen, these trees being grown solely for the manufacture of arrack from the sap or toddy, which, as I have already described, is obtained by cruelly beating the flower spathe to prevent the formation of embryo nuts. One result of this unnatural culture is that the very bats are demoralised; and when the toddy begins to ferment, the great flying-foxes assemble in flocks and help themselves to the contents of the chatties so freely that they literally become drunk and riotous!

While many beautiful types of foliage combine to produce an endless variety overhead and on either side of the red road, the undergrowth is no less varied and lovely. There are an infinite variety of ferns, including several exquisite climbing species, which bear the most delicate little fronds, sometimes fringed with seed on stems like black horse-hair,[1] and which grow so rankly as to veil tall shrubs and hang in fairy-like wreaths from tree to tree. In some parts of the island I have seen these growing so abundantly that they are cut wholesale and used for thatch as ruthlessly as we cut common brackens, the large hair-like stems acting as excellent rain-conductors.

Then there are a great variety of aroids, with handsome arrow-headed leaves, from the cultivated yam and the calla-lily to the crimson-veined and spotted caladium, familiar in our greenhouses, but of so much larger growth that a single leaf is often plucked as an effective and very pretty sunshade.

[1] *Lygodium scandens*.

In the neighbourhood of Galle a beautiful white lily,[1] like our virgin-lily, grows freely along the shore on stems fully six feet in height, and generally with a luxuriant growth of goat's-foot convolvulus, with shining green leaves and pink or delicate lilac blossoms, matting the shore to the brink of the sea, and invariably tenanted by innumerable tiny crabs, chiefly hermits—the "wise men" of the sea, who live in houses built for themselves by other creatures.

A charming feature of this drive, or indeed of any drive along the coast of Ceylon, is the great number of streams and rivers to be crossed by wooden bridges. Some are all fringed with feathery bamboos and palms; others, forming wide estuaries as they enter the sea, lose themselves in tidal swamps densely clothed with sombre mangroves, whose aerial roots form a labyrinth wherein myriads of crabs and shell-fish, water-snakes, crocodiles, and other unpleasant creatures, including swarms of mosquitoes, find a secure haven. A large proportion of these roots are thrown out from the stem at a considerable height above the mud, and bending downwards, act the part of buttresses to support the parent stem in the loose soil.

A very curious feature in the reproduction of the mangrove is that the seed does not fall from the seed-vessel when ripe, but therein remains and germinates, while the seed-vessel remains attached to the parent stem. The infant root grows out at the top, and continues growing till it reaches the mud, or till the seed-vessel drops off, in which case it equally lands in the mud, and there becomes established as a young mangrove to take its part in clothing the swamp, and by gradually extending the dense thicket of vegetation, reclaim more land from the neutral ground.

[1] *Pancratium zeylanicum.*

The bark of the mangrove is commercially valuable on account of the large amount of tannin it yields, and its timber is prized as firewood; but as population increases in the vicinity of mangrove-clad shores, it is a grave question whether the destruction of these maritime forests may not so disturb Nature's equilibrium as to prove a source of danger, as the tannin, which ceaselessly drops from leaves, bark, and seeds, is said to be a powerful antidote against putrefaction, and in places where wholesale denudation has been permitted, as in the case of the Brazilian mangrove swamp off Rio, the enormous deposits of dead fish and shell-fish, which are left to decompose in the burning heat on the now bare banks of black mud, are so offensive as to be deemed in at least some measure accountable for the terrible visitations of yellow fever and other epidemics of comparatively recent introduction.

Another tree which flourishes on these shores is the Baringtonia, a large handsome tree with dark glossy foliage and clusters of delicate white blossom edged with crimson. It bears large fibrous fruits of pyramidal form, within which lie seeds which are used in medicine, and from which an oil is expressed for lamps, which is also occasionally used by fishers, who mix it with bait, and so contrive to stupefy the fish, which are then easily captured.

One of the loveliest of these many rivers is the Kalu-Ganga or Black River, at the mouth of which is Kalutara, a large and pleasant village. We started from Bentota with the earliest glimmer of dawn, while fires were still gleaming in the fishers' boats, and so had full benefit of the deliciously cool morning air, and of the lovely early lights reflected in the calm waters of a long beautiful lagoon. We halted close to Kalutara to secure a rapid sketch of a very fine banyan-tree which formed a magnificent archway right across the road, aerial roots having dropped from the main branches and taken root on the farther side. The whole was bearded with a fringe of long brown filaments and overgrown by luxuriant parasitic plants and ferns, producing a most beautiful effect. Alas! it is reported that this very remarkable tree has been blown over in a fierce gale.

Very fascinating is the view from the old fort at Kalutara, where we halted for breakfast, looking up the beautiful Kalu-Ganga to the distant mountain range, crowned as usual by the Mount of the Holy Foot, which is distant about sixty-five miles. The river is navigable for boats as far as Ratnapura, whence many of the pilgrims to the Peak avail themselves of this easy mode of returning to the seacoast. Much of the estate produce is also brought by this easy waterway from the hills to Kalutara, and thence to Colombo either by rail or by further water-carriage through lagoons and canals, such as those by which we travelled to Kalpitya. The railway has the double advantage of speed and of security against dishonest boatmen, to whom the quiet of the lagoons offers almost irresistible temptations.

The river is here spanned by a wide bridge, below which lay moored many thatched boats, while seaward, fishers were drawing up their long seine nets and others were fishing from boats.

Strange to say, the laws of caste are as rigidly marked between the subdivisions of the fisher caste as between separate castes. There are five upper divisions, who are allowed to intermarry; each of these has a distinctive name, meaning "those who fish from the rocks," "those who fish from boats," "those who catch turtle," "those who cast nets," and "those who fish with a rod."

Besides these there are a number of divisions of fishers of lower social position, who must on no account aspire to marry with their betters, though some are engaged in lucrative trades, such as boat and ship building and cabinet-making. Some are carpenters and some are farmers—a curious blending of professions according to our British experience of the sharp line of demarcation which exists between our own fisher-folk and all others inhabiting even the other end of the same village.

Kalutara is one of the few places in Ceylon where that most delicious of fruits the mangosteen ripens well—a great point in its favour. The industry by which the town is most widely known is that of weaving baskets from the fibre of a palm leaf, which is split as narrow as fine grass, and dyed black, red, and yellow. The baskets are oblong, and are sold in nests of twelve, fitting inside of one another, very convenient to carry and very useful. They are wonderfully light and yet durable, and are made by women and children. Nearer to Colombo a good many Malays manufacture baskets and flower-stands from the rattan-cane, and at various villages in the interior we saw people weaving coarse rush-mats, but all finer ornamental mats used in Ceylon are imported from the Suvadiva group of the Maldive Isles, which are a dependency of Ceylon.

It is much to be feared that future travellers will miss much of the enjoyment of this lovely drive to Colombo, for the railway is now open as far as Bentota, with a station at the mouth of the Alutgama River—a beautiful line of railway, skirting still lagoons and generally running close along the shore, where the mighty waves break with a crash louder than the roar of the rushing train. But railway travel allows small leisure to realise all the beauties of the panorama so rapidly revealed, and in an Oriental land, where each moment we whirl past something of interest, it is the worst form of the aggravation of *tableaux vivants*, for at best we catch an unsatisfying glimpse of scenes which in the twinkling of an eye have vanished from our gaze.

Nothing is more remarkable in the history of all Oriental railways than the rapidity with which pilgrims of various faiths avail themselves of this mode of lightening the toil of their pilgrimage. The extension to Bentota proved no exception, for very soon after it was opened crowds of Mahommedans poured down from Colombo and elsewhere to worship at the Alutgama mosque.

Here, as elsewhere, the old life and the new flow side by side, sometimes in strange contrast. Thus while the railway from Kalutara to Bentota was in process of completion, three persons, including a native headman, were tried before the District Court for having subjected several persons to the torture known as the "ordeal by boiling oil," in order to extract a confession of the theft of some plumbago.

The accused, who did not attempt to deny the offence, were very much aggrieved that British law should interfere, and even punish them for an act sanctioned by ancient custom, and which, it appears, is still commonly practised in out-of-the-way parts of the Isle.

The ceremony is as follows. Oil from newly-gathered king cocoa-nuts is manufactured by a friend of the complainant, and is heated over the fire in a chattie. When boiling, each of the persons accused is required to dip his fingers thrice into the chattie, and, I believe, thrice also into a preparation of boiling cow-dung. If he can refrain from any exclamation of pain, he is held to be innocent, but any cry is equivalent to an admission of guilt. The only consolation of the victim is that he is at liberty to sprinkle over his adversary as much boiling oil as sticks to his fingers.

In the present case, though the five persons accused were all forcibly dragged up to the chattie and compelled to plunge their hands in the boiling oil, all managed to refrain from crying out except one young lad, though he was the least injured, consequently he was declared to be the thief and required to surrender the stolen property. All the five persons subjected to the ordeal were so shockingly scalded as to be unable to return to their work for three weeks.

Much to their indignation, the self-appointed torturers were each condemned to pay a fine of a hundred rupees, or undergo ten months' imprisonment.

At Pantura (or, as it is now called, Panadura), about half-way from Kalutara to Colombo, we crossed a backwater of the sea, which, stretching inland, forms the beautiful lake Bolgoda, all dotted with charming islands. These are the homes of innumerable waterfowl, and also are the scene of a curious phase of bird life, quite à la Box and Cox, affording a roosting-ground by day to flocks of large flying-foxes, which, after a night of marauding among the fruit-trees, come here at dawn to hang themselves up on secure boughs, just as the crows, who have slept here peacefully all night, as beseems respectable workers, are starting on their day of useful toil as scavengers.

As we drove cheerily on our way from Kalutara to Colombo, the excellence of "the Queen's highway" could not but call forth the usual encomium, as we contrasted our pleasant drive from Galle with the toilsome journey of the Governor's party when travelling over the same ground in the year 1800, when roads were non-existent.

Just think of the heat and of the dust stirred up by 160 palanquin-bearers and 400 baggage-coolies trudging wearily through the hot sand, to say nothing of the troop of fifty lascars, six horses, and two elephants who were necessary for the transport and care of the tents!

Now the coast-road, 769 miles in length, extends right round the island, the greater part of it being available for wheel traffic, though here and there portions still leave room for improvement.

Since we parted at Galle, the Bishop had been ordered to Malta on sick-leave, and the Campbells had most kindly offered me headquarters at their pleasant temporary home in Captain's Gardens, which is a promontory jutting into the Lake of Colombo, and clothed with most luxuriant vegetation—flowering trees gorgeous with fragrant blossom, kittool-palms seeming literally overladen with ropes of fruit, all reflected in the calm water, on which floated a wealth of lovely lilies.

At the entrance a fine banyan-tree formed an arch right across the road, somewhat in the style of the tree at Kalutara, but lacking its grace and its dainty tracery of ferns. Two fine india-rubber trees spread their wide arms and cool shade over the lawn in front of the comfortable bungalow, a one-storied house of the regular type, with a wide verandah and red-tiled roof, white pillars supporting the home of innumerable happy squirrels and little lizards.

A separate bungalow stood a little apart in the garden, and the large house was so full of little daughters that this separate "guest-house" was assigned to me, greatly to my pleasure, as it was charmingly situated on the very brink of the lovely lake, and shaded with cocoa-palms of all ages (which implies the loveliest variety of form), growing amid cool green grass, and catching every breath of air, whenever there was the faintest breeze from sea or lake. And it certainly was hot; every one around was gasping and craving for the "Chota monsoon"[1] to bring cool rain, though personally I gloried in what seemed to me divine weather; and certainly I was always up to anything, from gunfire till starlight.

It was fortunate that I was not troubled with nerves, for the house of which I was sole occupant had five outer doors and seventeen windows, not one of which could be securely closed, and so they all stood wide open day and night, for if they could not keep out thieves, there was no reason why they should keep out air! I confess to having experienced an occasional nocturnal qualm at the proximity of a large village of dhobies (laundry-men) not of the best repute, and sometimes awoke in the moonlight to make sure that there were no long poles coming in at the window to fish out my clothes in the approved fashion. However, no such evil befell; and, indeed, by reason of my host's office, police orderlies were always somewhere about to scare marauders.

[1] *Chota*, small.

CHAPTER XXIII.

NATIVE POLICE.

Native police—Frequency of stabbing and of perjury—Intricate division of property—Too many legal advisers—Regulations concerning cart and servant registration—Pearl-fishery—Cruelty to animals —Volunteers.

THE very fine body of native police, as at present constituted, is the creation of Mr. G. W. R. Campbell,[1] under whose command it continued till this year, 1891—a force of which he has good reason to be proud.

In September 1866, at the request of Sir Hercules Robinson, he resigned an excellent position in India to undertake the remodelling of the very unsatisfactory police force of that day.

He found it to consist of a nominal force of 560 men, but in reality there were only 470, quite untrained, and lacking in all *esprit de corps*. These were expected to keep order in a population of over two million people, by many of whom he found that crime was regarded with complete indifference, even in such horrible cases as that of a father lifting up his infant by the feet and dashing its brains out on the floor before its mother's eyes, merely to gratify his almost causeless rage against her; or that of a man brain-

[1] Now Sir George W. R. Campbell, K.C.M.G.

ing his own little girl on purpose to get his father-in-law hanged for murder. He found that even under the existing very imperfect system for detection of crime, no less than 81 cases of murder and 22 of manslaughter had been proven within the two previous years.

Where public opinion viewed such crimes with perfect apathy, it was no easy task for any body of police to work effectively. Nevertheless, in an amazingly short time Mr. Campbell had reorganised the whole force, and brought it into such excellent working order as to call forth the highest commendation from Sir Hercules, to whom Mr. Campbell then reported that his aim was to raise the police to such a point that the Ceylon Rifles (an expensive native regiment with European officers) might be altogether dispensed with.

However desirable, such a project then seemed quite beyond the range of possibilities. However, soon afterwards Mr. Campbell was sent to Penang as Lieutenant-Governor for eighteen months, and thence came to England on sick-leave. On his return to Ceylon, he found that during his absence the Ceylon Rifles had actually been disbanded as unnecessary, thereby effecting a very large saving for the colony.

A considerable number of the disbanded soldiers (mostly Malays) were drafted into the police, which incorporates men of very varied nationalities—British, Portuguese, Dutch, Singhalese, Tamils, and Burghers of mixed race, welding the whole into a remarkably fine and efficient force numbering about 1470.

The men are smart and soldierly, and may be described as civil police with a semi-military training. The thick tight-fitting jacket and trousers and stiff leather stock were at once discarded in favour of a suitable and becoming uniform, consisting of tunic and trousers of dark blue serge, with waist-belt and boots of dark brown leather, and scarlet forage-cap with a black top-knot. They are armed with Snider rifles and swords, and are regularly drilled, but except when on jail-guard or guarding convicts or treasure, they only carry batons.

Their total cost to the general revenue is set down at 401,831 rupees per annum; that of the old force was about 150,000 rupees. The present outlay includes many such items as the feeding and transport of prisoners and of sick paupers, cost of working the elaborate and very efficient systems of registration of servants and carts, and many other matters; and well may Mr. Campbell say, when pleading for a greatly strengthened detective branch, "No country in the East has so small or nearly so cheap a force as Ceylon." "Can it be expected that 1500 poorly paid police, more than half of whom are employed to guard convicts and treasuries and to keep order in the streets—can it be expected that this handful of men, scattered throughout a country nearly as large as Ireland, and with a population numbering nearly three millions, and *criminal to an unusual extent*, can bring a large majority of the worst criminals to justice?

"Whereas Ireland, with a population a little more than double that of Ceylon, has about 13,000 police with 300 officers, Ceylon (with only seven officers in receipt of upwards of 1500 rupees per annum, which, valuing the rupee at 1s. 6d., represents £112, 10s. per annum) has under 1500 police. Even this small force is employed on such duties as guarding convict gangs on public works, such as the saltpans at Hambantota, the Mahara quarries, the breakwater, &c. They are, further, the only relieving officers of the vagrant portion of the helpless poor ; they must attend to vaccination, sanitation of places of pilgrimage, the weights and measures of dealers, storage of kerosine, gunpowder, &c., and they are now the jailors of several of the minor jails."

Till within the last three years there were no habour-police, so that all work of this sort likewise fell on the regular force. Now the development of Colombo harbour has necessitated the appointment of a harbour-inspector with a couple of whaleboats and about sixteen men specially for this work. The police are now scattered over the country in ninety-four different detachments, and considering that there are on an average only four of the regular police at each station in rural districts to look after about a hundred square miles of cultivated land, all liable to crop-thieving, and that they have to escort and guard prisoners, keep order in one or two large village bazaars, and by their presence deter crop-thieves and purchasers of such stolen goods, take care of sick wayfarers, and serve all the countless summonses and warrants that may be issued, it is evident that they cannot eat the bread of idleness. In the whole force there is not a single mounted constable, so all the work must be done on foot. In each province, however, the Government Agent has a body of untrained and unpaid village police, who in some measure lighten the toil of the regular police.

Some idea of the miscellaneous work which falls on the police department might be gathered from a single detail of its office-work, namely, that about 70,000 documents are annually received and despatched from the two chief offices alone, *i.e.*, Kandy and Colombo.

At these two points the police barracks are a perfect triumph of ingenuity, so admirable is the result produced for the money expended, both as regards the construction of really handsome buildings at a very low cost, and also in the excellent taste displayed in the careful laying out of the grounds, with such profusion of flowering trees and shrubs, that the whole effect is that of luxuriant gardens.

This is especially striking at Kew, a peninsula on the Colombo Lake, formerly occupied by the Ceylon Rifles, whose barracks, with their dreary muddy surroundings, have been transformed by Mr. Campbell and his men into a scene of beauty. Here and at Bentota the gorgeous display of *Gloriosa superba* and other splendid climbing plants remains vividly impressed on my memory. The same care is shown wherever a police-station has been established in various parts of the Isle, and at elevations ranging up to 7000 feet, so that these are in a measure experimental gardens for new products.

It is greatly to be desired that these should quickly multiply, for as yet very many police-stations are still without any Government buildings, consequently ordinary dwelling-houses are hired to act as offices and lock-ups, while the constables have to hire quarters for themselves, often widely scattered, and sometimes in very undesirable company. The married men, who constitute more than two-thirds of the force, have to pay about one-eighth of their whole slender salary for the use of very wretched huts.

This is doubly hard, as not only are the necessaries of life much dearer in Ceylon than on the mainland of India, but the rate of pay in all ranks is from a quarter to half that of the corresponding rank in the Indian police. Even the Inspector-General, after serving ten years in the Bombay police, and after twenty-four years of ceaseless toil in Ceylon, has received only 1000 rupees a month, which is the average pay of a Superintendent of Police in India. But the generally low scale of pay is more apparent by comparing the weekly 31s. 6d. of a first-class London constable with the salary of the European constables in Ceylon, most of whom receive less than 10s. a week, *minus* several deductions!

Now, as regards our primary notions of the *raison d'être* of a police force, namely, the detection and suppression of crime, I confess it was to me almost incredible when I was first told of the deeply-rooted criminal tendencies of the Singhalese—these civil people, seemingly so mild and gentle, so courteous and sympathetic to strangers—to hear of many being savage and cruel to one another, cherishing anger, wrath, malice, jealousy, railing, and revenge, resulting in a terribly large proportion of robberies, violent quarrels, and murders, was certainly a grievous revelation. Yet alas! it is all too true, and the police reports present a dreadful catalogue of most callous murders, generally on account of the merest trifle, the victim being often some one to whom the murderer bears no ill-will, perhaps even his own near relation, and the sole cause is that a false charge of murder may be brought against some innocent person, against whom he has a spite! Imagine murdering a friend in order to throw blame on a foe!

But the larger number of murders are the result of momentary passion—it is a word and a stab, and these, alas! multiply only too surely with the ever-spreading curses of drink and gambling, "the prolific parents of Singhalese vice."

No one can fail to be struck with the singularly small proportion of women who find their way to the prisons of

THE TRUE CAUSES OF CRIME.

Ceylon. The daily average of convicted persons in prison in the last twelve years ranges from 1612 (of whom only 17 were women) to 3627 (of whom only 32 were women). Mr. Campbell questioned a number of the most intelligent prisoners as to what cause they attributed this difference to. "Our women do not drink nor gamble," was the reply.

All agreed that these two evils lay at the root of all their trouble. Not only do illicit drinking-houses provide gambling facilities to attract customers, but the men frequent secluded gardens, and arrange lonely meeting-places in the forest, whither each carries his own supply of liquor, and then they settle down to gamble, betting (heads-and-tails fashion) on the throw of certain shells, flat on one side, round on the other.

Some men, whose whole year's earning would barely exceed a hundred rupees, confessed to having lost or won two hundred at a sitting. Then, after this excitement, some are sulky, some desperate, and the majority more than half drunk. Then the beggared, reckless men begin quarrelling, and most cruel murders ensue, in which the victim is sometimes struck a score of times, the others probably going off to recruit their fortunes by robbery or cattle-lifting.

A large number of deaths are caused by blows from clubs or bludgeons, but a still larger proportion are due to stabbing with the sharp-pointed sheath-knife which a Singhalese habitually carries in his belt for pruning and other agricultural work, and which proves only too handy in every moment of passion. It is urged that a law forbidding the use of these implements, and enforcing that of clasp-knives, would be beneficial, as the moment required for opening a clasp-knife would give time for thought; especially if it happily closed on the fingers of the passionate man, might it tend to cool his ardour, the average Singhalese, like the brutal Briton, being very averse to pain. Hence the excellent deterrent influence of flogging—a tolerably liberal use of the lash or the rattan (cane) having been found highly efficacious in diminishing cattle-stealing in some of the worst districts.

That the ever-present, ever-open sheath-knife is largely responsible for Singhalese crime is shown by the fact that nearly all the murderers are of this race; whereas the Tamils, who do not habitually wear these knives, though continually being convicted of aggravated assault, almost invariably stop short of murder.

It is worthy of note that in almost all murder cases the victim and his assailant are of the same nationality—Tamil against Tamil, Singhalese against Singhalese, Malay against Malay—proving the absence of any race animosity.

I think a few samples of cases quoted from the police reports will be of interest, and in any case, the native names are characteristic.

First, then, I find that Ponambalam, a Tamil man, having been locked up for drunkenness, made a desperate rush to escape. Noordeen Bawa, a police-constable, stopped him, when Ponambalam seized Noordeen's thumb of the right hand in his teeth, and held it for half an hour. It could not be released till Ponambalam's teeth were forced apart with a chisel. Poor Noordeen, whose thumb was nearly bitten through, died of tetanus.

Puchirale, a Singhalese cultivator, was on a tree in the jungle picking fruit, when Appuhamy, also a Singhalese cultivator, fired and killed him. He said he had mistaken him for a monkey, but as they had been on bad terms, Appuhamy was put on his trial, but was acquitted.

Urugala, a wealthy Singhalese cultivator, aged sixty-five, having signified his intention of distributing his property among his children to the exclusion of his son Ukkurala, the latter beat his father *with a piece of sugar-cane*, so that he died.

At Batticaloa a man quarrelled with his mother about a cow, and killed her with a stick. For this he received four months' imprisonment.

Appuwa, a Singhalese cultivator, while drunk, stabbed with a knife and so killed his little daughter Kirihami, aged four years, owing to a quarrel with his wife for not having his food ready. He was acquitted.

Abaran, a Singhalese, was shot dead by Sirimalhami, whose mistress Abaran had carried off some months previously. Two young men helped Sirimalhami to remove the body to a jungle and there burn it. The two assistants were each sentenced to five years' rigorous imprisonment, but the murderer was acquitted.

Near Matara, eight Singhalese set upon one, and hacked him to death with choppers and sticks. Three were sentenced to ten years with hard labour, but the rest were acquitted.

Muttu Menika, a Singhalese girl of fifteen, was stabbed seventeen times by Dingirea, a Singhalese man twenty-four years of age, because she refused to marry him. He was sentenced to death.

Till recently all the inmates of a house were sometimes brutally murdered by robbers in order to get rid of inconvenient witnesses; but this was a characteristic of a form of gang-robberies now happily stamped out.

As examples of crime in 1889, Harmanis Soyza, a Singhalese fisher aged twenty-five, having deserted his mistress,

Siku, a Singhalese girl aged twenty, and being taunted by her and her mother, became infuriated, and entering their house, stabbed and killed them both, also stabbing and grievously wounding Siku's sister, Punchi Nona.

Balina, a Singhalese washerwoman, having quarrelled with Sunda, a neighbour, set fire to his house, and then stabbed him so that he died, for which she was sentenced to death.

That the amount of jewellery worn by children does not oftener lead them into peril is surprising. Here, however, is a case in point. Sinnasamy, a Tamil coolie, cut the throat of Ramer, a Tamil schoolboy aged eight, in order to steal his bangles, watch-chain, and two pairs of earrings. Sinnasamy was hanged, as he deserved to be.

Mataraye Samel, a Singhalese servant, struck Babie, an ayah, on the head with an areca-nut cutter, because she told her mistress of his intimacy with a girl in the house. Lockjaw supervened and poor Babie died, whereupon Samel was sentenced to ten years' hard labour.

Velen Sinnatambu, a Tamil, aged twenty-five, in a fit of rage hacked his wife, Sinnapillai, to pieces with a chopper. She was a girl under sixteen years of age. The murderer was hanged.

Even peaceful green pastures can be made the occasion of battle in Ceylon as well as in the Hebrides. Thus at Jaffna, Velan Kanapathi was killed and Arumugam Kanapathi seriously injured by being struck with stones in a quarrel about rights of pasturage. Ten men, all Tamils, were apprehended on this charge.

In the same district three Tamil men entered the house of a fourth, armed with clubs and a sharp-edged stone, and fractured his skull. Each was sentenced to ten years' rigorous imprisonment. Another skull was fractured by a heavy stone at beautiful Matara, in an altercation over the produce of a kitool-palm tree.

Most extraordinary cases of murder are those which are done solely in order to bring a false accusation against some one else. At Galle, Nicholas de Silva Madanayeke took his own child, twelve months old, and dashed it to the ground; then accused three young men of good character of having killed it. Happily they were acquitted, and the inhuman father was hanged within the walls of Galle jail.

Another case is that of a man who shot his own brother in order to bring a charge of murder against three enemies, while another knocked out the brains of his own little daughter in order to get his father-in-law hanged for the murder.

Near Kurunegalla, a Singhalese boy, aged twelve, was strangled by Hatuhami, a Singhalese man, in order that the murder might be attributed to some Buddhist priests with whom he was at enmity. For this, Hatuhami was sentenced to five years' hard labour.

Here is a more elaborate story of a case which occurred in 1879. A young Singhalese girl, possessed of some land, had just died. Two men induced another Singhalese girl to personate her, and to appear before a notary and make over the land to them. The fraud was discovered, and in order to prevent the whole story from being revealed, the men dragged the luckless girl night after night from one jungle to another, till she told them that life was a burden to her; whereupon they killed her, and cut off her head to prevent identification in case the body should be found. Found it was, and identified by the toes, which were partially webbed. The men were hanged.

One is struck by the pitifully small temptation which

results in such cruel murders. For instance, Babiela, a Singhalese villager, had a trifling dispute with a neighbour, and knowing that he possessed jewels worth about 200 rupees (less than £20), he stole quietly into the house at midnight, and cut the throats of the man, his wife, and four children. This miscreant was hanged.

I will only quote two more cases, each full of dramatic interest, only premising that though all the names are Portuguese, all the *dramatis personæ* are pure Singhalese. The first is that of Miguel Perera, a wealthy and influential Singhalese, living within ten miles of Colombo, and a man popular with Europeans because of his pleasant manners, and on account of his great energy and influence among his people. When anything had to be done quickly, such as the repair of a road or the decoration of a town to welcome a distinguished visitor, he was the man to be depended on. For these good services he received from Government the title of Mudaliyar of Ragama.

But there was a dark side to this attractive person. In his private life he was unscrupulous and tyrannical, both to men and women, and when one day he was found at high noon lying on a road on his own estate with his throat cut, the investigation proved that the crime had been committed by some of his own retainers, goaded to madness by his ill-usage, one detail of which was that after cruelly beating a man, he would lock him up for the night in stocks, which he kept at his own house.

Four men were apprehended, and the evidence would almost undoubtedly have proved them to be the murderers. But it seems as if the Singhalese could not leave justice to prove itself, so the two eldest sons of the dead man set to work to torture witnesses in order to fabricate further evidence, chiefly with a view to implicate an enemy of their father's, Louis Mendis. Tampering with witnesses is an everyday occurrence, but torturing them is going a little too far; so when this conspiracy came to light, the tables were turned—the murderers were acquitted, and the two brothers were each sentenced to three years' imprisonment with hard labour.

The Louis Mendis just mentioned was a cart-contractor, living at Nawalapitiya, in the Central Province, and the quarrel with Miguel Perera was due to the latter sending carters all the way from the coast to take away his custom. Mendis, not unnaturally, urged his own men to beat the intruders, and on one occasion, when he had primed his men with much arrack, a savage encounter occurred, in which a young carter from the coast, by name Juan Fernando, was *said to have been killed.* There was evidence of Fernando having been seen wounded, especially on the shoulder, but no corpse could be found, and Mendis and his party averred that the story of his death was a fabrication in order to damage Mendis, and that Perera was keeping Fernando out of sight.

Several months later the father came from his home on the coast to inform the police that he could point out the spot where his son's body was buried. He accordingly led them to a spot in the jungle some miles from Nawalapitiya, and there they found the headless and decomposed corpse of a young man with a broken shoulder-blade, and on the body was found the waist-belt of the missing Juan Fernando, with his initials scratched on the plate. It was assumed that the body had been carried to the jungle, and there buried by a carter in the service of Mendis, who, however, was not available as a witness, having in the interval been hanged for stabbing a police constable. Consequently Mendis and his men were punished only for assault, being sentenced to terms of imprisonment with hard labour.

They maintain, however, that Juan Fernando is still alive, and concealed by Perera's party, and that the body was one taken by Perera's order from some graveyard, adorned with Fernando's belt, and buried in the jungle in order to ruin Mendis, the head being removed in order to prevent its being proved that the body was *not* that of Fernando. (Of course Perera's people say the head was removed to prevent identification; but if that had been the case, it would have been a strange oversight to leave the belt with the tell-tale initials.)

These instances may suffice to give some idea of the chief difficulty which attends all judicial inquiries in Ceylon, namely, that of dealing with a race who, so far from attaching any disgrace to perjury, consider it as a fine art, and that the courts of law are the field where it may be most effectually and brilliantly practised. Mr. Campbell says, "Perjury is rampant and destructive, flooding our courts with false cases, paralysing their action, and producing grave deterioration of character."

In his recent report on the administration of police in Ceylon, Mr. Giles[1] observes: "The most dangerous form of crime in Ceylon, and that which perhaps involves the greatest moral turpitude, is the proneness of the people *to prefer false accusations and to bear false testimony.* No man can feel safe while this state of things continues; and the evils are by no means confined to the individuals falsely accused. The prevalence of perjury causes the judiciary to reject evidence which in a purer atmosphere would be

[1] Deputy Inspector-General of Police, Bengal.

unhesitatingly accepted, and criminals benefit by this reluctance. The courts are flooded with cases which should never come before them, *their time dissipated in vainly endeavouring to arrive at truth where all is falsehood,* and a virtual denial of justice often leads to the perpetration of fresh crime."

A somewhat striking illustration of this all-round falsehood was revealed to an astonished European by a grateful client, who had recently won a case to the utter amazement of his adversary. The latter had brought an action against him for the recovery of a large sum of money, for which he held defendant's bond. There were reliable witnesses to prove the debt, and the case was apparently quite clear, till the defendant produced the plaintiff's receipt in full for the sum advanced and duly repaid, and a tribe of witnesses to prove the authenticity of the signature. Nothing could be clearer, and the case, after patient hearing, was dismissed.

Now came the surprising revelation, which was that *there had been no money lent and none repaid;* but from the moment the defendant had learnt the charge that was to be brought against him, he had been perfectly aware that a bond must have been forged, and witnesses bribed to attest it; therefore (on the principle of "diamond cut diamond") he had at once secured the services of a skilful forger to prepare the receipt, and of witnesses to attest it, and had thus by foul means secured the justice which he could not have obtained by fair straightforward action.

This is a fair example of the manner in which the criminal law is employed as "an engine of oppression rather than of redress;" and to such an incredible extent is this perversion of justice carried, that in his report for 1881

Mr. Campbell says that from 95,000 to 110,000 persons are each year apprehended or summoned before the courts and never brought to trial, showing either the utter frivolity of the cases, or that the complainants or witnesses, or both, have been bought over.

"Even these figures," he says, "large as they are, give no idea of the extent to which the machinery of justice is misused by the people to oppress and harass each other, and actually to frustrate justice itself, until we take into account the cloud of witnesses who are also brought up by summons and warrants, and further take into account the multiplied postponements which characterise our courts, and unless we still further recollect the multitude of minor cases which are annually tried by the Gausabhawa or village tribunals. These, in the course of the year 1880, numbered no less than 26,748.

"The results of this inordinate misuse of the courts are the impoverishment of the people both by a waste of time and by actual expenditure on worthless crowds of self-styled lawyers, the fostering of their innate love of litigation, the encouraging of false witnesses and perjury, the general demoralisation which follows the prostitution of courts of justice, and the obstruction of the thorough investigation and punishment of serious crime. Better that a man should at his own proper peril strike a blow with a stick, or even with a knife, than that by making false and malicious charges he should make a court of justice an instrument for inflicting a cowardly blow. The blow by the court is quite as severe as the other, and the demoralisation of every one concerned is infinitely greater." It has been tersely said that "perjury is made so complete a business that cases are as regularly rehearsed in all their various scenes by the professional perjurer as a dramatic piece is at a theatre."

Of course, when it is so impossible for a judge to know who or what to believe, true evidence is constantly rejected, criminals escape, and innocent people suffer unmerited punishment, or at least retain a rankling sense of injustice which leads to retaliation, either in the form of false charges in court or of criminal violence.

This subject impressed itself strongly on Mr. Campbell on his first arrival in 1866, when, at the court at Panaduré, out of six hundred cases instituted there were only six convictions. Of course such immunity from punishment tends to prevalence of crime, the chances of conviction being so small that heinous offences are committed with little risk; for nothing is easier than to bribe all the witnesses, and probably the headman, whose duty it should be to prosecute, and sometimes even the plaintiff himself is bribed!

As regards the headmen, it is only natural that they should be amenable to bribes, for instead of receiving remuneration for helping in the detection of crime and the capture of criminals, by doing so they often have to incur serious expense out of their own slender means; so naturally it conduces both to their ease and profit to screen offenders.

The number of convictions fluctuates greatly, not from increase or decrease of crime, but according to the varied interpretation of law by successive Chief-Justices. In some years the interpretation has been such that convictions have been almost impossible, and so the most glaring criminals have been acquitted, and all their fraternity, openly laughing at the police, become bold beyond measure. Then comes a Chief-Justice who interprets laws differently; criminals find their deserts, and a comparative lull ensues.

Mr. Campbell has for years striven to effect the introduction of various simple measures with a view to lessening some of the evils complained of. Such are the preliminary investigation of cases ere granting warrants and summonses wholesale. This was instituted in 1872, as was also the payment of a trifling stamp-duty, amounting only to 15 cents on each criminal charge and 5 cents on each subpœna of an accused person, or of one summoned as a witness.

Incredible as it may seem, these petty and vexatious cases, which in 1871 had numbered 68,832, at once fell to 46,701 in 1872! That stamp fees amounting to a few pence should in one year have kept 22,131 cases out of court is good proof of how frivolous and false were the pretexts for litigation.

Unfortunately, in 1888 the process was in a measure reversed. The 25-cent duty was taken off of all charges of voluntarily causing hurt, consequently the list of one class of cases rose in one year from 6820 to 20,052, mainly owing to utterly frivolous, and certainly in most cases false charges; the lesson to be learnt being that "the trifling tax suffices to deter a large number of vindictive, idle, litigious people from using the courts as engines to oppress their neighbours."

In one very common class of accusation, against which no man can be safe, namely, that of grave immorality, the whole question turns on which man can bribe the largest number of false witnesses, and the innocent accused is very often obliged to purchase safety by paying his accuser to let the charge drop.

If the besetting sin of the Singhalese is their inordinate love of litigation, this certainly is fostered by their very troublesome law of inheritance, which results in such minute subdivisions of property that the 199th share of a field, or a 50th of a small garden, containing perhaps a dozen palms and a few plaintains, becomes a fruitful source of legal contention, quarrels, and crime. Emerson Tennant alludes to a case in which the claim was for the 2520th share in the produce of ten cocoa-palms!

As a sample of this sort of litigation, the Rev. R. Spence Hardy quoted an instance of an intricate claim on disputed property, in which the case of the plaintiff was as follows :—" By inheritance through my father I am entitled to one-fourth of one-third of one-eighth. Through my mother I am further entitled to one-fourth of one-third of one-eighth. By purchase from one set of co-heirs I am entitled to one-ninety-sixth, from another set also one-ninety-sixth, and from a third set one-ninety-sixth more. Finally, from a fourth set of co-heirs I have purchased the 144th of the whole." There is a nice question to solve ere a landowner can begin to till his field or reap its produce.

But though these difficult questions must always have proved a fruitful source of contention, it is only in recent years that the number of gentlemen of the legal profession has increased so enormously. Mr. Spence Hardy, writing in 1864, stated that sixty years previously there were in the Isle only two Dutchmen who did the whole work of advocates. Even in that time the number had increased to 16 advocates, 135 proctors, and 144 notaries.

Now, as we enter on the last decade of the century, there are about 300 advocates and proctors, and solicitors and notaries have increased in proportion, besides an incalculable brood of self-styled lawyers of the lowest species, who infest every village tribunal, "outdoor proctors," as they are called, who gain their own living by inciting the people to litigation, till the whole country is flooded with warrants and summonses, resulting in a large proportion of the population spending their time either in the courts or on the road between them and their houses, greatly to their own impoverishment.

It is, perhaps, not to be wondered at that so many favour a profession in which the highest honours are equally open to all without distinction of race—Singhalese or Tamil, Portuguese or Dutch, Eurasian or European, have equal chances in the race for distinction as barristers, magistrates, or judges.

In looking over the list of these legal names, I am much struck by observing how curiously certain names predominate in certain districts. Thus among the notaries in the Southern Province I find twenty-one De Silvas, distinguished by such high-sounding first names as Goonewardene, Sameresingha, Wickremanaike, Rajakuruna, &c. Turning to the Colombo district, I find in succession fourteen of the family of Perera with such Christian names as Andris, Juan, Paulus, Manual, &c. Of the multitude of De and Don there is no end, by no means necessarily implying Portuguese descent, but because so many of the families of purest Singhalese and Kandyan blood took these names from the god-father of their Christian baptism; thus we have Don Philip De Alvis, Don Charles Appuhamy, Don Carolis Senevaratna, Don Francisco Weresakara, Don Johanis Amarasakara, Domingo De Mendis.[1]

[1] I trust these gentlemen will pardon my quoting real names to illustrate an interesting subject.

As a sample of pleasant names for daily use, I cannot resist quoting a paragraph from a Ceylon paper which happens to be lying before me :—

"A MURDERER WANTED.—Induruwabadahelage Jema of Talawala, charged with the murder, on July 20th last, of one Pepiliyanebadahelage Barlis Barbos, has fled from justice. A large reward is offered for such information as shall lead to his apprehension and conviction."

Some historical suggestion may perhaps be gathered from the geographical distribution of these names. Thus in the list of notaries for the district of Colombo, I observe nine with the prefix De, and upward of forty with that of Don. In Kalutara, out of fifty-one, twenty-three own these honorific prefixes. Ratnapura has sixteen notaries, not one prefix. In the Central Province a dozen in a hundred are thus distinguished. In the Eastern and Northern Provinces, including Batticaloa, Trincomalee, Jaffna, and Manaar, there is not one. In the Southern Province, out of a total of about fifty, twenty-four are De and only one Don. In the North-West Province, Chilaw owns one in fifteen, and Kurunegalla, out of a list of twenty-seven, furnishes one Don.

It would be interesting to know whether the names accepted in the last century as a passport to State employment retain any special traditionary interest for their present owners.

Where so many have elected to earn their own bread by fostering the natural love of litigation among their countrymen, it follows that the blessing of the peacemakers is the last thing to be desired, and the longer a case can be spun out, and the oftener it is postponed, the better for the lawyers. In this respect matters have not mended since, in 1849, Major Thomas Skinner wrote: "The prevailing system of our district courts admits of the proctors feeding upon their clients for years. . . . I have seen instances wherein the judicial stamps have far exceeded the value of the case under adjudication, and which, by numberless vexatious postponements, have been protracted over a period of many years, to the ruin of both plaintiff and defendant— the proctors by their fees, and the Government by the sale of judicial stamps, being the only gainers."

For one thing, criminal cases are constantly brought to court so ill prepared as to necessitate being postponed again and again, thus wasting the time of magistrates, prosecutors, and witnesses.

Another thing by which the business of the courts is very unnecessarily delayed is by the invariable employment of magistrate's interpreters. In India, where in each Presidency there are so many different languages, each magistrate is bound to master whatever is requisite for the conduct of his own court, interpreters being only employed in the supreme courts. In Ceylon, although there are only two native languages, in which every newcomer has to pass examinations, every word spoken in court, every question and every answer, must be repeated through an interpreter, just doubling the work and the time expended.

Among the cases which call for considerable detective skill are those of forging bank-notes and coins, the former being generally the joint-work of professional engravers and surveyors, while the false rupees, though generally manufactured by Singhalese goldsmiths, are occasionally proved to be the handiwork of Buddhist priests, who have acquired the requisite skill by casting images of Buddha! The Buddhist priests are said to be the chief money-lenders and usurers, and it is whispered that they contribute rather a large proportion to the catalogue of felons, though, to avoid scandal, they are generally unrobed before trial. Some years ago, however, one was hanged in full canonicals, just to show that British law is no respecter of persons.

As regards deaths from violence or accident, the statistics for 1889 show that during that year inquests were held in the Isle on the bodies of 2166 persons. But there must have been many more whose deaths was never heard of—

men and women who from sickness or weakness perished by lonely roadsides, or were killed by wild beasts in jungles, or murdered and secretly buried, to say nothing of those drowned in the sea, the rivers, lakes, and tanks. Among the details of these deaths are 125 suicides, of whom 21 drowned themselves and the rest hanged themselves; 121 died from snake-bites, 87 by accidentally drowning in rivers and tanks, 134 by falling into wells, 383 by falling from trees, and 33 from gunshot wounds. (The increasing misuse of firearms forms a notable feature in recent police reports.) Almost every year wild beasts are responsible for a certain proportion of deaths; bears, elephants, chetahs, boars, buffaloes, alligators, and even hornets and bees, each doing their part in thus thinning the population.

To glance at the pleasanter aspects of police-work in Ceylon, one of Mr. Campbell's most successful schemes has been the Servants' Registration Ordinance, by which every servant is bound to have a pocket register, in which his antecedents are recorded, as are also the beginning and end of each new service, and the character he has acquired in each. The registrars are assistant-superintendents of police. The scheme has proved invaluable in the prevention of one of the commonest forms of burglary, made easy by the connivance of servants.

Alas! here as elsewhere familiarity with the white race does not always tend to raise them in the veneration of their brown brothers. Mr. Campbell says : " The days have gone by in which we could leave the house-door unbarred during the night. Much of the old contentedness and of the old respect for the European has gone, and new wants and excitements—amongst them drinking and gambling—must be satisfied."

In a country whose wealth consists so largely in its crops, these, of course, are a continual source of temptation to thieves, not only in the wide extent of growing crops, which it is scarcely possible for planters to guard, but still more when these are gathered and travelling from the store to the market. Take, for instance, the transport of coffee from a plantation in Uva to Colombo, a distance of perhaps two hundred miles, by road, river, and either lake or rail. Each cart-load is worth about 1000 rupees, each boat-load about 10,000 rupees.

Under the old system each cart-load was intrusted to the sole care of a carter, and each boat-load to that of a crew, of whom, in either case, "the senders generally knew absolutely nothing, and in whose honesty they had every cause to disbelieve!" The consequence was that whole cart-loads sometimes disappeared. In one case the police had the satisfaction of convicting a carter and a native agent who had thus appropriated 400 bushels of coffee, valued at 4500 rupees! Less audacious thieves were content with freely helping themselves from the coffee-bags. These carts were lost sight of for weeks; and the coffee which travelled from Ratnapura to Colombo by river, canal, and lake was at the mercy of the boatmen, who could halt for as many days as they saw fit, and call the aid of their families to manipulate it as they pleased.

So that throughout its long journey the coffee was subject to pilfering at the hands of drivers, boatmen, and other depredators, who sometimes stole half the good beans and filled up the sacks with inferior ones, or else made up weight and bulk by swelling the remainder with water, so that it reached the London market deteriorated in colour and in value.

To counteract this mischief, Mr. Campbell devised a simple and very effectual system of cart registration. He established police-stations at regular intervals along the road and river from Ratnapura to Kalutara (whence the sea-coast railway conveys the freight to Colombo), and each loaded cart or boat is compelled to report itself at each of these stations, whence the exact date of its arrival and start is intimated day by day to the Chamber of Commerce at Colombo. Thus the precious produce is under strict care throughout its journey, and theft becomes well-nigh impossible.

The regulation of pilgrimages and the strict sanitation of pilgrim camps is another of the schemes devised and excellently enforced by Mr. Campbell, thereby preventing a very large amount of suffering and mortality, and the too probable development of cholera in the Isle.

The system of police registration of all dogs is so rigidly enforced in the principal towns, that Ceylon is in a great measure exempt from hydrophobia. Each registered dog must wear a stamped municipal collar, obtained by his owner on payment of a small fee, and any luckless dogs not provided with this safeguard are captured and carried in a large cage on wheels to a pond, where, unless claimed within forty-eight hours, they are either shot or drowned (by bodily immersing the cage in water).

A matter which has involved much care and thought has been how to check cruelty to animals in this land, where (by the teaching of Buddha being carried out in the letter and utterly neglected in the spirit) life must not be taken —at least not the life of lower animals, for that of human beings is by no means so secure! But suffering is of no consequence. The cruelty so common in Ceylon is not wanton, as in too many countries, but seems to arise from sheer callousness to the tortures which are carelessly inflicted on poor suffering creatures. Thus deer, hares, snipe, doves, &c., badly wounded and with broken bones, are kept alive for days and hawked about in hopes of obtaining a sale. Six or eight fowls are tightly tied together by the feet, and are then strung, head downwards, from the ends of a stick balanced on the shoulder, and are thus carried for miles, cackling in anguish, till they are too weak and suffering to do so any more. Even the lovely little green parroquets are not exempt from cruel treatment. Large numbers are captured in the neighbourhood of Chilaw, and crammed into mat bags, the mouth of which is tied up, and these are carried, slung from the ends of a stick, all the way to Colombo, where the survivors find a ready market.

Fat pigs are thus fastened to a stick, carried between two men, the cord by which their poor legs are tied cutting deep into the flesh, and causing such pain that the wretched pig sometimes dies ere reaching his destination. The system of branding cattle by burning elaborate patterns all over them (to the destruction of the hide) is justified by the plea that doing so prevents rheumatism. Whether it does so or not, it assuredly causes the poor beast excruciating agony.

Worst of all is the barbarity, formerly commonly practised in the open market, and not yet wholly put down, of selling large live turtles piecemeal, each purchaser pointing out the exact slice he desired, while the wretched fellow-creature lay writhing and gasping in agony for hours, till the last-comer came to claim the heart and head, the latter being the only vital part; for, wonderful to tell, turtles continue to live and suffer after the heart has been cut out.

The commonest form in which cruelty is now apparent is in over-driving wretched worn-out horses, which are too often brutally beaten to make them drag weights far beyond their strength.

In 1862 a law was enacted for the protection of domestic animals, elephants, and turtles, but it does not appear to have been strictly enforced till about ten years ago. In 1881, however, the police were exhorted to greater diligence in this matter, with such excellent effect that since that date there have been upwards of 3000 convictions under this head. Moreover, a strong Society for the Prevention of Cruelty to Animals has now been formed, which it is hoped will prove a valuable auxiliary to the police. In the first six months of 1891 it secured convictions of cruelty against 229 persons in Colombo alone.

In addition to the regular duties of the police, a severe strain of work occasionally arises from external causes. Such was the famine in Southern India in 1877, from which time till 1880 thousands of poor starved creatures found their way to Ceylon, hoping to obtain employment on the estates, but who from weakness and illness were totally unable to work.

These helpless creatures, men, women, and children, reduced by starvation to mere apathy, were collected from the roadsides. Hundreds were found dead or dying, and received decent burial. The survivors were carried to temporary hospitals, where they were cared for and fed till they were able to work or travel, when they were helped on their journey, the naked being furnished with needful clothing, and free passages to India provided for such as longed to return to their own homes. So cheaply was this managed, that the average cost of the journey for each coolie was under two rupees. Food for the voyage was also provided, and a small sum to keep them from starvation on their journey from the coast to their own village.

A very onerous "occasional duty" is the care of the pearl-fishery, as may well be imagined, were it only in guarding the sanitation of the huge camp of 10,000 persons on the arid sea-beach, to which are daily brought millions of oysters to putrefy in the burning sun. The presence of about sixty police is required for about eighty days, during which they have charge of everything. They must strictly guard the only available drinking-water; they are responsible for the orderly and punctual start of all the boats, numbering about two hundred, and for seeing that each is escorted by a member of the civil boatguard, who must never sail twice with the same tindal and crew. The boats start at midnight and return the following afternoon, when the oysters are carried ashore in baskets, and the European police have to keep close watch during the unloading, and then, in all weather, to wade out and search the boats to see that no oysters have been secreted. They must also ceaselessly guard the enclosure within which the precious shells are stored, for when an uncomfortable oyster gapes, and reveals a tempting pearl, there are plenty of eager coolies ready to snatch it up and swallow it, or, if it is small enough, they might conceal it under a long finger-nail. But so well do the police guard the treasure, that there is no reason to believe that either the pearls or the large sums of money brought for their purchase are ever stolen.

Having discoursed at such length on the police and their manifold duties, I may add that Ceylon has now also a very efficient volunteer regiment—the Ceylon Light

Infantry Corps, which in 1885 numbered 930, including officers. Like the police, this force is composed of representatives of all the nationalities on the Isle, namely, 200 British-born, 454 Eurasians, 86 Malays, 53 Tamils, 107 Singhalese, and 33 others. The headquarters of the force are at Colombo, but companies are stationed at Kandy, Badulla, and Kurunegalla.

Long may it be ere they are called out to defend the beautiful Isle against foreign foes !

[1] Since the retirement of Sir G. W. R. Campbell from public service, the police force in each province has been placed under the direction of the Government Agent, who is held responsible for the suppression of crime and for the maintenance of order. Under these circumstances, there is room for hope that there will henceforth be less zeal in promoting a more extensive sale of arrack.

CHAPTER XXIV.

IN THE PLANTING DISTRICTS.

Kurunegalla—Monastery of Lanka Tileka—On Allegalla Peak—A footprint—Gangarowa—In the planting districts—The Wilderness of the Peak in 1849 and now—Lack of fuel—King Coffee *versus* King Tea—Insect foes—Cacao—A planter's cares—Sick coolies—Names of estates.

AMONG the various cities which in ancient and mediæval ages successively ranked as the capital of the Isle are Kurunegalla, anciently called Hastisailapura, and Gampola, formerly called Ganga-sri-pura, "the sacred city beside the river." The former, which is 58 miles from Colombo, was the Royal residence and that of the precious Tooth from A.D. 1319 to A.D. 1347, when Gampola had its turn.

Taking the train from Colombo to Polgahawella station, a crowded native coach carried me thence to Kurunegalla, "the beetle rock," which is so named from a huge almost bare mass of reddish gneiss rock, shaped like a gigantic beetle. The country hereabouts is doted with these enormous red rounded rocks, one of which bears some resemblance to a kneeling elephant, and is hence called Actagalla, "the rock of the tusk elephant." It is a goodly mass, three miles in length, and towers to a height of 600 feet above the plain and 1096 above the sea. The pretty little town and lake lie at the base of the great rock, which is of just the same character as that at Dambool and others which we had seen on the way to Anuradhapura. Here the zoological suggestions include an "Eel Rock" and a "Tortoise Rock."

The country from which rise these cyclopean boulders of red rock is a level expanse of fertile rice-land, interspersed with palms and all the vegetation of the hottest districts; for hot it is in truth, as is evident from the great tree-cactuses which flourish in the crevices of the rock.

An important industry of this district is plumbago-mining, or rather pit-digging, as it has hitherto been carried on somewhat superficially by native merchants. Hundreds of men are, however, employed, and thousands of tons are annually brought hence to Colombo.

The Government Agent's house, in which I was hospitably entertained—a pleasant red-tiled bungalow, with wide white-pillared verandah—occupies the site of the Maligawa, the ancient palace of the kings of Kandy, as is attested by suggestive sculptured stones and fragments of pillars, a favourite resting-place for peacocks of splendid plumage.

But more striking than these are the majestic trees which cover the ground as in a magnificent park, their huge stems supported by wide-spreading roots, which cover the ground for a very wide radius, forming buttresses like low walls. Some of these are so deep that a man standing near the base of the tree can only just rest his arm on one of the roots. The most remarkable of these are the Kon and Labu trees; there are also great India-rubber trees, whose roots, though not forming such high walls, are equally remarkable and labyrinthine.

The town is little more than a village with native bazaar and neat bungalows, each in a pleasant garden, inhabited chiefly by Burghers of Dutch and Portuguese extraction. Steep paths and rock-hewn steps lead to the summit of the rock, near which is a level space between two shoulders of rock—a green oasis of cocoa-palms and other fruit-trees, among which stands a large dagoba containing a model of the holy footprint on Adam's Peak (the Peak itself, about forty miles distant, being visible from this point). Pilgrims come here from all parts of the island, partly to visit some ruins on the extreme summit, which are those of a temple wherein Buddha's venerated Tooth was stored during four reigns, after it had been brought here from Pollanarua in A.D. 1319.

Of course, the view from this isolated height is very extensive and very fine, but the heat radiating from the sun-scorched rocks was well-nigh unbearable, and suggestive of sunstroke, which, however, strange to say, is of very rare occurrence in Ceylon. I was glad to descend to the cool shade of the great trees, and to drive at sunset beside the still lake and its lilies. We went to call on the Moodliar, to see a bright yellow parroquet, which is quite unique. It was captured in a flock of the usual bright emerald-green ones, which abound here, as elsewhere, throughout the low country.

A few days later found me at Gampola, which for a little season succeeded Kurunegalla as capital of Ceylon. It is a very pretty place, and I have happy memories of pleasant evenings of peaceful boating on the lovely bamboo-fringed river; but on this occasion I only halted here on my way with friends to visit the very interesting ancient Buddhist temple of Lanka Tileka, which was erected by King

Bhuwaneka-Bahu IV. in A.D. 1344. In Ceylon a temple which has only stood for five centuries is comparatively modern, but this one is at least old enough to be exceedingly picturesque, with walls, partly red, partly white, several storeys high, and high-pitched roofs with dull-red tiles.

It is most beautifully situated on the crown of a great mass of red rock, which rises in the centre of a rock basin like an inverted cup standing in a bowl. I own the simile is not romantic, but it just describes how the grand rock rises from the deep circular valley, all devoted to rice-fields, which at the time of my visit were flooded, like innumerable blue curving lakes, separated by their embankments.

With the exception of the bare summit, on which the monastery stands so conspicuously, the whole basin is densely clothed with the most luxuriant tropical vegetation that can be conceived. From a dense undergrowth of huge plantain and banana leaves tower clusters of tall areca, kitool, cocoa, and various other palms, with here and there a magnificent talipat-palm rearing its stately head far above its fellows, or else a dark bread-fruit or jak tree. (The kitool is the palm with fronds like gigantic maidenhair fern.) In short, all manner of fruit and flower bearing trees flourish in perfection in this sheltered valley.

We drove as far as wheels could travel, and there bearers, with a wicker arm-chair securely attached to bamboos, were in readiness to carry me the rest of the way. The Government Agent had kindly sent instructions to the Ratamahatmeya, the great local authority, who, with permission of the chief priest, had prepared for us the Bana Madoowa, or preaching-hall, which stands a short distance below the temple. Here we found two comfortable bedrooms and dining-room hung with calico, and otherwise ready for us. Strange to say, only one-fifth of this temple is in the hands of the Buddhists. The other four parts are *dewali* or Hindoo, to which, we were told, there was "no admittance," and that even the Buddhist priests might not or would not enter.

I regretted this the less, as the exterior is so picturesque that I gladly devoted all my time to secure a large sketch of the whole scene from across the valley, in presence of a crowd of Singhalese women and children, who, however, fled at every heavy rain-shower. The leeches were not so easily routed, and were most persistent in their attentions; but one cannot have such glorious vegetation without some drawbacks, and the loveliness of the clear moonlight fully compensated for the tearful day.

One of the temple buildings is edged with extremely effective hanging tiles edging the upper roof. Each forms a right angle, the ornamental front being about fifteen inches in length, decorated with a flower scroll and imaginary lion. Some of these had fallen (for the place was much neglected), and, with consent of the priest, I carried one back to Britain, thinking that some one would be glad of the design as a decorative touch for a school or fancy dairy; but it only found a welcome in a museum, I think at Inverness.

Returning by rail from Gampola to Kaduganawa station, I was there met by very kind friends, who had brought a chair fastened to bamboos, and a party of luggage-coolies to carry me and my goods to their delightful bungalow (Oolanakanda), perched far up the steep face of Allegalla Peak. The many pleasant days which on several occasions I spent in that sweet home, with its music and flowers and

sunny faces, are among my happiest memories of Ceylon. I only wish it were possible for words to convey something of the charm of such surroundings, of majestic crags, clear streams, and fruit-bearing trees, with varied cultivation, chiefly coffee, on the most impossible-looking ground—so steep and rocky; and all this at such a height that, looking up from the railway far below, one could only imagine an eagle's eerie perched at such a height.

Of course the outlook thence was a dream of delight, whether on clear days, when each field in the great cultivated plain well-nigh two thousand feet below us, and each farthest mountain peak, was faultlessly defined; or when, as occasionally in the early mornings, the whole valley was hidden by fleecy clouds of rolling mist, like a vast sea, dotted with dark wooded isles, which are the summits of hills. So steep was the hill-face, that it seemed as though we could almost have thrown pebbles from those cool heights to alight in the tropics only a trifle above the sea-level.

One day we climbed to the very summit of the Peak (3394 feet above the sea), there to inspect a large artificial hollow in the rock in imitation of Buddha's footprint on Adam's Peak. This one is well defined, and makes no pretension to being genuine. It is simply representative, and worshippers who cannot make pilgrimage to the true Sri Pada climb up here, to make their simple offerings, while looking towards Adam's Peak, which rises sharp and clear on the horizon.

At that high level even unsettled weather was a positive gain, for the radiant sunshine alternating with down-pours of rain produced endlessly varied cloud and storm effects, and certain sunsets remain stamped on my memory, when the uplifting of heavy curtains of purple cloud revealed dreamy glimpses of blue-green sky, and then gleams of fiery gold and lurid red shed an unearthly light on clouds and mountains.

Before each rain-storm there was a strange oppressive stillness, followed by an awakening breeze, with stormy gusts sweeping up chilling mists, which preceded the heavy rain. A few moments later and down it poured in sheets, transforming dry paths into beds of rushing torrents, and swelling tiny rivulets to impassable floods.

One day I was sitting alone under the shelter of some great masses of rock fallen from the crag overhead, and being absorbed in my sketching, took no heed of a terrific thunderstorm which broke right overhead, followed by pitiless rain. The friendly rocks sheltered me so effectually, that I purposed remaining in sanctuary till the storm was over, when suddenly down came a torrent from the hill above, pouring right through my nest.

In the sudden scramble to save my various possessions, I laid my paint-box on a high ledge and clambered back to rescue my picture and its waterproof cover. By the time I got out of this trap, the water was up to my knees, and all the way back the path was crossed by countless extempore streams, all above my ankles. It was a tiring walk, and I was glad to reach the friendly bungalow once more.

But imagine my dismay on finding that, in the hurry of flight, I had left the precious paint-box on the rocky ledge, whence in all probability it had been washed away by the flood! Such a loss would have been utterly irreparable; so there was nothing for it but to divest myself of all unnecessary raiment, and retrace my steps as quickly as possible, in the hope of retrieving this dear companion of my wanderings. To my inexpressible delight I found it high and dry, the spate having passed just below it, so I returned in triumph.

By the time these mountain torrents have reached the railway level far below, they have gathered such volume and such impetus, that a sudden thunderstorm sometimes renders the line impassable, owing to the rush of waters across it, or falling in muddy cascades right on to it. Trains occasionally receive shower-baths by no means in the programme, and the rice-fields in the valley are all suddenly transformed to lakes.

This was my first experience of a planter's home, one of many in all parts of the Isle, differing in many respects, according to situation, and consequent cultivation, but all alike in the warm-hearted cordial hospitality which made each successive visit so pleasant.

Another delightful home in which I found repeated welcome was Gangarowa, a most lovely estate on the banks of the beautiful Mahavelli River, opposite the Peradenya Botanical Gardens.

This was the first plantation started by Sir Edward Barnes in 1825, when he had opened up the country by making the road to Kandy. All planting being then experimental, a little of everything was tried, so that instead of the monotony of a large estate all devoted to one product, Gangarowa had the charm of infinite variety. Sad experience has now taught most planters the wisdom of not carrying all their eggs in one basket; but when I was in Ceylon, King Coffee reigned supreme, and in many districts literally nothing else was cultivated over an area of many miles. In every direction, as far as the eye could reach, up hill and down dale, it was all coffee, coffee, coffee.

Of course, such uniformity was singularly unattractive, and as I passed from one great coffee district to another in various parts of Dimbula, Dickoya, Maskeliya, Kalibooka, The Knuckles, Deltotte, &c., I confess to having often longed for some of the vanished glories of the forests of which I had heard so much from earlier settlers on the Isle, who had told me how between the clearings there remained hundreds of exquisite little nooks with streams trickling under tree-ferns, green dragonflies skimming over quiet pools and glorious forest-trees overhead; instead of which I found every ravine denuded, and the totally unshaded streams avenging themselves by washing as much soil as possible from the roots of the nearest coffee-trees.

But if those earlier settlers saw Ceylon in greater beauty than do those of the present generation, they also had to face very much harder conditions of life, living perhaps sixteen miles or more from even a cart-road, and feeding on salt beef and biscuit—never by any chance tasting milk, bread, or potatoes.

Now few need have such rough fare, and many of the married men have the cosiest of houses, enlivened by music and singing, new books and magazines, happy healthy children, excellent food, pleasant intercourse with neighbours— in short, all that can tend to make the wheels of life glide smoothly.

In truth, it is difficult to realise that it is less than half a century since the whole Central Province, right up to the very summit of the highest mountains, was clothed with dense impenetrable forests, so rapidly have they disappeared before the diligent and ruthless hands of indefatigable planters. Indeed, so precious has every acre become, that comparatively few men even allow themselves a garden round their own bungalows, though with the smallest care such a garden becomes a tiny paradise, where orange, lime, and other fruit-bearing trees, gardenias and scarlet lilies, and all manner of fragrant and gorgeous blossoms grow in endless profusion.

A few such gardens we did see, and therein lingered with delight beneath the cool shadow of large orange-trees, laden with blossom and ripe fruit, on which we feasted with all the more enjoyment after toiling for hours through dreary clearings. As a rule, however, such an oasis is rarely to be met with; and I grieve to say that even where some tasteful planters of the last generation had bordered their roads with hedges of delicious roses, a joy to all passers-by, new owners, in their thirst for gold, uprooted the blessed flowers in order to gain room for one more row of nasty little bushes (as I delighted in calling the young coffee-trees, to aggravate my friends of the planting community).

Of course, in a wholesale clearing, no precious morsel of forest *could* be reserved; so the man who craved for one shady tree to overshadow his house must plant it himself and wait till it grew, otherwise he could hope for nothing more imposing than his own coffee shrubs, whose allotted height is 3 feet or 3 feet 6 inches, according to their position; beyond this, the British planter does not suffer his bushes to grow, though round the native houses they attain to the size of Portugal laurels in this country, and notwithstanding this liberty bear a luxuriant crop of scarlet berries.

So the general effect of a district which has recently been taken into cultivation is singularly hideous. Far as the eye can reach, range beyond range of hills all show the same desolate expanse of blackened tree-trunks, for the most part felled, but a certain number still upright; a weird and dreary scene, as you would think had you to toil up and down these steep hills in the burning sun, thinking, oh! how regretfully, of the cool green forest shade which has been so ruthlessly destroyed.

Sometimes this contrast was brought very vividly before us when the path along which we were to travel formed a boundary-line between the reclaimed and unreclaimed land—the one so dismal, with scorching sun beating in all its fierceness on the black prostrate trunks, tossed in wild confusion among the rocks, the other fresh and pleasant to the eye, with an undergrowth of exquisite tree-ferns and a thousand other forms of beauty growing in rank luxuriance, and telling of cool hidden streamlets that trickle beneath the shade of great trees, many of them matted with brilliant flowering creepers, or studded with tufts of orchids—flowers of the mist.

Very soon the glory of the primeval forests will be altogether a tale of the past so far as the hill districts are concerned, for a few years hence, the tree-ferns and scarlet rhododendrons, and all such useless jungle loveliness, will have utterly vanished. Nature is very forgiving, however; for wherever a planter is found so careless as to suffer an encroaching weed (and I am bound to confess such graceful slovenliness is rare), she clothes the steep banks and cuttings along the road with a wilderness of dainty ferns of every sort, and the richest tangle of a magnified edition of our stag's-horn moss, which grows in wildest luxuriance.

After all, even while bewailing the destruction of beautiful forests, we were driven to confess that but for the labours of the planters the glories of the interior must have remained to us sealed books. As it was, we travelled hither and thither, and explored scenes which but a few years ago would have been to us simply unattainable.

When in 1840 Lieutenant Skinner ascended Adam's Peak, and looking down from that high summit on range beyond range all densely clothed with pathless forest, totally impenetrable save where elephants had cleared roads for themselves, he foretold that this region was destined ere long to become the garden of Ceylon—a garden of European as well as tropical productions, peopled with European as well as Asiatic faces—he was jeered at for his prediction.

Yet he maintained his conviction; for "who," he said, "can enjoy this perfect climate—thermometer at 68°—without feeling that it would be conferring a blessing on humanity, by clearing this trackless wilderness of from 200,000 to 300,000 acres of forest, to be the means of removing some 20,000 of the panting, half-famished creatures from the burning sandy plains of Southern India to such comparative paradise, and also benefiting our own Singhalese people inhabiting the margin of this wilderness, now compelled to hide in places scarcely accessible to man, in order to render their dwellings inaccessible to elephants, and many of them unable to cultivate a grain of paddy or to procure a morsel of salt?"

Major Skinner lived long enough to see the ancient inhabitants of the Isle, the immigrant labourers from the coast of Coromandel, and European planters all working peacefully side by side on reclaimed lands. But sad to say, the opening up of the country and the influx of foreign gold did not prove unmixed advantages. In 1849 Major Skinner had to report that "the most profligate of the low-country Singhalese had flocked from the maritime provinces into the interior, and spread their contaminating influences far and wide over a previously sober, orderly, honest race. Robberies and bloodshed had become familiar to the Kandyan in districts where a few years before any amount of property would have been perfectly safe in the open air."

Moreover, he had to report that the vice of intemperance had become an enormous evil, and one which was rapidly gaining ground. The system of the Government sale of arrack-farms was already in full force, and yielding a revenue of about £60,000 a year.

"It is, of course," he says, "the object of the renter to sublet as many of these taverns as possible; they are established in almost every village of any size throughout the interior, often to the great annoyance of the inhabitants, and in opposition to the headmen. To give the people a taste for the use of spirits, it is often, at first, necessary to distribute it gratuitously, the tavern-keepers well knowing that, with the use, the abuse follows as a certainty. I have known districts in which, some years ago, not one in a hundred could be induced to taste spirits, where drunkenness now prevails to such an extent that villagers have been known to pawn their crops upon the ground to tavern-keepers for arrack."

Forty years have elapsed since those lines were penned, and of those great forests, then known as "The Wilderness of the Peak," scarcely a vestige remains, fully 300,000 acres being now under cultivation, traversed by carriage-roads, and dotted over with European homes and such important villages as Maskeliya, Dickoya, St. Clair, Craigie-Lea, &c.

So fully has the prediction been carried out, that Nanuoya, the present railway terminus, which twenty years ago lay in the heart of untouched jungle, is now a centre of such busy life that last year it received and despatched no less than 21,090 telegrams on railway business, without counting private messages;[1] while a daily average of seventy goods waggons, laden with very varied products, were despatched thence, and as many more daily arrived from the low country.

Now that the steed has been stolen, and vast tracts totally denuded of forest, Government has wisely interfered to preserve some fragments in the remaining districts, and also by reserving a narrow belt of timber on the banks of streams and around their source; also by prohibiting the clearing of mountain ridges. But so ruthless and utterly improvident has been the wholesale destruction of the forests, that now, whatever timber is necessary for estate purposes, such as building or any form of carpentering, must be purchased, and planters in many districts have to employ coolies on purpose to fetch firewood from long distances.

Efforts are now being made to correct past errors by planting foreign trees, especially the quick-growing Australian trees, which adapt themselves most readily to the soil. Amongst these are the yarrah, casuarina, wattle, and other acacias. The wattle, however, from the extraordinary distance to which it spreads its roots, proved such an encroaching colonist, that it became necessary to eradicate it totally. But the various Eucalypti, *i.e.*, the Australian gums, have proved true friends in need, and develop in a manner worthy of their great Fatherland. On some estates at an elevation of 5000 feet, blue gums have been found to grow a foot per month in the rainy season, and about six inches per month for the other half of the year! So these

---

[1] At Colombo, in the same year, the railway telegrams received and despatched numbered 20,955, and post-office telegrams 50,187.

gigantic young Australians attain a height of upwards of sixty feet within five years!

As I have said, at the time of my visit to Ceylon, King Coffee held undisputed sway, and his name was on every lip. Coffee—coffee—coffee—its rise and fall in the market—its snowy blossoms—its promise of crop—the ravages of coffee-bug or leaf-disease, these were the topics on which the changes were rung morning, noon, and night—but especially at night over the pipes, which took (what seemed to us, vainly courting sleep) such an interminable time to smoke. For this is one disadvantage in the construction of all Eastern houses that I have ever seen. They are so built that every room has the benefit of all its neighbour's conversation, to say nothing of that which goes on in the verandah outside the windows. Moreover, to secure ventilation, the interior of most bungalows is merely divided by partitions reaching to a certain height, and above that is the tightly-stretched white canvas which checks the falling of fragments from the high-peaked roof.

In the mountain districts the houses are of a somewhat British type, having boarded floors, well raised above the ground as a precaution against damp, and fireplaces in most rooms. Where the carriage of brick from the low country, or even stone from the mountain quarry, would be too costly, these houses are chiefly built of wood trellised with bamboo, and the interstices filled with clay and plastered over.

Alas! very soon after the days of which I speak, King Coffee fell from his throne; the grievous leaf-disease appeared in all its virulence, and tens of thousands of acres on the most flourishing estates were left desolate, clothed with withered diseased shrubs scarcely fit for firewood.

This cruel disease (*Hemileia Vestatrix*) is a fungus which appears in the form of orange-coloured spots on the leaf, which presently drops off, and the shrub is sometimes left leafless and apparently dead. Perhaps soon afterwards it is again covered with leaves, but again the deadly fungus reappears. It was first observed in Ceylon in May 1869 on a few plants in one of the eastern districts, whence it attacked a few acres, then spread like wildfire over the whole coffee region. It appeared simultaneously in other Eastern countries—came and conquered—while grubs attacked the roots and brown bugs sapped the life-blood of the once flourishing shrubs.

Everything that ingenuity and despair could suggest was tried in vain—collecting and burning the diseased leaves, high manuring, wholesale pruning. The destructive fungus held its ground, and the sorely-tried planters in too many cases were literally driven to abandon the lands which they could not afford to work, and to seek employment under newcomers, who, after the lapse of a few sad years, brought fresh supplies of gold wherewith to test new products. Tea, cinchona, cacao, and various other crops were planted experimentally, with the result that Ceylon is now more flourishing than ever, with splendidly varied products, including coffee, which in some districts is now as fine and as healthy as ever, but the reigning monarch now is TEA, whose supremacy is scarcely likely ever to be disputed.

But before speaking of this new king, I will briefly glance at the history of coffee in Ceylon. To begin with, it is a singular fact that not only a very large proportion of all the coffee that once clothed these thousand hills in Ceylon, but also the coffee plantations of many other lands are all lineally descended from one plant, which, about A.D. 1690, was raised in a garden at Batavia by the Dutch governor, General Van Hoorne, to whom a few seeds had been presented by a trader from the Arabian Gulf.

These took so kindly to the soil of Java, that coffee plantations were established, and a plant was sent to the Botanic Gardens at Amsterdam. Thence young plants, reared from its seeds, were forwarded to Surinam, which in its turn sent a supply to various of the West Indian Isles. Wherever the young plants arrived, plantations were started, and meanwhile Java had sent supplies to Sumatra, Celebes, Bali, the Philippines, and Ceylon.

To the latter, however, the plant had already been brought, probably by Arab traders, but the secret of its fragrant berries had remained undiscovered. It was planted as an ornamental shrub about the king's palace and near the temples of Buddha, on whose altars its delicate starry blossoms were laid as offerings. A beverage was prepared from its leaves, which also found favour in making curry, but it was not till the Dutch revealed the hidden mystery that the art of roasting coffee-beans dawned upon them.

The Dutch, however, committed the blunder of making their plantations in the low-lying, thoroughly tropical districts of Galle and Negombo, both on the sea-coast. The result was highly unfavourable, and in 1739 the attempt to cultivate coffee was abandoned by the foreigners, but carried on by the Singhalese, who continued growing it on a small scale.

This continued till about the year 1825, when the English governor, Sir Edward Barnes, having opened up the hill-country by making a road to Kandy, bethought him of making an experimental plantation at this height. He obtained splendid crops from the virgin soil of those rich forest lands, and so successful an example was quickly followed. Free grants of Crown-land were so eagerly taken up, that 5s. per acre was charged, at which price some men abstained from buying.

Forty years later, choice land in full cultivation was sold at prices ranging from £100 to £130 per acre.

But ere then, the fortunes of coffee-planters were subject to strange vicissitudes. The golden harvest reaped by those first in the field attracted an eager throng of speculators of every rank, all hasting to secure Ceylon estates, and it has been stated that something like £5,000,000 was thus invested, when suddenly, in 1845, there came a terrible financial crisis in Europe, the effects of which on prices and credit shook the new industry of Ceylon to its very foundations.

Then, as a climax of evil, came the declaration of Free Trade, admitting the coffee of Java and Brazil to British markets on equal terms with that of Ceylon. These tidings of woe produced a panic which resulted in wide-spread ruin. In the consternation of the moment, estates were forced into the market and sold for a tithe or a twentieth of the money that had been expended on them. One estate, which three years previously had been purchased for £15,000, was sold for £440; two purchased for £10,000 apiece respectively realised £500 and £350; while for others no offer could be obtained, so they were abandoned and allowed to relapse to jungle. It has been estimated that probably one-tenth of the estates originally opened were thus abandoned.

Yet so quickly does time bring its revenges, that twenty years later the scale was reversed, and estates bought for a few hundreds were sold for many thousands sterling. In the midst of this lamentable crisis, the Bank of Ceylon stopped payment, losing heavily on large loans advanced to planters. Its business was, however, taken up by the Western Bank of India, which thereupon assumed the name of the Oriental Bank Corporation. It must be noted as a singular coincidence, that the career commenced under such adverse influences should have ended during the late almost equally calamitous time of commercial depression, in like manner rising Phœnix-like from its own ashes in the form of the new Oriental Bank Corporation.

By 1870 about 150,000 acres of mountain forest had been cleared and replaced by coffee, of which the annual export rose to 974,333 cwts., representing a value not far short of £5,000,000. That proved to be the highest point ever attained in the fulfilment of the coffee-planter's dream —a vision golden indeed, but, like the splendour of a gorgeous sunset, it heralded the stormy change which too quickly followed. A little cloud had been rising, at first scarcely deemed worthy of notice, yet all too quickly it had overshadowed the whole land, and the fair crops were all stricken by cruel blight. It was the old story of the seven lean kine which devoured the fat fair kine of previous years, for the years that followed were truly years of famine.

The destroying angel in the present instance came in the form of the humble fungus, of which I have already spoken —the orange-coloured spots on the leaves. At first it was hoped that it might prove merely local and be stamped out. That hope, however, proved delusive, for in an incredibly short period it overspread the whole land, and was unhappily exported even to the young colony of Fiji, where coffee, introduced with much care by Government, had previously been flourishing. To make matters worse, a green bug, as thirsty as the brown bug of past years, came to feast on the life-juices of the poor sick shrubs.

For some years the story of Ceylon was one cry of lamentation and mourning and woe. The fair Isle seemed sick unto death, and many gave up all hope of her recovery. Night seemed settling down to ever-deepening darkness, a night of chill mists, in which "poortith cauld" entered unbidden—the first guest that ever failed of a welcome to the ever-hospitable homes of the Ceylon planters. Then many a brave hard-working man, who had invested his whole capital, and probably borrowed money besides on the estate that seemed so secure, found it totally impossible to tide over the evil hour.

Where the calamity was so wide-spread as to cripple some of the great mercantile firms and involve all in serious anxiety, it became a hopeless matter for individuals to obtain credit, and when no money was forthcoming even to pay coolies' wages, there was in many cases no alternative but simply to abandon the land, and thousands of acres were thus left to relapse into jungle, and the estate buildings were left to go to ruin.

True to the axiom that misfortunes never come singly, the Oriental Bank, which in the terrible crisis of 1845 had so gallantly come to the rescue, now (partly owing to heavy insular losses) found itself compelled to stop payment, thereby adding so seriously to the general commercial complication as to threaten general bankruptcy. In this very grave complication, the Governor, the Hon. Sir Arthur Hamilton Gordon, took upon himself the responsibility of giving Government security for all the Bank's notes circulating in the island, to the value of 3,000,000 rupees—a prompt and energetic measure, which restored public confidence and averted untold mischief.

Never was there a more splendid instance of the advantage of acting for the best and asking leave afterwards. It was a tremendous responsibility for a Colonial Governor to undertake, and there is every reason to believe that had the question been referred first to the Home Government it would have been vetoed. As it was, it proved a splendid success, and saved many a house from ruin. Equally successful was the establishment of Government currency notes, which not only relieved the island from temporary difficulty, but already yield the colonial exchequer an annual profit approaching 200,000 rupees.

The darkest hour is ever next the dawning, and shortly before the coffee crisis had become serious, experimental tea plantations had been started at various altitudes, and all with complete success, the snowy blossoms of the tea shrubs—*Camellia theifera*—forming a pleasing variety on the monotony of the ever-present coffee, beautiful as it was, with its sheets of fragrant blossoms or its clusters of green, yellow, scarlet, and crimson cherries. Here then was a rainbow of promise for the future, and such planters as were still able to raise sufficient capital for another venture grasped the situation, and grappled with the new industry with the semi-despairing energy of men who knew it to be their last resource.

Happily on many estates it was decided not at once to uproot diseased coffee, but give it a chance of recovery, while tea shrubs were planted all over the ground; and well it is that this was done, as in many cases on estates which had been abandoned as past hope, the leafless bushes, which were apparently dead, recovered as if from a trance, and putting forth fresh leaves, yielded fair crops of berries, albeit struggling for existence with the too luxuriant weeds and scrub, which had been allowed to grow unheeded. On estates where it has been again taken into cultivation, excellent returns have been obtained, notably in Uva, where on a single branch, which in September 1890 was cut as "a specimen" of the crop on the Albion estate, no less than 954 berries were counted.

So there is now once more good hope for the future of coffee, and its advocates point out how scourges well-nigh as grievous as leaf-disease have ravaged certain crops in divers lands, yet have eventually worn themselves out. Thus in Ceylon about the year 1866 coffee was grievously afflicted by a black bug, which was first observed in 1843 on a few bushes in the district of Madulsima, but thence spread and multiplied till it had attacked every estate, and was officially recognised as a permanent pest; yet so completely has it passed away, that it now ranks as a comparatively rare visitor.

While searching for any natural cause which might account for the origin of a plague so virulent and widespread as the leaf-disease, it has been suggested that some such result very frequently follows the disturbance of Nature's system of blending innumerable varieties of vegetation.

Man clears great tracts of forest or plain, and plants the whole with one product, and ere long his vines develop phylloxera, his potatoes are attacked by blight or Colorado beetle, his great wheat plains are spoiled by rust. In Mysore a slimy leaf-disease attacks his coffee; in Brazil, and likewise in Dominica, great tracts of the same are destroyed by a burrowing grub; and so here in like manner vast districts hitherto clothed with all manner of trees, shrubs, ferns, and grasses, are suddenly stripped, to be henceforth devoted to the growth of one shrub, and that a shrub which requires the aid of divers manures to stimulate its growth.

It is self-evident that when once the special foe of such a product has discovered such unlimited feeding-ground, it is not likely to abandon the country very quickly. Nevertheless, as I have shown, such scourges do wear themselves out in time, and though coffee can never regain its former undisputed dominion in Ceylon, its cultivation is now once more taking a fair place among profitable industries.

A very remarkable feature in the successive cultivation of coffee and tea has been the discovery that these two plants derive their sustenance from totally different elements in the soil, so that an abandoned coffee-field is practically virgin soil as regards tea. The latter seems warranted to flourish in all soils and at all altitudes, plantations within half-a-dozen miles of the sea, and not 150 feet above sea-level, yielding as excellent returns as those at an altitude of 6000 feet. So extraordinary is the talent of this hardy shrub for adapting itself to circumstances, that although its habit is to send out lateral roots, which in some cases are as thick as a man's thumb, and extend ten or twelve feet from the stem, yet if it fails thereby to secure sufficient nourishment, it strikes a strong tap-root six or eight feet down to the lower soil, even penetrating cabook, and securing itself to the fissure of some subterranean rock, and drawing nourishment from land never reached by the coffee, which is a surface-feeder.

I have already referred [1] to the amazingly rapid extension of the tea industry in Ceylon, so need not now recur to that

[1] See vol. i. p. 6.

subject. Of course tea *may* develop a special disease, but as yet there has been no symptom of such a thing. Wherever it has been grown in other countries, it has proved remarkably hardy and free from disease. Certainly blights of green-fly and red-spiders have given some trouble on Indian estates, but so they do in English rose-gardens. A note of warning was sounded in 1884 when an insect named *Helopeltis Antonii*, which has proved a grave foe to tea in India and Java, and is the worst enemy of the chocolate-tree, appeared in Ceylon. Happily, however, it does not seem to have gained a footing in the Isle.

A more dangerous enemy is the ever-present, ever-active white ant, which was never known to attack living coffee bushes, but shows a great liking for flourishing young tea-trees, and has done grave damage in the Ratnapura district, and in some other places even 2500 feet above the sea-level.

In Southern India its chief foe is the porcupine, which has at least the merit of size (better than battling with myriads of scarcely visible foes). It goes about the tea-fields at night, cutting right through the roots, and grubbing up the bushes apparently out of sheer venom, as it does not seem to eat even the roots. But its love of potatoes gives the Neilgherry planter a chance; he prepares little enclosed patches of potatoes guarded with spring-guns, and thus disposes of a good many of these troublesome diggers, whose flesh is as highly acceptable to his coolies as is that of coffee-rats fried in cocoa-nut oil to the coolies of Ceylon, where swarms of the said rats sometimes attack a plantation and nibble off branches to get at the cherries.

Another foe which they turn to equally good account is the pig-rat or bandicoot, which grows to nearly two feet in length. It is a clean feeder, with flesh resembling pork,

and makes a much appreciated curry. In some districts—
e.g., Hantane—serious damage to coffee is due to wild pigs,
which grub up the bushes, and involve constant watching. These also are foes worth the trouble of slaying.
The merry, frolicsome little grey squirrel, with its handsome dark stripes and large bushy tail, is not often molested,
although rather a serious poacher, as he delights in the
ripe red cherries, or rather in the beans which he finds
within them.

Amongst other strong points in favour of tea *versus* coffee,
one is that whereas the harvesting of the latter is entirely
dependent on a few days of fine weather at certain seasons,
that of tea goes on more or less all the year round, the
warm steamy climate of Ceylon, produced by floods of sunshine alternating with heavy rain, being eminently suited
for the production of luxuriant foliage. The tree is no
sooner stripped of its leaves than it puts forth young shoots
in place of those gathered, which are immediately dried
artificially by processes so purely mechanical, that no handling is allowed; all is done automatically, thus securing the
most rigorous cleanliness—a very marked feature in favour
of Ceylon tea *versus* that of China.

An initial expense in the change from coffee to tea
cultivation has been owing to the fact that whereas coffee
is transported to Colombo, there to undergo its various
stages of preparation for the market, tea must all be prepared on the estates, involving new buildings and special
machinery. Moreover, the grave error of the wholesale
clearing of forests is thereby brought vividly home to
the planters, who are now compelled to buy fuel at a
high cost, not only for culinary purposes, but for tea-drying.

To supply this need, Eucalypti, blue gum, and many Australian trees have, as we have seen, been successfully planted on hills and patenas. But though the eucalyptus rapidly shoots up to a very great height, it has in many cases been killed by the ravages of a minute insect, myriads of which attack the tree and bore right through its stem.

Prominent among the industries which have only begun to develop since the temporary failure of coffee is the culture of the beautiful cacao or chocolate tree (*Theobroma Cacao*, "the food of the gods"), which had long been grown in Ceylon as an ornamental shrub, without a thought of its commercial value. And very ornamental it is, forming a very much more attractive plantation than either closely-pruned tea or coffee shrubs. In four years it grows to a height of about sixteen feet, with luxuriant masses of large handsome leaves, casting a dark cool shade.

It bears small pink and white blossoms, which develop into magnificent rough oblong pods as large as a man's two hands. These as they ripen, assume very varied and rich colours, the Caraccas cacao-pods changing from green to white and golden-yellow; that imported from Trinidad becoming crimson and maroon and purple. When open, they reveal a bed of sticky pulp, much appreciated by native children, wherein lie embedded from twenty to thirty of the precious beans or "nibs," which when roasted and mixed with sugar, vanilla, and other things, form the various preparations in which this "food of the gods" (as Linnæus so happily named it) is familiar to us.

To obtain these, however, the beans must first travel to Europe, amateur efforts at producing home-made cacao in Ceylonese homes having proved eminently unsatisfactory, whereas tea prepared on the estates is so perfect, that tea-drinking has been largely developed.

Of course there was much to learn regarding the conditions of successful cacao cultivation—the exact amount of shade required [1] and protection from wind, the necessity for good soil and sufficient rainfall—all these had to be learnt by experience, and the young industry received a severe shock in 1885 owing to the prolonged drought, which favoured the ravages of an insect pest, causing the death of many young trees and inducing some planters to abandon this culture. This, however, proved but a temporary check, as Ceylon cacao now commands a high price in European markets.

Of all the new products, none gave such rapid and valuable returns at the time of the most grievous depression as cinchona, the bark of which yields the quinine so precious as a tonic and preventive of fever, as also in counteracting the craving for opium and other stimulants. Some seeds imported from South America had been sown in the Government garden at Hackgalla in 1861, and chemical analysis had proved the island-grown produce to be of such excellent quality—fully equal to that sold by English and French chemists at a guinea and thirty francs per ounce—that its cultivation had been encouraged by the offer of free gifts of young plants; but so entirely were the whole community under the dominion of King Coffee, that even when a planter of an experimental turn of mind converted a corner of his

---

[1] These problems have to be puzzled out with regard to each separate product. For instance, with regard to coffee, it is found that on elevations of from 2000 to 6000 feet above the sea no shade is required, as the clouds suffice. But at lower levels moderate shade is found advantageous, especially if afforded by remunerative trees, such as cacao shrubs, which in their turn can be shaded by tall cocoa-palms.

estate into a cinchona plantation, the next proprietor rooted it out, grudging every inch that was not devoted to coffee.

But when that failed, men bethought them of the hitherto neglected cinchona, the value of which in their eyes was perhaps further enhanced by the fact that the young plants were no longer offered at the Government nurseries as a free gift, but at the rate of five rupees per thousand. Within six years about four million young plants were thus disposed of, and plantations were formed throughout the hill-country on all manner of soil and at all possible altitudes, both above and below the coffee zone.

The methods of cultivation and of obtaining the largest quantity of bark without killing the poor trees in the process of partial flaying were so very experimental, that in some cases this cinchona-planting proved a failure.[1] It is a peculiarly uncertain crop to raise, as there is no security that good plants will grow from even the best seed taken from the best plants. But the plantations on suitable soil and judiciously treated yielded very large returns, as may be inferred from the rapid development of the export of cinchona bark, which in 1872 amounted only to 11,547 lbs., but by 1887 had reached well-nigh 15,000,000 lbs.

These figures, however, do not represent unalloyed profit. For, strange to say, whereas in past years cinchona-trees three years of age have been known to yield upwards of ten per cent. of sulphate of quinine, the average produce now shipped does not exceed two per cent. This deterioration of quality, combined with the enormously increased supply now thrown

[1] Planters more than most men, can only learn in the hard school of experience. Thus in 1884 half a million of cinchona trees, some of which were sixteen years of age, were killed by an unusually hard frost at Ootacamund, in the Madras Province. By this unexpected visitation several well-established plantations were almost wholly destroyed.

on the market, has tended very seriously to reduce the commercial value of Ceylon bark, the price of which has fallen so low, that except in certain specially favourable localities it does not pay to collect the crop. And yet some country chemists still sell quinine at a very small reduction on the old exorbitant price. It is said that quinine manufacturers combined against the producers and the consuming public in order to keep up the price; but whatever is the reason, the planters find it impossible to obtain a remunerative price for bark, though thousands of fever-stricken people and of Chinamen struggling to shake off the bondage of opium crave quinine as their one hope of salvation.[1]

When young trees have been recently stripped or shaved, a careful planter supplies them with an artificial garment of dried grass or old newspaper! That any plant should tolerate such a substitute for lungs seems incredible; nevertheless these seem to flourish under this treatment, even when repeated in successive years. Certainly the cinchona is a most forgiving shrub!

Besides these, which are of course the leading industries, many smaller cultivations are being tried experimentally,

[1] Mr. J. Ferguson, of the 'Ceylon Observer,' writes to the Secretary of the Society for the Suppression of the Opium Trade showing how much opium-eating (laudanum and morphia or pure opium) may be counteracted by a liberal use of quinine. It is known to be practised to a very serious extent in the Fen districts of Cambridge and Lincolnshire, about Gravesend on the Thames, and in other malarial districts, as well as by underfed men and women in unhealthy houses in great cities.

He quotes Mr. Archibald Colquhoun, in his "Journey Across Chrysê," to show how many Chinamen, victims to this curse, realise the efficacy of quinine in superseding the need of opium, and possibly curing the craving for it; and how both mandarins and people craved for a pinch, as the best gift he could bestow on them. He shows how beneficial this tonic would also be to horses and cattle in malarial regions, if only it could reach the consumer at anything approaching the modest price which would pay the cultivator.

such as india-rubber, cardamoms, croton-oil seed, aloes, on account of their fibre, &c.

It is no life of idleness which awaits a young planter. Early and late he must be at his post, in foul weather and in fine; sometimes for weeks together living in a continual state of soak, with rain pouring as it can only do in the tropics, finding out all the weak places in the roof, and producing such general damp that nothing is dry, and boots and clothes are all covered with fungus. Up and down the steep mountain-side he must follow his coolies, often battling with fierce wind, scrambling over and under great fallen trees and rocks and charred branches, for wherever a little bush can find a crevice, there he must go to see that it has been duly tended. For it is not enough to plant a bush and leave it to take its chance; what with manuring and handling, pruning and picking, there is always something to be done. In the case of coffee, however, the great mass of work comes on periodically in crop-time, when for several consecutive weeks the press and hurry continue, and Sunday and week-day alike know no rest.

Nor will the substitution of tea culture for that of coffee lighten the planter's work; on the contrary, the former involves more constant care. Coffee crops were only gathered at definite seasons, and work on the plantation, in the store, and in the pulping-house was all cut and dry, the rush of work being compressed into two or three months. It was simple work, requiring less special training and care than tea cultivation.

Tea-picking goes on all the year round, and the curing requires the greatest care and nicety of manipulation, and constant European supervision. The work involves long hours nearly every day of the whole year, and is a great and continuous strain on both physical and mental powers.

One of the sorest difficulties with which the planter has ceaselessly to contend is the washing away of his precious surface soil by the annual heavy rains, which carry down hundreds of tons of the best soil, possibly to enrich some one else in the low country, but more probably to be lost in the ocean. This might in a measure be obviated by more systematic drainage, but that of course means more coolies and more outlay, and both of these are serious difficulties.

Amongst a planter's varied anxieties is the care of his coolies when they fall sick, as these natives of the hot dry plains of Southern India are very apt to do in the cold dreary rainy season of the mountain districts. Occasionally a very serious outbreak of illness occurs, when perhaps the nearest doctor is far away, and the young planter is thrown on his own resources. Such was the outbreak of cholera which occurred in July 1891 (a terribly rainy season) at Lebanon in Madulkele.

An epidemic of dysentery ripened into cholera of so virulent a type that in many cases death ensued within six hours. Some coolies who had turned out at muster at 6 A.M. were dead at ten the same morning. There were in all forty *bonâ fide* seizures, besides a crowd of frightened men and women who were doctored on chance, and twenty-five died in such horrible cramps that their bodies could not be straightened, and the survivors were so terrified that it was difficult to compel them to bury the dead.

Imagine how terrible a charge to be suddenly thrown on a young planter.[1] He proved equal to the emergency, however; physicked, blistered, and rubbed down all the

[1] Mr. Thomas Dickson.

patients with his own hands till an experienced cholera doctor came to his aid from Kandy. Two poor fellows died in his kitchen-verandah. It was somewhat remarkable that of the twenty-five deaths only six were women.

Happily such a terrible experience as this is rare, but there are continual occasions for care and the exercise of much discrimination to discern between illness and idleness —a quality which does sometimes assert itself even in these energetic and industrious Tamil coolies, who are the backbone of all island labour. In days of old these immigrants from the mainland invaded Ceylon as ruthless conquerors; now they come as valuable helpers in every enterprise.

How important a place they occupy may be gathered from the fact that there are always from 200,000 to 300,000 at work on the plantations (in the time of the Madras famine in 1878 about 400,000 contrived to make a living in Ceylon). When at home in Southern India, their average earnings are between £3 and £4 a year, on which they maintain themselves and their families, always reserving a margin for temple-offerings.

In Ceylon they have regular work and regular pay, earning about four times as much as they do on the mainland, besides receiving certain extras in kind—a roof, a bit of garden in which to grow vegetables, a blanket, and medical attendance in sickness. Their staple food is rice, of which an enormous supply is imported from the mainland. A man's wages range from 9d. to 1s. a day; a woman can earn about 7d., and a child 3d.; so they are well off and generally content, their relations with their employers being almost invariably kind. On every estate there is a long row of mud huts, which are " the coolie lines," and very uninviting quarters they appear to Europeans.

The Singhalese furnish a very small proportion of the estate labourers, and are chiefly employed when extra hands are needed for light work, such as plucking tea-leaf in the season; for although no one can get through hard toil better and quicker than the Singhalese, they have a fixed belief that all work is derogatory save that which produces food for their own families. So although they work well on their own paddy-fields (and send hardy deep-sea fishers to the north of the Isle, while the Tamil fishers stick to the shore), they contrive to earn a general character for indolence, and go about their work in a style which often reminded me of a certain Ross-shire boatman, who was supposed to provide fish for the laird's table, but therein frequently failed. One day his mistress ventured to compare his ill-filled creel with that of a visitor on an adjoining estate, mentioning how many fish he had brought home. "Oh! 'deed, I weel believe it," was the reply. "*Puir man! he'll just be making a toil of it!*"

The Singhalese are said to be somewhat more conscientious than the Tamil coolies as regards doing well what they undertake. At the same time, if it is work which can possibly be done by women and children, these will certainly be deputed to do it. I think, however, that, as regards the employment of deputies, the palm must be awarded to a Malay conductor, who was asked whether he was observing the fast of Ramadan. He replied that he was not, as he was working hard and required his food, but that *he was making his wife keep it!*

Of course, on estates employers take care that their coolies do work energetically, but as a specimen of really indolent occupation you should watch a gang of Government coolies working on the roads—those excellent roads which overspread the country in every direction like a network. In spreading metal, one powerful man fills a very small basket, which another strong man lifts on to the head of a woman, who walks a few yards, empties it on to the road, and then returns for another load.

Then when the roads are to be pounded, a gang of able-bodied men stand in a group, while one of them sings a long monotonous ditty rather like a Gaelic song, and at the end of each verse of four lines all simultaneously raise their pounding blocks and let them drop with a thump on the road. It has been calculated that if they make thirty strokes in an hour, they are above the average!

As I have said, these poor coolies are utterly miserable in rainy weather, although the planters do their best to clothe them. I never guessed till I saw these gangs what becomes of old regimental great-coats. But when the sun shines and their scanty drapery has been recently washed, and large, bright turbans well put on, they look as cheery as one could wish, and the women especially are most picturesque, with their fine glossy black hair, large dreamy black eyes, and numerous ornaments on ears, neck, arms, and ankles—some indeed only of painted earthenware, and the majority of bell-metal, but others of real silver, massive but of coarse workmanship. Their gay drapery is worn in most artistic folds.

Many of their merry little brown children wear no clothes whatever, even their heads being shaved and oiled, all save one little tuft of black hair. Shaving, by the way, is generally done with bits of broken bottles! Sometimes you see pretty little girls (Tamil) whose sole decoration is a silver fig-leaf (*Ficus Religiosa*), very suggestive of the legend that here was the Paradise of our first parents!

Some poor little girls are weighted with a short, heavy, leaden chain passed through a slit in the ear where European women wear their small earrings. By long weighting in this fashion, the poor ear can be lengthened so as literally to touch the shoulder, and is then loaded with rings—truly hideous in our eyes, and involving much suffering in youth. But pride, they say, feels no pain, so we must hope that this is a case in point. The top of the ear is adorned with a small, close-fitting stud, like that often worn on one side of the nose.

One of the first things that struck me as strange on reaching the planting districts is the fact that the names by which estates are known to Europeans convey nothing to the minds of the men who work on them. My first experience of this difficulty was when *en route* to Mrs. Bosanquet's pleasant home at Rosita in Dimbula, and my Tamil driver, not having received his instructions before starting, drove stolidly on for fully six miles beyond the turning, totally ignoring my vain expostulating queries, "Rosita?" "Bosanquet dorré" (*i.e.*, master). It was quite useless; so there was nothing for it but to drive on till I espied a European bungalow, to which I sent a written message, which happily brought a tall white man stalking down through the coffee to say we *must* bait the horse and breakfast at his house; where, accordingly, we were most hospitably entertained, and then duly forwarded to our destination.

Considering that all the coolies are Tamils imported from Southern India, one would naturally suppose that they would accept whatever name the owner of an estate has been pleased to give to the piece of forest he has cleared; but so far from this being the case, there is scarcely an estate in the island which is not known to Europeans and their labourers under totally distinct names, so that even in the rare case of a Tamil coolie understanding English, he could not direct you to an estate unless you spoke of it by its Tamil name, and these are sometimes very confusing.

Thus, supposing I wish to visit the estate of Didoola, I must direct my coolies to *Palla Kaduganara;* but supposing I am on my way to Kaduganawa, I must bid them carry me to *Mudaliyarthottam.* I scarcely wonder at finding that places called after homes in Britain retain Singhalese names. Thus Abercairney in Dickoya, and Rosita in Dimbula, are both known as *Sinne Kottagalla;* Feteresso continues to be known as *Anandawatte,* Glen Cairn as *Manickambantotte,* Gorthie as *Hindagalla,* Blair Athol as *Sinne Darrawella,* Braemore as *Kooda Malleapoo,* Fassifern as *Ayra Patena,* Waverley as *Bopatelawa,* Craigellachie as *Puthu Road,* Malvern as *Partambasi,* Windsor Forest as *Rajah Totam,* Duffus as *Pusila Tottam,* Forres as *Nagawattie,* &c. But it *is* strange to find that even genuine Singhalese names are not accepted; as, for instance, Gangaroowa, which to the coolie is known as *Raja Tottam,* while Oolanakanda is *Ulankanthai,* Wewelkellie is *Veragodde,* Ouvahkellie is *Kayagalla;* while in some cases the coolies know estates only by their name for certain firms or companies, *e.g.,* Diyagama is only recognised as Company Totum; Edinburgh and Inverness estates are both Nilghery Totum. As this system of double names applies to about fifteen hundred estates, the new arrival in any district must find the study of his " Estates Directory " an essential part of his education.

In looking over a list of these Highland homes, I am struck by the predominance of Scotch names, as suggestive of the clinging to dear old associations which is always supposed specially to characterise men born in hilly countries. In the low country this inspiration seems to be lacking, for in a list of about 350 cocoa-nut estates, I only find four Scotch names.

I will not attempt to give details of the pleasant months I spent in the various planting districts, for I fear I must have already tried the patience of my readers. I can only say that in each district I found the same hospitable welcome, and was struck with the cordiality and good-fellowship which forms so marked a characteristic of life among the planters.

Of course a lover of beautiful nature cannot but mourn over the bleak ugliness of range beyond range of mountains all totally denuded of any vegetation whatever except the very monotonous carefully-pruned bushes, growing amid the blackened or sun-bleached stumps of what but a little while ago were noble forest trees, now standing like headstones in some vast cemetery.

Day after day we witnessed marvellous effects of opal light and strange blue mists, telling of great forest burnings, and, on favourable days, marked on every side the column of dense lurid smoke rising from some glen or valley that was about to be "improved." At several of these "burns" we were actually present, when tracts of two or three hundred acres were committed to the flames, and for hours we watched the wild conflagration raging—a scene of indescribable grandeur. Sometimes the great burnings so affected the atmosphere as to bring on tremendous rain-storms, and on one occasion, when we had to ford a river, we got across only just in time before the stream came down in flood.

Out of so many thousand acres of beautiful timber ruthlessly destroyed, one tree excited my special regret. It was a majestic banyan-tree, which had occupied the only piece of quite level ground at the Yoxford. That ground was the only suitable spot for the erection of a bungalow, so the grand old tree had been felled, and the ground was strewn with its huge trunk and arms—a sorry sight!

As regards social meetings, men gathered from far and near for church services, especially at Christmas and New Year, as also for occasional cricket-matches, never allowing their energies to be damped by any amount of rain. And sometimes, as a very great event, there was a cheery ball, when the principal coffee-store in the district was swept out and elaborately decorated as a ball-room, and the nearest bungalow was given up to the ladies to dress and sleep in, as they had probably ridden over hill, valley, and torrent for many miles to attend the unwonted festivity.

At the time of my visit to Dimbula, there were actually thirty-five ladies in the district—a true sign of prosperity—and a ball was not a matter of indifference to either sex; indeed, the hearty honest enjoyment of existence among the planters, and the zest with which they enter into whatever business or pleasure is the order of the day, is one of the pleasantest features of life in the mountain districts.

CHAPTER XXV.

ASCENT OF ADAM'S PEAK.

Adam's Peak—The Sri Pada, or Holy Foot—Footprints in Britain—
In Sicily—Of Vishnu—Of St. Thomas—Of Hercules—Of Montezuma—Of Buddha and Siva—Adam and Moses—Ascent of Allegalla, Kurunegalla, and Adam's Peak.

THE first impressions of the traveller approaching Ceylon must in a great measure depend on the state of the atmosphere. In some seasons he will see only the monotonous levels of the low country; at other times the mountain ranges of the interior are clearly visible, the whole crowned by one sharp pinnacle, about fifty miles inland from Colombo.

That pinnacle is pointed out to him as Adam's Peak; but if he knows aught of the story of the Isle, he will know that is only the name given to it by foreigners, and founded on the legend as taught them by some Mahommedan; but though called by many names, each denoting sanctity, it is emphatically known to all inhabitants of Ceylon, of whatever creed, as THE SRI PADA—THE HOLY FOOT, so named on account of a natural mark on the extreme summit, which, to the eye of faith, was in remote ages in some degree suggestive of a huge footprint, and was accordingly revered as a miraculous token of the place having once been visited by some supernatural being (it must have been in the days when giants walked the earth).

As various creeds developed, the adherents of each claimed THE FOOTPRINT as that of their own ideal, and so this particular mark has attained a celebrity far above those on any of the numerous rocks similarly reverenced in other lands.

And very curious it is to note in how many parts of the world certain rocks have from time immemorial been places of sacred pilgrimage on account of some natural indentation bearing some resemblance to a gigantic human footprint.

These have generally been somewhat elaborated by pious hands, which define the toes and perfect the outline, and the footprint then becomes an object of the most devout homage to thousands of human beings, who believe it to be the true spot of earth, hallowed for evermore by the fact that it was the first or the last touched either by the founders of their religion (whatever that may happen to be) or by some venerated hero.

We need not go far for one example, for in our own little isle our favourite British hero is thus commemorated. At Tintagel, in Cornwall, where the ruins of King Arthur's castle stand, on the summit of a projecting crag rising from the sea, and connected with the mainland only by a narrow neck of land (a spot once well-nigh inaccessible, and only to be reached by steep steps cut in the rock), a large unshapely mark, deeply impressed on a big boulder, is said to be the footprint of the great pure king.

Not far off a modern footprint is shown, which, as years roll on, will doubtless be revered as that of the great good queen, for on the pier at St. Michael's Mount an inlaid brass marks the first footprint of Queen Victoria on the occasion of her visit with the Prince Consort in 1846.

Students of Hindoo mythology, or travellers who have ventured to invade the temples of Vishnu, will doubtless remember the reverence accorded to many footprints ascribed to that god, whose votaries are distinguished by curved lines daily painted on their forehead in white, red, or yellow lines, as the symbol of his sacred foot or feet, as the case may be, as different sects dispute as to the propriety of thus indicating one foot or two. So the sect which is in favour of only one foot indicates it by one curved line of white between the eyes, crossed by a red mark in honour of his wife. Another sect indicates both feet resting on two lotus blossoms; and so bitter are the disputes concerning these frontal emblems, that as the same images are worshipped by both sects in the same temples, ruinous lawsuits sometimes arise between the two factions as to which mark shall be impressed on the images![1]

Thus painted or engraved representations of Vishnu's feet enter largely into his worship. At the great annual festival held in his honour in the month of May at Conjeveram (forty miles to the south of Madras)—a festival which is attended by an incalculable multitude of worshippers—one of the priests in immediate attendance on the image of Vishnu carries a golden cup within which is engraven the likeness of Vishnu's feet; and the chief craving of each individual in that vast surging throng is to struggle for a place so close to the procession that the priest who bears the cup may let it rest for one moment on his head—a touch ensuring blessing in this and in all

[1] See "In the Himalayas," pp. 23, 24. Chatto & Windus.

future lives. "Wilt thou not come and place thy flowery feet upon my head?" is the fervent prayer of each longing soul.[1]

Knowing the policy which has led the Church of Rome in all heathen countries as far as possible to adapt Christian legends to all objects specially venerated by the people (thus sanctioning their continuance of a homage which could not be at once uprooted), we need not wonder to find Portuguese writers attributing these revered rock-marks to Christian saints; and De Couta records how, in his time, a stone at Colombo bore the deep impress of the knees of St. Thomas, who had previously worn a similar hollow on a rock at Meliapore, near Madras. How his poor knees must have ached![2]

Even at the present day, the Roman Catholic Christians of Ceylon make pilgrimage to the footprint on Adam's Peak, as to that of St. Thomas, though some Portuguese writers attribute it to the eunuch of Candace. In Valenteyn's account he says the mountain was esteemed most sacred by the Catholics of India, while Percival related that "the Roman Catholics have taken advantage of the current superstition to forward the propagation of their own tenets, and a chapel which they have erected on the mountain is yearly frequented by vast numbers of black Christians of the Portuguese and Malabar races."

Of an early Christian saint of the Western Church it is

[1] I scarcely like to compare words from Holy Scripture in this connection, but there is a curious example of Oriental phraseology in Isaiah lx. 14, 15, where it is written, "All they that despised thee shall bow themselves down at the soles of thy feet. . . . I will make the place of My Feet glorious."

[2] At Anuradhapura two marks on the granite pavement of the Ruanwelli Dagoba are pointed out as having been worn by the knees of the devout King Bátiya-tissa, who reigned from 19 B.C. to A.D. 9.

recorded by Willebad (an Anglo-Saxon, who in the year A.D. 761 journeyed in Sicily) that he was shown "her shoeprints" in the prison at Catania.

In the Church of the Ascension on the Mount of Olives a rock is shown within the chapel having a natural cavity, described as the footprint of our Lord. The earliest record of this mark is that by Arculf, who mentions the impression of two footprints. Now there is only one, with no resemblance to any foot.

In days of old, Herodotus told of a gigantic footprint on a rock near Syras in Scythia, and which was believed to be that of Hercules; and in the New World we find the Mexicans revering a mark on a huge block of porphyry which they suppose to have been imprinted by the imperial foot of Montezuma.

Few who have entered the British Museum can have failed to note the casts of sculptures from the ancient Tope of Amravati in Southern India which adorn the walls of the grand stairs, and the attention of many has doubtless been arrested by two slabs on each of which are sculptured only two footprints. To the devout Buddhists these double footmarks are said to have symbolised the invisible presence of Buddha—a tenet, however, wholly unwarranted by his own teaching.

Passing up these stairs to that corner of the new gallery which is devoted to Buddhist mythology, we note a great stone slab on which is sculptured one huge footprint nearly five feet in length. The whole is covered with elaborate symbolic carving, and each toe is adorned with a curious object like a large spiral shell. The outline of this foot is defined by a raised border, originally carved in a pattern like scale-armour, but at a later period this has been coated with plaster and encrusted with bits of looking-glass and coloured glass representing gems. All that is known of the history of this once-venerated object is that it was brought from Burmah by Captain Marryat; but by what means he obtained it, or to what mountain or temple it formerly attracted devout worshippers, there is unfortunately no record.

Happily for the archæologist, the most celebrated of these great footprints are on immovable rock-boulders.

It seems probable that there are, or have been, a considerable number of rocks thus sanctified wherever the religion of Buddha has held sway, for Hiouen-Thsiang, the celebrated Chinese pilgrim, who devoted the years between A.D. 629 and 645 to visiting all the most noted shrines of India, makes continual allusion to having seen among their sacred objects the footprints left by Tathagata (by which name he describes Buddha), where he walked to and fro preaching the law.

Such preaching was described as "turning the wheel of the law;" hence a simple wheel, sometimes overshadowed by the honorific umbrella, is a frequent symbol in Buddhism;[1] and among the very ancient sculptures at the Sanchi Tope and elsewhere we find representations of Buddha's feet, on which are depicted the symbolic wheel and the *swastica* (the latter is a peculiar mark, something between a cross and a Greek fret).

Hiouen-Thsiang also relates strange legends concerning the actual feet, telling how, when the body of Buddha was about to be burnt at Kusinagara, after it had been swathed in a thousand napkins and enclosed in a heavy coffin,

[1] "In the Himalayas," "The Sacred Wheel," pp. 430-434. Chatto & Windus.

which rested on a funeral pyre of scented wood, lo! at that moment Tathagata revealed his feet, causing them to project from the coffin, and his favourite disciple, Kasyapa, saw that they bore the sign of the wheel and other marks of various colours; and as he marvelled what these could be, the dead spoke, and told him that these were the marks of tears, which gods and men, moved by pity, had wept because of his death. (I may observe that two lotus blossoms bearing the marks of Buddha's feet are among the subjects which are most frequently represented in the sacred pictures of Japan.)

At the present day, in the province of Behar in India, and also in Siam, at Prabat, near Bangkok, several temples glory in the possession of rocks exhibiting these revered traces of Gautama Buddha—doubtless the very rocks of which Hiouen-Thsiang wrote.

A still more ancient Chinese traveller, Fa Hian, who visited Ceylon A.D. 413, tells of two sacred footprints of Fo (i.e., Buddha), one of which lay quite in the north of the island. More recent Chinese writers attribute the mark on Adam's Peak to Pwan-koo, the first man.

Fourteen hundred and sixty years later I too followed the pilgrim path to visit several such footprints. The one mentioned by Fa Hian in the far north is now forgotten, but I found one on the summit of Allegalla Peak, another on a mountainous mass of red rock at Kurunegalla, and a third (which is emphatically THE FOOTPRINT) on the summit of Adam's Peak.

I was also shown marks—confessedly artificial—in the Buddhist temples at Cotta and at the Alu Vihara, where they are simply revered as models of the True Footprint on the summit of the Peak. Another at the temple of Kelany, near Colombo, has the credit of being genuine, and is declared by the sacred Buddhist books to be so, having been imprinted by Gautama Buddha when he appeared on his third visit to Ceylon to preach to the Nagas or Snake-worshippers. But this mark is imprinted on a rock in the middle of the river, and the cool rushing waters circling around it in ceaseless homage overflow and conceal it from the eyes of men. This is the legend told of a deep eddy in the Kelani-Ganga.

Yet another, confessedly of recent manufacture, is shown on the summit of the great rock of Isuru-muniya, a very ancient rock-temple at Anuradhapura. It is reached by a flight of rock-cut steps.

A peculiarity of all these footprints is their gigantic size, the smallest which I have seen being that on the western summit of Allegalla, which is *only* 4 feet 6 inches by 2 feet! Those on Kurunegalla and on Adam's Peak are each 6 feet in length, as I proved by lying down full length on them in absence of the guardian priests! But to the eye of faith this is no hindrance, for according to Mahommedan tradition, Adam was the height of a tall palm-tree (the tomb at Yeddah, near Mecca, which is reverenced as that of Eve, is 70 feet in length). Buddha likewise is said to have been 27 feet in height, and this is about the proportion which he bears to other saints in Japanese pictures. But in every country where he is worshipped, especially in China and Japan, there are cyclopean images of him far taller than that.[1]

As regards Siva and Saman, who also receive credit for the big footprint, they, being gods, could of course assume any size they pleased.

[1] See page 125.

Most of the world's revered footprints have been appropriated by the Buddhists, who have not scrupled to manufacture a considerable number. I visited one of the latter class in China, on a rock within the Temple of the Five Genii, in the heart of the city of Canton—a temple where the homage bestowed on the footprint is quite secondary to that accorded to five rough-hewn stones, which represent five celestial rams, on which the five good genii descended to Canton.[1]

Even the grave Mahommedans, with all their theoretic abhorrence of everything savouring of superstition or idolatry, reverence various rock-marks which they affirm to have been the footprints of prophets or great saints. Of course the most venerated relic of this class is that at Mecca, where, within the sacred enclosure of the Kaaba (that little temple which to all Mahommedans is the holy of holies), there is a small building erected over a sacred stone, which they believe to have been brought thither by Abraham, and on which he stood while building the Kaaba. It bears the impress of his two feet, the big toes being deeply indented. Into these, devout pilgrims pour water, and drink thereof, and also wash their faces as a symbolic purification. This stone is always kept covered with a veil of pure silk; it must on no account be mixed with cotton. Three different veils are kept for use in different years, one green, one black, and one red; all are embroidered in gold.

Another greatly revered Mahommedan relic is the footprint of Moses at Damascus. Over this sacred rock has been built a mosque, which more than five hundred years ago bore the name of "The Mosque of the Foot." It was visited about the year A.D. 1324 by the celebrated Moorish

[1] "Wanderings in China." C. F. Gordon Cumming. Vol. i. p. 49.

pilgrim, Ibn Batuta, who, fired with a desire to visit every place deemed sacred by Mahommedans, started from his native city of Tangiers, and for twenty-eight years (when travel was a very different matter to our easy journeys now-a-days) wandered in ceaseless pilgrimage from shrine to shrine.

At Shiraz he visited the tomb of the saintly Abu Abd Allah, who, he says, first "made known the way from India to the Mountain of Serendib," *i.e.*, Adam's Peak in Ceylon. As this saint died early in the tenth century, it is evident that Mahommedans had ere then accepted the footprint on the summit of the Peak as that of Adam—an idea which, strangely enough, they seem to have adopted from the corrupt semi-Christian Gnostics, who borrowed a little from every creed, not even omitting snake-worship, and who gave special pre-eminence to Adam, as the original man.

In a Coptic manuscript of the fourth century, which is attributed to Valentinus the Gnostic, there occurs a most curious passage, in which our Saviour is represented as telling the Blessed Virgin that he has appointed an angel to be the special guardian of the footstep impressed by the foot of Ieû (*i.e.*, Adam). It is understood that this passage has reference to Adam's Peak, and it is the oldest record we possess of its sanctity.

The legend thus attached to it by the Gnostics was adopted by the Arabs, and so it came to be accepted by Mahommedans in general, all of whom reverence Adam as the purest creation of Allah, and so rank him above all patriarchs and prophets—the first of God's vicegerents upon earth.

As a matter of course, this Gnostic legend of the footprint was rejected by the early Christians of purer creed, and so Moses of Chorene, Patriarch of Alexandria, writing in the fourth or fifth century, affirms it to be undoubtedly the mark of Satan, who alighted here when he fell from heaven!

According to the orthodox teaching of the Koran, Paradise was not on this earth, but in the seventh heaven; and when Adam was ejected thence, it was he, and not Satan, who alighted on the Peak, and here he remained standing on one foot for about two centuries, striving by penance to expiate his crime; hence the mark worn on the rock. Poor Eve tumbled into Arabia, and landed at Yeddah, near Mecca, whither, when these centuries were ended, the Archangel guided Adam, who brought her back to live in Ceylon, as the best substitute for Paradise that earth could give. Both, however, are said to have been carried back to Mecca for burial.

Whatever the varieties of creed that exist in this fair Isle, all alike agree in their reverence for this one high pinnacle, and, most marvellous to relate, all meet to worship side by side on the sacred summit in peace and amity.

While the Mahommedans crowd here to do homage to the memory of Adam, the Tamils[1] believe that the footprint is that of one of their gods, the worshippers of Siva claim it as his mark, while the votaries of Vishnu ascribe it to Saman, who, in India, is worshipped under the name of Lakshmana. He was the brother of Rama, one of the incarnations of Vishnu, whose invasion of Ceylon to rescue his beautiful wife, Sita, from the demon-king, Ravana, is celebrated in the Ramayana, a nice little epic poem of

---

[1] Some of these are the descendants of the old Malabar conquerors of Ceylon; others are constantly being imported from the mainland by the planters as labourers. Most of these are of the Hindoo religion.

96,000 lines! Being a descendant of the sun, Saman's image is always painted yellow, and to him are consecrated the scarlet rhododendron blossoms which glorify the mountain summit.

It is in his honour that the butterflies—true children of the sun—bear the name of Samanaliya. They are supposed to be especially dear to him because of the vast flights which sometimes stream from all parts of the Isle, all tending in the direction of the Peak; hence it is supposed that they too are on pilgrimage to do homage to the holy footprint. (If it seems strange that the Singhalese should call their exquisite butterflies by the name of a Hindoo god, we must remember that Buddhism is so very accommodating and all-absorbing that many Hindoo idols are worshipped in Buddhist temples.)

Very various are the names bestowed by all these religious bodies on the shapely cone, which has been so well described as the sacred citadel of ancient religions. To the Hindoos of all sects it is the Mount Swangarrhanam, "The ascent to heaven;" but the Sivites distinguish it as Siva-noli-padam, while to the Vishnuvites it is Samanala or Saman-takuta. To the Mahommedan Moormen it is Baba-Adamalei, which is the equivalent of the European name Adam's Peak, while to the Buddhist the term SRI PADA, "THE FOOTPRINT," is all expressive.

Thus as clouds ever float around the loftiest mountain summit, so have the legends of many races gathered round this high pinnacle, which consequently possesses for Oriental minds a concentrated essence of sanctity altogether indescribable.

To the most careless traveller its natural beauty offers an irresistible attraction, and never shall I forget my first glimpse of it as seen from the sea, when we were still some miles distant from the coast, the mountain apparently (though not really) far overtopping all others. There, in the early dawn, it stood revealed—a deep blue peak cutting clear against a golden sky. To reach this high point became the desire of my heart, but many months elapsed ere I accomplished it.

Meanwhile I found welcome in a lovely home nestling high on the face of a mountain scarcely less beautiful than Adam's Peak, though its name is comparatively unknown to the world in general. This is Allegalla Peak, which towers majestically above the low wooded hills and the rice-fields of the lowlands, its own slopes being clothed with the richest vegetation and the lovely foliage of many varieties of palm.

On a glorious day, when not a cloud veiled the tranquil blue heaven, we reached the summit of this Peak, which we found to be really a double summit, connected by a rock-saddle. The eastern peak is crowned with palms, as beseems so brave a mountain, but our steps were attracted to the western peak, for there, on a rounded slab of rough red rock, is imprinted the footmark to which the inhabitants of this district do homage. I do not believe that it has any pretension to be a genuine article, but it is a convenient representative of the true footprint on the summit of Adam's Peak, which, though about forty miles distant, we saw clearly on the horizon, towering above a sea of low-lying white mist.

This is a perfect footmark, 4 feet 6 inches in length by 2 feet in width. Before it is a rude stone altar, on which some worshippers had laid their offering of flowers and fruit, and the clear water, which lay in a hollow of the scorching rock, suggested that it had been carried thither and poured out on the footprint as an act of worship. As we looked across the sea of white mist enfolding the base of the distant Sri Pada, a long line of swiftly advancing light rounding the face of the precipice far below us marked the express train rushing down from Kandy to Colombo, suggesting a strange contrast between the pilgrims who through so many centuries have toiled up that hill of difficulty, and the luxurious travellers of these later days rushing on in their ceaseless race against time.

About twenty miles to the north of Allegalla [1] is Kurunegalla, which foreigners used to call Kornegalle, and which is said to derive its name from a gigantic rounded mass of red rock shaped like a beetle.

Here, in the court of an ancient temple, the object of special veneration, is a "Holy Foot" cut in the rock. It is the right foot; it is six feet in length, and points northeast. It is avowedly only a model of the true footprint, but it has the advantage of being several hundred years old, having been cut to assist the devotions of the ancient kings of Kandy and the ladies of that royal house, when, in the first half of the fourteenth century, Kurunegalla was the capital of the kingdom, and the royal residence was situated at the base of the crag, where, beneath the shadow of noble old trees, carved stones and broken columns still mark the spot.

From this rock Adam's Peak is visible in a direct line to the south, and one of my most delightful reminiscences of Ceylon is of a moonlight night spent on its summit. I

---

[1] *Galla* means rock. I had occasion to refer to these two crags in the last chapter, but I trust my readers will excuse my recalling them in this connection.

think part of its charm lay in the knowledge that probably not half-a-dozen white women had accomplished the ascent, for though it really is not very difficult to a good scrambler, it is the fashion to consider it a very great feat, and almost all the gentlemen, who had themselves been to the summit, jeered at the idea of my accomplishing it. It occurred to me, however, that I could probably climb quite as well as the Singhalese and Tamil women of all ages, who year after year toil up here for the good of their souls.

In China I heard how, among the crowds of pilgrims who annually travel from most distant districts to worship on the summit of the sacred Mount Tai-Shan, in the province of Shantung, and who end their toilsome journey by five miles of steep climbing, a spectator observed a company of old women, of whom the youngest was seventy-eight and the oldest ninety years of age. With infinite pain and toil these earnest pilgrims had accomplished a journey of 300 miles from south of Honan, their special object being to plead the merit of their life-long fast from fish and flesh, and to crave a happy transmigration for their souls.

Naturally I thought that if poor old women of fourscore and ten could accomplish such feats as these, I need not be discouraged; so I kept this aim ever in view during the most pleasant of pilgrimages, travelling by easy stages from one coffee estate to another, halting at bungalows which bear such names as Blair Athol, Glen Tilt, Moray, and Forres, strangely homelike sounds to my ears, and suggestive of the colony of genial Scotchmen whom I found settled in every corner.

I prefer, however, to speak of "Britons," for my kind entertainers included men and women from England, Scot-

land, and Ireland. One of these I had last known in London as a smart "man-about-town," whose special vanity lay in his "gardenia button-holes." Here the gardenias formed a fragrant and luxuriant hedge, but the busy planter cared more for the snow-white flowers and scarlet cherries of the bright green coffee bushes which he and his regiment of coolies had planted with so much toil among the charred stumps of the burnt forest—tiny green bushes in a blackened waste.

In every direction save one, we looked out on an endless expanse of undulating mountain ranges, all clothed with the same monotonous little bushes, replacing the beautiful primeval forest, which, however, happily still remained almost intact on the ranges close to the Peak, which seemed to tower from these lower ranges right up to heaven, while in the foreground beautiful groups of trees, spared as yet by ruthless axe and flame, lay mirrored in the clear waters of the Mahavelli-Ganga.

One comfortable home in which I was hospitably entertained has been aptly named "Bunyan," in irresistible allusion to the "Pilgrim's Progress," being right on the pilgrims' path.

When my friends found I was really bent on making the ascent, a little band of stalwart planters soon arranged all details for a pilgrimage, and a very pleasant one it proved. It was in the month of January, and we were favoured with ideal weather and a faultlessly clear atmosphere.

Starting from Glen Tilt, in the Maskeliya district, we walked or rode as far as "Forres,"[1] where we slept, in order

[1] To me a very familiar name, the town of Forres, in Morayshire, being only three miles from Altyre, my birthplace.

to be fresh for a very early start next morning. It lies at the very foot of the Peak, or rather of a long shoulder, along which we toiled for four hours, till we reached an ambulam, or pilgrim's rest-house, at the foot of the actual cone.

I had hoped that I could have been carried thus far in a dandy, which is a strip of canvas hung on a bamboo,—a mode of travelling the advantages of which I had often proved in my Himalayan wanderings,—but as the track lay up and down frightfully steep ravines, or else through forest so thick that the long bamboo pole could not make its way, I had soon to give up this attempt, and join the walkers, consoling myself for the extra fatigue by the beauty of the undergrowth of ferns, and the wonderful variety of lovely tints, rich madder, sienna, crimson, delicate pink, and pale green, all due to the young foliage, which here is ever developing all the year round.

Gay caladium leaves mingled with a profusion of delicate maiden-hair fern, while here and there wild bignonias or brilliant balsams claimed admiration, as did also a luxuriant sort of stag's-horn moss, and an occasional tuft of violets or forget-me-nots.

Having started at daybreak, we were all very glad of a halt for breakfast beneath the rough shelter of the said rest-house, which is merely an open shed. Happily we had brought mats of talipat-palm leaf, which we spread on the floor, and thereon rested. Only for our eyes there was no rest, as we gazed upwards at the majestic cone shaped like a gigantic bell, and towering right above us, cutting sharp against the deep blue sky. The other side of the ravine presented a front of mighty precipices.

At this halting-place there are a few tiny shops, chiefly for the sale of curry-stuffs for the pilgrims, and much we marvelled to see the multitudes of bottles of eau-de-cologne —genuine Jean Marie Farina—at one shilling a bottle. Of course I invested, thinking it would at least do to burn in my Etna, but little did I guess what a villainous compound it was, which the very irreligious merchant pawned off on devout pilgrims as a meet offering wherewith to anoint the holy footprint.

The pilgrims are a never-failing crop. All the year round they come and go, but their special season is at the spring festival in April and May, just when the rains are at their height, and mountain torrents are liable to rise suddenly and detain them for days, subject to all manner of hardships; but these, I suppose, only add to the merits of the pilgrimage, for the sanctity of the season prevails, and the pilgrims press on in a continuous stream amounting to thousands annually. The feebleness of old age is no drawback—grey-bearded grandfathers and wrinkled, toothless old hags are escorted by all their family, and sometimes a tottering old granny is borne on the back of a stalwart son,—a true deed of filial devotion,—while mothers help their toddling little ones up the steep ascent which is to secure for them such special blessing.

Some have travelled from the mainland of India, others from the farthest districts of the Isle, long and toilsome journeys; and when they reach the base of the holy mount, they are so near the accomplishment of their heart's desire, that all weariness is well-nigh forgotten, and ever and anon the stillness of the dense forest is broken by the echo of the shout of praise, "Saädu! Saädu!" which is the equivalent of "Hallelujah! Hallelujah!"

The great mass of pilgrims approach the mountain from the south *viâ* Ratnapura, "the city of rubies," which, unless the accounts which have been published are very highly-coloured, must involve far more difficult climbing and scrambling than anything we had to do. When they have ascended about 150 very ancient rock-hewn steps, attributed to good King Prakrama Bahu I., himself a pilgrim, they come to a most romantic bathing-place overshadowed by large trees. This is just above a granite precipice, over which the Sita-Ganga[1] hurls itself on to the boulders far below.

In these chill waters the pilgrims must bathe, and so purify themselves ere completing the ascent of the Holy Mount along precipitous faces of rock, where their only safety lies in gripping the iron chains which adventurous climbers have placed here for the benefit of weaker heads.

As a matter of course, traditions, legends, and myths attach to each rock and turn on the pilgrim path; each overhanging cliff, each gushing spring, each rippling rivulet that rushes down the water-worn ravines has its own story, in many cases vague and dreamy as the mists which float around the towering pinnacle. But as regards practical details, it is well to consult a trustworthy pilgrim; and as Lawrence Oliphant ascended the Peak from the Ratnapura side, I may as well quote what he says on the subject, for the benefit of any one who may be undecided as to which route to select. He says:—

"We passed the night at a native house in one of the higher villages, and leaving our horses there, on the following morning pursued our way on foot amid scenery which at every step became more grand and rugged, the path in places skirting the edge of dizzy precipices, at the base of which foamed brawling torrents.

[1] *Ganga* means river.

"The way was often rendered dangerous by the roots of large trees, which, having become slippery by the morning mist, stretched across the narrow path, and one of these nearly cost me my life. The path at the spot was scarped on the precipitous hillside; at least 300 feet below roared a torrent of boiling water, when my foot slipped on a root, and I pitched over the sheer cliff. I heard the cry of my companion as I disappeared, and had quite time to realise that all was over, when I was brought up suddenly by the spreading branches of a bush which was growing upon a projecting rock. There was no standing ground anywhere, except the rock the bush grew upon.

"Looking up, I saw my companion and the natives who were with us peering over the edge above, and to their intense relief shouted that so far I was all right, but dared not move for fear the bush would give way. They, however, strongly urged my scrambling on to the rock; and this, with a heart thumping so loudly that I seemed to hear its palpitations, and a dizzy brain, I succeeded in doing.

"The natives, of whom there were five or six, then undid their long waistcloths, and tying them to each other, and to a piece of cord, consisting of the united contributions of all the string of the party and the packages they were carrying, made a rope just long enough to reach me. Fastening this under my armpits, and holding on to it with the energy of despair, or perhaps I should rather say of hope, I was safely hauled to the top.

"This adventure was not a very good preparation for what was in store for us, when not very far from the top we reached the *maurais pas* of the whole ascent. Here again we had a precipice with a torrent at the bottom of it on one side, and on the other an overhanging cliff—not metaphorically overhanging, but literally its upper edge projected some distance beyond the ledge on which we stood; it was not above forty feet high, and was scaled by an iron ladder.

"The agonising moment came when we had mounted this ladder to the projecting edge, and had nothing between our backs and the torrent some hundreds of feet below, and then had to turn over the edge and take hold of a chain which lay over an expanse of bare sloping rock, to the links of which it was necessary to cling firmly, while one hauled one's self on one's knees for twenty or thirty yards over the by no means smooth surface.

"My companion was so utterly demoralised that he roundly declared that nothing would induce him to made the descent of the same place."

I am happy to say that no such difficulties attended our ascent from the Maskeliya, Dickoya, and Dimbula side.

Our ascent of the actual cone commenced immediately after leaving the aforesaid rest-house. We crossed a clear crystal stream rushing downward from the summit (such as when swollen by sudden storm might well prove a serious hindrance to returning pilgrims). Then entering a deep fern-clad ravine, we struggled steadily upward, and a very stiff climb it proved, like that of the very steepest stair up an old cathedral tower a thousand feet high. This continued for two and a half miles, sometimes in dark, cool forest, sometimes along a face of bare precipitous rock exposed to scorching sun. The path is like the bed of a watercourse, coming straight down from the summit, with thick jungle on either side. The ravine is so narrow that it is necessary to go single file, and it really is a serious difficulty to meet pilgrims on their downward way. At intervals on either side of the road there are cairns of small stones heaped up by pilgrims, just like those on the summit of Fuji-yama, and in the Himalayas and in Scotland.

I got some help by passing a rope round my waist and sending two coolies ahead with the ends of it, which gave some support and a gentle upward impetus. Happily some royal pilgrims of old had flights of steps cut on the almost vertical slabs of slippery rock. Some of the steps certainly are very high, but the difficulty is greatly overrated, and in fair weather there is no danger whatever, though the iron chains which hang along the face of a precipice at the summit are said to be really necessary for the pilgrims to hold on by on stormy days; indeed, the great iron chains by which the roof of the little shrine is affixed to the rocks all round tell the same story of the wild sweeping of tempestuous winds and storms, which often rage around the summit and invest the Peak with dread.

These chains are said to have been originally placed here by Alexander the Great, whom the Mahommedans affirm to have climbed the pinnacle about B.C. 330, to do homage to the footprint of Adam. Ibn Batuta, describing his ascent of the Peak in the fourteenth century, tells how a ridge at the base of the cone bears the name of the Conqueror, as does also a water-spring, at which all pilgrims slake their thirst; and Ashref, a Persian poet of the following century, tells how, in order to facilitate the difficult and dangerous ascent, Alexander caused stanchions to be fixed in the face of the cliff to sustain iron chains, by holding on to which they were able to scale the precipitous rock without danger. Whoever has the merit of first placing the chains, there they remain to the present day.

We accounted ourselves rarely fortunate in being favoured with a day of calmest sunshine, for most evenings, both before and after our expedition, closed with terrific thunderstorms, and for hours together the Peak was veiled in dark clouds, so we had fully reckoned on the possibility of such a night of awe. Instead of this, on reaching the summit, our eyes were gladdened with a magnificent view of the whole island, outstretched on every side. All around lay a vast expanse of forest-clad mountain ranges—the wholesale destruction of the forests to prepare the way for cultivation being less conspicuous from this point than from many others; and far away, beyond wide sweeps of parklike country, traversed by silvery lines which mark the course of rivers, and vanishing in a soft blue haze, a line of glittering light revealed the presence of the encircling ocean.

All this we beheld at a glance, when, after a final steep climb up the huge naked rock, about forty feet high, which forms the mountain crown, we reached a morsel of level ground which lies about ten feet below the summit, from which point a level pathway has been constructed, forming an oval of about 65 by 45 feet, passing round the Peak, so as to enable pilgrims to perform the three orthodox turns, following the course of the sun, by keeping the right hand next to the rock all the time. The outer edge of this path is happily protected by a low stone wall. Sorely, indeed, must the sunwise turns have tried dizzy heads ere this was built by some pious pilgrims.[1]

So steep are the precipitous sides of this mighty cone,

---

[1] I have noted numerous instances of "sunwise turns" round all manner of sacred objects, in "In the Himalayas," pp. 4, 250, 359, 430, 529, 551, 584, 590. Also "In the Hebrides," pp. 241-245. Published by Chatto & Windus.

that one marvels how the gnarled old rhododendron trees
have contrived to gain, and continued to retain, their hold
on the rock, or how they find sustenance. There they are,
however, with their glossy leaves and crimson blossoms, as
gay as though rooted in the richest peat soil, instead of
being fed chiefly by the dews of heaven.

A final ascent of about ten steps brings us to the extreme summit of the Peak, 7352 feet above the sea. It is crowned by a picturesque little wooden temple, consisting merely of a light overhanging roof, supported on slender columns, and open to every wind of heaven—such winds as would carry it to the sea were it not for the strong iron chains passing over it. Beneath this canopy lies THE FOOTPRINT, revered not only by about four hundred million Buddhists, but also, as I have just stated, by Hindoos and Mahommedans without number, and even by Roman Catholic Christians.

Happily for us, ascending at the end of January, we arrived before the annual stream of pilgrims, so we found only a handful—a very varied selection, however, beginning with our own party, which included divers European nationalities, while the Oriental creeds were represented by an old Hindoo Yogi in saffron-coloured robes, and wearing a large rosary of black beads; he had come from the Punjab to worship Siva, while his neighbour, a Mahommedan priest, had travelled all the way from Lahore, in Northern India, to do homage to Adam on this sacred spot. He found the mountain air exceedingly cold, and crouched over his fire, wrapped in a gorgeous patchwork quilt, smoking his hubble-bubble. Several Christians from the Malabar Coast were intent on the worship of St. Thomas.

Strange to say, the only representative of Buddhism

present was a small boy of the Amarapoora sect, who slept apart beneath an overhanging rock near our hut, where we heard him singing his midnight prayers most devoutly. He was a pretty little fellow, and the yellow robes of Buddha harmonised well with his clear brown skin and dark eyes. A wretched little hut, on the level just below the summit, is reserved for the use of the senior priests, who, however, have more comfortable quarters at the foot of the mountain when not on duty here. We were told that the venerable high-priest of the Peak lives up here a good deal during the pilgrim season.

While I made a careful drawing of the scene, my companions were hard at work preparing our night quarters. Happily there still remained the walls of a hut which was built on the occasion of Lady Robinson's ascent; so this was quickly cleaned out, thickly carpeted with bamboo grass, and roofed with the large mats of talipat-palm leaf which we had so fortunately brought with us; so in the course of a couple of hours we had a capital two-roomed house ready. This had the merit of standing a little apart from the pilgrims, and was perched upon rocks fringed with ferns and sweet pink orchids, and overshadowed by rhododendron trees.

Suddenly, about twenty minutes before sunset, to our intense delight, the far-famed shadow of the Peak fell eastward athwart the plain, like a blue spirit-pyramid resting, not on the ground, but on the atmosphere; for instead of assuming the forms of the mountains, it lay in a faultless triangle ("an isosceles triangle," observed one of the party, last from Oxford), the lines as straight as if they had been ruled, although the object casting the so-called shadow is a ragged cone.

I suppose it is due to the fact of the sun being so much larger than the earth that its level rays, divided by the base of the mountain, seem to meet again on the opposite horizon. But such prosaic speculation as to its cause found no place in our thoughts while gazing spell-bound on this wondrous apparition, which each moment grew wider at the base, while lengthening till it touched the ocean on the eastern horizon, and the sun sank beyond the western waves.

When the last glories of the afterglow had faded away, we had a most cheery dinner by a moonlight so clear that we could distinguish the whole island outspread far below us right away to the sea. Our thinly-clad coolies suffered much from cold, and so tried to warm themselves by dancing round their fires—a curious wild scene. The gentlemen encouraged the dancers, and strove to warm them by administering small drams of brandy, which they received in the palm of the hand, crouching at the feet of the *dorre*— *i.e.*, " master."

While this was going on, I crept up to the now deserted shrine, and stood there alone beside the rock-mark, which in all ages has inspired such amazing reverence in millions of my fellow-creatures. During the regular pilgrim season the shrine is all hung with white cloths, and the sacred footprint is covered by a model of itself made of brass, inlaid with pieces of coloured glass, which is the modern substitute for the original, which was of pure gold, inlaid with precious gems, and which was seen here by Dutch travellers who ascended the Peak in 1654.

In Valentyn's account of the Sri Pada in March 1654 he says, " The priests showed our people a gold plate representing the length and breadth of the foot, on which were various figures, which they said were formerly to be seen on the footprint itself; but that after the priests allowed them to be engraved on the gold, *they disappeared from the stone*. These figures were sixty-eight in number, and may be seen figured by Baldæus in his description of Coromandel, fol. 151, with other matters relating thereto."

Perhaps the very elaborate symbols sculptured on the Burmese footprint in the British Museum may afford some clue to these vanished figures.

Strange to say, among the offerings presented at the shrine fifty years ago was an embossed silver covering for the great footmark, the gift of Sir R. W. Horton, who held office as British Governor from 1831 to 1837, and who thus emphasised the proclamation made in the name of His Majesty King William IV., that protection would be continued to all rites and usages of the Buddhist religion.

When Hoffmeister made the ascent in 1844, he found the footprint enclosed within a golden frame studded with gems of considerable size, of which, however, he pronounced that only a few were genuine.

I had the better fortune to see the rock unadorned, and, if the truth must be confessed, being anxious to measure it accurately for myself, I lay down full length on it, and found it to be $4\frac{1}{2}$ inches longer than myself, whereby I proved it to be just 6 feet in length. I was told that the breadth at the toes is 32 inches; that at the heel is 26 inches. The natural mark is merely a slight indentation, 8 inches deeper at the toes than at the heel, but the imaginary outline of the foot has been emphasised by a rim of plaster, coloured to match the rock. The toes have also been defined. The footprint points north-west.

According to a tradition quoted in Chinese records of the

sixteenth century, the hollow of the footprint should contain a never-failing supply of fresh water, supplied from heaven, and which cures all diseases. I am told that many sick folk make this toilsome pilgrimage on purpose to drink of this water of life. I can only hope that they do not often find the rock as dry as it was on this occasion! There is, however, a well at the foot of the mountain, which, although its waters are less sacred, is nevertheless credited with miraculous cures, and this also has been duly recorded by observant Chinese travellers of the fourteenth century. So you see, the farther you travel, the more surely you will prove that there is nothing really new under the sun!

After a while chilling mists began to arise from the deep valleys and to creep up the mountain-side, and I was glad enough to join the merry party beside the blazing fire, and then to seek rest in the little hut, truly thankful for the kind forethought which had supplied so goodly a store of warm blankets.

Ere the first glimmer of dawn I stole forth to look down upon the wondrous sea of white mist, which seemed to cover the whole Isle with one fleecy shroud, a strangely eerie scene, all bathed in the pale spiritual moonlight. Ever and anon the faint breeze stirred the billowy surface, and a veil of transparent vapour floated upward to play round the dark summits of the surrounding hills, which seemed like innumerable islands on a glistening lake. One of these, bearing the name of Uno Dhia Parawatia—a grand square-shaped rock mass—towers high above the surrounding ridges of densely wooded hills.

The stars were still shining brilliantly, while eastward the pale primrose light was changing to a golden glow. Sometimes the uprolling clouds floated as if enfolding us, drifting beneath our feet as though the solid earth were passing away from under us.

Wonderful and most impressive was the stillness. Just before daybreak my ear caught the ascending murmur of voices, and peering down the mountain-side, I discerned the glimmering torches which told of the approach of a pilgrim band toiling up the steep ravine, bent on reaching the summit ere sunrise.

Judging from my own experience, I should have thought they could have little breath to spare. Nevertheless, they contrived to cheer the way with sacred chants, and very wild and pathetic these sounded as they floated up through the gloom of night.

At last the topmost stair was reached, and as each pilgrim set foot on the level just below the shrine, he extinguished his torch of blazing palm-leaves, and with bowed head and outstretched arms stood wrapped in fervent adoration. Some knelt so lowlily that their foreheads rested on the rock. Then facing the east—now streaked with bars of orange betwixt purple clouds—they waited with earnest faces, eagerly longing for the appearing of the sun, suggesting to my mind a strikingly Oriental illustration of the words of the poet-king, "My soul waiteth for the Lord *more than they that watch for the morning.*"[1]

Gradually the orange glow broadened, and the welling light grew clearer and clearer, until, with a sudden bound, up rose the glorious sun, and, as if with one voice, each watcher greeted its appearing with the deep-toned "Saädu! Saädu!" which embodies such indescribable intensity of devotion.

Beautiful in truth was that radiant light, which, while

[1] Bible version of Psalm cxxx. 6.

the world below still lay shrouded in gloom, kissed this high summit and the glowing blossoms of the crimson rhododendron trees, and lent its own brightness to the travel-stained white garments of the pilgrims.

But while these gazed spell-bound, absorbed in worship, we quickly turned westward, and there, to our exceeding joy, once more beheld the mighty shadow falling right across the Island, and standing out clear and distinct—a wondrous pyramid whose summit touched the western horizon. The world below us still lay veiled in white mist, now tinged with a delicate pink, as were also the mountain-tops, which rose so like islands from that vaporous sea. But, right across it all, the great spectral triangle, changing from delicate violet to clear blue, lay outspread, its edge prismatic, like a faint rainbow.

We watched it for three hours, during which it gradually grew shorter and more sombre, so that it was actually darker than the forest-clad hills which lay in shadow before us, and across which it fell. As the sun rose higher and higher, the blue pyramid gradually grew narrower at the base, till finally it vanished, leaving us impressed with the conviction that to this phenomenon must in some measure be attributed the sanctity with which, in early ages, a people always keenly addicted to nature-worship invested this mountain-top. Their modern descendants seemed to have no room for it in their full hearts.

I may mention that I have witnessed this identical phenomenon at sunrise from the summit of Fuji-Yama, the holy mountain of Japan, and I have heard it said that a similar effect is to be seen from Pike's Peak in Colorado, a mountain 14,157 feet in height, but not remarkable in form. I have, however, seen a picture which merely shows the sunset shadow of the mountain on the eastern sky—not at all a triangle. From the summit of Mount Omei, the holy mountain of the Chinese Buddhists, a very peculiar shadow is sometimes seen, capped by a marvellous prismatic halo, which is known as the "Glory of Buddha." Occasionally, when the shadow of Adam's Peak falls on mist, the spectral shadow seems to stand upright, taking the conical form of the mountain, and a rainbow-girt halo rests on its summit.

One traveller only, so far as I am aware, has had the good fortune to see this wonderful shadow as a moonlight phenomenon, which, of course, could only occur when an almost full moon was very near the horizon, either rising or setting. This fortunate observer was Lawrence Oliphant, whose description of the scene is so striking that again I cannot refrain from quoting his words.

"By the light of a moon a little past the full, in the early morning, I looked down from this isolated summit upon a sea of mist, which stretched to the horizon in all directions, completely concealing the landscape beneath me. Its white, compact, smooth surface almost gave it the appearance of a field of snow, *across which, in a deep black shadow, extended the conical form of the mountain I was on, its apex just touching the horizon*, and producing a scenic effect as unique as it was imposing.

"While I was watching it, the sharpness of its outline gradually began to fade, the black shadow became by degrees less black, the white mist more grey, and as the dawn slowly broke, the whole effect was changed as by the wand of a magician. *Another conical shadow crept over the vast expanse on the opposite side of the mountain, which, in its turn, reached to the horizon*, as the sun rose over the tremulous mist; but the sun-shadow seemed to lack the cold mystery of the moon-shadow it had driven away, and scarcely gave one time to appreciate its own marvellous effects before the mist itself began slowly to rise and to envelop us as in a winding-sheet. For half an hour or more we were in the clouds and could see nothing; then suddenly they rolled away and revealed the magnificent panorama which had been the object of our pilgrimage."

Intently as we watched each change in this wondrous vision, we did not fail to note the proceedings of our fellow-pilgrims, who, previous to paying their vows at the holy shrine, walk thrice sunwise round it, following the well-worn level footpath, and carrying their simple offerings of flowers, chiefly the scarlet blossoms of the rhododendron and the fragrant white champac and plumeria, raised on high in their joined hands. Then a second time they performed the three sunwise turns, this time bearing on one shoulder a brass lota filled with clear icy water from a spring which lies about twelve feet below the summit, and in which leaves wafted from Paradise are sometimes found floating,—so the pilgrims believe. A second spring lies about forty feet lower down.[1] (Two silver bells were the gift of certain Moormen to the honour of Adam, as were also two large brass lamps.) The pilgrims then kneel in lowliest adoration whilst the priest pours out their offering of water upon the footprint, on which they also lay their gift of flowers, and a few small coins for the use of the

[1] It always seems strange to find water-springs in the hard rock at a great altitude. I saw two similar springs on the extreme summit of Fuji-Yama in Japan, which is simply a dormant crater, and others on the summit and in the crater of Haleakala in the Sandwich Isles. See "Fire Fountains of Hawaii," vol. i. p. 264. Published by Blackwood.

priests. Then dipping their hands in the water thus sanctified, they wash their faces in symbolic purification.

Afterwards it is customary for each pilgrim to tear a fragment from his scanty raiment and knot it to one of the iron chains, to remind Heaven of the petitions offered on this sacred spot. These rags, old and new, form a fringe of many colours, enlivening the rusty chains which secure the temple to the crag. Some of the links in these ancient and modern chains are inscribed with the name of the donor, who has thus presented a more enduring memorial than the rag of his poor brother. Strange, is it not, how this identical custom of rag-offering prevails in all regions of the earth, from Ireland's holy wells to Himalayan mountains and sacred bushes!

Some of the pilgrims had brought with them long strips of white calico, wherewith the little priestling covered the mystic rock, and on each of which he traced with saffron (sacred yellow) an exceedingly well-defined footprint. These were hung up to the eaves of the temple, and thence fluttered flag-like till thoroughly dried, when the devout pilgrims would carry them to distant lands, for the edification of less fortunate believers. These are deemed a charm against the evil-eye and sundry diseases.

Various travellers have noted a graceful detail of family life at the conclusion of the appointed worship, namely, that husbands and wives, children and parents, salute one another most reverently and affectionately with lowly salaams; the grey-haired wife, moved to tears, almost embracing the feet of her venerable husband, and he raising her lovingly —younger men simply exchanging salutations and betel leaves.

Thus year after year, from the earliest ages of human

history, have pilgrim bands climbed this lofty summit to worship on the pinnacle which, though we believe it to be no nearer to heaven than the murkiest street of our crowded cities, is certainly far uplifted above the levels of earth.

To say that the aboriginal native worshippers of the Isle revered this rock-pinnacle long before the days of Gautama Buddha, is nothing; for though he is said to have appeared here more than five hundred years before Christ, he was only the most recent of a series of Buddhas—holy beings who are supposed to have honoured this earth with their presence in divers ages. I believe the Singhalese legends tell of twenty-five Buddhas who have visited Ceylon, of whom four are said to have revealed themselves on this spot.

The first of these was Kukusanda, who appeared about B.C. 3000, and found the Peak already known as Deiwakuta, "Peak of the God."

The second Buddha who here revealed himself was Konagamma; he appeared B.C. 2099, and even at that early date the mount (so they say) was already known as Samantakuta, in honour of Saman, who three hundred years previously had, as I have already observed, accompanied Rama when he conquered Ceylon.

The third Buddha, known as Kasyapa, appeared about B.C. 1000, and then, B.C. 577, came Gautama Buddha, the prince of Lucknow.

Since then, successive kings and nobles have come here from far distant lands on solemn pilgrimage, and many a picturesque company (some robed in all the gorgeousness of Oriental splendour) has wended its way from the coast through the dense beast-haunted forests which clothed these wild mountain ranges, to toil up these self-same rock-hewn steps since, in the year A.D. 24, Meghavahana, king of Cashmere, came all the way hither to worship on this summit.

That the kings of Ceylon should be numbered amongst the pilgrims is only natural, though doubtless it was a notable event that they should make the journey on foot, as did the great Buddhist king, Prakrama Bahu I., who, about A.D. 1153, "caused a temple to be erected on the summit of Samanala" (so it is stated in the Rajavali).

Thus through each successive age has the ceaseless offering of prayer and praise ascended from this majestic mountain-altar to the great All-Father, whose tender mercy enfolds all His children, albeit so many can but feel after Him through the blinding mists of heathenism. But we, who KNOW His all-enfolding love, and grieve to see these weary ones pleading with "unknown gods," can but echo the hope of him who wrote:—

> "What if to THEE in THINE Infinity
> These multiform and many-coloured creeds
> Seem but the robe man wraps as masquer's weeds
> Round the one living truth THOU givest him—THEE!
> What if these varied forms that worship prove
> (Being heart-worship) reach THY perfect ear
> But as a monotone, complete and clear,
> Of which the music is (through CHRIST'S NAME) LOVE?
> For ever rising in sublime increase
> To 'Glory in the Highest—on Earth peace.'"

CHAPTER XXVI.

THE TUG OF WAR—THE BATTLE OF DIVERSE CREEDS
IN CEYLON.

Nestorian Christians—St. Francis Xavier—Portuguese—Dutch—Table of British Missionaries—Roman Catholic—American Mission—Need of a Medical Mission for Women—Jaffna College—High-caste students—Commencement of Wesleyan Mission—Its Mission to Burmah.

I DOUBT whether in any other corner of the earth so small an area has proved the battle-field for creeds so diverse as those which have successively striven for the mastery in Ceylon. Certainly there is none in which successive mercenary invaders, whether heathen or Christian, have more unscrupulously used the cloak of religion as a political engine for the furtherance of their own designs, or with more lamentable results.

This fair Isle, somewhat smaller than Ireland, has for centuries been distracted by religious and political conflicts, subject to the caprice of successive rulers of diverse race and faith, each imposing its own secular and spiritual government on the conquered islanders, and all alike unstable. From the days when pure, cold, atheistic Buddhism first sought (quite ineffectually) to drive out the devil-worship which prevails to this day, and through Hindoo and Malay invasions, bringing alternate waves of polytheism and monotheism, till Portuguese and Dutch conquerors came, each in turn determined to enforce their own creed, the people have been subject to such conflicting teaching, that to a very great extent all these faiths have partly blended and partly neutralised one another.

At the present day, although, out of a population of somewhat over 3,000,000, 1,800,000 are professedly Buddhists, 630,000 are Hindoos, 220,000 are Mahommedans, and, according to the latest census, 283,000 are Christians, the great mass of these people are still in the thraldom of the aboriginal devil-worship, which is a system of ceaseless propitiation of malignant spirits.

As regards the effect on the Christianity of the Isle, it is evident that creeds enforced by conquerors could not fail to be odious in the eyes of the people. As to winning their hearts, that was never attempted until the present century, unless, perhaps, in very early days when Christianity was introduced from Persia by Nestorian missionaries. Of this mention is made by Cosmas, a Nestorian Christian, who, writing in the time of Justinian, tells that in Taprobane (which was the ancient Greek name for Ceylon) there existed a community of Persian Christians, tended by bishops, priests, and deacons, and having a regular liturgy.

These are understood to have been merchants attracted by commerce to this Isle of gems, ivory, and precious timber, which was then the great emporium of Oriental trade. They are supposed to have established their head-quarters on the shores of the Gulf of Manaar, but by the close of the sixth century Eastern trade seems to have languished, the Persian merchants no longer frequented the Isle, and no more is heard of these Persian colonists. Their influence, however, remained, for when Sir John Mandeville visited the North-West Province in the fourteenth century, he states that he there found "good men and reasonable, and many Christian men amongst them."

Some lingering trace of their teaching doubtless predisposed the Tamil natives of that district to the Christian faith, for when[1] St. Francis Xavier (like his MASTER preaching to the fishers on the Lake of Galilee) made his earliest proselytes among the fisher-folk of Cape Comorin, those of Manaar sent him an invitation to come and teach them also. Though unable to come in person, he sent one of his clergy, through whom about seven hundred received baptism—a baptism which was straightway crowned by martyrdom, as these early converts were forthwith put to death by the Rajah of Jaffna, who was a worshipper of Siva. This martyrdom was followed by the usual results, for ere long the sons and other relations of the persecuting ruler embraced the Christian faith and fled for protection to the mainland, to the court of the Christian Viceroy of Goa.

Soon afterward the Rajah himself, terrified by the encroachments of the Portuguese, declared himself a convert, and induced St. Francis to secure for him a political alliance with these irresistible invaders, who accordingly established a sort of protectorate in his realm, which soon resulted in the assertion of absolute power and the expulsion of the tyrant from his dominions.

To this day the majority of the Singhalese and Tamil fishers are members of the Roman Catholic Church, and members, moreover, who pay their tithes in so liberal a fashion, that when, in 1840, the British Government abolished the tax on fish, which had previously been an item of revenue

[1] A.D. 1544.

equivalent to about £6000 per annum, the fishers simply transferred their payment to the priests, by whom it has thenceforth been collected. The Portuguese seem to have discovered the Island by accident, while pursuing trading vessels. They found Moorish ships laden with cinnamon and elephants, and straightway their covetousness was awakened. They found a people weakened by dissensions, amongst whom they came in threefold character, as merchants, missionaries, and pirates. They craved an inch, they quickly took an ell, and in truth a knell they sounded throughout the weary land.

So soon as they obtained possession of Colombo and the adjoining districts (A.D. 1505), Don Juan de Monterio was consecrated first Roman Catholic Bishop of Ceylon, and every effort was made to induce the Singhalese to declare themselves converts. So great was the official pressure, enforced by the indescribably brutal cruelty of fanatical soldiers, that multitudes yielded and submitted to baptism. Amongst these nominal converts were the kings of Kandy and of Cotta, but this was not till the former had been driven from his throne, and the latter compelled to seek the aid of the Portuguese to retain his kingdom. The example of their kings was followed by many of the nobles, who carried compliance so far as to adopt the names of the Portuguese nobles who stood sponsors at the holy font—a circumstance of which we find a curious survival at the present day in the Portuguese Christian names combined with native surnames borne by so many of the people of pure blood, such as *Gregory de Soyza* Wijeyegooneratue Siriwardene, *Don David de Silva* Welaratne Jayetilleke, *Johan Louis Perera* Abeysekere Goonewardene, &c.

Although the influence of Portuguese gold, the hope of

official honours, and the dread of barbarous torture combined to produce a general outward conformity, it stands to reason that the majority of the people continued secretly attached to the Buddhist and Brahman faiths; and so great were the concessions made by the Roman Catholic teachers in the way of assimilation as to call forth serious remonstrance from some of the stricter Orders.

Thus matters continued till, in the beginning of the seventeenth century, the Dutch obtained the upper hand in the struggle for supremacy, and in A.D. 1642 they proclaimed the Reformed Church of Holland to be the established religion of the Isle. Then followed a period of most cruel persecution. Many of the Portuguese priests were deported to India, one was beheaded, all were insulted and oppressed, as were also the native Roman Catholics, many of whom, however, had now become so thoroughly in earnest that no amount of persecution could make them abjure their faith. These were Singhalese, Tamils, and descendants of the Portuguese.

By way of exhibiting their superiority to childish reverence for images, the Dutch indulged in such unworthy diversions as mutilating the sacred figures in the churches, especially that of St. Thomas, the patron saint of the Isle, into which they knocked great nails, and then shot it from a mortar right into the Portuguese quarters. Thus Christianity was presented to the islanders solely as the ground for bitter contentions between these two bodies of those professing it. The Portuguese persuasives having been the sword, the stake, and the spear, the Dutch tried bribery, Government office, and emolument of various kinds.

In curious contrast with their contemptible sacrifice of Christianity to trade in Japan, the Dutch here set to work with a high hand to establish the Reformed Faith. Issuing stringent penal proclamations against the celebration of mass and every other office of the Roman Catholic Church, they took possession of the churches, established Reformed schools, and by the close of the seventeenth century they reckoned their nominal adherents among the Tamil population in the north of the Isle at about 190,000. Nevertheless, Baldæus, one of the earliest Dutch missionaries, who in 1663 records this triumph, has to confess that, though Christian in name, they retained many of the superstitions of their Hindoo Paganism.

But the Singhalese of the Southern District were by no means so ready to adopt another new creed at the bidding of strangers; so to quicken their intelligence, proclamations were issued to the effect that no native who had not been admitted by baptism into the Protestant Church could hold any office under Government, or even be allowed to farm land. Of course, upon this there was no limit to the numbers who pressed forward to submit to the test thus sacrilegiously imposed, Brahmans claiming their right to do so without even laying aside the outward symbols of their heathen worship.

And no wonder that they assumed the test to be merely an external form, when in A.D. 1707 they saw the Dutch actually securing peace with the Kandyan king by a loan of ships to convey messengers to Arracan, thence to bring Buddhist priests of sufficiently high ecclesiastical rank to restore the *Upasampada* order in Ceylon and reinstate Buddhism, which had fallen into decay during the long-continued wars.

The Dutch, however, had every intention of really educating the people to an understanding of Christian doctrine, so free schools were established everywhere throughout the maritime provinces over which they held sway, and attendance was made compulsory and enforced by a system of fines. The natives made no objection to sending their boys, but that girls should be compelled to attend in public was then deemed scandalous.

Even under the pressure of the new edict, the southern Buddhist districts never yielded half so many nominal converts as did the Hindoo population in the north. There was nothing in the prosaic forms of Dutch Presbyterianism which appealed to their imagination. But the Church of Rome received a fresh impetus from the fervent preaching of Father Joseph Vaz, of the Oratory of St. Philip Neri at Goa, who (protected by the reinstated Christian king of Kandy, who backed his advocacy by the persecution and imprisonment of non-compliant subjects) gained 30,000 converts from the ranks of those who had hitherto continued staunch Buddhists.

The Roman Catholics had now resumed worship in four hundred churches throughout the Isle, and the Dutch deemed it necessary to reassert themselves by issuing fresh penal laws, resulting in bitter contentions between these two bodies of the Christian Church, while all the time heathenism continued rampant, the Dutch themselves declaring that multitudes of their nominal adherents were incorrigible Buddhists, who regulated every act of life by the teaching of astrologers, always calling in the aid of devil-dancers, rather than that of the clergy, wearing heathen charms, and making offerings in the idol-temples.

But the penal laws which subjected Roman Catholics to all possible civil disabilities, and even refused to recognise marriage by a priest as valid, continued in force till 1806, when they were repealed by the British Government, and religious liberty established. At the present day scarcely a trace remains of the influence of Dutch Presbyterianism, whereas the numerous descendants of the Portuguese converts continue to be devout members of the Roman Catholic Church (combined, however, with much of the grossest superstition of their heathen neighbours). A very debased form of the Portuguese language is also extensively spoken, and, in fact, was till recently in common use amongst all the mixed races, whereas the Dutch language has entirely died out.

That the Dutch Church, so forcibly established, should have failed to obtain any real footing in the hearts of the nominal converts is no wonder, inasmuch as their clergy would not even take the trouble to master the language of the people, but taught through interpreters. In 1747 there remained in all the Isle only five ministers of the Reformed Church, and only one of these could even understand the language.

After this, however, they were ably assisted by Schwartz and other members of the Danish Mission at Tranquebar, who undertook to train young men for the ministry in Ceylon. But a Church which was so entirely built up on a basis of political bribery and coercion could not stand when these incentives were removed, and so this outwardly imposing Dutch Church has faded away like a dream.

For some time, however, after the British annexation of Ceylon, Dutch Presbyterianism was recognised as the Established Church of the colony, and Mr. North (the first British Governor, afterwards Lord Guildford) not only took active measures for restoring 170 of the Dutch village-schools all over the Island, but also offered Government assistance to the clergy if they would itinerate through the rural districts, and so keep alive some knowledge of the Christian faith.

How little the Home Government cared about the matter was proved by the refusal to sanction the sum expended by Mr. North on the schools, which accordingly had to be considerably reduced—a parsimony which was deemed grievously out of keeping with the high salaries granted in other departments.

Meanwhile, however, seeing the interest thus taken in the matter by their new rulers, and expecting that religious profession and political reward would continue to go hand in hand, the number of the nominal converts, both Roman Catholic and Presbyterian, increased rapidly, but only to be followed by wholesale apostasy so soon as they realised that their creed was a matter of absolute indifference to their official superiors. Thus, whereas in A.D. 1801 no less than 342,000 Singhalese professed the Protestant faith, ten years later that number was diminished by one-half, the rest having returned to the worship of Buddha!

Likewise in the northern districts, where in A.D. 1802 upwards of 136,000 of the Tamil population were nominal Presbyterians, the cloak of "Government religion" was thrown off so rapidly, that, four years later, the fine old churches were described by Buchanan as having been abandoned, and left to go to ruin, the Protestant religion being extinct, and the congregations having all returned either to the Church of Rome or to the worship of the Hindoo gods. The clergy of the Presbyterian Church had left a district where they were as shepherds without sheep. Only one Tamil catechist remained in charge of the whole province of Jaffna, while priests from the Roman Catholic college at Goa divided the field with the reinstated Brahmans.

So feebly rooted was this Dutch Christianity, that there was reason to fear that those who continued to profess the "Government religion" were really those who cared least about any faith; and though they and their descendants have ever been willing to bring their children to holy baptism, the very term which describes that sacrament, "*Kulawadenawa*," "admission to rank," recalls the notion of secular advantage which it conveys to their minds.

Of course, a country in which religion had been thus misused presented the most disheartening of mission-fields. Nevertheless, in the beginning of the present century, the London Mission, the Wesleyans, and the Baptists each sent representatives to try what could be done; but their early efforts seemed to themselves altogether without fruit. The Church of England likewise sent chaplains to minister to the British settlers.[1] About the same time the American Board of Foreign Missions sent its emissaries to commence work at Madras. On their way thither their vessel was wrecked off the north-west of Ceylon. This they accepted as an indication of the Divine will that they were to go

[1] I may here quote Mr. Ferguson's Chronological Table of Missions in Ceylon:—

A.D. 1505. Portuguese visit Ceylon.
— 1544. Roman Catholicism first preached at Manaar.
— 1642. Dutch Presbyterian Ministry commenced.
— 1740. Arrival of Moravian Missionaries.
— 1804. Arrival of London Missionaries.
— 1812. Baptist Mission commenced.
— 1814. Wesleyan Mission commenced.
— 1816. American Mission commenced.
— 1818. Arrival of Church Missionaries (C.M.S.).
— 1840. Arrival of Church Missionaries (S.P.G.).
— 1854. Tamil Coolie Mission commenced.

no farther. They accordingly established themselves at JAFFNA, which was then a very different place from the civilised town and province of the present day, with gardens and lawn-tennis grounds, its network of first-class roads and travelling facilities. At that time there were no roads, only footpaths over heavy sand, which in the rainy season became impassable. The salt lagoon was not bridged, and the only means of travel was by canoe and palanquin. Bullock-carts were unknown luxuries, and where vast cocoa and palmyra palm plantations now flourish, all was gloomy jungle, haunted by innumerable leopards, black bears, and other dangerous foes. Packs of jackals infested the suburbs, making night hideous with their cries, troops of monkeys and large grey wanderoos boldly stripped the gardens, while gangs of robbers kept all honest folk in terror.

At this very uninviting spot the shipwrecked Americans took up their quarters near the old Dutch fort, and devoted all their energies to the evangelising of the Tamil population—an effort which has been carried on without ceasing up to the present time with very marked success.

These pioneers were closely followed by the English Church Missionary Society, whose first messengers commenced work at Nellore, in the immediate neighbourhood of Jaffna, and there studied, taught, and preached for twelve weary years ere their patience was rewarded by making a single convert. Ere that year closed, however, a little band of ten had renounced idolatry, and formed the nucleus of the future Church, which, from that small beginning, has very slowly but steadily developed, and has now just attained that stage of vitality when a Church begins to recognise its own responsibility towards its heathen neighbours—a conviction which inevitably results in self-extension.

Of course mission-work was now commenced on an entirely new footing. So far from aiming at wholesale conversions, all inquirers were henceforth individually subjected to most searching probation, and a rigid standard of character has been maintained, with the result that though the recognised adherents of each Mission are comparatively few, they are of true stuff, and many are of the kind which seeks to win others.

Thus the position of Ceylon in regard to Christian missions is that of a canvas on which successive artists have tried their skill, each striving to obliterate the work of his predecessors, resulting in an undertone of heavy neutral tint; whereon at the present moment many draughtsmen are simultaneously endeavouring to work out a Christian design, although sorely at variance concerning the detail and colour of its several parts.

The various Protestant sects do indeed seek to work in harmony, though of course their differences must sorely perplex the heathen who is half inclined to forsake his ancestral faith. But reckoning all together, Episcopalians, Wesleyans, Presbyterians, Congregationalists, and Baptists, these, even according to the census, only constitute a total of about 70,000, and of these only about 35,000 are recognised adherents of any Protestant mission. Here, as in India, many who would be no credit to any creed can assume the name for their own ends. The Roman Catholics, who are content to acknowledge very nominal conversions, reckon their co-religionists at upwards of 212,000, but a very large number of these are Christians solely in name, descendants of converts of bygone generations, and absolutely ignorant of even the distinctive outlines of Christian faith.

Of these two great branches of the Church Catholic, it

can certainly not be said that they are working in union in their Master's cause, but never does their estrangement appear so grievous as when thus displayed in presence of an overwhelming majority of the heathen, whom each seek to lead to the same Saviour—at least we would fain believe that such is the object of the whole Catholic Church, though practically even the largest charity must admit that a vast number of the Roman Catholic converts merely exchange one idolatry for another. I have already mentioned having myself seen in one small chapel the image of Buddha on one side and that of the Blessed Virgin on the other, receiving divided worship; and as to the processions in the Tamil districts, it is scarcely possible to distinguish those of so-called Christian images from those of the Hindoo gods (which are worshipped alike by Buddhists and Tamils), to say nothing of the fact that each are escorted by companies of riotous devil-dancers and truly diabolical musicians, both hired from heathen temples.

But even a most orthodox Roman Catholic festival is startling when considered as a legitimate feature in the worship of ONE who has revealed Himself as "a jealous GOD," saying, "MY glory will I not give to another, neither MY praise to graven images." Here, for instance, is an account of the Midsummer Pilgrimage of Our Lady of Maddu as described by the 'Jaffna Catholic Guardian' in 1884:—

"The annual festival of this celebrated sanctuary was solemnised with the customary pomp, fervour, and devotion. As the fame of this holy spot spreads, so does the number of pilgrims increase from year to year. This year the number assembled on the festival day was calculated to be between fifteen and twenty thousand. Yet the order and quiet that reigned throughout the time the festival lasted was simply admirable. The cheerfulness and resignation of the people amidst the discomforts and privations of a jungle life, far away from any human habitation, and especially in a place where water is scarce, was a source of edification to every one. Nothing could be more touching than to see the pious fervour with which the pilgrims, *both Catholics and Hindoos, Buddhists and Moors*, from early dawn till late in the night, flocked around the altar of our Holy Mother *to thank her* for favours received, and *to supplicate her* for the grace they stood in need of. The temporary church could not contain the crowds that gathered at the morning and evening services."

The mixed multitude of pilgrims here represented as worshippers at the shrine of the Blessed Virgin is certainly remarkable.

Perhaps we need scarcely wonder that the Protestant catechists, who insist on a radical change of creed, sometimes meet with more serious opposition from the Roman Catholic priests than from the heathen. For instance, a catechist was recently selling books and tracts from village to village in the Negombo district. The purchasers included sundry Roman Catholics, who in that neighbourhood are numerous. One of these invited the catechist to bring his books to the verandah of his house, and sent a private intimation to the priest, who in the course of a few minutes arrived, angrily denouncing the sale of such pernicious literature. The catechist vainly pointed out that the books he was selling were all the simplest teaching about Jesus addressed to Buddhists, but the irate priest refused to hear him, and informing him that he had already collected and burnt more than a hundred of the books sold in other villages, he confiscated the whole remaining stock. Reckoning the prices marked on those for sale, he paid down the money, but appropriated all that were for gratuitous circulation, and, notwithstanding the protestations of their owner, he carried off the whole lot to burn them. During this scene a crowd of Romanists gathered round, and were worked up to such excitement, that the catechist was thankful to escape from the village without personal injury.

Of the three races whom both Catholics and Protestants seek to influence, *i.e.*, the Singhalese, Tamils, and Moormen, the most satisfactory mission results have been obtained amongst the Tamils of the Northern Province, Jaffna, as I have already stated, having long been the headquarters of the American Congregational Mission, as also of a Church of England and a Wesleyan branch, all happily proving their love to one Master by working in sympathy shoulder to shoulder, as beseems loyal soldiers of the Grand Army, who are too deeply engrossed in a real war with dark idolatry to contend over small differences of regimental uniform.

Each of these missions has its own schools and chapels, scattered over the many villages of the surrounding districts. The most notable feature in all three is the recent recognition of the tremendously antagonistic power of the heathen wives and mothers, "the backbone of the nation," whom it is always so difficult to reach on account of Oriental customs of feminine seclusion; not that these are by any means so stringent in Ceylon as on the mainland. So a great effort is now being made by each of these missions to establish schools, and especially boarding-schools for girls, and in every possible way to win the women.

This effort was indeed commenced at the very beginning of the AMERICAN MISSION, when it was found that Tamil parents were willing to send their boys to school, but declared that it was absurd to send girls, as they could no more learn than sheep! One day, however, a heavy tropical rainstorm came on so suddenly that two little girls sought shelter in the mission-house. As the storm continued, they could not leave till evening, and they were hungry and began to cry. The missionary lady gave them bread and bananas, and the younger sister ate, but the elder refused.

Presently their parents came to seek for them, and when they learnt that the youngest had eaten bread prepared by any one not of their own caste (worst of all by a foreigner), they were very angry, and declared that the child was polluted, and that they would be unable to arrange a suitable marriage for her. They were in sore perplexity, but decided that the lady had better keep the child and bring it up.

To this she gladly agreed, and the little one was soon quite at home. Her new friend sprinkled sand on the floor of the verandah, and thereon wrote the 247 letters of the Tamil alphabet, a few every day, till her young pupil could write them all herself. Some little Tamil playmates came to see her, and were so delighted with this new game that they came again and again, and very soon they were all able to read, to their own great delight and the surprise of their parents.

Seeing how happy and well-cared-for the first little girl was, other parents consented to intrust their children to the foreign lady, and thus in 1824 commenced the Oodooville (or, as now spelt, Uduvil) Girls' Boarding School, probably the earliest effort of the sort in a heathen land.

(I may remark in passing, that in 1887 several girls in the Oodooville training-school passed far ahead of any of the boys, a circumstance which proved quite a shock to the Tamil believers in feminine incapacity for intellectual studies!)

This school grew to very great importance under the care of Miss Eliza Agnew, "the mother of a thousand daughters," as she was lovingly called by the people.

When herself a child only eight years of age, at home in New York, her school-teacher, in giving a geography lesson to her class, pointed out the large proportion of the world which is still heathen. Then and there one little pupil resolved that, if God would allow her, she would go and teach some of these to love her Saviour.

Domestic duties tied her to her home till she was a woman of thirty, when the death of her only near relations left her free to follow her early impulse, and she was allowed to join the newly-established American Mission at Jaffna. There she worked without intermission for forty-three years, loved and loving, and teaching successive generations, the children, and even some grandchildren, of her first pupils. Upwards of a thousand girls studied under her care, and of these more than six hundred left the school as really earnest Christians.

These became the wives of catechists, teachers, native pastors, lawyers, Government officials, and other leading men in the Jaffna peninsula, so that the influence exerted by this one devoted Christian woman has been beyond calculation. Hundreds of these families attended her funeral, sorrowing as for no earthly mother.

The two sisters who told me these details, and who themselves carried on her work and tended her last hours, added: "In hundreds of villages in Ceylon and India there is just such a work waiting to be done by Christian young women as that which, with God's blessing, Miss Agnew accomplished in the Jaffna peninsula. Heathen lands are open to-day as they have never been open before; the stronghold of heathenism is in the homes. It is the women who are teaching the children to perform the heathen ceremonies, to sing the songs in praise of the heathen gods, and thus they are moulding the habits of thought of the coming generation. If we are to win the world for Christ, we must lay our hands on the hands that rock the cradles, and teach Christian songs to the lips that sing the lullabies; and if we can win the *mothers* to Christ, the *sons* will soon be brought to fall at the feet of their Redeemer.

"Zenanas, which forty years ago were locked and barred, are to-day open. We have been told by Hindoo gentlemen that there are many educated men in India to-day who are convinced of the truth of Christianity, and would confess Christ, were it not that a wife or mother, who has never been instructed about Him, would bitterly oppose their doing so."

They added that in India alone there are 120,000,000 women and girls; that in Great Britain alone there are about 1,000,000 more women than men, and yet the total number of women who have as yet volunteered for this honourable work in India, counting all in connection with every Protestant Missionary Society, is barely 500; and knowing from full personal experience the gladness of life and fortune consecrated to this grand cause, they ask, "Cannot many more women be spared from their homes, and cannot more go who are possessed of private means, and here realise how satisfying is this life-work?"[1]

From their own personal knowledge of pitiful cases of the terrible suffering of women, owing to the total lack of the very simplest medical skill, and to the barbarous system of so-called "sick-nursing" (which makes one marvel how sick persons ever survive), these ladies specially plead for trained

[1] For most interesting details of the work of these two sisters, see "Seven Years in Ceylon," by Mary and Margaret Leitch. Published by S. W. Partridge & Co. Price 2s. 6d., post free.

medical women to come to the aid of their sisters in Ceylon and India. But on this subject I cannot do better than quote part of a letter from Dr. Chapman, a native Christian doctor at Jaffna, who, speaking of the need for a Medical Mission for Women in Ceylon, says:—

"A favourite prescription is a pill made of croton-seed. One pill will act perhaps forty times! The stronger the pill is the better, so they think. Sometimes one pill is enough to kill a person. Two cases of such mistreatment, and death from that cause alone, happened recently to two Christian women, both of whom were teachers in mission schools."

He also writes at some considerable length about the heathen doctors not allowing their patients water or sufficient food, and speaks of many cases of death simply from starvation.

Speaking of barbarous native customs in regard to childbirth, he says:—

"A few days ago I was asked to go to a house where a woman was being confined. The woman was tied to the roof of the house by a rough rope, and kept standing upon her knees. She was also supported by other native women. The room was very small, and as no ventilation was allowed, was very hot. The poor woman and her friends were in profuse perspiration. She was held up in this position *three days and two nights*. She was not allowed to rest or lie down at all. The friends of the woman, who were holding her up, took turns with each other and rested themselves, but the poor woman had no one to change with.

"When I reached the house, her limbs were cold, and she was not able to hold up her head, and was fast sinking. I ordered that they should take her down and let her lie on the ground, and that they should give her brandy and ammonia. . . . I did everything in my power to save her, but she died the following night.

"*In all such cases of confinement the women are held up in this standing posture for days and nights until the child is born or the woman dies.* The reason of this great superstition, among the poor and the rich, among the educated and uneducated, among the Christians and heathen, all alike, is that they think gravitation will assist the mother in the birth of the child. By thus being held up for days without rest or food, the mother loses her whole strength, and, in many instances, becomes unable to bring forth her babe.

"However, if a child is born, the mother is taken to another room and is bathed, that is to say, she is laid on a cold mud floor and cold water is dashed all over her till she is thoroughly chilled. This is immediately done with all possible haste, without letting the mother rest a moment, of course causing a fearful shock to the system.

"If she escapes this crisis, she is laid on a mat, and a strongly spiced paste is given her to eat, which is made of pepper, garlic, and ginger. Nothing else is given her for three days. No water is given. On the fourth day rice is given, with hot spices and dried fish. She is daily bathed in hot water, spices and oil are freely given her to eat; not a drop of water is she allowed to drink. The mother is allowed to nurse the child only on the fifth day. Every woman must get fever on the fifth day. Fever is good, they think. Before the fifth day the child is fed with some decoction.

"The population of the province is about 316,000, and taking the birth-rate at 3 per cent., there must be some 9480 births every year, and yet there are no trained midwives to assist in such cases."

The fact that this doctor was only called after the woman had been tied up to the roof of the house for three days and two nights, and when it was too late for him to render any aid, shows the extreme reluctance of the people to call for the help of a male doctor at such times.

Miss Leitch tells me that in such cases she has gone into homes where the poor exhausted woman was lying shivering on a cold mat and literally dying for want of a warm drink, while the house has been crowded with relatives bewailing as for one already dead. By turning them all out and applying needful warmth, she has had the happiness of seeing the poor mother recover, but knew that, however exhausted she herself might be, she dared not leave the house, as all the relatives would at once return, and pandemonium would again surround the sick-bed. In many houses devil-dancers are called in to exorcise the evil spirits supposed to be present, and the wretched patient is distracted by the beating of tomtoms for hours at a time.

Here then is one grand field of work for Christian women, as yet wholly unoccupied, and assuredly, of all phases of work, is that which most closely assimilates to His, the merciful MASTER, Who won men's hearts by healing all manner of sickness and disease.

A very important step was taken this year when Dr. Kynsey, the principal medical officer of Ceylon, sought the Governor's sanction for the admission of female students into the Medical College at Colombo, there to be trained as doctors for their countrywomen. The College will be open to them from May 1st, 1892, when they will attend the same lectures as male students, but have separate class-rooms for anatomy, their studies being directed by Mrs. Van Ingen, a fully qualified lady-doctor, herself trained in the Indian Medical School for women, founded by Lady Dufferin in 1885.

That great scheme has already resulted in the establishment of 38 hospitals specially for women, with 40 lady-doctors, while 204 female students are now being educated to aid the suffering women of India.

Scholarships and other inducements will be offered to attract students in Ceylon; and, as in India, the scheme will be worked on entirely unsectarian lines, no attempt being made to influence the religion of either students or patients.

It is certainly much to be regretted that Christian medical missions should have been unable to occupy this field, and secure so important a means of influence, instead of its becoming an altogether secular agency.

As regards the quiet extension of purely spiritual work, many of the native Christian women now recognise the duty of trying to influence their heathen sisters by visiting them in their homes; and though such work implies very great effort on the part of those in whom the second nature of custom has exaggerated natural timidity, a considerable number are now doing excellent service as Bible-women, even making their way in the wholly heathen villages.

Some of the Tamil women who have undertaken this good work are the wives of Government officials, doctors, or lawyers, so that their words are the more certain to carry weight with their countrywomen, who invariably receive them with respect, and acknowledge that only a strong conviction of religious duty combined with a remarkable love to their unknown neighbours could possibly have induced them to come forth from the privacy of their own homes. This movement was commenced in Jaffna in 1868 by the Wesleyan Mission, and was successfully adopted by the English Church and American Missions there. The latter has upwards of forty of these good pioneers now working in various parts of the peninsula.

From one district the superintendent writes: "The Bible-readers teach in the forenoon, and every afternoon go from village to village, collecting the women and holding meetings. Thus twenty villages are visited. The great interest of our work consists in the willingness of the women of all classes to learn to read for themselves. There are now in this district 373 women under instruction. One hundred can now read the Bible, and all the rest are learning. The majority of the women are of the Vellala or farmer caste.

Last year we had nine Brahman women, now we have twenty-two. Of other classes we have a few from the barber, carpenter, washer, and tree-climber (*i.e.*, toddy-drawer) villages. Many of these attend the weekly meetings of the 'Helping Hand Society' for study and recitation."

Another superintendent of ten Bible-women tells of their weekly visits to 375 women in their respective village-homes. Each of these women undertakes to learn by heart[1] each week four verses of the Bible and part of a hymn, the portions selected being those assigned in the village day-schools, in order that the little girls, on their return home in the evening, may thus become pupil-teachers, helping their mothers and grown-up sisters to learn their lessons. In truth, the story of the Mission records some very pathetic instances of how the ewes follow the lambs—in other words, how the simple faith of little children has resulted in the conversion of their parents. Of course, the primary object of each visitor is to teach every woman to pray, and they have reason to hope that a very large proportion of their pupils do so, many having had the courage openly to confess their conversion.

In addition to this house-to-house visitation, these ten Bible-women teach sewing to upward of 250 girls at twelve day-schools; they also teach in the Sunday-schools, and otherwise make themselves useful in arranging women's meetings.

Similar reports, more or less encouraging, come from the other districts, in one of which, at a meeting of heathen women, one told how fifty years ago, when quite a child, she had been for six months at one of the Mission boarding-schools, when her parents removed her in consequence of

[1] "To memorise" is the expressive American abbreviation.

an outbreak of whooping-cough, and she had not been allowed to return. But those six months seemed to remain in her memory as the one bright spot of life.

To some of the high-caste women, the fact that the Bible-women are mostly of low caste is in itself an objection to submitting to their teaching, which is only overcome by the ambition of learning to read; the fact, too, of having to sit on equal terms amongst pupils who are also of low caste is at first a great barrier to women of the higher castes attending any meeting. In many cases, however, this difficulty has been overcome, and a kindliness hitherto undreamt of seems to herald the dawn of the faith which teaches unselfish loving-kindness.

Remembering how the first girl was given to the care of the missionaries, because, having eaten of their bread, she was polluted, it is touching to hear now of an annual meeting at Batticotta of the Native Missionary Society, at which upwards of a thousand communicants assemble, the native Christians of the town providing an abundant meal of curry and rice for all visitors—a putting aside of caste prejudices which is indeed a triumph of grace.

Formerly some heathen families who sent their daughters to the mission-schools used to insist on elaborate ceremonial ablutions before allowing them to re-enter their home in the evening!

The regular work of the American Mission at Jaffna is carried on by eleven native pastors and about sixty assistants, under the supervision of five married missionaries. Here, as in the Hawaian isles, the venerable American missionaries, several of whom have here toiled ceaselessly for half a century, are affectionately designated "Father" of their flock. Thus the late much-loved Principal of the

College, Father Hastings, is succeeded in office by Father Howland. Father and Mrs. Spaulding, and I think Father Smith, also each gave upwards of fifty years' work to Jaffna, and have left sons and daughters who follow in their steps. Each district has at least one chapel, but great efforts are made to carry on systematic preaching in as many villages as possible, and it is hoped that the numerous books, Bibles, and portions of Scripture sold by colporteurs will prove silent teachers in many homes. Not only all the schools, but also the police-courts are found to be suitable preaching centres, on account of the large number of people who generally congregate in the neighbourhood.

It is also hoped that much good may result from the multiplication of what are called "moonlight meetings," which are informal meetings in the homes of any of the people who care to call together their friends and neighbours for religious discussion or instruction. The workers of all denominations agree as to the advantage of diligently prosecuting this system, which seems to find much favour with the people, who in some districts assemble to the number of several hundreds. In some of the Singhalese districts even Buddhist priests sometimes attend these meetings in quite a friendly spirit.

Naturally, however, this is not always the case, the zeal of the Christian preachers sometimes awakening a corresponding energy in the more rigid Buddhists. For instance, the marked success of the moonlight meetings in the neighbourhood of Cotta, near Colombo, induced the Buddhists to commence holding opposition services. The majority of the people, however, refused to countenance these, declaring that the Christians "were only doing their own work and trying to do good, and that to commence such meetings simply out of spite or envy showed a very bad spirit!"

As regards open-air preaching in the streets or other public places, Buddhists and Christians being alike protected by the British Government, have precisely the same liberty and security.

The total number of Church members in connection with the American Congregational Mission is as yet only about 1300, but the attendants at public worship are about 7000; and there is reason to believe that a very much larger number are converts at heart, although the fear of domestic persecution, and the difficulties of strict Sabbatical observance and of disposing of extra wives, prevent many from professing themselves Christians.

One of the most remarkable Christian institutions in Ceylon is the College for Tamils at Batticotta, in the Jaffna peninsula, which originated in a purely spontaneous effort made in 1867 by the native Christians in that district to secure for themselves and their descendants a superior education both in English and Tamil. They succeeded in raising £1700—a large sum in a land where the wage of a labourer is but 6d. a day. This nest-egg was supplemented by £6000 from America, and in 1872 the college was started under the control of a board of directors. These are the Government Agent of the Northern Province, eleven representatives of the native Christian gentlemen of the community, and the senior missionaries of the three Christian regiments which work in that province in such admirable brotherly union, namely, the CHURCH OF ENGLAND MISSION and the AMERICAN and WESLEYAN MISSIONS, all of whom are in full sympathy with the work of this noble institution.

While the college is undenominational, it is essentially Christian, and the form of worship adopted is Congregational. Not one heathen teacher has ever been employed in it, and all students are required to live on the premises, and are thus continuously under strong Christian influence. It might be supposed that Hindoo young men of high caste would object to paying full price for board and lodging in a college where a standing rule is that all inmates shall refrain from heathen practices, and from wearing idolatrous marks on their foreheads; but so highly is the education prized, that no objection to these conditions is ever made,[1] and the Hindoo students not only eat, sleep, and live with the Christians, but unite in the

[1] Perhaps I ought to say "no objection by those really concerned." In point of fact, a party-cry of "religious intolerance" was raised a few years ago by certain wealthy Hindoos, who, although too indifferent to establish schools for themselves, made this a ground of attack on missionaries, who rightly insist on all children who attend Christian schools coming with clean faces, that is to say, without the temple marks of cow-dung ash on their foreheads.

So many Europeans seem to think that they cannot yield sufficiently courteous recognition to heathen customs, that the strong words of Bishop Copleston on this question may well be remembered. "It matters everything what we teach by our action to our heathen neighbours and to our Christian people. Let us teach that the symbol of Siva—if it means anything but a dirty face—is an outrage on the majesty and love of the One True God, that it is what Scripture calls 'an abomination,' to be abhorred by all loyal children of the One Father. And let us remind our own people that THERE IS SUCH A THING AS A SOUND AND TRULY RELIGIOUS INTOLERANCE, WHICH IS NOT TOLERANT OF AFFRONTS TO OUR GOD; WHICH WILL NOT TREAT AS ONE AMONG MANY FORMS OF RELIGION THE WORSHIP OF IDOLS AND THE DENIAL OF OUR LORD. . . . Our heathen neighbours will have reason to thank us in the end, and in the meantime will respect us, if we are determined both to speak and act the truth in love."

daily study of the Bible, and are present at morning and evening prayers, the Sabbath-school, and church services of the American Mission.

This college takes no grant-in-aid from Government, and until June 1891 it was not affiliated to any university,[1] as experience proves that students who are working for passes grudge the time bestowed on Biblical study, which does not count in their examinations. Naturally a college which recognises the training of Christian catechists and schoolmasters as the primary object of its existence prefers to be independent of a purely secular superior.

The result of this system has been, that out of about 350 students who have been educated here, fully 150 have gone out into the world as Christians and communicants, and are leading such consistent lives as tend greatly to uphold the honour of their faith.

In India, on the other hand, where in the Government schools absolutely secular education is given, with entire disregard to religion—even Bible-reading being set aside —the statistics of the four universities show that only between four and five per cent. of the graduates are Christians ; the rest, for the most part, while learning to despise heathenism, drift into agnosticism, and even atheism.

I cannot refrain from quoting a paragraph on this subject from a non-Christian Bombay paper. The writer says: " Education provided by the State simply destroys Hindooism ; it gives nothing in its place. It is founded on the benevolent principle of non-interference with religion, but in practice it is the negation of God in life. Education

---

[1] The directors state that the decision of Government to give up Cambridge and introduce London, has compelled them to affiliate the Jaffna College to that of Calcutta.

must destroy idolatry, and the State education of India, benevolent in its idea, practically teaches atheism. It leaves its victims without any faith."

This lamentable result, which is flooding India with a multitude of highly-educated utter sceptics, was vividly brought home to the Christian workers in Jaffna when they found the existing college totally inadequate for the number of promising young men in the schools, who were consequently compelled to cross over to India, and there seek the "higher education" in Government schools.

Many of these were apparently on the verge of professing themselves Christians, but after a course of two or three years in totally heathen and grossly immoral surroundings, they invariably returned either as bitter heathen or atheists; a state of matters all the more distressing as they were in many cases betrothed to Christian girls in the mission schools.

It was evident that the Christian college at Jaffna must be placed on such a footing as to enable it to meet this ever-increasing need. A sum of £30,000 was required for its immediate extension, and it is delightful to know that this has been almost raised by the efforts of the two sisters of whom I have already spoken, and who came to Britain and to America for this purpose.

There is every reason to believe that this college is destined to fill a very important part in the evangelisation of India, for this reason, namely, that a singularly large proportion of the Tamils resident on the peninsula of Jaffna are of very high caste, and the 15,000 children attending the Christian day-schools and the 2500 communicants connected with the three missions are mostly of high caste. It is scarcely possible for Europeans to realise how deeply ingrained in Hindoo nature is the reverence for all members of the upper castes, however poor they may be, and the natural tendency to look with contempt on low-caste men. Now it so happens that in India the majority of converts are of low caste, and these, as a general rule, are not only intellectually inferior to the higher castes, but are generally too poor to afford the highest course of education. Consequently Brahman teachers, whose caste secures unbounded reverence, are frequently found even in the Mission colleges and high-schools, with the badge of heathen gods on their foreheads, instructing the students in the highest classes, while native Christian teachers take the lower subjects. Possibly the native pastor who gives the Bible-lessons is by caste a Pariah, and however excellent he may be, is, as such, despicable in the eyes of the Hindoo student.

Thus the social barrier of caste enters even into the Mission colleges, acting as a very serious drawback. Of course the various Missions would gladly replace the Hindoo and Mahommedan teachers by thoroughly educated and influential Christian men, could such be procured. The Principal of the Lucknow High School alone states that he would thankfully engage two hundred Christian teachers for the schools of the American Mission in that district, were such available; but as it is, heathen teachers are engaged of necessity.

Now in these respects Jaffna is very remarkably favoured, and is apparently destined to become to Southern India what Iona once was to Scotland—the school for her teachers. It must be borne in mind that Tamil is one of the four great Dravidian tongues, and is the language of 13,000,000 of the inhabitants of the Carnatic, extending from Cape

Comorin to Madras. Glorious indeed is the prospect thus unfolded, that (as has been said) "after having received its two false religions from India, Ceylon shall, by a Christlike retribution, send over her sons to preach the one true religion to India's millions."

Already a large proportion of the students trained in Jaffna College (men whose attainments fully qualify them for secular work on salaries of from £5 to £10 a month, with prospects of promotion) have voluntarily chosen to devote their lives to Christian work as teachers, catechists, or pastors on a salary of £1, 10s. to begin with, and no prospect of ever rising above £4 a month.

Several of the most able have volunteered to leave their beloved Isle in order to undertake posts in mission-schools at Rangoon, Singapore, Madras, Madura, Bombay, Indore, and many other parts of India, where they are working most successfully, thus profitably trading with their birthright talent of good caste. One of these young men, who for some time has been working in Ahmednugger on a salary of £4 a month, was offered £10 a month if he would accept work elsewhere. He refused, saying that he believed he could do more good where he was, and where he has won extraordinary influence with a large class of high-caste young Hindoos.

It would be well if some of those who are ever ready to sneer at the imaginary pecuniary advantages which are supposed to influence native Christians, could realise the full meaning of a few such details as these, and also the extraordinarily generous proportion of their salary, or other worldly possessions, which is almost invariably set aside by the converts in Ceylon (and in many other lands) as their offering for some form of Church work—tithes, which we are so apt to deem excessive, being accounted quite the minimum to be offered.

It is quite a common thing in the gardens of Christians to see every tenth palm or other fruit-bearing tree specially marked in token that its whole crop is devoted to some sacred purpose. Poultry is reared for the same object, and the eggs laid on Sunday are set apart as an offering; and even the very poor families who possess no garden find a method of contributing their mite; for when the mother is measuring out so many handfuls of rice for each member of her household, she ends by taking back one large handful from the common store, and places it in "the Lord's rice-box," the contents of which are periodically emptied, and being added to those of many neighbours, make up a considerable item in the teacher's store.

I have already referred to the well-developed missionary spirit of these Jaffna Christians. So early as 1848 this showed itself in providing funds to work a purely native mission to the 28,000 heathen inhabitants of the large group of islands lying to the west of the peninsula. One of these isles, Ninathevu, is the special care of the Christian students in the college, who there built a school, and now continue to raise the funds for the support of their own missionary and his wife by devoting many of their recreation hours (while the others are playing cricket and other games) to cultivating a garden and selling its produce.

These young men also do their utmost for the conversion of the Hindoo students in the college, and on Sunday afternoons they disperse themselves over eight or nine of the neighbouring villages, holding Sabbath-schools, which are attended by about 400 children. One of the young men invested £5 in an American organ to enliven the services in one village—an extravagance which called forth remonstrances from his relations, till he proved that he had simply abstained from spending it on tobacco.[1]

The Blue Ribbon Army are also doing good work, and have successfully established brotherhoods at Jaffna, Galle, and Kandy.

There are at present seventy-six young men in the college, nine students of divinity, and about 400 boys and girls attending the schools. The total attendance at the village day-schools under the management of the Principal of the college is about 2500, and the American mission has about 8000 children in other schools, of whom it is certain that a large proportion will grow up as Christians, notwithstanding the disadvantage that about one-third of the teachers employed are unavoidably heathen.

The happy results of the hearty co-operation of the English and American missionaries at Jaffna are especially observed in the union of all Young Men's Christian Associations throughout the peninsula, and in their healthy tone. The special value of such associations may well be imagined when each member composing it has had to nerve himself to come out from the idolatrous worship of his kinsmen, and to endure the cross of their ridicule and persecution; and to many this has been meted in full measure and bravely and patiently borne.

[1] In looking over missionary subscription lists, I see that several sensible men have sent considerable sums under the very suggestive heading of "SAVED FROM SMOKE." I could not but think how much pleasanter many of my acquaintances would be if only they would follow this example, and leave the atmosphere untainted. Considering that men in general do not work harder than the majority of women, and their diet and drink are certainly not more stinted than that of their sisters, can there be any valid reason why, in every household, the lords of creation should expend on this item of self-indulgence a sum which, were it devoted to missionary purposes, would entitle that family to rank high among contributors to the good cause?

The three Missions also hold union Bible-meetings, at which the people are addressed by representatives of all three Missions, and are thus spared the confusion which is so often entailed by the antagonistic attitude of Christian sects one towards another. Here, while each retains its individuality, all unite in one common cause, which surely is the true solution of that much-talked of phantom, Church union.

It seems to me that a very fit emblem of the Christian Church is that of a mighty WHEEL, of which CHRIST is both tyre and axle-tree, and HIS true servants in all the Christian regiments are the spokes. All are bound together in HIM, and so, although they may not touch one another, all unite to do HIS work in the progress of HIS kingdom. So the Wheel, which for ages has been the symbol alike of Buddhism and of Sun-worship, seems to me a most appropriate emblem of the true SUN OF RIGHTEOUSNESS.

Though the WESLEYAN MISSION in this island cannot record such startling success as has attended its work in the fallow fields of the Fijian and some other Pacific groups, it has a special interest as being *the very first Oriental station of this denomination.* Its commencement was so strongly advocated by Dr. Coke, that the Wesleyan Conference consented to sanction his collecting funds and selecting companions willing to accompany him thither.

Accordingly, on December 30, 1813, he embarked with six missionaries, two of whom were married. But the voyage, then in slow-sailing vessels, was a very different business to the pleasure trip of the present day by swift steamers. To reach Ceylon they had to travel *viâ* Bombay, a voyage of about six months, and ere they sighted the Indian land two of that little company had been called home. The first of these was Mrs. Ault, wife of one of the missionaries. She died in February. But a yet sorer trial awaited the Mission in the sudden death of their leader, the zealous and energetic Dr. Coke, whose master-mind had originated the whole movement, and whose death, ere even reaching their destination, proved sorely bewildering to the survivors, the more so as they were unable even to cash his bills, and so provide money for their maintenance. They found good friends, however, in Sir Evan Nepean, Governor of Bombay, and Lord Molesworth, Commandant of Galle, where they finally arrived on the 29th June 1814, having left Bombay nine days previously.

The Dutch Church being virtually dead, there was at that time no other mission of the Reformed Church in Ceylon, or rather none had secured any footing; therefore, after a fortnight's consideration and much prayer and consultation, they resolved to divide the land, three of the six being sent north to commence work in the Tamil districts at Jaffna and Batticaloa, while the other three were to remain in the southern districts among the Singhalese Buddhists, establishing their headquarters at Galle and Matara. The former had, of course, to begin by learning the Tamil tongue, while their brethren in the south had to acquire that of the Singhalese.

In the three years that followed, the arrival of six other missionaries enabled them to commence work at Trincomalee, Negombo, Kalutara, and Point Pedro, and to spare one of their number to commence a mission at Madras. One is reminded of "the grain of mustard-seed" on learning how small were the beginnings of the work which, though it has not yet "overshadowed the land," has certainly taken firm root in every province. At Port Pedro the first seed was sown in 1818, when a piece of land on the seaside was rented for the equivalent of 9d. a year, and thereon was commenced a school attended by twelve boys.

In 1819 these scattered workers met at Galle to estimate their progress. They found that in the past five years 249 persons had become Church members, which of course implied a very much larger number of attendants at Christian services, and included several Buddhist priests. Seventy-five schools had been established, at which 4484 children were receiving instruction. Mission-houses and chapels had been built, a considerable number of native catechists had been trained to teach their countrymen, and a printing establishment in Colombo was pouring forth thousands of portions of the Scriptures and of tracts.

Wherever it was found possible so to renovate the old Dutch churches as to make them safe, these were occupied, but the majority had gone so far to ruin and decay that the walls had to be taken down and rebuilt, so that it was in most cases found simpler to build afresh. One of the most important of the new churches was that built in 1839 at Batticaloa, where progress was particularly satisfactory, and was marked in the four following years by no less than 758 baptisms, of which 447 were of adults.

The Batticaloa station embraces a large number of villages scattered along the seaboard for a distance of eighty miles, and is worked from two mission centres—one at the capital, which is known to the natives as Puliantivu, and the other at Kalmunai. The latter, however, seems as yet to have afforded comparatively small encouragement; but recently an awakening seems to have commenced, a symptom of which is the largely increased attendance of native women at the village meetings, after one of which the native minister was surprised and gladdened by the remark of a heathen man of good position, " I verily believe that your religion will soon overspread this place, and surely stamp out ours."

The opening at Kalmunai of a girl's boarding-school is in itself a sure detail of success, as has been well proven by a similar school at Batticaloa, in the immediate neighbourhood of which the Wesleyans have also nine day-schools for girls and about twenty for boys, with a total of about 2500 pupils.

At Trincomalee, Port Pedro, and most of the other stations, the same care is extended to the girls; indeed at Jaffna the Wesleyan Mission established a boarding-school for their benefit so early as 1837. Certainly it could only accommodate six girls, but it has gone on steadily increasing, and now numbers upwards of 100 boarders. Parents of the upper class, who will only allow very young girls to attend day-schools, do not object to send their daughters to boarding-schools, paying a moderate fee towards their expenses, and so well pleased are they to see them turn out so neat, clean, and punctual in their habits, so well instructed in the art of needlework, and especially in making their own clothes, that they are content to accept the probability of their becoming Christians, a result which very frequently follows, so that such schools are likely to exercise an ever-enlarging influence on the homes of the next generation.

In many parts of the country, however, mothers, and especially grandmothers, who themselves have had no education, fail to see its advantage for their descendants, and many girls who were converts at heart have been removed from the schools and compelled again to kneel before idol shrines. Of course here, as in all other heathen lands, a very large number of hearers are convinced of the truth of Christianity, and many are practically Christians at heart, but have not yet found courage to face the inevitable domestic persecution that awaits them when their inward conviction results in outward profession.

One thing certain is that, sooner or later, every school yields some converts, and the testimony of all the Missions is that more than half the adults who eventually become Christians attribute their conversion to teaching received in the schools, which they had ignored at the time, but which, like well-laid fuel, was ready to ignite in due season. In many cases these early impressions smoulder on through half a lifetime ere the convert finds courage openly to confess the faith which must subject him to such severe domestic persecution. For instance, amongst those who have recently sought baptism from the Church Mission at Jaffna, one was the hereditary manager of a famous Hindoo temple, who for thirty long years had vainly striven to silence the inward voice which first spoke to his conscience at the mission-school.

Another is an old man seventy-five years of age, who in his boyhood attended the American school. He was a very hopeful pupil, and was the subject of much special prayer. He was, however, removed by his relations, all of whom were strict worshippers of the Hindoo gods. From the time he left school he never entered a heathen temple, but, like Nicodemus of old, he sought God secretly by night, dreading the persecution which he knew would result from confessing his Lord. Sometimes he spoke to his wife about Christianity, but she called him a madman, and so he still shrank from taking up such a cross as that of open avowal. At last, when attacked by a severe illness, he vowed that if he recovered he would confess himself to be a disciple of Christ. He did recover, and kept his vow; whereupon his own daughters turned him out of the house, and the old man would have been left to starve had not a still older Christian catechist, who was a distant connection of his own, offered him a home under his roof, thus securing a little interval of peace ere this true friend, "Old Philips," was himself called to his rest—a good and faithful servant, who since his own baptism in 1830 had never ceased working diligently and successfully for the conversion of others.

Remembering all the prayers that were offered sixty years ago on behalf of that promising school-boy, one cannot but think how apt is the illustration of the husbandman who "with long patience" waits for the precious fruit.

The aim of the Society is to establish in every village a school with an able teacher, who, while fulfilling all requirements of the Government code of education, shall make the religious instruction of the children his primary care. To provide such Christian teachers, and also local preachers to keep up a constant series of services for the heathen in all the villages, the Wesleyan Mission has established at Jaffna a Training Institute for male teachers, which shall supply native agents for the building up of a healthy native Church in the Tamil districts.

To those who have noted how sure a test of vitality in any branch of the Church is its recognition of the duty of winning others, it is especially interesting to note that the Native Wesleyan congregations at Jaffna and Batticaloa (having for many years entirely supported their own pastors) have now established among themselves societies which send out catechists to preach in certain jungle-villages. These are maintained by funds locally subscribed by the native Christians as thank-offerings for having themselves been called out of heathen darkness.

The Wesleyan Church at Jaffna also sends Tamil ministers to Colombo and its neighbourhood to minister to their countrymen who have migrated thither.

For the southern districts, namely, Negombo, Colombo, Kandy, Galle, and Matara, the native ministers are, of course, either Singhalese or Burghers. They are said to be not only eminently good men, but in many cases so well versed in Buddhistic learning as to prove more than a match for such priests as have sought to draw them into controversy. As an instance of the excellent work done by some of these men, I may refer to that of one now gone to his rest—the Rev. Peter De Zylva, a Singhalese bearing a Portuguese name. He was appointed to begin work in the district of Moratuwa Mulla (commonly called Morottoo, which lies between Colombo and Kalutara), as being a part of the country notorious for its ignorance and the prevalence of devil-worship. Here he commenced visiting from house to house and conversing in the bazaars with all who would speak with him, but many months elapsed ere he was rewarded by any symptom of success. At length, however, his words, exemplified by his own good life, began to take effect, and at the end of twenty years he had the joy of knowing that, out of a population of about 4700, 600 of the villagers had become faithful followers of his Lord.

One of his earliest converts was the Kapurala or priest of a devil-temple, close to which he had established a preaching-station. Without leaving his temple, the old man could not choose but hear the hymns and prayers and preaching which began so strangely to influence those who had hitherto been his own followers. Ere long he himself was convinced that He of whom De Zylva preached was a better Master than his cruel devil-spirits; so locking the temple, which was his own property, he presented the key to the Christian teacher, and bade him do as he saw fit with all the poor idols, for that thenceforth he would worship only the Saviour, of whom he had now heard. And the old priest proved a faithful and an earnest helper.

The good work thus begun has continued to prosper, the converts proving their faith by the self-denying liberality of their alms. They now support two Singhalese pastors, and have built chapels and mission-houses. One of the former, which was recently opened, is a large substantial building, erected from a native design under native superintendence. All labour for the roof and windows was contributed gratuitously, a hundred carpenters (not all Wesleyan converts) each freely giving a week's work; they commenced on Monday morning, and finished on Saturday night, the Christian women of the district bringing gifts of food for all the workmen.

Although such purely voluntary work as this is probably exceptional, the members of this Mission have found the people so wonderfully ready to afford help in every village where a school or chapel has been erected, that the Mission has rarely borne more than half the cost of the building. For instance, in the Port Pedro district, near Jaffna, several handsome school-chapels have been erected almost entirely through the liberality of natives who still bore on their foreheads the symbolic marks of the Hindoo gods, and who not only granted the sites, but also presented all the palmyra-palm trees for rafters, the plaited palm-leaves for the thatch, and handsome gifts in money. Of course, in such cases it may be assumed that the educational advantages thus secured outweigh their antagonism to the teacher's creed. Besides, in many cases the assistant-teachers are heathens, and consequently the majority of the pupils continue to worship the Tamil gods.

With regard to Wesleyan educational work in the Southern Province, there are two important training colleges, namely, the Richmond College at Galle, and the Wesley College at Colombo, where there is also a high-school for girls, as well as one for boys. An industrial school for girls has recently been established at Kandy, where the daughters of poor parents are instructed in sewing, knitting, and biscuit-making. Badulla also has an excellent school for girls.

At Colombo an industrial home for destitute boys and girls supplies willing workers for the cotton-spinning mills. In the same city the Mission owns a valuable printing establishment. It has also established a mission to seamen, which provides for visiting the ships in harbour and inviting the sailors to special Sunday services. Comparatively few, however, are able to come ashore, as merchant vessels in harbour recognise no day of rest, and the hot, noisy toil of discharging and receiving cargo goes on night and day without intermission, Sunday and week-day alike.[1]

The workers in this Mission have latterly been very sorely hampered by pecuniary troubles, serious and repeated reductions in the grants from headquarters in England having put them to great straits in order to find the means of subsistence for the native agents; for, apart from the grief of being compelled to abandon the half-cultivated mission-fields, such retrenchment would necessarily imply casting into destitution

[1] In the busy harbour of Hong-Kong Sunday labour is now reduced to the minimum by the strictly-enforced requirement for a special license at very high rates for all Sunday-work. Thus sailors and officers may enjoy the exceptional privilege of a Sunday at rest. What a boon similar harbour regulations would prove in other ports!

men who had served the Mission faithfully. Of course this lack of funds has seriously hindered extension, the Mission having been compelled to refuse the services of various promising young men, who wished to enter the native ministry.

This is the more to be regretted as the Wesleyans have but recently commenced a work which promises immense success if only the labourers were forthcoming, namely, that in the hitherto uncared-for province of Uva, where, as I have already mentioned,[1] the people of about 800 villages are sunk in the most degrading ignorance and superstition.

The Rev. Samuel Langdon, chairman of the Wesleyan Society in Ceylon, writes from his "Happy Valley Mission" that he has not a tenth of the men or the funds necessary to do justice to the work in that province. Could Christian schools be at once established in all those villages, a very great step would be gained. Otherwise, under the energetic leading of English Theosophists, Buddhist schools will be opened by teachers trained in Government schools, and will secure the Government grant. It will then be far more difficult to secure a footing in this now vacant field.

The Wesleyan Mission in Ceylon to all nationalities at present numbers seventeen European clergy, with about 200 native assistants of all sorts. The total number of Church members does not exceed 4000, but the regular attendance at school and public worship is about 20,000.

There is one detail of progress which I must not omit, (believing as we do that the truest evidence of life in any branch of the Christian Church is its readiness to seek extension by undertaking mission work), and that is, that in

[1] Page 31.

the autumn of 1887 the Wesleyan Church in Ceylon commenced a mission to Upper Burmah, which by its annexation to Britain in the previous year was for the first time practically open to such effort. Two European missionaries, accompanied by two young Singhalese, went to begin work among the Buddhists of Mandalay, with its 5000 priests. Truly a tiny band to attack so strong a foe!

They landed without one friend to welcome them, and totally ignorant of the language; but they immediately secured three advantageous sites for mission-stations, with ample space for extension. So earnestly did they commence the study of the language, that very soon they were able to address the people in their own tongue, and found that the totally new idea of God as our ever-present loving Father soon attracted attentive hearers. They illustrate their indoor teaching by good magic-lantern views, all of Scripture scenes, so that the truth may reach the mind by eye and ear simultaneously.

The beginning made by the two young Singhalese has been so satisfactory, that it is greatly hoped that others, both men and women, themselves converts from Buddhism, will volunteer for the work, and that England and Australia will furnish the requisite funds for their support.

Note.—I have often been struck by the manner in which, on their return to England, some men who have lived in various countries without taking any personal interest in Christian work, authoritatively decry the practical results, and even the very efforts, of those who are devoting their lives to mission work.

Such an one had been for some time indulging in this strain about a district where he had been stationed for a considerable period, and where he declared "the missionaries did nothing." Presently a Bishop who overheard him came forward, and very gently asked him how long he had been resident in his present quarters in one of our Midland cities? "About two years," was the reply. "Ah, then," said the Bishop, "I shall be so very glad to have your unbiassed opinion of the working of the Young Men's Institute there. You never heard of it? Dear me, I wonder at that; it is such a very wide-spreading organisation. I hope you like the system of our Schools, and especially of our Industrial and Night Schools, where so many rough lads and wild hoydens are transformed into comparatively respectable members of society?"

Once more the "accuser of the brethren" had to confess his ignorance, and his interrogator continued: "Well, what do you think of the system of our Working-Men's Provident Institution? of our Free Hospital? of our Orphanage and Asylum? of our Night Refuge? of our Ragged Church, crowded with poor tattered creatures who never show in our streets? of our Band of Hope and our Home for Strangers? And what is your personal impression of the workers in our Home Mission?" Of course there was but one reply to all these questions. Then said the Bishop, "Do you not think that possibly it may have been the same at —— Station in India?"

CHAPTER XXVII.

CHRISTIAN WORK IN CEYLON.

Salvation Army—Work of the Society for the Propagation of the Gospel —Work of the Church Missionary Society—Cyclone in 1884—Work in Pallai and the Wannie—Converts from Hindooism—Tamil Coolie Mission—Christian lyrics—Kandyan itinerancy—Converts from Buddhism—Mission at Cotta—Trinity College, Kandy—Summary.

However deeply we sympathise with the efforts of "all who love our Lord in sincerity," we cannot but regret that, considering the number of agencies [1] already at work in this Isle (where Christian growth has been so cruelly impeded by the jealousies of successive gardeners), the Salvation Army should have introduced a fresh element of confusion by selecting for their campaign, not purely heathen villages, but several in which much good work had already been done. Still more unfortunately, a marked characteristic of some of their leaders has been such violent antagonism to other Christian denominations, that one who has hitherto been a subscriber to the funds of the Army has recently declared their position in Ceylon to be that of persecutors and hinderers of Christian workers.

[1] I regret that lack of space compels me to omit all details of the Presbyterian and Baptist Missions. The latter numbers about 6000 adherents, of whom 550 are communicants. The former has 2500 adherents, of whom about 1000 are communicants.

Sad as such dissensions must ever be, they are tenfold more distressing in presence of those whom we would fain win from the worship of idols and sacred cattle and the reverent use of cow-dung, and who very justly think that Christians should at least agree amongst themselves before they try to teach others.

For the same reason it is deeply to be regretted that even within the fold of the Church of England the converts should have been perplexed by " High Church " and " Low Church " questions, resulting for a while in serious difficulties. These happily have in a great measure subsided, and though it is certain that this division of the house against itself expedited the disestablishment of the Anglican Church from its position as the Established Church of the Isle, there is good reason to hope that in this, as in other matters, apparent evil has been overruled for good, the necessity for united action having led to a more perfect fusion of the interests of all members of the Episcopal Church, and to such resolute effort to meet the consequent pecuniary difficulties, that there is now little doubt that when the last props of State support are removed, the Episcopal Church of Ceylon will be found stronger and healthier than in her previous condition. Already she has her own Synod, her own constitution, and is generally well afloat.

It is worthy of note that she has thus been compelled to take up the self-same work which she has for many years been urging the Native Church to undertake, namely, not only the entire support of its own institutions, but also the duty of contributing the needful funds for sending teachers to its heathen countrymen.

So since the 30th June 1886 all State aid has been withdrawn, with the exception of the stipends of such Government chaplains, Episcopal and Presbyterian, as were appointed prior to 1st July 1881, such aid, of course, ceasing with the individual lives.

The total number of clergy of the Episcopal Church in the diocese of Colombo (in other words, in Ceylon) is now seventy-one. Of these, thirty-four (*i.e.*, eighteen European and sixteen native) are in the service of the Church Missionary Society, and fifteen (including nine natives) in that of the Society for the Propagation of the Gospel. The native clergy are Singhalese, Tamil, and Burgher; some are half-Burgher, half-Singhalese.

Let us briefly glance at the work of the two great Societies whose representatives have striven so earnestly to build up this Church.

The Church Missionary Society began work here in 1818. The Society for the Propagation of the Gospel, generally known as the S. P. G., followed suit in 1840.

The S. P. G. has from the beginning imported very few European clergy. It has rather aimed at assisting the Government chaplains (whose recognised official duty was simply to minister to such as were already Christians), and by enabling them to extend their sphere among the surrounding heathen, give a missionary character to their work also.

In 1845 the Isle, which had previously been included in the See of Madras, was made a separate diocese, and Dr. Chapman was consecrated first Bishop of Colombo. By his exertions and liberal gifts, aided by the S. P. G., St. Thomas College at Colombo was founded and endowed with a special view to training native clergy and schoolmasters.

Here English, Singhalese, and Tamil lads receive most careful religious teaching, combined with such high secular education as may fit them for any profession; but the College maintains its original missionary character, inasmuch as it furnishes almost all the native clergy in the employment of the Society, and also supplies the ever-increasing demand for schoolmasters.[1]

A high-class school for girls has for some years occupied a pleasant bungalow close to the Cathedral, and the Society has also established a female boarding-school at Matara, which is a very important centre of mission-work; the attendance at the various schools being upwards of 1100.

A very interesting S. P. G. work is the large orphanage of Buonavista, near Galle, of which I have already spoken.[2] It supplies Christian teachers, both male and female, for the surrounding village schools. About one-sixth of the children attending these are Christians, and a much larger proportion are removed by their relations so soon as they evince a strong bias in favour of Christianity. Then Buddhist priests are called in, and a period of home persecution ensues, which, however, rarely succeeds in extinguishing the light thus early kindled.

Apart from these centres, a quiet work is progressing in many places, such as Badulla, and several of the neighbouring villages, where a special effort is now being made for the extension of mission-work in the hitherto neglected province of Uva. About 400 children have been gathered into the Anglican schools in this district.

To return to the earliest efforts on behalf of Ceylon by the Church Missionary Society. Between 1818 and 1821 work was commenced at four points, which have ever since been important centres. These were Jaffna, in the extreme

---

[1] For details of this college see chapter ii.
[2] See p. 175.

north; Kandy, in the centre of the Isle; Cotta, near Colombo, and Baddigama, in the extreme south.

In the first instance, the Rev. Joseph Knight was sent to commence work at Jaffna. Finding the Americans and Wesleyans already in the field, he established himself at Nellore, in the immediate neighbourhood. There six years later he was joined by the Rev. W. Adley, and together they studied, and taught, and preached; but seven more years of patient work elapsed ere their hearts were cheered by making a single convert.

At length, in 1830, Mr. Adley's Tamil horse-keeper renounced idolatry and sought baptism, and ere that year closed a little band of ten Christians formed the nucleus of the future Church. One of these, named Matthew Philips, who had been working with Mr. Knight as his pundit ever since his arrival in the Isle, became the first catechist, and from that day till the hour of his death at Christmas 1884 (when he had completed his ninetieth year), he proved a zealous and eloquent preacher and most devoted Christian.

Such was the story of this Mission for the first twelve years. Ten more elapsed, and the Church members had increased to twenty-five, but as yet *did not include a single woman*. Ten years later the congregation at Nellore had increased to eighty, a new station was opened at Kopay in the immediate neighbourhood, and an old Portuguese church at Chundicully, also in the neighbourhood, was made over to the Mission, together with its congregation of Protestant Burghers. By degrees other stations have been included, and a large number of schools both for boys and girls have been established, and in these all the teachers are Christians; and thus the tree whose early growth was so slow has fairly taken root. A very important detail was the commencement in 1842 of a girl's boarding-school at Nellore. Here about 270 girls have received careful training, and many have become wives of the native clergy and school-masters.

The Jaffna peninsula is the extreme north-west corner of Ceylon, a dead level, palm-clad plain, twenty miles wide by thirty-six in length. A glance at the map will show better than pages of description how strangely the sea has intersected the land between this plain and the main Isle, forming truly labyrinthine lagoons.

In October and December 1884 this district was devastated by terrible cyclones, which, following on a period of prolonged drought and short crops, proved terribly trying to the people. The first of these appalling tempests was heralded by a pale-green sunset sky, flushing blood-red on the western horizon. It resulted in the total destruction of 66,000 cocoa-nut, palmyra, and areca palms, and about 7000 other valuable trees, chiefly fruit-trees. On the morning after the cyclone the peninsula resembled a newly-felled jungle, and even the streets were blocked by fallen trees, including about a hundred of the beautiful yellow suriyas,[1] torn up by the roots. About 120,000 plantain and banana bushes were ruined. Even the trees that survived were stripped of foliage and appeared as if scorched by fire. Fourteen thousand head of cattle, sheep, goats, and buffaloes were killed, as were also twenty-eight human beings. Thousands of crows were found dead with their wings all twisted.

The great breakwater which protected the town, the embankment, and sea-wall were alike destroyed; the road skirting the sea for many miles was washed away, as were also bridges and culverts, and thousands of houses of the poorest sort were damaged. Twenty-seven vessels

[1] *Thespesia populnea*, formerly called *hybiscus*.

are known to have been wrecked; some brigs and small schooners were carried miles inland, and the town was strewn with wreckage. Small craft innumerable perished, and hundreds of fishing and cargo boats were found in gardens and fields, while some were left in the streets or on the half-ruinous verandahs of houses! Others, which were recognised as belonging to neighbouring islands, were found washed ashore.

Equally lamentable was the destruction of the rice-crops. In the October storm hundreds of acres of paddy-land, which had been carefully ploughed and manured, and were all ready for sowing, were so flooded as to resemble only a vast lake. When the waters subsided, the wretched farmers did their best to repair the damage, but the December cyclone effectually blasted their hopes. Though in point of fury it was but as an echo of the first, nevertheless the prevalence of unseasonable rain destroyed the rice-crops and ruined the gardens.

A curious incident of the cyclone was the fall of the steeple of Kopay Church, which was blown over, and in its fall exactly filled up an adjacent well, a very grave loss in that region of droughts.

For a considerable period after this the poverty of the people was such that many of the children used to come to school half-famished, and for some time attendance was seriously diminished.

In this extremity many of the school-teachers shared their pittance with the hungriest of their flock, but the suffering of all was severe. Of course, diminished school attendance involves a reduction in Government grants and in the salaries of the teachers, and this again in the American Mission reacts on the modest income of the native pastor, which is partly dependent on the offerings of the teachers, who, it seems, are in the habit of devoting one-tenth of their salary to the service of the Church.

About twenty years ago very decisive efforts were made by the missionaries in order to root out any lingering idea that temporal advantage attached to the profession of Christianity. In order still more strongly to counteract such an impression, the native Christians, were urged so far as lay in their power, not only to undertake the support of their own institutions, but also to contribute the needful funds for sending teachers to their heathen brethren. The result of this movement has been that whilst a limited number of mere professors relapsed into heathenism, the majority have become very much more decided and zealous, and the native Church has become in every respect healthier and stronger.

This has notably been the case in the Northern Province (of which Jaffna is the capital), where the effects of mission-work on Hindooism present a striking contrast to the results effected in the south of the Isle, where only, as it were, the fringe of Buddhism has as yet been touched. And yet those most practically acquainted with the work say that even in North Ceylon "heathenism is still so gross and rampant that mission agencies can hardly count the battle there to be much more than begun." But those who are Christians are in real earnest; and so, notwithstanding the poverty of the people, a Native Missionary Association was formed in the autumn of 1883, which now supports several native teachers to assist in the work commenced in 1862 by the Church Missionary Society in two of the dreariest and hitherto most neglected districts of the Isle, namely, the Wannie and Pallai.

The latter is only about twenty miles from Jaffna, a sandy tract of cocoa-nut plantations and malarious fever-haunted jungle. So unhealthy is the climate, that of all the mission agents who have been sent to work here, not one has escaped the jungle-fever. The population numbers about 10,000 persons, and in all this district there is but one medical man, whose primary duty is to look after the planters. As for the people, finding small benefit from their own medicine-men, and assuming all manner of sickness and trouble to be the visitation of offended evil spirits, they at once call in diviners and devil-dancers, who distract the poor sufferer with their truly "infernal" noise, or else they make a pilgrimage to some favourite devil-temple. Anxious relations bring the patient a drink of foul water, which has washed the feet of some filthy fakir, and which is deemed precious medicine.[1]

Here indeed is a fallow field awaiting medical missionaries endowed with such love for their suffering fellow-creatures as to induce them to face existence in such uninviting surroundings. It is, however, certain that men born in the Isle might face the climate with less danger than Europeans, and it is to be hoped that the Medical College at Colombo, which is training so large a number of students, may yield the right men. Certainly no other form of mission is so certain to go straight to the hearts of these poor villagers, and it is satisfactory to learn that the Jaffna Medical Mission has now been commenced in real earnest, and is to be under control of the directors of the Jaffna College (*i.e.*, missionaries and native Christians in connection with the three Missions).

[1] For astounding details of sorcery and criminal preparation of charms by a native doctor, see Emerson Tennant's "Ceylon," vol. ii. pp. 544–548.

Dr. Marston, formerly of Mildmay (London), has gone out to assume charge of this great work, but as yet is the only missionary-physician among the 316,000 inhabitants of the Northern Province; and what that means may be inferred from the fact that within two months in 1888–1889 no less than 2000 persons died in Jaffna during an epidemic of malignant fever, and such visitations of fever, small-pox, and cholera are by no means rare, and invariably carry off thousands, who perish from ignorance of the simplest laws of medicine.

Still more unattractive than Pallai is the dreary Wannie district, a name chiefly associated with that of the virulent Wannie fever, which not only incapacitates its victims at the time, but is very difficult to shake off. This district comprises an area of about 14,000 square miles, and its population, which averages one to the square mile, is scattered along the sea-coast, and in about 200 small villages inland, each surrounded by swampy rice-fields, the irrigation of which is a constant care, as any failure of the water-supply from the village tank involves famine. Most of these villages take their name from the tank; hence the frequent termination of "Colom," a tank, e.g., Choendic-Colom, Sundi-Colom.

These wretched people suffer terribly from pleurisy and from a swelling in the glands of the throat, but worst of all from the fearful parangi or karayo, that horrible disease, somewhat resembling leprosy in its most loathsome form, which is aggravated by bad water and scanty fare. Wherever the restoration of the ancient tanks has blessed a district with a renewed water-supply and consequent abundant crops, then this awful disease in a great measure disappears.

The people are described as being sunk mentally, morally, and physically to the deepest degradation. Their faith is Hindooism of the very lowest type, with a large admixture of devil-worship.

In this unpromising field, agents of the Church Mission were sent to commence work at Mullaitivo, a town on the east coast about seventy miles south of Jaffna, and at Vavania-Velan-Colom, a large inland village, about fifty miles from Mullaitivo. From these centres, evangelistic work of all sorts has been carried to the surrounding districts. Here, as in the Pallai district, schools have been established, and several of the most promising converts have been taken to the Training Institution at Kopay, that they may eventually return as teachers to their own countrymen. Thus an influence has gradually been created, and prejudice so far overcome that now no opposition is offered to the Christian teachers; on the contrary, their message is heard with eager attention, and in several cases devil-dancers, and even the priests of the devil-temples, have been among the earliest converts, although their acceptance of Christ involved the sacrifice of their sole means of living—a very strong test of faith.

Indeed, if the offertory by which this Native Mission is supported could tell the story of self-denial by which many of its small sums have been obtained, no better proof could be given of how thoroughly in earnest these poor Christians are; in fact, in the year when extreme poverty was aggravated by cyclones, the subscriptions, so far from diminishing, actually increased. Amongst its items are gifts from several young men who have been trained in the Institution of sums equal to one-half, one-third, or one-twelfth of their first year's salary as schoolmaster.

In the records of this work we occasionally obtain a touching glimpse of some of the difficulties which beset the Hindoo, whose reason and heart alike incline to the Christian faith. Foremost among these are the claims of deceased relations, and the supposed cruelty to these involved in omitting the ancestral offerings; for as the dead of the last three generations are believed to be entirely dependent on the living for their supplies and deliverance from purgatory, and as only a son can officiate at the funeral rites of his father, it is evident that when, by becoming a Christian, a man incapacitates himself from fulfilling these obligations, he is doing a grievous wrong to the dead, whom he is most bound to reverence. Hence we hear of the "great fortitude" shown by a convert in refusing to take his part in the heathen rites at his father's funeral, and we know what tears, entreaties, and persecutions he must have withstood from all the women of the family.[1]

Moreover, when a Christian is taken ill, his sufferings are often greatly aggravated by the persistent determination of his relatives to perform noisy devil-ceremonies on his behalf, and also by the fear lest after his death they should forcibly burn his body with heathen rites. If some other members of the family are Christians, they can generally succeed in preventing this dishonour to the dead, but very painful scenes sometimes offend this solemn presence, as in the case of a young school-mistress, whose deathbed was a striking instance of calm Christian peace, but

[1] In "The Himalayas and Indian Plains" I have given full details o the requirements of *Ancestral Worship among the Hindoos.* See pp. 187-190, also 574, 575. And in "Wanderings in China" I have entered minutely into the still more extraordinary ramifications of the same worship in that vast Empire.

no sooner had her spirit passed away, than her heathen relatives commenced a terrible uproar in their determination to enforce heathen rites. Her father and brothers, however, being also Christians, stood firm; whereupon all their kinsfolk forsook them, refusing to have anything further to do with them.

Very striking is the manner in which these poor caste-ridden people occasionally apply some story of our Lord's tenderness and humility, as contrasted with the harsh arrogance of the Brahmans. Thus a poor coolie chanced to hear the story of Christ's visit to Zacchæus. Next time he visited the temple and presented his accustomed offering, he felt how different was the action of the proud priest, who bade him lay his money on the ground, and who then poured water over it and washed it with his foot before he would take it up. So he went back to the house where he had heard those good words, and stood outside listening during the morning prayers, and one who saw him, bade him enter, and taught him, and soon that man became a working Christian. Like St. Andrew, he "first found his own brother, and brought him to Jesus;" then he persuaded his wife, and so the leaven of good has spread.

But very often when a man resolves to take this great step, he is rejected by all his relations; his own wife and sons utterly despise him. Yet again and again such an one has persevered in prayer for their conversion, and although years may elapse ere one will join him, sooner or later the change is wrought, and the patient convert has the gladness of bringing his family to crave Christian baptism. Amongst those who have thus been added to the Church was one of the most notorious devil-dancers of

Pallai, whose delight it was to ridicule the preaching of the Gospel. Nevertheless, that he might be the better able to cavil, he bought a Bible and began reading it, with the oft-told result. Light entered into his heart so fully, that not all the prayers and tears of his kinsfolk could shake his new-born faith; and so eager did he now become to confess Christ in presence of all men, that those who witnessed his baptism begged that he might be named Paul Vayrakiam (Paul the Zealous). With him was baptized another young man, whose conversion was due to the efforts of another recent convert from the devil-dancers.

For in these fever-stricken districts, and on those burning sandy plains, the old, old story comes home to these poor neglected ones with just the same love and power that it has done to myriads in all corners of the earth wheresoever this Gospel has been preached. In the life of many of the converts there is abundant proof of their having fully realised their Saviour's love, and of their living in the blessed consciousness of His abiding presence; and there is just the same earnest longing to lead others to a personal knowledge of the only source of light and life, with apparently less of that shyness—perhaps selfish shyness—which leads our more reserved Western natures to shrink from speech on the subjects which we recognise as most vital to ourselves, and yet often guard as jealously as though our neighbour had no concern therein.

Grand enduring work has been done by many such loving disciples—work known only to their Master—in the gradual upbuilding of His Church.

I must, however, turn to a less pleasant topic, to show how not only the good leaven spreads, but also the evil; for, sad to say, here, as in Japan and other countries, the bitter leaven of infidel teaching is working with pernicious effect, and the writings of the leading "free-thinkers" and atheists poison the minds of many a would-be-wise young student. So the preachers of the Gospel have not merely to contend with the systems of a debased Buddhism or Brahmanism, but with all the oft-repeated, oft-refuted difficulties and objections which are deemed so doubly wise because they are imported from Europe.

For instance, one of the chief Hindoo festivals in this district is annually held at an ancient temple near Nellore, in honour of Kandaswami, the youngest son of the god Siva. The festival continues for twenty-five days, and on the tenth day the idol is brought forth and placed on a splendid car, and so drawn triumphantly in sunwise circuit round the temple. The most fanatical observances of olden days are now prohibited, and here, as at the great Juggernath Temple of India, devotees may no longer throw themselves beneath the wheels of the car, but have to satisfy their zeal by rolling in the dust in its wake. This is done by hundreds of the vast multitude who annually assemble from all parts of the country in very earnest pilgrimage.

Such a gathering affords an opportunity of sowing good words broadcast, which is not neglected by the Christian teachers who mingle freely in the crowd, and do what they can by preaching and the sale and distribution of books. Latterly they have been gladdened by hearing comments on the good which Christianity was acknowledged to have effected in Jaffna, and some were heard to say that doubtless forty or fifty years hence all the population will have become Christian. But though many listened with interest, an organised system of molestation and interruption has now been set on foot by a party of young men, who go about, not to defend the insulted dignity of Kandaswami, but to distribute pamphlets and tracts compiled by themselves from the works of atheistic Europeans.

In like manner, quite the most serious bar to the acceptance of the Gospel by Buddhists is the energetic teaching of European exponents of Theosophy and Esoteric Buddhism.

A very important branch of Church missionary work amongst the Hindoo population of Ceylon is that known as the Tamil Coolie Mission, which has for its object the instruction of all the legion of immigrants from Malabar, who come generally for a term of five years or more, chiefly to labour on the plantations, and do all the hard work of the Isle. This Mission was commenced on a small scale about thirty years ago, and has been mainly supported by the coffee-planters, who raise more than £1000 a year to maintain catechists and schools,—a clear proof of their estimate of this good effort.

Upwards of forty native agents are now thus employed; but so numerous are the estates, that each catechist has to visit from forty to sixty, and so can only go to each about once in three months, which does not allow much chance of gaining individual influence with the utterly ignorant heathen.

The Mission is superintended by three European and two Tamil clergymen, whose lives are spent in one long round of difficult hill-travelling, over an area so vast, that on an average they can only go over the ground once in six months. Their district is about as large as Wales, and much more mountainous; so this mission may well be described as under-manned, the more so seeing how many plantations lie beyond the reach of any English service, save on these rare occasions.

To supply even this scanty spiritual fare involves an exhausting life of ceaseless locomotion. Some folk in England might think it hard work to be up and out every morning by 5 A.M. to attend the muster of coolies, and preach to them before starting on a four or five hours' walk, beneath a blazing sun, over steep hills without one scrap of shade. Then the native Christians on the estate, and perhaps some in the nearest village, must be visited, and candidates for baptism or confirmation examined and taught, and the catechist, if there be one, must be cheered by a talk about his work, and on the morrow the same round must be repeated on the next estate. And so each day of the week repeats itself till Sunday, when there is a Tamil service for as many coolies as can be mustered, and English service for the planters, many of whom come a very long way to be present.

Small chapels are indeed scattered at wide intervals over the mountain districts where the plantations chiefly lie, and in these, two of the Diocesan clergy minister regularly, and others occasionally, but many estates are so remote that they are only visited at very rare intervals. When we think of the multiplicity of church-going luxuries offered for our selection in this country, we can perhaps realise how very much neglected we should feel—in fact, how easily we might lose the mere habit of Sunday observance—were our religious privileges limited to two or three meetings in a coffee-store or a drawing-room in the course of a year. Certainly it does seem a very unequal division of the Church's workers which leaves so wide a field with such limited pastoral care.

Even Sunday does not necessarily bring rest from travel; for instance, the native clergyman (Tamil) at Pelmadulla holds an English service at 8 A.M., and then one in Tamil, after which he either travels twelve miles to hold an English service at Ratnapura, or to some other district. But in truth, neither clergy nor people spare themselves in this respect, the distance which some of these people walk to be present at a service being almost incredible; as, for instance, at Rackwane, in the south, to which some of the congregation were in the habit of walking fifteen miles every Sunday, till a Christian conductor undertook to hold service in one of the coffee-stores. (The Principal of Trinity College, Kandy, mentions that one of his late pupils travelled 130 miles in order to be present at the early morning service on New Year's Day.)

As a matter of course, the work of this Mission is greatly helped or impeded by the attitude of the authorities on each estate. In some cases the planters themselves, or their superintendents, take a hearty interest in its progress, and I have recently heard of one who, being present at the baptism of five of his own coolies, addressed them in their own tongue in such plain, manly words as they were not likely to forget, especially exhorting them so to live that they might be the means of bringing others also to Jesus. That speaker's words are so happily illustrated in his own life, that one of his Singhalese neighbours expressed a devout hope that he may eventually become a Buddha!

Happily, within the last few years, a considerable number of the planters have awakened to the duty and privilege of thus exerting a strong personal influence on the men in their employ, while on other estates much is done by earnest Christian *Kanganis*, *i.e.*, coolie overseers, who supplement the work of the catechist by reading the service on intermediate Sundays, or in some cases by holding prayer-meetings (for many catechists have charge of a very much larger district than any one man can work satisfactorily). In at least one district the habit of family evening-prayer is now general amongst the Christians, though to assemble in the morning is impossible, owing to the early hour when work begins.

On the other hand, where the *Kangani* is a heathen and antagonistic to the Christians, he can greatly impede the work of the catechist and embitter the lives of the converts. Thus in one district, where till recently there were four Christian *Kanganis*, a change in the management of the estates has led to their being all replaced by heathens— a very grievous matter for the little band of converts whose taskmasters they are.

A considerable number of conversions have been entirely due to the influence and persuasion of Christian fellow-coolies. This has notably been the case in Uda Pussellawa, where, about twelve years ago, a Canarese man and his wife were converted. They had for many years been working on Ceylon estates, and probably had a large acquaintance among their fellows. Every evening since their baptism, when the long day's work is done, they have assembled in their house as many as they could collect for Bible-reading and prayer, and it is mainly due to this effort that a congregation of upwards of a hundred persons now meet for worship every Sunday in a pretty stone church, towards the building of which "Isaac" and his wife contributed the first hundred rupees. The congregation prove their zeal by walking from six to ten miles from other estates, no small effort on this their only day of rest. These are only poor coolies, but somehow I fancy that in the Great Hereafter many of us who now daily *say* (I doubt if we as often really *pray* that oft-said prayer) THY KINGDOM COME, will vainly wish that in all our lives we had done as much to prepare the way for our Lord's coming as these humble folk have done.

Certainly it is enough to make us all think, to note how often a few words of Scripture or of exhortation have so impressed poor ignorant heathen Tongans, Fijians, or Chinamen, that they have returned to their own villages and endured persecution for years staunchly, never resting till they have persuaded others, and so each has become the nucleus of a church; whereas we, on whom all teaching and Christian privileges have been lavished from our cradles, what have we individually ever done to induce one from without the fold to enter?

I never hear the story of Ebed-melech, the Ethiopian eunuch (whom so many white men would contemptuously have described as "only a nigger," but to whom alone the prophet was bidden to convey the Divine assurance of safety amid all the horrors of the capture of Jerusalem and the slaughter of all the princes and nobles of Judah[1]), without a thought of that day of surprises, when so many great lords, temporal and spiritual, will have to take the lowest places, and others who are now last and least will find themselves first and greatest in THE KINGDOM.

In another case recently reported, eighteen persons came forward to ask for baptism, all of whom had been very carefully instructed by another Christian couple. Thirteen of these had walked thirty miles through a continuous downpour of rain to present themselves to the clergyman on his visiting the district. Of course all candidates are subject to most searching examination to prove their sincerity, and the answer of one suggested how truly he had grasped

[1] Jer. xxxviii. 7, 8; and Jer. xxxix. 6, 7, and 16–18.

the principle of the new life. "Doubtless," he said, "some may be Christians in name only, but such have only joined Christianity without being united to Christ."

Of course the difficulty of obtaining a permanent influence over these coolies is greatly enhanced by their migratory habits, which often take them from one district to another, or back to India, before much appreciable good has been done. Nevertheless, some of the workers are convinced that, even as the dawn advances to high noon—imperceptibly —so the Light is radiating silently but surely, and though as yet only about fifteen hundred of the Tamil coolies now on the Isle have received baptism, a considerable number have returned as Christians to their own country, and very many listen with earnest attention, and some say they are convinced of the truth of the Gospel, but dare not face the anger of their relations should they openly embrace Christianity. It would be difficult to find a more remarkable proof of their goodwill than is shown by the generosity with which they sometimes contribute to purely Christian objects, as, for instance, the building of a substantial church at Rackwane, where the congregation is very small and very poor, and about three-fourths of the requisite sum has been given by heathen overseers and coolies!

Among what I may call "insensible influences" for good are some exceedingly popular Christian lyrics, something in the style of "The old, old story," composed by a Tamil poet. They are Christian stories told in the native style of poetry, and set to native tunes, which find great favour with the people. Many of the converts who cannot read know these by heart, and their companions, attracted by the melody, learn them also; and so the story is sung, and often well sung, by those who as yet know little of its meaning.

Thus one whose heart is in his Master's work, chanced to be travelling by coach to Kandy, when one of the passengers commenced singing Hindoo songs so cheerily that his companions begged him to continue. One at least of his hearers was considerably astonished when the next song selected was one of the most beautiful of these lyrics, " Jesus carrying His Cross," a text which furnished the subject for earnest words to an attentive audience of Hindoos and Buddhists. The singer said he had learnt the lyric from hearing it sung by a Roman Catholic convert in a distant part of the country.

When we remember that in the Jaffna peninsula alone the three Missions have 15,000 children in training, all of whom are taught to sing sacred stories, it is evident what a far-reaching agency for good this must prove. The schools have periodical concerts, when all the relatives come to hear and admire, and the children and Biblewomen teach the mothers, who like to sing them in their own homes, so that they are gradually replacing the very objectionable mythological songs even in homes which are not yet altogether Christian.

To those who have not noted elsewhere how often a mighty tree grows from a tiny seed, the feeble first-fruits of work in some large centres of heathenism may seem almost contemptible. Thus in the town of Kurunegalla, the Tamil Christian congregation consists of three very poor families; one is that of a fisherman, another of a man who climbs palm-trees to draw "toddy," while the third householder is a road-coolie, who at his baptism selected the name of Zachariah, his wife naturally assuming that of Elizabeth. The latter tends a flock of sheep—a few sheep we must assume, since at night she folds them all in the largest room of her little hut, she and her husband contriving to stow themselves away in the other room, which measures 5 feet by 6 feet! Truly a tiny flock, both pastoral and spiritual, but as regards the latter, its shepherd is satisfied that it will erelong prove the nucleus of an ever-widening congregation.

I must repeat that I am speaking only of the Tamil Christians of Kurunegalla, the Singhalese and Burgher congregations being of course quite distinct. Of the former, a recently acquired member is a native headman from an outlying village, converted through the instrumentality of his brother. These two men, being the only Christians in that neighbourhood, have had to face considerable opposition; indeed, before his baptism this young man had given very strong proof of his determination, in resolutely refusing to offer incense in the great temple at Kandy, where he was obliged to be present in his official capacity, his refusal gave great offence to his superiors. To those who can realise the scene within that beautiful temple—the crowd of devout worshippers bearing their offerings, the gorgeously dressed headmen, the throng of yellow-robed priests urging the recreant to compliance with this simple ceremony—only the burning of a little incense—such an incident suggests a picture of wondrous interest.

Indeed, in all Oriental scenes the picturesque element presents itself at every turn in a manner undreamt of by those who insensibly illustrate these outlines from their own Western thoughts. Thus in the case of the tiny Tamil congregation of which I spoke just now, the reader whose mind sees only three very poor English families would conjure up a very different picture from the little group of turbaned brown men and of women whose brilliantly-coloured drapery is worn so very effectively, and whose poverty must be dire indeed if it forbids the display of rings and bangles, always in good taste, however base the metal. Even the sheep lying in the shade on the verandah of that humble hut are quaint lanky animals with long drooping ears, very much more attractive to the artist than those approved of by British farmers.

While the TAMIL COOLIE MISSION seeks to reach the Hindoo immigrants, a corresponding organisation known as the KANDYAN ITINERANCY works over nearly the same area of hill-country in the three central provinces. It appeals especially to the Singhalese village population, supplying (to the best of its ability) Christian schoolmasters and catechists, under the superintendence of two European and two Singhalese clergymen of the Church of England.

But considering over what a vast expanse of mountainous and forest country these four men must travel in order occasionally to minister to their widely-scattered flock, we can well believe that this Mission also suffers from being "under-manned." Nevertheless a wide-spread influence for good has been established; in many districts a spirit of interest and inquiry now replaces the dull apathy of sleepy Buddhism, and a multitude of tiny congregations form so many little spots of leaven in the great mass of heathenism.

It is not to be supposed that the paths of the converts are always paths of peace, for even the non-persecuting Buddhists contrive to make life very unpleasant to relations who venture to differ from them; young converts especially are occasionally removed from school and beaten to induce them to kneel once more at Buddhist altars, and the dread of being so treated prevents many from expressing their convictions. For instance, two youths who ventured to say they wished to become Christians were at once compelled by their parents to assume the yellow robe and prepare for the Buddhist priesthood.

The contemplative life, however, sometimes results in a more absolute conversion, as in the case of a lad who had for four years attended the mission-school at Baddigama, when he was inveigled away by the priest of a neighbouring village, who painted in glowing colours the easy life and abundant food of the priesthood, and the honour and homage he would receive from the people would he but take upon him the vows of Buddha. The influence of the parents was secured by the promise of an annual gift of twelve bags of rice from the temple. So the lad yielded, and was duly shaven and invested with the sacred yellow robes, and for three years he continued in the service of the temple with an ever-reproachful conscience.

At length his spiritual conflict was evident to all his companions, and every means, fair and foul, was tried to hold him fast. Some tried bribes, and one man threatened to stab him if he would not say that Buddha and the priests were the most high refuge. But the lad gained courage, and throwing off the yellow robes, he returned to his first teachers, and after due probation was baptized and confirmed, and is now a communicant. His parents were present at his baptism, and there seemed every reason to hope that they would follow his example.

In various parts of the Isle men who were once priests of Buddha have likewise found the True Light, and are now working steadfastly under Christ's banner.

At the present moment, when a leaning to Buddhism and its twin-brother Agnosticism, has become a sort of fashion in England, it is interesting to note the reasons for renouncing the former which are given by men born and bred in that faith. One says he does so "because Buddha nowhere says a word about the Eternal God; all things in heaven and earth declare His wisdom and power, but as concerns loving, obeying, and believing in Him, Buddha is dumb. Hence communion with God in prayer, which is the very life of the soul, is absolutely ignored, since, according to this teaching, there is no one to whom prayer can be offered—no one to hear and no one to answer."

An old man about seventy-five years of age said that all through his long life he has been seeking rest. He wrote out sacred books, he gave large alms, and performed long pilgrimages to Adam's Peak and Anuradhapura and other holy shrines, hoping thus to heap up merit; but it was all to no purpose till at last Christ came to him (for truly, he says, it was not that he had sought Christ), and in Him he found the rest he craved. The old man was one of a congregation of upwards of seventy communicants in a village where a few years ago there was not one Christian.

Now, note the reply of a young convert, who, when urged by his father to return to his ancestral faith, replied, "I cannot go back to Buddhism. I must believe that there is a Creator of the world. I need forgiveness of sin, and there is no Saviour, no forgiveness in Buddhism. There is no one who has the power to forgive, therefore every one must of necessity endure all the consequences of his sins. I want to be happy after death, and there is no hope in Buddhism—but in Christianity I find all these." The latter is the son of a rigidly Buddhist family, and had been brought from another province by the priest at Kurunegalla on purpose to teach a school which he had opened in opposition to that of the Mission. This young man's uncle was sent for to reason with him, but instead of reclaiming the wanderer, he confessed the validity of all his arguments, and presented himself as a candidate for baptism.

It is also instructive to note that the aforesaid priest, in urging his neighbours to withstand the teaching of "those lying fools the Christians," instead of himself preaching pure Buddhism, recommends the villagers to join the Society of Theosophists. There is, unfortunately, no doubt that Buddhism has received a real impetus from the example of certain foolish Europeans, who (most assuredly lacking any personal knowledge of "THE MASTER" whom they so dishonour) have thrown in their lot with the teachers of so-called Theosophy and Esoteric Buddhism—systems which those who understand them best, classify as "Bedlamite balderdash," "blatant humbug," and "impudent imposture."

I would shrink from quoting such expressions regarding any phase of true Theosophy or "Divine knowledge," but the leaders of this society in Ceylon (well aware that there could be no fellowship between seekers after knowledge of God and the atheistic system of Buddhism, which does not acknowledge any God) were wise in their generation, and adopted as their title the Paramawignanartha, or Supreme Knowledge Society. Consequently it embraces whatever may be the individual ideal of highest good, whether it be how best to enjoy this world, and how to get on in it and get wealth, or how best to attain to Nirvana and the extinction of all desire.[1]

---

[1] Taking Theosophy even at its best, as now preached in Europe, an unbiassed student of its teaching writes: "There is no note which vibrates more constantly in the soul of every true man than the prayer, 'Lord, be merciful to me a sinner!' . . . To that heartfelt cry I do not find any answer in Theosophy. I find, on the contrary, an almost exultant assertion that GOD is not a Being with a Father's heart, that for sin there is no expiation, and for the sinner no forgiveness."

I think the European disciples of these schools would be rather startled were they to realise the practical working of the systems for which they are content to abjure Christianity. For instance, in the neighbourhood of the mission-station at Cotta, Colonel Olcott succeeded in stirring up the Buddhist priests to such hostility, that for a while the attendance at the Christian schools was sensibly diminished. In the village of Udumulla the priests under this influence opened a rival school, and pronounced a very singular form of excommunication against all who should persist in sending their children to the mission-schools. Such offenders were to be fined a rupee and a half, and were further admonished that "the dhobie shall not wash their clothes, the native doctors shall not attend any of them in sickness, *the devil-dancers shall not perform demon ceremonies for them (!), and the astrologers shall not consult the planets for them on the birth of their children, or concerning marriages and other important events!*"

We need scarcely wonder that those who have escaped from this debased system are proof against all arguments of the Theosophists. Colonel Olcott did his utmost to persuade a Buddhist priest who had become a Christian to resume the yellow robe. When he had exhausted his arguments, the ex-priest replied, with more force than polish, "I am not a dog that I should return to my vomit. Pray spare your pity. If you can believe that there is no right, no wrong, no soul, no conscience, no responsibility, no God, no judgment, you need for yourself all the pity you possess and more."

Yet it is to this system that so great an impetus has been given even in Europe and America by the agency of so beautiful a writer as Sir Edwin Arnold, who, in his passionate admiration for the good and noble, depicts things not as they really are, but as he would have them to be; for truly what he calls "The Light of Asia" has most practically proved to be only bewildering darkness.

Surely such an ovation as was accorded to him by the Buddhists when he visited Ceylon in 1886 was doubtful honour for a Christian. At one Buddhist college near Colombo well-nigh three thousand Buddhists assembled to testify their gratitude to the poet who has painted their leader in colours all borrowed from the life and teaching of Him Who is the true LIGHT OF THE WORLD. The honoured guest was placed on a raised platform beneath an honorific canopy, while Buddhist ecclesiastics robed in yellow satin chanted chorals, litanies, and anthems in Pali and Singhalese, Sir Edwin replying in Sanskrit.

One of those best acquainted with practical Buddhism in Ceylon describes it as "the most cunningly-devised system of atheism and negation, of idol-worship, tree and serpent worship, demon-worship, and pessimism which has ever held the human mind in bondage"—a system exactly answering to the awful Scriptural summary, "Having no hope, and without God in the world."

Archdeacon Farrer says, "Buddhism, as it appears, not in 'The Light of Asia,' but in the original 'Life of Gautama,' is but a philosophy of despair, which knows no immortality, no conscience, and no God. Humanity has groped in blindness after its Creator; in Christ alone has it learned the love of His Fatherhood and the riches of His salvation."

Here are the two creeds. The Buddhist Gospel of Misery teaches that all is vanity and all is suffering, and that complete cessation of craving for existence is the only cessation of suffering, and therefore the one thing to strive after.

He "who is able to keep us from falling" says, "Be ye perfect, even as your Father which is in heaven is perfect." And His Apostle says, "Work out your own salvation with fear and trembling, for it is God which worketh in you both to will and to do of His good pleasure." And, as the goal for which we strive, he says, "AND SO SHALL YE EVER BE WITH THE LORD."

Christ bestows now on all who truly give themselves to Him, the gift of a spiritual life, one with His own, which shall exist in conscious, perfect union with Him throughout eternity.[1]

Can anything more pitiful be conceived than that human beings born within the pale of the Christian Church can deliberately sacrifice the privilege of individual personal communion with the ever-present Almighty Friend who cares for each one of us, in exchange for an utterly irresponsive negation—a theory of perfection only to be attained through self-conquest, at which poor weak human beings are advised to aim through ages of lonely life-long struggles extending over many transmigrations, without one prayerful look to the Divine Helper who alone can keep our wayward wills from wandering after all manner of evil? And all this in order to gain the cessation of their individual life.

Buddha made no offer of the Divine Gift of Life, for it was not his to bestow.[2] Of Christ it is true now as of

---

[1] Jesus says, "He that hath the SON HATH LIFE. He that hath not the SON OF GOD HATH NOT LIFE. I am come that they might have Life, and that they might have it abundantly. Where I am, there shall also My servant be."

[2] When Prince Gautama was born, the world had still six centuries to wait ere man might again have access to the Tree of Life (the tree of which, according to the old allegory, Eve failed to eat, and the approach to which was thenceforth guarded, lest, having sinned, she should nevertheless eat of

old, that "as many as receive Him, to them gives He power to become the sons of God," who shall dwell with Him for ever and be like Him. Buddha offers no power nor help of any sort. He merely gives rules how so absolutely to conquer every natural instinct, that, after untold ages of weary agonising, men may attain to a cessation of their very undesirable individual existence, in other words, to Nirvana, *i.e.*, the condition of a flame after it has been blown out. The highest ideal of bliss is the attainment of perfection in the colourless, loveless condition of a dewdrop falling into the ocean, thenceforth to exist only as merged in the Infinite. It is not a very inviting goal for which to agonise, except as a means of escape from the prolonged miseries of innumerable transmigrations. Surely not worth even a passing thought from any one who has received Christ's gracious offer of immortality—His own gift of Eternal Life in Himself.

I think if good Prince Gautama had been born 600 years later, and within hearing of the truth as revealed in Jesus Christ, he would assuredly have been the most earnest and devoted of His apostles, and he would now be spared the grief of seeing dim-eyed men turn from the fulness of the True Light to grope after the pale glimmer which, when he kindled it in the black night of unmitigated idolatry, was so eagerly blessed, even as the weary watcher prizes the feeble rushlight if he has nothing better; but candle and lamp alike pale before the glow of the Eastern dawn.

its fruit and live for ever in estrangement from God); and so the Redeemer reveals Himself not only as the Life, but as the Life-Giver. "To them who by patient continuance in well-doing seek for . . . immortality, He giveth Eternal Life." "To him that overcometh will I give to eat of the Tree of Life, which is in the midst of the Paradise of God." "THIS IS LIFE ETERNAL, that they may know Thee, the Only True God, and Jesus Christ, whom Thou hast sent."

To us Christians the whole of life is glorified and gladdened by the consciousness of living union with our ever present loving Lord, and the certainty (too often proved in our own experience to leave any room for doubt) of His sympathy and care for all that concerns us. But for the Buddhist there is no such companionship, only lonely striving after a perfection unattainable to the weakness of unhelped humanity.

He seeks absolute perfection here. The Christian knows his life here to be but the embryo of what it shall be; of the next stage he knows no more than the dull grub working out its little round of existence dreams in what perfection of life and radiancy of colour it will emerge from its crysalis coffin. Our life here is that of the chick cradled within the egg-shell—a life hid (but hid with Christ in God), and even now being formed and developed, soon to burst the shell and pass through whatever stages may yet be needed to bring us to perfection.

"It doth not yet appear what we shall be," any more than a vast collection of bird's eggs of all nations can suggest the myriad forms of beauty which they represent—the soaring eagles, swift sea-birds, jewelled humming-birds flashing in the sunlight, too quick for sight to follow, bright birds of paradise, all varied types of radiant plumage and musical song, and all developed from a lot of empty egg-shells. So from the soul-cases in which we now dwell shall go forth the living us to be perfected, each after his kind, and dwell for ever in His presence, which is fulness of joy.

Of course one radical difference between the striving after perfection enjoined on the Christian and on Buddhists, Parsees, Brahmans, and Mahommedans lies in the motive for good works. The Christian knows he is bound to do his very utmost as a thank-offering for the free gift bestowed on him, whereas in all other creeds the one idea is that of purchasing salvation by works. Multiply acts of self-denial, external rites, pilgrimages, prayers (though Buddhism ignores God), and by these means weave a robe of self-righteousness —the dearest of all to human pride.

In the case of Buddhism, repeat the name of Buddha as a perpetual charm. You can never say it often enough; so go on and on all your life. If you could be sure that you had thus, or by any other means, acquired sufficient merit, there would be no occasion to pay the monks for reciting endless acts of devotion (which cannot be prayers) on your behalf, to get your soul out of the many purgatories in which devils will delight in tormenting it. Oh! the hopelessness of such a creed, with its weary prospect of successive transmigrations, each carrying forward the account of good or ill from the previous state of existence.

Kandy, as might be expected in the city of the sacred tooth, has as yet proved a rocky soil, unfavourable to the growth of Christian seed; and though the Episcopal Church, the Wesleyans, and the Baptists are all at work, it has been well said that the atmosphere is as full of heathenism as it is of heat. Seeing the very important bearing on this subject of female education, it is somewhat remarkable that, with the exception of the Wesleyan industrial schools for poor girls, no female boarding-school should have been established in the mountain capital. Mission-agents send their daughters from here to Cotta, but for those of influential Kandyan gentlemen no such education is available, though it has been proved that wherever such schools are opened, parents willingly send their daughters, though well aware that a considerable number invariably embrace Christianity. This subject is one of increasing importance, not merely on account of the influence which might thus be acquired in many influential homes, but as the surest hope of providing suitable wives for such converts as may be won from among the high-caste Kandyan boys who are now being trained at Trinity College, Kandy.

Such is the anxiety for a good English education, that the parents of these lads and young men are eager to secure it, notwithstanding a well-grounded impression that it will probably result in the renunciation of Buddhism. The college is under the direction of two English clergymen and a staff of ten masters. The two hundred day-scholars and the forty boarders are of all denominations, but the majority are professedly Christian, as are also all the masters; and when we hear of these scholars holding prayer-meetings by themselves, and that in one year eight of the senior students dedicated themselves to active Christian work, it is evident that the tone of the college must be encouraging to any Buddhist lad who is inclined to think seriously on the subject.

I have already spoken[1] of the great school at Cotta, commenced by the Church Missionary Society in A.D. 1822, with its boarding-school for girls and training institution for native clergy.

In addition to these varied duties, the Principal of Cotta, the Rev. R. T. Dowbiggin, has also the general superintendence of upwards of fifty village-schools, twenty-seven for girls and twenty-five for boys. These are scattered over an area of five hundred square miles, and have an average daily attendance of 1100 girls and 1600 boys, most of whom are Buddhists. This extension of girls' schools is deemed a most satisfactory feature, full of promise for the future,

[1] Vol. i. p. 151.

were it only for the breaking down of caste prejudice. As in the schools for Hindoo girls in the Northern Provinces, so here Singhalese girls of four distinct castes now sit on the same benches and learn the same lessons. This result has been achieved with far greater facility in the boys' schools than in the girls'. But the fact that girls should be allowed to live in the houses of Christians, and eat food cooked by them, proves that caste in Ceylon is a less grievous yoke than it is in Northern India.

This caste question, however, does prove a very serious difficulty, not only among the Tamil people, who of course keep up the regular Hindoo caste distinctions, but also among the Singhalese. One of their own pastors, the Rev. L. Liesching, writes, that although born and bred in Ceylon, he could not have believed how strong its influence really is. He says that even the Duriya (low-caste) Christians, on whose behalf he has to combat the prejudice of their higher-caste neighbours, show just as much unwillingness to associate with those who are of inferior caste to themselves. And as regards the highest castes, this is undoubtedly the greatest obstacle to their conversion. This is the more remarkable as caste is not a sacred institution among the Singhalese, for Buddhism does not recognise any such distinction of rank, and the Buddhist priests, to whom all yield reverence, are admitted from every caste. Here the distinction is simply social; nevertheless the line of demarcation is so marked, that no amount of wealth can overcome it, or induce the native aristocracy to admit a man from a lower caste to social intercourse, far less to intermarriage.

Thus, of all the races who people Ceylon, the Moormen alone are apparently free from caste trammels, at least I suppose they are as free as average Christians, which, after all, is not saying much, especially in free America, where the general interpretation of social equality seems to lie in being the equal of all superiors and the immeasurable superior of all of lower degree!

The Church Missionary Society did not commence work in Colombo till 1850. Three years later a large church was erected on the Galle Face Esplanade, in which English, Singhalese, and Tamil services have been constantly held for the three races. Here the Society also has district schools for boys and girls, and a boarding-school for Tamil Christian girls. It also carries on all manner of evangelistic work among Hindoos, Mahommedans, Buddhists, and Portuguese.

The work amongst the latter is most discouraging, the majority being so steeped in hopeless poverty that their life seems to have lost all spring; and as Ceylon has no poor-laws, all such are dependent for relief on a voluntary association called the Friend-in-Need Society, which, at best, can merely mitigate the sufferings of the most needy. Though of Portuguese descent, many of these poor Burghers living in the lanes and alleys of Slave Island are absolutely heathen; so the Wesleyans have latterly commenced holding services in Portuguese for their benefit, while the Church of England endeavours to reach some by means of a ragged-school and special services in Singhalese, which the majority can understand better than English. Their own language is a very debased Portuguese. Of course the well-to-do Dutch Burghers form a large and very important class of the community. As may be guessed by a glance round any of the churches one may chance to enter, they fill all sorts of responsible positions, but the Portuguese seem never to have got over the crushing oppression to which their ancestors were subjected by the Dutch, and to this day few rise high in the social scale.

In the Southern Province, where the population is principally Singhalese, and consequently Buddhist, the Church of England Mission is carried on chiefly by the S. P. G. and Diocesan clergy, the only station of the Church Missionary Society being that at Baddigama, which was commenced about A.D. 1820. Here one European and two native clergymen superintend the work of fifty male and female lay teachers. Baddigama is a large district, extending as far north as Bentota, and including a population of 100,000 souls, of whom only 526 are as yet professedly Christian. Twenty-six church-schools, with an average attendance of about sixty-seven children, are, however, so many centres of good influence, though there are villages where the schoolmaster himself is as yet literally the only Christian. Yet even in these the people seem quite willing to listen, and many profess to have lost all belief in Buddhism.

These villages are generally in the poorest districts, which have been almost abandoned by the Buddhist priests, and the temples left to fall into decay. This points to the fact that in the low country there are few rich temple endowments in land, such as were bestowed on the priesthood by the Kandyan kings, and which make the priests of the Central Province altogether independent of the people. That the people themselves desire education is certain, and at one of these low-country villages the Bana Maduwa (Buddhist preaching-place) was offered to the Mission by the village headmen, to be converted into a Christian school; and when this was declined because it adjoined the *pansala, i.e.*, temple-school, they at once erected a new building for the purpose.

It is, however, to be feared that the present "Buddhist revival," so diligently fostered by Europeans, will awaken much priestly activity in regard to long-neglected schools. Thus, in September 1890, a Buddhist school was opened at Welligama, the temple south of Galle, which was endowed by "the Leper King," apparently for no other purpose than to draw away the children from the Wesleyan and S. P. G. schools there. Sixty were allured from the former, and twenty from the latter, and a few days later a dastardly attempt was made to burn down the Wesleyan schools.

That a period of renewed struggle and difficulty may be at hand seems only too probable. Yet, on the whole, there is good ground for encouragement. In summarising the present position of Ceylon in regard to Christianity, it must be borne in mind that, apart from actual conversions, a very much wider work has been accomplished in the softening of prejudices, the general loosening of the far-reaching roots both of Buddhism and Brahmanism, and especially in awakening a real interest in religious questions in place of the former utter apathy. This last change is doubtless due to the amount of careful Scriptural training which has for so many years been imparted to many thousand children in the schools of all the Protestant Missions. These at present number over forty thousand.

Consequently, in any district where mission-schools have been at work for any length of time, a Christian preacher may be sure that many of his hearers have some previous understanding of the subject, which in itself is an immense help. Moreover, Christian teachers are more and more supplanting the heathen teachers in all the schools, so that all influence is in the right direction.

It is quite evident that the way is now open for real

progress, if only the mission-field were provided with a sufficient working staff. Whether these can be supplied must depend in a great measure on the pecuniary support placed at the disposal of the various working societies. Of Ceylon, as of so many other lands, it must be said, "The harvest truly is plenteous, but the labourers are few."

From the present position of Buddhism, it is evident that every month of delay in occupying any fresh mission-field in Ceylon will increase the difficulties and diminish the prospect of success; therefore it is surely the plain duty of English Christians to rouse themselves to a resolute effort on behalf of the beautiful Isle where such a multitude of England's sons are striving to earn their living.

Now here, it seems to me, is one of the most practical bits of direct work that could well be found. There lies the beautiful land, with, IN ONE SINGLE DISTRICT, TENS OF THOUSANDS of neglected villagers, weary of their own dark ignorance, and ready to be taught by whoever will first enter the field. Earnest workers, who have gladly devoted their lives and consecrated every energy to ploughing and sowing in neighbouring districts, look longingly on this great field which now lies white to the harvest, and from their lonely stations they send home to rich Christian England such a cry for help in this great need as must surely arouse the most indifferent to a true understanding of their privilege in being allowed to help such a work, from those funds which we know we each hold in trust, to be accounted for hereafter, as we so often need to remind ourselves, as we say "Both riches and honour come from THEE, and of THINE own do we give THEE."

Our MASTER has deputed us to offer to all men throughout the whole world His priceless gift of SPIRITUAL LIFE;

and yet there are millions to whom His message of love has never been delivered, because they to whom He has intrusted His talents of gold and silver are either squandering them on themselves, or hoarding them for other purposes than that of sending messengers to carry this great light to the nations who still dwell in the darkness of heathenism.

The funds at the disposal of the various societies being quite insufficient to supply the means of livelihood for even the native catechists, schoolmasters, and Bible-women so sorely needed for the work, it is evident that Europeans possessed of sufficient private means to support themselves would be especially welcome. Surely there must be some —and many are needed—who will recognise in this glorious work for eternity a better use for God-given talents than that of shaping the pleasantest career in England.

Why should not two friends who realise the true purpose of their lives agree that whereas their companions are starting in couples in search of big game in far countries, they too will start together as fishers of men, to cast the Gospel-net in waters teeming with life? Assuredly in no other career will they find so true a spring of joy and gladness for their own lives as in this ceaseless effort to draw all around them to the knowledge and love of their Saviour.

And of all mission-fields, few offer greater attractions than this beautiful Isle, with its mountains and forests, its bold crags and picturesque rivers, its gorges and waterfalls, its lower hills and wide verdant plains. Furthermore, as compared with such vast mission-fields as China or Africa, this has the charm of a simple language, a people gracious and kindly to Europeans, the protection of the Union Jack, and the possibility of at any time securing a day with some fellow-countryman who will welcome the sound of his own mother-tongue.

Here then are the inducements:—A healthy open-air life in a lovely country, ploughing and sowing fields which assuredly cannot prove barren, inasmuch as the Lord of the harvest is Himself with His servants to direct their work; and when the angel-reapers have garnered their ripened grain, the patient sower will realise such everlasting gladness as all the fleeting honours of earth fail to secure.

INDEX.

Aboriginal worship, ii. 143, 146.
Actors, Tamil, i. 367.
Adahana Maluwa, a sanctuary, i. 304.
Adam's Peak, ii. 310.
Admiral De la Haye, ii. 149.
Adult baptisms, ii. 80.
Aetagalla, ii. 272.
Agnew, Miss Eliza, ii. 360.
Agnosticism, ii. 412.
Alexander the Great, ii. 331.
Alexandrite, ii. 14.
Allegalla Peak, life on, ii. 277—footprint on, *ib.*—rain-storm on, 278.
Alu-Vihara rock-temple, i. 337.
Amalgamated religions, i. 81, 277, 297 ; ii. 45-48.
Ambetteyos or barbers, outcasts, ii. 101.
Ambulam, ii. 5.
American Mission, ii. 359.
Amherstia nobilis, i. 52.
Ancestral worship great hindrance to conversion, ii. 401.
Ant-eater and ant-lion, ii. 40.
Ants, red and black, i. 2, 61, 114.
Ants, white, i. 59-62 ; ii. 39—eat dead timber, ii. 25.
Anuradhapura tanks, i. 356, 361, 428—origin of name, 372 note, 373—ruins, 377—buried, 392—history, 400 note, 401-403—bo-tree, 406-415.
Arichandra, i. 368.

Ark, sacred, i. 404 note ; ii. 6.
Arnold, Sir Edwin, ii. 4, 417.
Arrack, ii. 156, 181, 234—trade, 185-187—farms, Skinner on, 185, 284.
Arrows of gods, i. 304—of Saman, ii. 6—of Maha-Sen, 129.
Artist's difficulties, i. 264, 384, 385.
Artocarpus incisa and *integrifolia*, i. 167.
Ashes of cow-dung, ii. 48—of sandalwood, use sanctioned by Rome, *ib.*
Astrologers, i. 279 ; ii. 417.
Aukana Vihare, i. 374.
Australian gums, ii. 285, 297.
Avissawella, ii. 1.
Axis, i. 242.

Badal-wanassa, i. 257.
Baddegama, ii. 176.
Badulla, ii. 30, 32—church, 38.
Baker's, Sir Samuel, farm, i. 194—sport, 241.
Balalu-wewa, i. 352, 364.
Bamboo, gigantic, i. 269—gregarious flowering, 215.
Bana Samanala, ii. 2.
Banana plant, i. 44.
Bandarawella, ii. 29.
Bandicoot, ii. 295.
Banyan-tree at Negombo, i. 145--on the Nerbudda, 146 ; ii. 237, 241.
Baptisms, adult, ii. 80.
Barber, Tamil, i. 38.
Barringtonia, ii. 236.

Basawa-kulum tank, i. 356, 364—oldest, 428.
Bats, nitre, i. 337, 428.
Batticaloa, ii. 76, 169—the harbour-bar, 172.
Batticotta College for Tamils, ii. 370-376.
Bears, ii. 68, 217.
Bêche de mer, i. 132.
Bees, i. 213, 214.
Belligama, sand village, ii. 194.
Bentota, ii. 227—oysters, 230.
Betel-chewing, i. 44.
Bible-women, ii. 366.
Bintenne, ii. 90.
Birds' nests, edible, i. 133.
Bishop of Colombo, first, i. 39—first Roman Catholic, 52.
Blended faiths, ii. 357.
Blue-bells, i. 192.
Boar, wild, ii. 72.
Boatmen, picturesque, i. 19, 120.
Bolgoda Lake, ii. 240.
Botanical gardens, Hak-galla, i. 216—Peradeniya, 267, 272—Henaratgoda and Anuradhapura, 271—Badulla, 271; ii. 38.
Bo-tree, sacred, i. 147, 406-415—prophecies concerning, 410—cremation of branch, 411—of leaves, 412.
Bow and arrows of gods, i. 304; ii. 6.
Branding cattle, i. 36.
Brazen temple, i. 394, 396.
Bread-fruit tree, i. 167.
Bridge of boats, i. 81.
Buddha as a roast hare, i. 297 note—relics of, 385, 432.
Buddha or CHRIST? ii. 418-422.
Buddha's dreary negations, i. 429—birthday, 96.
Buddhas, twenty-five, in Ceylon, i. 409 note; ii. 348.
Buddhism incorporates Hindooism, i. 81, 277, 297—is Atheism, 84—and State patronage, 87, 90, 96—and serpent-worship, 128—and Roman Catholicism, ii. 45-48 — reasons given for abjuring, 415-417—esoteric, 416.

Buddhist rival sects, i. 81—robe, how worn, 82, 374—temporalities, 87—cosmology, 93—fighting priest, 99—reverence for animal life, 222 note—heavens, 418—railing, 419.
Buffaloes, i. 153; ii. 60, 63, 69, 133, 217—hunting, 59.
Bulan-kulum, i. 364.
Bungalow, i. 57—temporary, 260; ii. 36, 102, 132—beside the lake, 241.
Buona Vista Orphanage, ii. 174.
Burning forest, ii. 41, 43, 309.
Busy officials, ii. 220 note.
Buttercups, i. 192.
Butterflies, i. 208; ii. 104—Samanaliya, 321.

Cable-rattans, ii. 133, 134 note.
Cacao and chocolate, ii. 297.
Cacti, i. 126, 130, 339; ii. 51.
Calpentyn, i. 130.
Camphor, oil of, i. 64.
Canals, i. 109—ancient, 363, 364.
Candle-nut tree, i. 159.
Canoes, i. 19, 120.
Cape Barberyn, westernmost land, ii. 227.
Car festival, ii. 7, 23.
Cashew-nuts, i. 134—bark, 423.
Cassia, i. 68.
Cassia fistula, i. 421.
Caste, ii. 81 -- persecutions, 83, 86—prejudices, 97—Singhalese, 98—Singhalese, its strength, 424.
Caste and outcast, ii. 98-101.
Castes, subdivisions, fisher, ii. 237, 238.
Cat's-eye, ii. 13.
Cattle, humped, i. 37—estate, ii. 88, 89.
Centipede, i. 115.
Ceylon Rifles disbanded, ii. 244.
Chandivelle, ii. 87.
Chanks, temple trumpet, i. 260.
Charms, i. 278, 280; ii. 195, 196.
Chekku oil-mill, ii. 182, 183.
Chena-farming, ii. 50.
Chetahs, i. 237; ii. 57, 59, 61, 64, 217.

INDEX.

Chilaw, i. 134, 137.
China, early trade with Ceylon, ii. 126 — Ceylon tributary to, 127 — modern trade, ib.
Cholera, ii. 225, 302.
Chrysoberyl, ii. 16.
Chunam, i. 57, 391.
Cinchona plantations, ii. 299.
Cinnamon gardens, i. 52, 62, 69 — laurel and oil, 63, 65 — doves, 63 — sensitive, 65 — peelers, 67 — in jungles near Negombo, 149 — stone, ii. 15.
Clearing the forest, ii. 41-43, 49.
Climbing plants, ii. 51, 131.
Close season for game, ii. 52, 216.
Clothes, smart, i. 207.
Cobra reverenced, i. 128 — five- or seven-headed, 128, 412, 417, 432 — tame, 129, 413 — and tic polonga, 413 bite remedies, 425.
Cock, red, sacrifice, i. 282.
Cocoa plantation, life on a, ii. 71, 87. See Palm.
Coffee, ii. 26, 43 — stores as churches, &c., 44 — thieves, 266 — disease, 287 — history of, 287-290.
Coffin, stone, i. 418.
College, St Thomas's, i. 39, 40 — Royal, at Colombo, 41 — Vidyodaya, 92.
Colombo Cathedral, Anglican, i. 39 — Roman Catholic, 98.
Colombo harbour, i. 9, 10 — ironworks, 12 — cotton-spinning, 13 — churches, 41 — fort, 46 — siege of, 48 — lake, 53 - derivation of name, 54.
Convolvulus, marine, i. 125; ii. 162.
Coolies, ii. 303.
Coral-tree and cotton-tree, 169.
Cotta mission - station, i. 151; ii. 423.
Cottiar Bay, ii. 148.
Cow-catcher, i. 155.
Cow-dung plaster, i. 43; ii. 40, 88 — ashes, 48 — boiling, 239.
Crabs, i. 140; ii. 161.
Cremation of a Buddhist priest, i. 101

Crime regarded with indifference, ii. 243, 248 — causes of, 248.
Criminals, few women, ii. 249.
Crocodiles, i. 360, 428; ii. 69, 70, 134, 213 — longevity of, 135 — skin, 136.
Crops, two, annually, i. 154, 369.
Crow Island, ii. 194.
Cruelty to animals, ii. 267-269.
Curry, i. 43.
Customs, Singhalese and Tamil, i. 118.

Dagoba, various kinds of, i. 296, 378 — Ruanweli, 378, 381, 391 — Miriswetiya, 379, 380 — Abhayagiria, 381 — Thuparama, 383 — Lankarama, 386 — Jetawanarama, ib. — of two classes, 387 — circle on a square, 388 — Hanguranketa, contents of, 389 — Seta - Chaitiya or Lajjikavihara, 390 — Kiri Wihara, ib. — derivation of word, ib. note — at Buddha-Gaya rebuilt, 408 — Etwehera, 432 — Maha-Seya, 433 — Ambustele, ib. — Rankot or Ruanwelle-saye, ii. 122 — Kiri, at Pollonarua, ib.
Dambulla rock-temples, i. 338 — scene of last insurrection, 350.
Datura blossom, i. 180, 187.
Days of the week, i. 309.
De and Don, Portuguese prefixes, ii. 262.
Deaths, falling from trees, ii. 158 — accidental, 265.
Decoration, church, i. 200.
Delada-Maligawa at Kandy, i. 246, 284, 292, 311 — at Anuradhapura, 383 — at Pollonarua, ii. 121.
Delada-wanso, i. 309.
Demon-worship, i. 278, 282; ii. 89.
Detractors of missionaries, ii. 388.
Devil-bird, ii. 114, 115.
Devil-dancers, i. 258.
Devils, how to deceive, i. 280.
Dewenipiatissa, King, i. 356, 385, 408, 431.
Dhatu-Sena and Mahanamo, i. 352, 366.

VOL. II. 2 E

Dhobie, village laundryman, ii. 102
—prepares bungalows for travellers, ib.
Dimbula district, i. 191.
Dondra- or Dewa-nuwara, i. 402; ii. 192, 198-201.
Doves, ii. 230.
Dragonflies, ii. 25.
Drama, i. 368; ii. 163, 164.
Duel, historic, i. 342.
Dutch missions, ii. 175 — invasion, 349.
Dutugemunu, i. 342, 373, 378, 379 note.

Ebed-melech, the Ethiopian, ii. 409.
Ebony wood durable, i. 59; ii. 159
—raft of, i. 79.
Egg-shells, ii. 421.
Eiswara, ancient worship of, i. 417.
Elephant Plains, i. 191.
Elephant, Tom Skinner's first, i. 173
—war, pre-Christian, 373—shooting, ii. 58, 68, 71—a midnight adventure with an, 218-221—charmer, professional, 221.
Elephants as surveyors, i. 176—climbers, 217 — natural history, 219-236—tender feet, 231—export of, 235—in full dress, 299—bridge-building, ii. 54—close season, increase, 216.
Elk, i.e., sambur deer, i. 238, 240; ii. 52, 67.
Ella Pass, ii. 35.
Elu, high Singhalese, i. 289.
Encroachments of the sea, ii. 201-205.
Eribudda, i. 110.
Esoteric Buddhism, ii. 416.
Eucalyptus, ii. 285.
Euphorbia, ii. 221.
Evil eye, dread of, ii. 97.
Evil spirits, how to deceive, i. 281.
Eye flies, ii. 54, 104.

Fa Hian, Chinese traveller, i. 383, 407.
False accusation, murders to cause, ii. 233.

"Father" American mission, ii. 368.
Feet of Buddha, i. 387. See Holy Foot.
Female medical students, ii. 365.
Ferguson, A. M., editor, i. 72—William, botanist, 73.
Ferns, tree, i. 190 — maidenhair, 435—climbing, ii. 2, 234—basket, 132.
Ficus religiosa, *indica*, and *elastica*, i. 147, 148, 265, 407.
Field-hospitals, ii. 35.
Filter necessary, i. 125; ii. 104—for village, 105.
Fire, sacred, i. 85.
Fire-flies (beetles), i. 28, 113, 185; ii. 7, 165.
Fish of gorgeous colours, i. 38, 137, 140—culture, 196, 197—in boiling springs, ii. 154.
Fishers, Roman Catholic, i. 19, 121
—pay tithes, ii. 347 — drawing nets, 206—separate castes, 237.
Fishing by torchlight, i. 110-131; ii. 79—with baskets, 136.
Flamboyant, i. 52.
Floral offerings (case of fraud), i. 85, 285, 393.
Flowers, profusion of, i. 58, 181, 204, 211—at Nuwara Eliya, 199-201.
Flying foxes, i. 272; ii. 131—squirrels, i. 272—fish, ii. 166, 173.
Foliage, brilliant young, i. 17, 119, 186.
Footprints, ii. 310—Christian, 312
—on Allegalla, 322—on Adam's Peak, 333, 336.
Forest Department, ii. 49.
Forres, ii. 325.
Fort Austenburg, ii. 140.
Fort Frederick, ii. 142, 147.
Frequent removal of officials, ii. 192 note.
Frescoes in rock-temple of Dambulla, i. 341—at Sigiri, 345.
Frogs, i. 53—embedded in stone, 95
—green, ii. 131.
Fruit supply, i. 38—cool when first gathered, 433.
Fungi, ii. 24.

Gal Vihara, ii. 124.
Galgé, priest's cell, i. 417, 435.
Galkulum, i. 377.
Galle, i. 9, 23; ii. 174—harbour, i. 9; ii. 178—lighthouse, ii. 178—coral reefs, ib.
Galle to Colombo, road, ii. 233—ninety years ago, 240.
Gambling, Singhalese love of, i. 23—leads to crime, ii. 248.
Gampola, i. 181, 403; ii. 274.
Gangarowa, ii. 279.
Gem notary, ii. 8—legislation, 19.
Gemming, i. 210.
Gems, list of, ii. 10.
Gems and gem-pits, ii. 8-20.
Giant's tank, i. 354—canal, 363, 372.
Gigantic bean, ii. 131—images, 125.
Glacial marks on rock, none, i. 435.
Gloriosa superba, ii. 234, 246.
Glow-worm, ii. 7, 8.
Goats, long-legged, i. 415.
Gobbs, i. 103.
Gogerly, the Rev. J., i. 289.
Goldsmith's curse, i. 257.
Gordon, Sir Arthur Hamilton, i. 363-366.
Gordon Cumming, John, 1st chena Inspector, ii. 49—diary, 56.
Grain on dry soil, i. 359.
Grammars in rhyme, i. 291.
Grasshoppers, ii. 25.
Grassy downs, i. 191.
Grave-stones, domestic use for, ii. 39.
Green, predominance of (submarine), ii. 178—prevalence of, in birds and butterflies, ii. 229.
Gregory, Lake, i. 196.
Gregory, Sir William, i. 361-363.
Grove of the Tank Gods, ii. 129, 130.
Gutta-percha, i. 266.

Habsidum or retention of breath, i. 418.
Hak-galla, i. 215.
Haldummulla, ii. 23, 26.
Hambantota, ii. 211, 214.

Hanomoreyos outcasts, ii. 101.
Hanwella, ii. 1.
Happy Valley Mission, ii. 30-34, 387.
Haputale railway, i. 157; ii. 28, 29—pass, 27.
Hare, Buddha, mark on moon, i. 297 note.
Hat-bodin, seven bo-trees, ii. 198.
Head-covering, i. 119.
Hedgehog-grass, i. 124.
Hibiscus, i. 45.
Hindo-galla, i. 249.
Hindoo-Buddhist procession, i. 297; ii. 6.
Hindoo images in Buddhist temples, i. 81, 277, 341.
History, Dutch, French, British, ii. 149.
Holy Coat, i. 327.
Holy Foot, ii. 310, 333, 336—or feet? 312—to whom ascribed, 320.
Holy Footprint, ii. 310.
Holy Girdle, i. 326.
Holy oil, essence of Tooth, i. 321.
Holy places in the forest, ii. 129, 130.
Holy teeth, a complete set, i. 318.
Holy Tooth, i. 291-321—burnt, 312—manufactured, 314, 317.
Holy Trousers, i. 333.
Home-sick Britons, i. 40.
Honey-sucker, i. 275.
Horoscope, i. 278.
Horse-keepers, i. 36.
Horses, sacred, ii. 76.
Horton Plains, i. 189.
Hospitals, ii. 35.
Hot springs, ii. 153.
Hounds, i. 240.
Hydrophobia, i. 77.

Ibn Batuta, Moorish traveller, ii. 198, 331.
Idol's eyes, i. 97, 98.
Iguana, i. 111; ii. 176.
Images, Hindoo, in Buddhist temples, i. 81, 277.
India-rubber tree, i. 148—avenue at Peradeniya, 264—how collected, 265.

Industrial homes, i. 14—schools, ii. 33.
Infidel books, ii. 404.
Inheritance, law of, ii. 261.
Inscriptions on rock or slabs, i. 344, 436—"Galpota," ii. 118.
Insects, noisy, i. 27.
Iramative, snake-temple on, i. 127.
Iron-wood, i. 52, 187.
Irrigation works, i. 351-371.
Ixora, ii. 112.

Jackals, ii. 57, 64.
Jaffna, ii. 355—College, 370-376—the Iona of Southern India, 374—cyclone, 395.
Jak-tree, i. 167.
Jambu-tree, ii. 80.
Jay, blue, i. 210.
Jetawanarama temple at Pollonarua, ii. 121, 122, 128.
Jinrikisha, i. 11.
Juggernath car, ii. 7, 23.
Jungle fever, remedy for, i. 156.
Jymkana, i. 202.

Kaasyapa the parricide, i. 346.
Kabragoya, i. 111; ii. 177.
Kaduganawa, ii. 276.
Kaduganawa Pass, i. 156, 171, 179.
Kala-wewa tank, i. 351—its feeders, 352.
Kalpitiya, i. 130.
Kalutara, ii. 237.
Kandy, ancient approach, i. 171-173, 284—history, 243—king's funeral ceremonies, 248—chiefs' dresses, 251—ladies', 254—four Hindoo temples, 303.
Kannya hot-springs, ii. 153.
Kanthalay tank, i. 353-361; ii. 128, 137.
Kapok, i. 169.
Kapua (devil-dancer), i. 259-277.
Kapurales, i. 303, 304.
Karajo or parangi, ii. 399.
Karative salt-pans, i. 134.
Kattadia (devil-priest), i. 278, 279.
Kattregam, i. 356; ii. 129, 223, 224.
Kelani ferry, i. 53—bridge of boats,

79—temple, 80—town anciently inland, ii. 203.
Kiklomani, i. 196, 207.
Kingfishers, ii. 77, 138.
Kirti Nissanga, King, ii. 109, 119.
Knox, Robert, captive, ii. 148.
Kopay Church, fall of steeple, ii. 396.
Kurukkan (grain), i. 359.
Kurunegalla, i. 339; ii. 272.
Kushta, Rajah, ii. 194.

Lagerstræmia regina, i. 160.
Lagoons, how formed, i. 53, 103; ii. 77—very salt, 212
Lake Gregory, i. 196.
Lakes, artificial, i. 53, 353.
Langdon, the Rev. Samuel, ii. 30, 32, 387.
Lanka, i. 407; ii. 109, 202.
Lanka Tileka, ii. 274.
Lantana, ii. 51.
Layard, Sir Charles Peter, i. 72.
Leeches, i. 116, 261-264.
Legends and folk-lore, i. 342.
Lemon-grass, i. 191-193.
Leopards, i. 236-238.
Leper King, ii. 194, 195—hospital, 195.
Lettuce-tree, i. 32.
Lighthouses, ii. 200.
Lilies, water, i. 113, 421—on the sea-shore, ii. 161.
Lily (climbing), ii. 234—(Virgin), 235.
Lizards, i. 111, 112; ii. 131, 134, 207, 208.
Lotus blossom, i. 421; ii. 113—gold and silver, i. 292, 296, 404.
Lowa-maha-paya, Great Brazen Temple, i. 394-396.
Luminous creatures, ii. 7.
Lunatics, i. 36.
Lyrics, Christian songs, ii. 410.

Madoolseme, ii. 41.
Madulsima mountains, ii. 215.
Maha Eliya (Horton Plains), i. 189.
Maha-Sen, King, i. 353; ii. 128-223.

INDEX. 437

Maha - Wansae, great dynasty, ii. 108.
Maha-wanso chronicles, i. 289, 378, 400.
Mahadova, ii. 41.
Mahagam, ancient city, ii. 215.
Mahindo, royal missionary, i. 431-433—Mahindo's bed, rock-ledge, 435.
Maidenhair fern, i. 435.
Mail-cart to Edinburgh, i. 3.
"Makin' a toil of it!" ii. 304.
Malaria in Dekanda Valley, i. 156.
Maligawa, Tooth temple at Kandy, i. 246, 284, 292.
Mana grass, i. 191, 192.
Mangosteen, ii. 238.
Mangrove swamps, ii. 77, 235.
Mantis, praying, i. 273.
Manuscripts, ancient, i. 288-291.
Maradankadawalla, i. 376.
Maravilla, i. 144.
March, on the, ii. 54.
Marine convolvulus, ii. 235.
Masks, hideous, i. 259.
Matale, i. 336, 337.
Matara, ii. 192, 197.
Mavalipuram submerged, ii. 205.
Memecylon tinctorium, i. 422.
Meritorious water-jars, ii. 231-233.
Midwifery, ii. 363.
Migration of butterflies, i. 208.
Mihintale, i. 382, 391, 430; ii. 132 —1840 steps, i. 431.
Mildew, i. 58, 385.
Milk not used, i. 113—offering, 127, 410—charm, ii. 113.
Millepedes, i. 274.
Mimosa sensitiva, i. 268.
Minery Lake, i. 353-355; ii. 108, 128.
Miracle plays at Chilaw, i. 141.
Mission, native home, ii. 383 Happy Valley, 387 Tamil coolie, 405— Kandyan Itinerancy, 413.
Missionary detraction, ii. 388 note.
Missions, chronological table, ii. 354 — summary of, 356 — American, commenced, 359 Wesleyan, 378 —Native, to Burmah, 388—Baptist and Presbyterian, 390 note— Salvation Army, 390—Episcopal, 391 — to Portuguese burghers, 425.
Models of hands, arms, eyes, ears, offered, ii. 223 note.
Mohammedan festival, i. 96—mosque, 130.
Monara or Mayura-paya, i. 394.
Monastic records graven on rock, i. 437.
Mongoose, i. 105, 106 note.
Monkey, i. 109, 121-123—mischievous, ii. 103.
Monoliths, i. 378, 385, 387, 396.
Monsoon, seasons of, i. 56.
Moondim Aar lake, ii. 87.
Moonstones, gems, i. 210; ii. 13— ancient sculpture, i. 391, 393, 406; ii. 117.
Moormen, i. 20, 130, 131; ii. 8, 9.
Mosquito, i. 110—prolific, 197.
Motive for striving, ii. 421.
Mouse-deer, i. 239.
Mudaliyar, dress of, i. 252.
Mulgirigalla, Buddhist monastery, ii. 209, 211.
Murders to cause false accusation, ii. 253.
Murray, inventor of clay sluice-pipes, i. 368.
Musical instruments, i. 259, 376— shell-fish, ii. 78, 79.

Naga Pokuna, i. 432.
Naga-dipo, isle of serpents, ii. 98.
Nainativoe, snake-temple on, i. 127.
Nairs, peculiar undress of high-caste women, i. 349.
Names, descriptive, i. 211; ii. 262— of estates, 306-308.
Nanuoya, i. 180; ii. 27.
Nationalities, divers, in Ceylon, i. 21.
Nattoor river, ii. 95.
Navatkuda, ii. 80.
Negombo lake, i. 109, 110, 145—fort, 149.
Nellore, ii. 355.
Nest of a moth, i. 274.

Nestorian Christians in Ceylon, ii. 346.
Nests, peculiar birds', i. 275, 276.
New Year, Tamil and Singhalese, i. 96.
Nillo, i. 213, 215.
Nine and three, i. 301, 303, 307, 308.
Nipple hills, ii. 216.
Nirvana, definition of, i. 375 — or eternal life, ii. 418-422.
Nutmeg-tree, i. 71.
Nuwara Eliya, i. 180, 195—climate, 198, 202.
Nuwara-Kalawiya, i. 361; ii. 112.
Nuwara-wewa, i. 428.

Oath-stone at Pollonarua, ii. 129.
O. B. C., failure of, ii. 291.
'Observer' newspaper, i. 72.
Ola palm-leaf book, i. 165, 288-291 —copy-book, ii. 95.
Olcott, Colonel, ii. 417.
Oliphant, Laurence, ii. 328.
Oodooville, first girls' school, ii. 360.
Opera-glasses in the temple, i. 294.
Orchids, Wanna Rajah, i. 108— yellow ground, 192.
Orchilla, lichen, i. 132.
Ordeal by boiling oil, ii. 239.
Oriental Library, i. 92, 285, 288.
Otters, i. 197, 242.
Owls, ii. 114.
Oysters at Bentota, ii. 230.

Padda-birds, i. 126.
Padivil tank, i. 353, 354 note.
Pali, i. 289.
Pallagolla, i. 183.
Pallai, ii. 397-399.
Palm-leaf books, i. 165.
Palm-leaf umbrella, i. 163, 403.
Palms as lightning-conductors, ii. 189.
Palms blossom like wheat, i. 133.
Palms, cocoa, i. 31; ii. 180-191—at high elevations, i. 120; ii. 185— with several heads, i. 150—plantation, ii. 71, 87, 169-171 — leaf used as a charm, 191—areca, i. 31, 161—palmyra and banyan, 120—jaggery or kitool, 161—
talipot, 163 — date, thorn, oil, sago, 267—*coco de mer*, 268—palmyra, ii. 154-160.
Palms multiplied by foreigners, i. 371; ii. 179, 180.
Pandals, erection of, i. 257.
Pandanus, i. 109.
Panduwaasa, King, i. 428.
Pansala schools, i. 88, 417; ii. 30.
Panther, i. 237.
Pantura or Panadura, ii. 240.
Papaw, i. 168.
Paradise in Ceylon, ii. 310.
Parangi or karayo, i. 363, 369, 429; ii. 221, 399.
Park-country near Batticaloa, ii. 35, 52, 90.
Patenas, i. 192-194.
Patipola dividing range, ii. 27.
Peacock Palace, i. 394.
Pearl-fisheries, i. 7 — police regulation of, ii. 270.
Peepul, i. 147, 406, 409.
Pelicans' nests, i. 354 note; ii. 69.
Pengolin or ant-eater, ii. 41.
Peradeniya Gardens, i. 267, 272.
Peradeniya Station, i. 179.
Perahera at Kandy, i. 284, 297, 300, 306—date of, 300—at Ratnapura, ii. 5—at Dondra, 200.
Periyakulam, ii. 153.
Perjury rampant, ii. 257.
Pettah native bazaar, i. 36, 39.
Phosphorescence, i. 29, 131; ii. 165-168.
Pidaru-tala-galla, i. 196, 203.
Pigeons, ii. 229.
Pig-sticking, ii. 73.
Pilgrimages, regulation of, ii. 224.
Pilgrims, aged, ii. 324, 327.
Ping-chattie (water-jar), ii. 231, 233.
Pioneer corps, i. 175.
Plains, Elk, Agra, i. 192, 206— Horton, 189 — Maturata, 205 — Matale or Maha-talawa, 336.
Planet-worship, i. 278, 308, 309.
Planter's aid to Mission work, ii. 407.
Planter's life, ii. 301, 309.

INDEX. 439

Play, ancient Buddhist, i. 384—
 Tamil, 368; ii. 163.
Plumbago, ii. 21, 22.
Plumeria acutifolia, i. 84.
Poet Kalidas, ii. 197.
Poinciana regia, i. 52.
Pokuna, Kuttam, i. 427.
Pokuna, Kumara, ii. 123.
Police work, ii. 243 *et seq.*
Pollonarua, i. 401-403—derivation of name, 414; ii. 108.
Polyandry, ii. 203 note.
Porcupine, ii. 72, 73, 124—foe of tea, 295.
Portuguese invasion, ii. 348—present condition, 425—names, 348.
Potato-tree, i. 187; ii. 37.
Pottery, offerings of red, ii. 139.
Prakrama Baku, i. 344, 374; ii. 108, 109, 110—Seas of, i. 355; ii. 109—his statue, ii. 116.
Precautions in tropical countries, i. 423.
Prescriptions, native, i. 423-427.
Prickly heat, i. 115.
Processions, Buddhist and Roman Catholic, i. 99—Roman Catholic at Chilaw, 141—Roman Catholic in coffee districts, ii. 43.
Progress in Ceylon, i. 3, 6.
Proverbs, i. 419.
Provinces, i. 256.
Pussilawa, i. 182.
Puttalam, i. 130, 136.

Quarries, i. 391.

Races, diversity of, i. 20, 118.
Ragalla, i. 205.
Rag offerings, ii. 342.
Railway, Colombo to Gampola, i. 155.
Rainbow, rose-coloured, ii. 25.
Rain-charms, ii. 113, 120.
Rajah-kariya, i. 8, 175, 245, 356-359.
Rajah Singha, i. 291.
Rama and Ravana, i. 189; ii. 320.
Rama, Prince of Oude, ii. 202.
Ramayana poem, ii. 320.
Rambutan, i. 38.
Ratnapura, ii. 2.

Rats and rat-snakes, i. 57, 129.
Ravana, ancient king or demon. ii. 202.
Razors, cheap, ii. 305.
Red-deer, i. 239.
Red rain, ii. 197 note.
"Red thread" to keep off witches, i. 343.
Reformatory, ii. 34.
Regimental coats for coolies, ii. 44—great-coats, 305.
Registration of dogs and carts, ii. 267—of servants, 265.
Relic-shrines, i. 296, 389.
Relic-worship, i. 321—blood of Thomas à Becket, *ib.*—Father Arrowsmith's hand, 322—arm of St Augustine, 322—the True Cross, 323—toe-nails of St Peter, 324—corpse of the Bishop of Ischia, 326—Sainte Ceinture, *ib.*
Relics, recently discovered, i. 91-95—several, 338.
Religious conflicts, Roman Catholic, i. 99, 141.
Religious intolerance, ii. 371 note—orders, i. 51.
Reptiles, i. 73.
Rest-houses, ii. 4, 137.
Rhododendron trees, i. 187, 188.
Rice cultivation, i. 153.
Rice-fields, terraced, i. 336.
Rice from wrecked ships, i. 371.
Rice-name, baby's, i. 279.
Rita-galla, i. 351.
River, the Kelani, i. 53, 179—the Maha-welli-ganga, 96, 102, 179; ii. 103—the Maha-Oya, i. 111, 145, 179; ii. 54—the Ging-Oya, i. 111, 145—the Luna-Oya, 113, 119, 143—the Dedroo-Oya, 124—the Moondalani, 126—Puna-Ella and Garunda-Ella, 182—Sita-Ella, 189—Nanuoya, 196—Fort M'Donald river, 241—the Ping-Oya, 336—the Kala-Oya, 352—the Malwatte, 355, 370, 420—Ambanganga, 355; ii. 112—the Kalu-Ganga, 2, 236, 237—the Manick-Ganga, 16, 225—the Kataragama, *ib.*—the Belihul-

Oya, 25—the Welawe-Ganga, ib.
—the Magama, 35—the Dambera-
Oya, 54—Nattoor, 95—Gindura,
176—Nilwalla-Ganga, 192, 196—
Kumukkan, formerly called Kom-
bookgam, 216—Alutgama, 227, 238
—Sita-Ganga, 329.
Road bungalows, ii. 4.
Roads when non-existent, ii. 240.
Robert de Nobili, Jesuit, ii. 46-48.
Robin of Ceylon, i. 144.
Robinson, Sir Hercules, i. 90, 361.
Rock frescoes at Sigiri, i. 347.
Rock snake, ii. 62, 70.
Rock-temples, Hindo Galla, i. 249—
Alu-Vihara, 337—Dambulla, 338
—Isurumuniya, 417—Ella Pass, ii.
36—Mulgirigalla, 209.
Rocks, huge dark masses, i. 339.
Rodiya outcasts, ii. 99-101.
Rogers, Major, i. 219, 225.
Rogers' Memorial Church, ii. 37.
Roman Catholic Mission, ii. 45, 357, 358.
Roots of trees, buttressed, ii. 55, 273.
Rounded rock-masses, i. 339, 434; ii. 272.
Royal maiden, a, ii. 204.
Rubies, ii. 10, 12.
Ruby sand, ii. 225.
Rugam tank, ii. 55.

Saami Rock, Trincomalee, ii. 142-146.
Sabaragamua, ii. 10, 17.
Sack-tree, i. 117.
Saints, their great stature, ii. 317.
Salt-works, north-west coast, i. 134-136—south-east, ii. 212-214.
Saman, brother of Rama, ii. 320.
Sambur deer (Elk), i. 239, 240; ii. 52.
Sanghamitta, i. 409.
Sanscrit, i. 289.
Sapphires, ii. 9-12.
Satin-wood bridge, i. 180.
Saved from smoke, ii. 377.
Schools, Wesleyan Industrial, at Colombo, i. 14.
Scorpions, ii. 194.

Scotchmen, ii. 324.
Screw-pine, i. 109.
Seas of Prakrama, i. 355.
Seeds carried by rivers, i. 124.
Seeds which purify water, ii. 105.
Sensitive plant, i. 268.
Serendib, ii. 165.
Serfdom on temple lands, i. 89, 357.
Serpent and tree worship, i. 412, 413.
Serpent-bite remedies, i. 425.
Serpent "for broken bones," ii. 39.
Serpents, i. 59—propitiated, 127.
Service Tenures Ordinance, i. 90, 357.
Seven- or five-headed cobra, i. 128, 412, 417.
Shadow of Adam's Peak, ii. 334, 339
—of Fuji-Yama, 339.
Shark-charmers, ii. 213.
Shark in harbour, ii. 141.
Shell-beds, ii. 222.
Shrine of St Anna, i. 142—of the Tooth, 294.
Sigiri, fortress of, i. 345.
Singhalese homes, i. 42—children, 118.
Sita, wife of Rama, ii. 202.
Skinner, the roadmaker, i. 172—his rations, 177—his work, 179—on district courts, ii. 263—his prophecy, 283.
Skylarks, i. 242.
Slave Island, i. 53.
Sluice-pipes of clay, i. 368, 376.
Smallpox, first appearance of, in Ceylon, i. 174—goddess of, propitiated, 283—terrible visitation of, ii. 111.
Snake's fangs, i. 127.
Snake's Isle, i. 127.
Snake's temples, i. 127.
Snake, rat-, i. 57, 129—sea-, 132.
Snake-worship and Buddhism, i. 128, 412—and Siva, 128.
Snipe, ii. 89, 90.
Southernmost known land, ii. 201.
Soysa, Charles de, i. 77, 144.
Spence Hardy, the Rev. R., i. 289.
Spice-laden breezes, i. 17, 35.
Spiders, ii. 104, 206-208.
Sportsman's paradise, ii. 74.
Spotted deer, i. 242; ii. 52.

INDEX. 441

Squirrels, ii. 206.
Sri Pada, Holy Foot, ii. 310.
Sri-patula, sacred footprint, i. 417.
Stag's-horn moss, i. 257.
Stick-insects, i. 273.
Stilts, i. 260.
Stone bulls, i. 405.
Strychnine-tree, i. 125.
Sula-Wansae, or lesser dynasty, ii. 108.
Sun-birds, ii. 151.
Sunday cargo-work checked, ii. 386 note.
Sunwise turns, i. 403, 405, 412; ii. 7, 332.
Suriya-trees, i. 45.
Suriya-Wansae, or Solar Dynasty, ii. 108.

Tailor-bird, i. 275.
Talla-goya lizard, i. 112.
Tamankaduwa district, ii. 112.
Tamarind-tree, i. 169.
Tamblegam, brackish lake, ii. 138.
Tamil ladies, i. 137—coolies, ii. 303.
Tangalle, ii. 205, 209.
Tanks, restoration of, i. 361-371—at Batticaloa, ii. 77—restoration around Pollonarua, 112.
Tea in 1660 and 1890, i. 3—"golden tips," 7—how to cool, for traveller's drink, ii. 106—introduction of, 292—adaptive to soil, 294.
Teeth, a complete set, i. 318.
Theosophy, ii. 416.
Thespesia populnea, i. 45.
Thorny plants, i. 114.
Three and nine, i. 301, 303, 307, 308; ii. 23.
Thunbergia, i. 264.
Ticks, ii. 53.
Tic polonga and cobra, i. 413.
Timber, beautiful woods, i. 79.
Time and tides, i. 55.
Tiripane tank, i. 377.
Tissamaharama tank, ii. 221, 222.
Tissawewa tank, i. 356, 361, 363, 428.
Titles, official, 253-255.
Toddy, ii. 185-187—drawers, 82, 156,

158—and arrack, 156, 181-187, 234.
"Tooth and State," i. 288, 317.
Tooth, the original, i. 291-321—its many temples, 311.
Toparé (Pollonarua), ii. 107.
Topa-Wewa, ii. 106, 108.
Topaz, ii. 14.
Tortoises, i. 74-77, 105.
Tortoise-shell, i. 22.
Totapella Plains, i. 191, 193.
Tourmaline, ii. 16.
Transmigration, i. 274—of Buddha as a hare, 297 note.
Travellers' tree, i. 45.
Tree and serpent worship, i. 412.
Tree of Life (palmyra), ii. 159.
Trincomalee, ii. 140—additional fortification, 150.
Tulip-tree, i. 46.
Turtles, i. 74, 105.
Turtles' eggs, ii. 172.

Umbrella, honorific, i. 163 note, 296, 298, 304, 344, 378; ii. 6.
Umbrellas, low caste dare not carry, ii. 82, 86.
Uva, i. 191; ii. 30, 34, 428.

Varied vegetation necessary, ii. 293.
Vavuniya-vilan-kulam tank, i. 353.
Vaz, Father Joseph, ii. 351.
Veddahs, rock, ii. 90—kindle fire, 93—village and coast, 94—high caste, 94, 99—archers, 96.
Vendeloos Bay, ii. 95.
Venomous creatures, i. 115.
Vicarton Gorge, i. 336.
Vidyodaya College, i. 92-95.
Vigita-pura, i. 372, 373.
Village hospitals, i. 9.
Violets, i. 192.
Votive offerings at Kattaragama, &c., ii. 223 note.

Wakwella, ii. 177.
Walagam-bahu, King, i. 336, 382.
Wanderoo monkey, i. 109, 121.
Wanna Rajah orchid, i. 108.
Wannie, the dreary, ii. 399, 400.

Wanny, the, i. 354; ii. 216.
Wansac, Maha-, ii. 108 — Suriya-, Solar Dynasty, ib.—Soma Suriya, Luni-Solar race, 119.
Ward, Sir Henry, i. 361; ii. 49.
Wata Dágé, ii. 117, 118.
Watch huts, ii. 128.
Water purified by seeds, i. 125; ii. 105—cutting the, i. 305—deficient, 359, 360—must boil and filter, ii. 104.
Water-cress, i. 184.
Water-lilies, i. 113.
Water-spouts, i. 55.
Weaver-bird, i. 275.
Wedding procession, i. 117.
Weight in gold, i. 344; ii. 119, 120.
Welligama, ii. 193.
Wellington, the Duke of, at Trincomalee, ii. 149.
Wesleyan Mission commenced, ii. 378.
Wheel as an emblem, ii. 378.

White cloth, honour of, i. 260, 295, 303, 412; ii. 6, 81, 102.
Wijeyo the Conqueror, i. 342, 343, 371, 372 note—his capital, 402.
Wilderness of the Peak, ii. 284.
Wind, land, i. 148.
Witchcraft, i. 425, 426.
Wood, ornamental, for cabinets, i. 79.
Work for women, ii. 362.
Workers wanted, ii. 428, 429.
Worms, gigantic, i. 275; ii. 133.
Wytulian heresy, i. 396.

Xavier, St Francis, ii. 347.

Yakkas, ii. 98.
Yellow parroquet, ii. 274.
Yodi Ela, i. 363, 429.
Yoga-stones, i. 418; ii. 118.

Zebu, i. 37.
Zircon, ii. 15.

THE END.

PRINTED BY WILLIAM BLACKWOOD AND SONS.

www.ingramcontent.com/pod-product-compliance
Lightning Source LLC
Chambersburg PA
CBHW022116300426
44117CB00007B/731